Springer Texts in Business and Economics

For further volumes:
http://www.springer.com/series/10099

Yeming Gong

Global Operations Strategy

Fundamentals and Practice

 Springer

Yeming Gong
EMLYON Business School
Ecully
France

ISSN 2192-4333   ISSN 2192-4341 (electronic)
ISBN 978-3-642-36707-6   ISBN 978-3-642-36708-3 (eBook)
DOI 10.1007/978-3-642-36708-3
Springer Heidelberg New York Dordrecht London

Library of Congress Control Number: 2013938038

Printed on acid-free paper

Springer is a part of Springer Science+Business Media (www.springer.com)

Preface

This book has grown from courses in operations strategy and operations management, taught to graduate students and executive managers in different countries. The objective of this book is for students and managers to understand the fundamentals and practice of global operations strategy. I have two primary audiences in mind for the book.

The first audience comprises various students. The core readers are graduate-level students. Executive programs can use part of this book for executives who want to focus on specific topics of global operations strategy, for instance, global supply chain, and cross-value global operations strategy, or to combine global operations strategy with a specific industry or company, for instance, global operations strategy of a telecommunication company. The book can be used by undergraduates who wish to enhance their understanding of global operations strategy and Ph.D. students who wish to read a literature review of global operations strategy and lay a foundation for further research in this field. The student audiences are:

- Master of Science students
- Master of Business Administration students
- Master of Philosophy students
- Students in executive (open and custom) programs
- Undergraduates
- Ph.D. students

For experienced practitioners, this book serves as a suitable reference for the fundamentals and practice of global operations strategy. The manager and practitioner audiences are:

- Managers in operations management or operations strategy
- Managers in international business
- Consultants
- Managers in marketing, finance, accounting, human resources, retailing, and logistics who are considering interface problems with global operations

Focus of the Book

I do not intend to cover all topics in operations strategy. "Global" operational problems are my focus. I focus on the global elements of global operations strategy, including global competency, global resource-based operations, global process-based operations, and global operational practice.

I also do not try to present all global decisions; hence, the book focuses on decisions at the "operations strategy" level. In a global environment, it is difficult to identify decisions at this level since a great number of decisions on global problems are at the "corporate strategy" level or the "business strategy" level. Separating decisions at the "operations strategy" level and at the "operations management" level is also difficult since their decision time horizons are close.

With a "focus strategy," I may have overlooked some topics in operations strategy or global strategy. Given the constraints, I welcome any suggestion for improvement.

Features of the Book

The book reviews the newest theories in global operations strategy. For the covered topics, I conducted a literature review up to 2012.

All case information is updated to 2012. Except for a few classical cases, such as Coca-Cola for globalization and Toyota for operations strategy history, the newest cases are selected from recent years, including the Samsung versus Apple war in 2012, the shipbuilding crisis in 2012, the Bosch EFQM award 2012, Huawei globalization in 2012, the Foxconn–Apple supply chain crisis in 2011, the Japanese earthquake of 2011, and global supply chain 2011. The locations of cases are global: about one-third of cases and case examples are from Europe, one-third from North America, one-third from Asia Pacific, with many embedded examples from the rest of the world. The features of the book are:

- Underpinning by updated theory
- Illustrations using new management practice
- Inclusion of part objectives
- Inclusion of chapter objectives
- Case examples from recent years
- The newest cases tested by students
- References and further reading
- Supportive teaching materials including slides and teaching notes for all cases and case examples, teaching videos, syllabuses, exercise sets, and exam papers

Organization of the Book

The current literature in global operations strategy is fragmented and varied. To facilitate its understanding, I have organized the book with a "triple triangles" structure (see Fig. 1.9).

Part I introduces global operations strategy with a structure of "3I" triangles (see Fig. I). Chapter 1 introduces the concept of global operations strategy, mainly addressing the question "what is global operations strategy?" Chapter 2 introduces the methods of operational globalization, mainly answering the question "how are operations globalized?" Chapter 3 introduces the rationale behind operational globalization, mainly addressing the question "why are operations globalized?"

Part II addresses the fundamentals of global operations strategy with a "3V" structure from three views (see Fig. II). The fundamentals in the competency-based view are addressed in Chap. 4, fundamentals in the resource-based view in Chap. 5, and fundamentals in the process-based view in Chap. 6.

Part III discusses the practice of global operations strategy by a "3C" structure (see Fig. III). Cross-border practice is addressed in Chap. 7, cross-function practice in Chap. 8, and cross-value practice in Chap. 9.

EMLYON Business School   Yeming GONG
April 2013

Acknowledgments

Several years ago, I wrote many lecture notes on global operational problems to answer questions from my global students. These students are highly globalized and their interesting questions cannot be easily found in classical textbooks without focusing on global operational problems. It was their strong demands that drove me to integrate my lecture notes into a book. About 400 graduate students have used case materials in more than ten rounds of teaching in operations strategy or operations management courses and have provided valuable feedback.

I am grateful to more than 20 professors of operations management, operations strategy, and global strategy for many theoretical suggestions and several professors of finance, marketing, human resources, and information management for sharing their knowledge of the cross-functional problems presented in Chap. 8. Several Ph.D. students have carefully read the whole book and provided detailed feedback.

This work is supported by NSFC (No.70901028). I have greatly benefited from valuable comments, encouragement, and guidance from Christian Rauscher, editor of Business and Economics at Springer, and the support from Springer's professional team. I would like to express my gratitude to the support and stimulating environment of EMLYON.

Finally, I would like to thank my family, Rona, Ruiqi, and Alex, for allowing me to dedicate a significant amount of time to the work.

Yeming GONG

Contents

Part II   Fundamentals of Global Operations Strategy

Part I

Introduction to Global Operations Strategy

Part I introduces global operations strategy through a "3I" or "W-H-W" triangle (see Fig. I). Chapter 1 introduces the concept of global operations strategy, mainly addressing the question "what is global operation strategy?" Chapter 2 introduces the ways of operational globalization, mainly answering the question "how are operations globalized?" Chapter 3 introduces the rationale of operational globalization, dealing mainly with the question "why are operations globalized?" The objectives of Part I are as follows:

- To introduce basic concepts and the evolving process of global operations strategy.
- To discuss basic principles and basic decisions global operations strategy.
- To introduce milestone literature for further reading and learning.
- To explain the structure of the book.
- To describe globalization modes for global manufacturing and global services.
- To introduce basic theories and framework for operational globalization.
- To discuss drivers, risks and benefits of operational globalization.

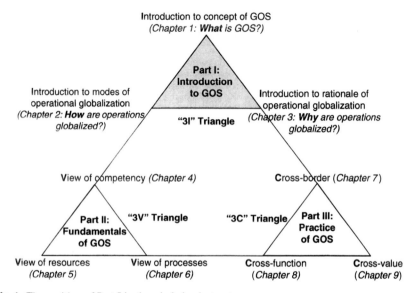

Fig. I The position of Part I in the whole book structure

Basic Concepts of Global Operations Strategy

1

Chapter Objectives

- To introduce the evolving process of global operations strategy.
- To define key concepts: manufacturing strategy, service operations strategy, and global operations strategy.
- To discuss international operations management and global operations strategy.
- To present basic principles in global operations strategy.
- To discuss basic decisions in global operations strategy.

1.1 Strategy, Operations Strategy, Global Operations Strategy

1.1.1 From Strategy to Manufacturing Strategy

Strategy is "the determination of the basic long-term goals and the objectives of an enterprise, and the adoption of courses of action and the allocation of resources necessary for carrying out these goals" (Chandler 1962). There is a hierarchy of strategy, with three major levels (Hofer and Schendel 1978):

1. Corporate Strategy: What set of businesses should a corporate be in?
2. Business Strategy: How should a corporate compete in a given business?
3. Functional Strategy: How can this function contribute to the competitive advantage of the business?

Manufacturing strategy is one of such functional strategies. Corporations usually use three basic strategies: low-cost production, differentiation, and cost or differentiation focus (Porter 1985). Here operations are firstly regarded as one of the functions to support competitive business strategy, and used to enhance the competitiveness of the business. However, the main emphasis of functional strategies has previously been placed on finance and marketing. During the oil embargo of the 1970s, Japanese automobile companies – including Toyota and Nissan – used a manufacturing strategy, providing automobiles to decrease fuel consumption, as a competitive weapon. This event has changed the view of functional strategies. Wickham Skinner is usually regarded (see, e.g., Anderson et al. 1989) as the first to advocate using manufacturing to strengthen a corporation's competitive ability (see Skinner 1969, 1978, 1985).

Wheelwright (1978) presents basic manufacturing decisions, and points out trade-offs among various criteria. In his words, "the basic problem is that most decisions, particularly those in manufacturing, require trade-offs among criteria". The demand for productivity, time, quality and customer service cannot be simultaneously satisfied at the same level, forcing sacrifices and compromises within these dimensions.

Hayes and Wheelwright (1984) define manufacturing strategy as a consistent pattern in decision-making, and propose a framework for manufacturing strategy. In particular, they list eight major areas in which a corporation can seek a competitive advantage in manufacturing: the workforce, vertical integration, facilities, capacity, quality, production planning and control, organization, and technology.

In a later book, Hayes et al. (1980) go beyond the structural decisions (the "bricks and mortar" of facilities and equipment) to the infrastructure decisions of a manufacturing company: the management policies, systems, and practices that must be at the core of a world-class organization. They address the difficulty of creating that infrastructure, emphasizing the management leadership and vision that are required. A truly superior manufacturing company seeking to build a competitive advantage through manufacturing excellence should build continuous learning ability, take a holistic perspective, relentlessly pursue customer value, and realize that management makes the difference.

Hayes and Wheelwright (1984) separate decisions into two categories: structural decisions and infrastructural ones. Structural decisions refer to decisions related to structural practices, which have a long-term impact and are not easily reversible. Structural decisions need substantial financial investment and strongly influence physical assets. Typical structural decisions are: facility capacity, vertical integration, manufacturing process, factory capacity, and plant location.

Infrastructure decisions refer to the systems, policies, practices, procedures, and organizations which support the manufacturing processes. Infrastructure decisions are related to infrastructure practices, and have relatively short-term effects on corporation performance. Infrastructure decisions usually do not need substantial financial investment and strongly influence physical assets. Typical infrastructure decisions are: quality management, work force management, organization structure and design, production and inventory planning and control systems, and environment management systems.

In a competitive environment, a corporation usually has a unique operational capability help it to build a competitive advantage. We call this unique operational capability "distinctive competence". Distinctive competence is a "notion that each company should identify and exploit those resources, skills and organizational characteristics that give it a comparative advantage over its competitors" (Hayes and Wheelwright 1979b). A good manufacturing strategy should transfer distinctive competence of business strategy to distinctive competence of functional areas of manufacturing. Typical distinctive competencies of a manufacturing system are time, quality, cost, and flexibility.

Considering the relationship between manufacturing strategy and competitive strategy, manufacturing strategies are usually classified into four stages (Hayes and Wheelwright 1984), from relatively passive to relatively aggressive:

1. Internally neutral. Manufacturing simply provides products.
2. Externally neutral. Manufacturing only meets the requirement from competition.
3. Internally supportive. Manufacturing tries to be unique and separate from its competitors.
4. Externally supportive. Manufacturing pursues uniqueness worldwide and becomes world-class manufacturing.

Table 1.1 shows main literature in evolving GOS. To sum up, mainly based on the statement above and the research of Skinner (1969), Wheelwright (1978), Hayes and Wheelwright (1979a, b, 1984), and Hayes et al. (1980), we define manufacturing strategy as:

> A consistent pattern of structural and infrastructural decisions, determining the resource and process of a manufacturing system to achieve a set of manufacturing competencies alignment with business strategy.

1.1.2   From Manufacturing Strategy to Service Operations Strategy

(1) The distinction between product and service

Thomas (1978) is among the earliest to advocate that strategy is different in service businesses. Siferd et al. (1992) provide a review of strategies of service systems. Evolving from manufacturing strategies to service strategies is firstly a result of the difference between the natures of product and service. The distinction between product and service is seen mainly in the following four aspects:

1. Inseparability and simultaneity

While product process and customer experiences happen simultaneously in the service business, this is not true for products, which may first be manufactured and then put in distribution centers. The service provider is an integral part of the service. The customers participate in the service, and affect the service outcome.

2. Heterogeneity

Since a service is produced and consumed simultaneously and individuals make up part of the service delivery, a service is always unique. The delivered service can vary in quality, quantity, and delivery time. For example, although the menu may be fixed during a specific period in a restaurant, its taste, material weight, cooking time, food temperature, smell, and associated

Table 1.1 Main literature in evolving global operations strategy (1)

Categories	Literature	Contributions
Strategy	Chandler (1962)	Provides a general definition of strategy
	Hofer and Schendel (1978)	Present a hierarchy of strategy with three major levels, including functional strategy
	Porter (1985)	States that corporations use three basic strategies: low-cost production, differentiation, and cost or differentiation focus. Operations are used to enhance the competitiveness of the business
Manufacturing strategy	Skinner (1969)	One of the first to advocate using manufacturing to strengthen a corporation's competitive ability
	Skinner (1978)	Studies the role of manufacturing in the corporate strategy, and argues the dangers of overlooking manufacturing for corporate growth
	Wheelwright (1978)	Presents basic manufacturing decisions, and points out trade-offs among various criteria
	Hayes and Abernathy (1980)	A call for American managers to remain technologically competitive in the long run
	Hayes et al. (1980)	Goes beyond the structural decisions to the infrastructure decisions of a manufacturing company
	Hayes and Wheelwright (1984)	Defines manufacturing strategy as a consistent pattern in decision-making, and proposes a framework for manufacturing strategy
	Miller and Roth (1994)	Proposes taxonomy of manufacturing strategies
	Hill (2000)	A systematic introduction to manufacturing strategy
Service strategy	Thomas (1978)	Advocates that the strategy is different in service business
	Chase (1978)	Categorizes different types of service systems
	Heskett (1986)	Proposes methods for formulating service strategies
	Roth and van der Velde (1991)	Proposes a service strategic framework based on customer/account base matrix
	Hayes and Chase (1992)	Applies operations strategy to service firms
	Fitzsimmons and Fitzsimmons (1994)	Introduces service management to win competitive advantage
	Karmarkar and Pitbladdo (1995)	Provides a framework for describing, analyzing, and explaining service competition
	Kellogg and Nie (1995)	Proposes a service strategic framework based on service process/service package matrix

service attitude will vary slightly, dependent on customers, chefs, waiters, and service environment. Products are homogeneous, at least in the same batch – once produced, the quality is uniform across all line of products.

3. Intangibility

   Most services are intangible and products are always tangible objects. The intangibility indicates that the ability to touch, smell, taste and see is absent in services, which can deter the service receiver from gauging service quality.

4. Perishability

Most services are perishable and they do not have a long life or cannot be stored for repeat use. For example, an empty hotel room on one specific night is perished; the use of that room in that time slot cannot be repeated. Only some products are perishable, and they can be stored in warehouses.

(2) Service categories

To formulate service strategies, we need to distinguish not only product and service, but also internal categories of service. Chase (1978) has categorized service systems into four types – pure service, mixed service, quasimanufacturing, and manufacturing – by the extent of required customer contact in the creation of the service. From an operational perspective, Lovelock and Yip (1996) categorize services into the following three types, which lay a foundation for developing global service strategies.

1. People-processing service

In this service, customers are integrated with production processes. For example, in Hilton hotels, customers need to enter the hotel to enjoy the service. In a tourism agency, a tourist needs to sign up to a cruise to experience the processes.

2. Possession-processing service

This type refers to customer involvement with the production process without directly following production, via tangible actions to a service object to improve the value. For example, for a public storage warehousing service, a customer will rent a storage unit, but not follow the whole service process.

3. Information-processing service

This refers to creating value by collecting, processing, and transferring information. Bloomberg, for example, collects and delivers updated business news, economic data, and financial information to global customers.

(3) Service competences

An appropriate service operations strategy should keep alignment with business strategy in terms of distinctive competences. Partially different from manufacturing systems, typical distinctive competencies of a service system are as follows: speed of service, quality, price, flexibility, availability, reliability, uniqueness, and range of services.

(4) Service concept

Different from manufacturing strategy, it is a core task to identify the service concept when formulating a service operations strategy. A service concept is a service product bundle including explicit and implicit services and specific service goods. A service concept is a statement of service nature, including customer service experience of the service process and service outcome of benefits, emotions, and values. For example, a Swedish company offers the service concept of an ice hotel, providing customers with the exciting and fun experience of residing in a hotel made of ice. One of the strategic roles of

Fig. 1.1 An outcome/
experience competitive
service strategy framework

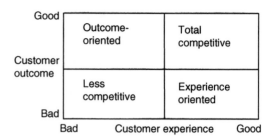

operations is to design a service delivery system to support the desired service concept.

(5) Service packages

Unlike products, service is often delivered with a form of service package. A service package consists of the following four elements (Fitzsimmons and Fitzsimmons 1994):

1. Supporting facility: This consists of physical resources that support the service; for example, a building for a restaurant, a swimming pool, a warehouse for public storage.
2. Facilitating goods: These are goods consumed or used by customers; for example, towels and shampoo in a hotel.
3. Explicit service: These are benefits quickly noticed by customers and are the intrinsic or essential features of a service: for example, the accommodation and feeding of customers in a hotel, and surgery in a hospital.
4. Implicit services: These are benefits sensed by customers vaguely – extrinsic features ancillary to service. Examples include the romantic atmosphere in a bar.

(6) Competitive service strategy frameworks

The distinction between manufacturing strategy and service strategy is relevant to inseparability and simultaneity, and is one of the differences between product and service. A service competitive strategy considers both customer outcome and customer experiences. Figure 1.1 shows a customer outcome-experience matrix, which is divided into four quadrants characterizing four service competitive strategies.

1. Customer outcome-oriented service strategy

   With this strategy, customer outcome is excellent but customer experience is not good. Some consulting firms, for example, are in this quadrant. They provide world-class consulting services, and guarantee a good consulting outcome. But customer experience may be unpleasant and customers may even find it difficult to access this consulting service. The engineering education provided at French elite graduate engineering schools (grandes écoles d'ingénieurs) adopts this strategy: first-class engineers are produced, but the training process is usually tough and not enjoyable.

2. Customer experience-oriented service strategy

   Customer experience-oriented service strategy refers to a strategy that focuses on or is good at customer experience, but the customer outcome is bad. This is an unstable strategy: while customers may feel good during the

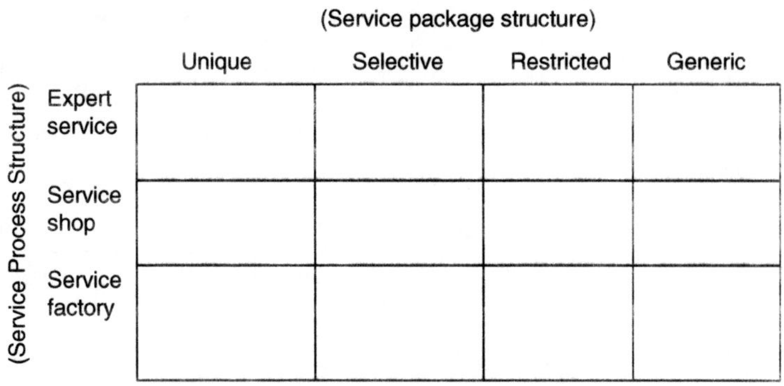

(Service package structure)

	Unique	Selective	Restricted	Generic
Expert service				
Service shop				
Service factory				

(Service Process Structure)

Fig. 1.2 Kellogg and Nie SP/SP competitive service strategy framework

service, they will hardly revisit it if they find the service outcome not good enough.

3. Less competitive service strategy

   This is an unsuccessful service strategy which can achieve neither good customer outcome nor customer experiences.

4. Total competitive service strategy

   Total competitive service strategy competes with players along both dimensions. For instance, Starbucks scrutinizes details to enhance the mood and ambience of the store, going to great lengths to make sure the store fixtures, the merchandise displays, the colors, the artwork, the banners, the music, and the aromas all blend to create a consistent, inviting, stimulating environment to improve customer experiences. Meanwhile, Starbucks stores offer a wide choice of regular or decaffeinated coffee beverages to improve customer outcomes.

Another competitive service strategic conceptual framework (see Fig. 1.2) is based on the service process/service package matrix (Kellogg and Nie 1995), linking service process structure with service package structure.

Service process structure is about customer influence on the service production and service process. Kellogg and Nie (1995) categorize service process into expert service with high degree of customer influence, service shop with medium degree of customer influence, and service factory with low degree of customer influence.

Service package structure is featured by the degree of customization of service package. Kellogg and Nie (1995) categorize service packages into unique service package with full customization, selective service package with considerable customization, restricted package with limited customization and generic package with little or no customization. This matrix is used to align

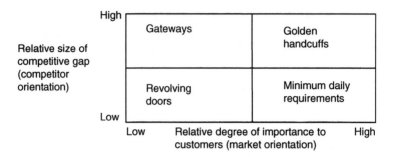

Fig. 1.3 Roth and van der Velde competitive service strategy framework

the types of service package with the types of process to gain better strategic insights.

Similar to the manufacturing strategy put forward by Hayes and Wheelwright (1984), Roth and van der Velde (1991) propose a framework based on the customer/account base matrix (see Fig. 1.3) to evaluate the relative competitive positions. They propose the following four stages of service strategy development:

1. Revolving door
   At this stage, just like a "revolving door", operations make little value-added contribution to service delivery. Relative degree of importance to customers is low and relative size of competitive gap is small.
2. Minimum daily requirement
   In this strategy, the critical success factors are highly important for customers but display small capability gaps among competitors. The corporation just maintains parity with competitors.
3. Gateway
   The gateway capabilities provide service differentiation to enhance the market attractiveness of service. The term "gateway" is used to describe a strategy to attract new customers to enter service systems. This is a strategy which is perceived by the majority as less important, but can display large competitive gaps. Given appropriate implementation policies, this strategy can win the competitive edge in the long term.
4. Golden handcuff
   "Golden handcuff" is used to describe a strategy to hold long-term customer loyalty. In this strategy, the success factors are not only perceived to be important by customers, but also create a large competitive gap.

(7) Definition

In summary, based on the statement above, we define service operations strategy as:

A consistent pattern of structural and infrastructural decisions, competing on customer outcome and/or customer experience, to develop service concept for people-processing, possession-processing, or information-processing services, and to achieve a set of service competencies aligned with business strategy.

1.1.3   From Operations Strategy to Global Operations Strategy

(1) Operations strategy

Anderson et al. (1989) conduct a literature review on operation strategy, mainly based on manufacturing strategy. Anderson et al. (1989) were among the earliest to use terminology "operations" strategy, and also mentioned service operations. At that time, as they pointed out, the literature on service operations strategy was not rich.

When Hayes and Upton (1998) propose operations-based strategy, they treat naturally both manufacturing and service operations since the research on service operations keep increasing from 1989 to 1998. Hayes and Upton (1998) argue that operations effectiveness is difficult to imitate and operations-based competitive advantage is sustainable. Hayes and Upton (1998) identify three operating capabilities which are helpful to understand operations strategy.

- Process-based operating capacity
  This is a type of capacity to achieve operating advantage, including low cost and high quality, during the process of transferring material or information to a product or service.
- Coordination-based operating capacity
  This is a type of capacity to achieve operating advantages, such as short lead times, product and service ranges, and customization, through coordination excellence throughout the entire operating system.
- Organization-based operating capacity
  This is a type of capacity to introduce new technology, design new products, and build new facilities faster than competitors.

  Hayes et al. (1996) is one of the earliest textbooks in operations strategy. Hayes et al. (2004) present principles for the development of a powerful operations organization, and describe how a company's operating and technological resources can be used to create a sustainable competitive advantage in a global and IT-intensive environment. Hayes is an important researcher in operations strategy, whom publisher Wiley claims to be "a founder of the Operations Strategy field" (overview of Hayes et al. 2004).

  For an updated review of operations strategy in a general application environment, we refer readers to Van Mieghem (2008), who provides a comprehensive treatise on operations strategy, introduces the principles and practice of operations strategy, and proposes a framework for operations strategy.

(2) Global strategy

Studies on global strategy are abundant and relevant principal theories include eclectic theory, transaction cost approach (TCA), competitive advantage of nation (CAN), competing for future, resource-based view (RBV) theory, core competency theory, interorganizational network theory, strategic groups theory based on industrial organization economics, and cognitive communities theory based on psychology (for further discussion on global strategy, see Sects. 2.1, 3.1 and 3.2). We only introduce several researches of direct relevance to global operations strategy.

- Dunning eclectic theory

  Dunning (1977) provides the first statement of the "eclectic" approach, later refined and extended in books and papers by the author and his collaborators. According to Dunning, a firm will engage in international production when each of the three following conditions is satisfied. First, the firm possesses an "ownership advantage", some unique competitive advantages not possessed by competing firms in other countries. Second, there is a "location advantage": Undertaking the value adding activities must be more profitable in a foreign location than undertaking it in a domestic location. Third, there is a "internalization advantage": the firm must benefit more from controlling the foreign business activity than from selling or leasing them to other companies.

  This framework integrates various strands of theoretical approaches for international production. Therefore Dunning labels his approach "eclectic". The framework has strongly influenced global operations strategy, including location strategy, and inspired many applications.

- Kogut comparative advantage-based competitive advantage

  The key concept of comparative advantage-based competitive advantage imposes influence on studies of global operations. Kogut (1985a) highlights the difference between comparative advantage (or location-specific advantage) and competitive advantage (or firm-specific advantage). Kogut (1985a) thinks the design of global strategies is based on "the interplay between the comparative advantage of countries and competitive advantages of firms".

- Ghoshal framework for global strategy

  While Levitt (1983) argues the effective global strategy stems from product standardization, Hout et al. (1982) think it comes from multiple methods, and Hamel and Prahalad (1985) think the effective global strategy is provided by a broad product portfolio. To assimilate these different views, based on an idea of "mapping means and ends", Ghoshal (1987) presents a conceptual framework for global strategy and introduces a map for research in global strategy. Ghoshal (1987) points out that a multinational has three means (sources of competitive advantage): national differences, scale economies, and scope economies. A firm can use these three means to achieve three goals or "ends": achieving efficiency in current operations, managing risks, and innovation learning and adaptation.

- Yip total global strategy

  With a systematic and practical introduction to global strategy, Yip (1992) provides an approach of total global strategy to diagnose industry globalization potential, to design global products and services, to locate global activities, to build a global organization, and to measure the use of global strategy.

(3) Global operations strategy

We firstly introduce global operations strategy from three perspectives proposed by Van Mieghem (2008), and then expand the perspectives to the setting of global operations.

1. Competency-based global operations strategy

In this view, managers consider competency in global competition in terms of cost, time, quality, and flexibility, among other competencies. In a global environment, the competency is often achieved through the competitive advantage based on comparative advantages of countries (see Kogut, 1985a). First of all, flexibility competency is vital for the multinational corporation, which is a network of activities located in different countries, benefiting from the coordination of subsidiaries. Kogut and Kulatilaka (1994) model this coordination as the operating flexibility to shift production between two manufacturing plants located in different countries. The value of operational flexibility is usually relative to exchange rate risks (Huchzermeier and Cohen 1996). Second, in a global setting, quality problems in outsourcing are paid high attention. For example, Mattel and Toyota have recalled products because of risks associated with outsourcing. Third, via outsourcing manufacturing and service, a corporation can achieve cost advantage with global operations. For example, Apple outsources manufacturing to suppliers like Foxconn to achieve cost competency. Fourth, global operations impose higher requirements regarding time competency. For example, while it is relatively easy for online retailers (like Amazon) to achieve fast response times (the time from order acceptance to product delivery) within a small geographic region, it becomes challenging to achieve fast response times in global operations. Finally, in a global setting, a company may pursue other competencies like uniqueness, availability, and ubiquity.

2. Resource-based global operations strategy

Here managers mainly consider how to develop a bundle of real assets or resources. Typical resource-based problems include capacity size problems, capacity investment and expansion time problems, resource-type problems, and resource location problems. Global capacity strategy is an important topic. Karabuk and Wu (2003) have studied the coordination of strategic capacity planning in the semiconductor industry, while Cohen and Lee (1989) have undertaken resource deployment analysis of global manufacturing and distribution networks. Second, the global location problem is vital for long-run success. For example, Lowe et al. (2002) study location strategies to reduce exchange rate risk. Hodder and Jucker (1985) study international plant location under price and exchange rate uncertainty. Third, to succeed globally, companies must choose correct global expansion strategies. For example, Henderson and Cool (2003) examine how firms may learn to better time their capacity expansion strategies through past experience with an empirical analysis of the worldwide petrochemical industry.

3. Process-based global operations strategy

Managers mainly configure the global activity network or processes, including the supply process, technology management process, demand and revenue management process, and innovation processes. First, global sourcing, global supply chain, and global purchasing are important business processes. Kouvelis (1999) examines global sourcing strategies under exchange rate uncertainty, and Ettlie (1998) evaluates and examines the role of R&D in global manufacturing. Second, risk management and operational hedging is an active topic in process-based global operations strategy. For example, Huchzermeier (1991) studies global manufacturing strategy planning under exchange rate uncertainty, while Kazaz et al. (2005) study an aggregate production planning problem in a global manufacturing network under exchange rate uncertainty. They formulate the problem as two-stage recourse, and feature two forms of operational hedging. Finally, the innovation process plays a critical role in a global environment. Knight and Cavusgil (2004) highlight innovative culture in the born-global firm.

4. Integration decisions of global operations strategy

Besides the structural and infrastructure decisions proposed by Hayes and Wheelwright (1984), global operations strategy needs to consider integration decisions, which determine how the operational function will strategically interface with various functions, borders, and values. The main decisions are as follows:

- Cross-border global operational decisions
  Cross-border decisions consider operational problems across political separation, cultural separation, physical separation, developmental separation, and relational separation.
- Cross-function global operational decisions
  Cross-function decisions consider the interface between operations and marketing management, finance management, taxation management, human resource management, R&D management, and IT management.
- Cross-value global operational decisions
  Cross-value decisions consider global operational problems across economic, environmental, and social values.

Table 1.2 shows main literature in evolving GOS. In summary, based on the statement above, we define global operations strategy as:

A consistent pattern of structural, infrastructural, and integration decisions, in a global competitive environment, determining the resource and process of a manufacturing or service system to achieve a set of optimal competencies alignment with business strategy.

Case Example: Global Operations of IKEA

IKEA, the world's largest furniture retailer – founded in 1943 by 17-year-old Ingvar Kamprad in Sweden – is a privately held, global home products company that designs and sells ready-to-assemble furniture featuring Scandinavian modern design and accessories.

Table 1.2 Main literature in evolving global operations strategy (2)

Categories	Literature	Contributions
Operations strategy	Anderson et al. (1989)	An early literature review on operations strategy
	Hayes et al. (1996)	An early textbook on operations strategy
	Hayes and Upton (1998)	Proposes operations-based strategy, identifies process-based, coordination-based, organization-based capabilities, and studies sustainability of an operations-based competitive advantage
	Hayes et al. (2004)	Describes how a company's operating and technological resources can be applied to create a sustainable competitive advantage in global economy
	Van Mieghem (2008)	Introduces operations strategy, particularly its principles and practice, and summarizes the competency-based view, resources-based view, and process-based view
Global strategy	Dunning (1977)	Proposes OLI (Ownership-Location-Internalization) triad framework, which strongly influences global operations strategy and inspires a great deal of applications
	Hout et al. (1982)	The effective global strategy stems from multiple methods
	Levitt (1983)	The effective global strategy stems from product standardization
	Herbert (1984)	Develops several strategies and multinational organization structures
	Hamel and Prahalad (1985)	The effective global strategy stems from a broad product portfolio
	Ghoshal (1987)	Presents a conceptual framework for global strategy, and introduces a map for research in global strategy
	Yip (1992)	Provides the first systematic, comprehensive, balanced, and practical approach to developing a global strategy
Global operations strategy	Kogut (1985a)	Puts forward differences between comparative advantages and competitive advantages
	Kogut (1985b)	Studies the role of operational flexibility in global strategies
	Lovelock and Yip (1996)	Develops global strategies for service business
	McLaughlin and Fitzsimmons (1996)	Identifies strategies for globalizing service operations
	Young and Nie (1996)	Reviews the research on global operations management, and particularly study cultural and technical success factors

Despite an aggressively promoted Swedish identity, IKEA set up headquarters in the Netherlands. The corporation structure (see Fig. 1.4) is very complicated, and roughly consists of two parts: (1) INGKA Holding, a private, for-profit Dutch company, manages most of IKEA's operations, including purchasing

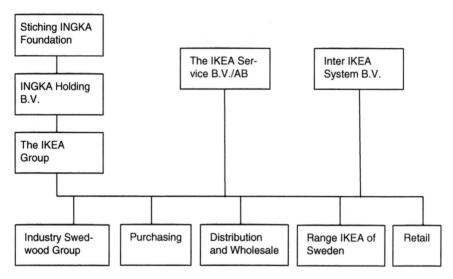

Fig. 1.4 The organization structure of IKEA

and supply chain management, design, manufacture, and store management. INGKA Holding is owned by the Stitching INGKA Foundation, which Kamprad established in 1982 in the Netherlands as a tax-exempt, not-for-profit foundation registered in Leiden, Netherlands. The INGKA Foundation is controlled by a five-member executive committee chaired by Kamprad; (2) Inter IKEA Systems, a Dutch company, owns the IKEA trademark and concept. Every IKEA store pays a franchise fee of 3 % of its revenue to Inter IKEA Systems. Inter IKEA Systems is believed to be controlled by Ingvar Kamprad.

IKEA's value proposition is at the core of "Affordable Solutions For Better Living". IKEA targets customers seeking furniture items with good design and excellent quality at relatively low prices, who are willing to do a little work – serving themselves during shopping, order picking, checkout, transporting products home, and assembling the furniture. The typical customers are working-to middle-class and relatively young. To achieve the competency of low price, IKEA reformulates its global operations, including (1) global service strategy and (2) global manufacturing.

In service operations innovation, IKEA widely applies self-service options and moves activities from the front desk to customers. IKEA combines back-desk warehouses and front-desk retailing stores. During the shopping tour, customers use an operation called self-picking – that is, they, not IKEA staff, pick items. This reduces warehousing operation costs, since it is well known that in some warehouses, about 50 % of warehousing costs stems from order picking. IKEA controls the layout of the shopping tour to efficiently deliver products and enhance customer experience. After their shopping tour, customers may choose to use self-checkout stations. This reduces IKEA's retail labor cost, since checkout staff usually comprises a large proportion of the workforce in large retailers. After shopping, customers will self-assemble furniture from IKEA.

Table 1.3 shows IKEA's internationalization process in terms of market entries. As of April 2011, IKEA operates about 321 stores in 38 countries, and widely adopts global sourcing in both developed and developing countries and regions. IKEA has a network of 2,700 furniture subcontractors in 67 countries, sourcing a range of around 11,200 products, and has a European logistics center in Dortmund, Germany and an Asian logistics center in Singapore. Its suppliers are usually based in low-cost countries or have proximity to raw materials or reliable access to distribution channels. The products are highly standardized and intended for the global market, with consideration of economies of scale. IKEA studies the comparative advantages of different regions and transfers the comparative advantages of locations to corporation competitive advantage via integrating low costs, standardization, and high quality. IKEA has indeed met many challenges during its global sourcing. In 1994, TV media reported its suppliers in Pakistan used child labor. The company appointed a third-party Scandinavian agent to monitor child labor practices at its suppliers in India and Pakistan.

Case Questions

1. Why did IKEA, which originates in Sweden, set its headquarters in Netherlands? What is the relation between INGKA Holding B.V. and Inter IKEA Systems?
2. The IKEA business strategy is at the core value of "affordable solutions for better living". Does its global sourcing strategy keep alignment with this core business strategy?
3. With global sourcing, how does IKEA transfer comparative advantages of locations to corporation competitive advantages? Which competencies have they achieved?

1.2 International Operations Management and Global Operations Strategy

1.2.1 Introduction to International Operations Management

International operations management (IOM) is the set of activities of an international organization seeking to transform kinds of input (materials, labor, and so on) into final goods and services. IOM is a well-established foundation of global operations strategy.

Prasad and Babbar (2000) conduct a literature review on international operations management, and propose a framework with two dimensions: topics and scope. In terms of topics, IOM includes strategy, location, capacity, flexibility, technology, productivity, layout, forecasting, scheduling, aggregate planning, purchasing, distribution, inventory, JIT (Just-In-Time), quality, reliability and maintenance, work

Table 1.3 IKEA's internationalization process in terms of market entries

Year	IKEA first store/market entry	Number of stores in 2011
1958	Sweden: Almhult	17
1963	Norway: Oslo (Nesbru)	6
1969	Denmark: Copenhagen (Ballerup)	5
1973	Switzerland: Zurich (Spreitenbach)	10
1974	Germany: Munich (Eching)	46
1975	Australia: Artamon	7
1976	Canada: Vancouver (Richmond)	12
1977	Austria: Vienna (Vosendorf)	7
1978	Netherlands: Rotterdam (Sliedrecht)	12
1978	Singapore: Singapore	2
1980	Spain: Gran Canaria (Las Palmas)	13
1981	Iceland: Reykjavika	1
1981	France: Paris (Bobigny)	28
1983	Saudi Arabia: Jeddaha	3
1984	Belgium: Brussels (Zaventem and Ternat)	6
1984	Kuwait: Kuwait City	1
1985	United States: Philadelphia	38
1987	United Kingdom: Manchester (Warrington)	18
1989	Italy: Milan (Cinisello Balsamo)	18
1990	Hungary: Budapest	2
1991	Poland: Platan	8
1991	Czech Republic: Prague (Zlicin)	4
1991	United Arab Emirates: Dubai	2
1992	Slovakia: Bratislava	1
1994	Taiwan: Taipei	4
1996	Finland: Esbo	5
1996	Malaysia: Kuala Lumpur	1
1998	China: Shanghai	9
2000	Russia: Moscow (Chimki)	12
2001	Israel: Netanya	1
2001	Greece: Thessaloniki	3
2004	Portugal: Lisbon	3
2005	Turkey: Istanbul	5
2006	Japan: Tokyo (Funabashi)	5
2007	Romania: Bucharest	1
2007	Cyprus: Nicosia	1
2009	Ireland: Dublin	1
	Total	321

(*Source*: Jonsson and Foss 2011)

measurement, service, and project management (Prasad and Babbar 2000). In terms of scope, IOM consists of three issues: mono-country/region study, cross-country/region, and global studies (Prasad and Babbar 2000).

1.2.2 The Difference Between IOM and Global Operations Strategy

(1) Internationalization and globalization

The terms "international" and "global" are often used interchangeably. While an "international" business, could be a simple trade between USA and Canada, however, a "global" corporation often does business in both developed and developing countries, in different political systems, and for heterogeneous customers with different cultural and religious views. Yip (2003, p 7) states the difference between relevant terms as follows:

> The term "worldwide" will be used as a neutral designation. "International" will refer to anything connected with doing business outside the home country. "Multilocal" and "global" will refer to types of worldwide strategy.

A global strategy emphasizes an integrated approach across borders. This book will highlight the approach of global integration, including integration across different borders and integration between operations strategy and other functional strategies, including marketing, finance, human resource, technology management, and information management strategies.

(2) Operations management and operations strategy

Operations management refers to controlling, managing, evaluating, and improving daily and repetitive operational practices, which mainly handles individual processes and given resources set. Operations strategy is one of the functional strategies and refers to not one practice but collective operational practices, which mainly relate to choosing resources and processes and building future capabilities. Operations strategy needs to consider integration with other functional strategies and keep alignment with business strategy. For further readings in global operations strategy, see Birkinshaw et al. (1995), Buckley and Ghauri (2004), Chase and Uday (2007), Doz and Kosonen (2008), Porter (1980, 1987, 1996, 1990/1998, 1991), Prokesch (1995), Slack and Lewis (2011).

Case Example: HSBC – "The World's Local Bank"

HSBC is a global banking and financial services company headquartered in London. HSBC (abbreviation from the "Hongkong and Shanghai Banking Corporation") was founded in Hong Kong and Shanghai by Scotsman Sir Thomas Sutherland in 1865. From its origin, HSBC has been a product of globalization. It has around 7,200 offices in more than 80 countries and regions across Africa, Asia, Europe, North America and South America. As of 30 June 2010, it had total assets of \$2.418 trillion, of which roughly half were in Europe, a quarter in the Americas and a quarter in Asia.

HSBC has launched a worldwide campaign to define a distinct personality and introduce itself as "the world's local bank". Through the campaign, HSBC tries to balance its philosophy of valuing international organizations and global services and its operations strategy of respecting diverse cultures and delivering individual customized service. With the strapline "the world's local bank", HSBC tries to show customers can benefit from both its international experience and its local knowledge.

To reduce global operations cost, HSBC is outsourcing processing work, including data processing, customer service, and internal software engineering, to locations such as Pune (India), Hyderabad (India), Vishakhapatnam (India), Kolkata (India), Guangzhou (China), Curitiba (Brazil), and Kuala Lumpur (Malaysia). Currently, HSBC operates service centers (e.g., call centers) out of eight countries. The group service centers play a key role in delivering consistent customer experience and try to create a seamless service delivery proposition. However, risks arise from these offshoring operations. For example, on 27 June 2006, HSBC reported an employee at the Bangalore call center supplied confidential customer information to fraudsters. Trade unions in the US and UK have also blamed these centers for job losses in developed countries.

Case Questions

1. Although HSBC claims itself to be "the world's local bank", part of its operations and service (facility layout, basic service procedure at the front desk, offshoring call centers, ATM operations) is relatively standardized in most regions. What do you think about this "inconsistency"?
2. Why did HSBC outsource processing work to developing countries? What are the comparative advantages of these countries? Which operating advantage can HSBC achieve by offshoring?

1.3   Basic Principles in Global Operations Strategy

1.3.1   Global Integration Principle

In order to win competitive advantages and achieve corporations' goals, it is imperative to integrate operations strategies and business strategy. There are two opinions about the relationship between these strategies. Researchers from one school of thought think the role of operations is to support corporate objectives. Hayes and Schmenner (1978) think "manufacturing functions best when its facilities, technology and policies are consistent with recognized priorities of corporate strategy". Researchers of another opinion think that operations strategy can lead corporations to some extent, and that operational capacity can determine business strategy in order to achieve competencies. Although there are two views of the relation between operations strategy and business strategy, the necessity of building linkages between operations strategy and corporations and keeping them in alignment is beyond doubt.

1.3.2   Global Coordination Principle

The complexity of coordination for global operations is higher than for regional operations. When a corporation goes global, geographic dispersion is a complexity-adding factor. It is associated with the need for a new structure (see Herbert 1984), and a new structure requires additional conditions. Global operations, managing global networks of human, resources, and processes, require coordinated organizational branches in different regions, coordination among business functions (see page 6, Porter 1986), and coordination across political separation, cultural separation, developmental separation, and relational separation. In particular, Young and John (1996) (a chapter in Young and Nie 1996, p. 153) point out that marketing-manufacturing is "aggravated by complex structural, geographic, and cultural considerations that give the coordination task an added dimension of complexity".

The complexity and difficulty of coordination are associated with global strategy and organization structure. Based on the research of Herbert (1984) and Martinez and Jarillo (1989), Young and John (1996) summarize five strategies with an international organization structure and note that global coordination varies according to the organization structures:

1. Volume expansion

   The corporation just exports products made domestically, with an objective of increasing revenue. The coordination between product and outbound logistics and order management coordination increases.

2. Resource acquisition

   In this strategy, in order to assure reliable availability of materials for use in domestic manufacture, the corporation may build a foreign subsidiary. Coordination between product and inbound logistics and purchasing management coordination increases.

3. Reciprocity

   Herbert (1984) defines reciprocity strategy as a two-way materials flow: A corporation might ship low-value raw materials or semi-finished products to a developing country, and complete processing or final assembly in that nation. Finally it ships the finished product out to developed countries. In this mode, the coordination between product and inbound logistics, assembly and outbound logistics, and purchasing management coordination increases.

4. Integration

   In this strategy, operations are fully integrated. The complexity and difficulty of coordination among demand and order management, purchasing, manufacturing, and logistics are high.

5. Complex global

   Bartlett and Ghoshal (1989) propose a complex interdependence consisting of collaborative problem solving, resource sharing, and information sharing. Martinez and Jarillo (1989) call this strategy "complex global". Young and John (1996) think the difference between reciprocal and complex global lies in "the stability of the organization structure and predictability of the coordination requirements".

The most common coordination mechanisms (Martinez and Jarillo 1989) for multinational corporations are as follows:

1. Departmentalization or grouping of organizational units.
2. Centralization or decentralization of decision-making.
3. Formalization and standardization (e.g., written policies, rules, job descriptions and standard procedures).
4. Planning (e.g., strategic planning, budgeting).
5. Output and behavior control (e.g., financial performance, technical reports, sales and marketing data).
6. Lateral or cross-departmental relations (e.g., direct managerial contact, committees).
7. Informal communication (e.g. personal contacts).
8. Socialization (e.g., building an organizational culture).

1.3.3 Global Trade-off Principle

A corporation usually sets multiple objectives and may try to achieve multiple competitive advantages. Unfortunately, it is often impossible to excel simultaneously in all aspects of operations, and in many cases the corporation has to make trade-offs, treating one objective or competency preferentially over another, since there is inherent contradiction between the factors under consideration. Skinner (1969) identifies five decision fields, including plant and equipment, production planning and control, labor and staffing, product design, and organization management, which a manager may need to make a trade-off among.

There are trade-offs particularly relevant to global operations. Ghoshal (1987) thinks a global strategy tends to increase centralization levels and transfer power from subsidiaries to the headquarters. This transfer contradicts the advantage of local knowledge learning by demotivating subsidiaries' managers. Strategic flexibility, as suggested by Kogut (1985b), will sacrifice efficiency-based competencies. While the INSEAD business school chooses Singapore, an international environment, in which to locate its Asia campus, this may mean it loses the chance to directly enter larger Asian economies like China, Japan, and India. While Airbus inaugurates its A320 final assembly line in Tianjin, closer to China, the second largest aviation market, this also exposes it to large risks. Essentially due to limited capability of resources and processes, the competencies of global operations are governed by various trade-offs.

Not all researchers completely accept the trade-off principle. Ferdows and De Meyer (1990) try to avoid trading off one capability for another. They identify that some companies can outperform their competitors in multiple dimensions in terms of quality, dependability, responsiveness, and cost. Ferdows and De Meyer (1990) propose a "sandcone" model, arguing that, with a sequence in which operational capacities should be developed, certain operational capabilities can enhance one another, enabling operations excellence to be built cumulatively. They suggest firstly enhancing quality, then enhancing dependability while efforts to enhance

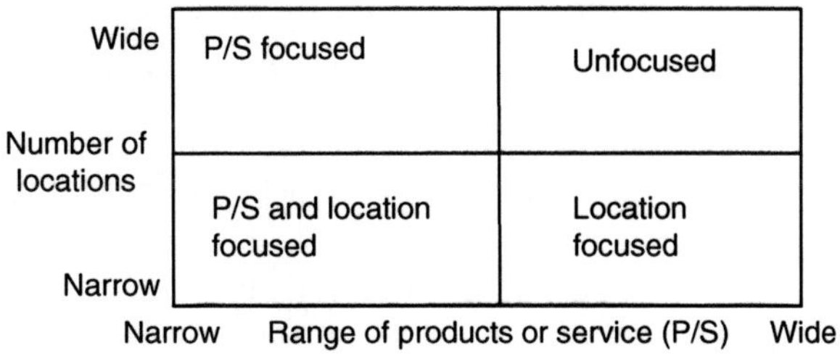

Fig. 1.5 Global product/
service-location focus matrix

	Range of products or service (P/S)	
Wide	P/S focused	Unfocused
Number of locations		
	P/S and location focused	Location focused
Narrow		
	Narrow Wide	

quality are further expanded, then enhancing flexibility while quality and dependability are further enhanced, and then enhancing cost while all efforts are further enlarged.

In their consideration of the strategic problem associated with social responsibility, Porter and Kramer (2011) also lack appreciation for the trade-off principle. While the theory of CSR (corporate social responsibility) thinks social value will impose constraints on corporate economic objectives, making it necessary to make a trade-off between economic and social value, Porter and Kramer (2011) propose a new theory of CSR (creating shared value) and think corporations should expand the overall amount of social and economic values, going beyond trade-off principles.

1.3.4 Global Focus Principle

Also due to the multiple objectives and multiple competitive advantages targeted by corporations, an unfocused strategy may make corporations noncompetitive. Skinner (1974) was among the earliest to propose the concept of focused manufacturing, suggesting that "a factory that focuses on a narrow product mix for a particular market niche will outperform the conventional plant, which attempts a broader mission". The key characteristics of the focused factory are focused process technologies, focused market demand, focused product volume, focused quality levels, and focused manufacturing tools.

Focused strategy in a global setting involves competition in industries that extend across national boundaries and comparison of strategic resources in multiple locations. A common trade-off is between global integration and local focus of specific activities. Focus strategy may be formulated at different geographic levels. In Fig. 1.5, we study the focus strategy in a global setting along two dimensions of focus: the number of locations and the range of service. We identify the following different geographic focus strategies:

- Product/service focused strategy. Focus on a narrow range of products or service, but access to multiple locations – even to the world.
- Location focused strategy. Focus on a narrow range of locations, but offer a bundle of products or service packages.

- Product/service and location focused strategy. Focus on a narrow range of products or services in one or few locations.
- Unfocused strategy. Offer a bundle of products or service worldwide.

Case Example: INSEAD – The Business School for the World

INSEAD is an international graduate business school, offering a full-time MBA program, a PhD in Management program, and several executive education programs. INSEAD's flagship MBA program is ranked No. 1 by Forbes and Bloomberg BusinessWeek in the category of Top Non-US one Year Business Schools. INSEAD regards itself as "the business school for the world" and its mission is "to promote a non-dogmatic learning environment that brings together people, cultures and ideas from around the world, changing lives, and helping transform organizations through management education".
- Three campuses and one center
In 2000, INSEAD opened a campus in Asia and became the first business school to have two fully-fledged campuses with permanent faculty – one in Europe, the other in Asia. INSEAD's location selection was not easy, taking in Singapore, Hong Kong and other Asian cities. Kuala Lumpur in Malaysia was one of the candidate locations since it was possible to get support from a major conglomerate, Sime Darby. INSEAD finally excluded Kuala Lumpur due to the impact of the economic downturn in Malaysia and the school's wish not to be tied to a particular company. Hong Kong was also considered but INSEAD thought there were uncertainties before Hong Kong's return to China. Although today, particularly after the rapid development of China and Hong Kong's growth after 1997, people wonder whether INSEAD has missed a larger opportunity, Singapore seems to fit the culture of INSEAD well. "INSEAD considered twelve locations in the entire Asia-Pacific... but in the end, Singapore won," said INSEAD Asia's former Dean Hellmut Schütte. "Singapore wanted us, courted us and finally convinced us. No regrets so far. If we would have to take a decision today, we would choose Singapore again." In 2000, the Graduate School of Business at the University of Chicago made the same choice, boosting the local education landscape with its prestigious programs.

However, not all Western business schools take the same opinion in their Asian location selection. For example, Harvard built Harvard Center Shanghai, the first such presentation and research space of its kind outside Boston and Cambridge. New York University built NYU Shanghai, a comprehensive research university in China's financial capital – the first American university with independent legal status approved by the China Ministry of Education. President Sexton of NYU said this decision: "New York and Shanghai enjoy a natural affinity as world capitals; as vibrant, ambitious, and forward-looking centers of commerce and culture; as magnets for people of talent. As we did in Abu Dhabi, here in Shanghai we have found visionary partners, and our joint effort to create NYU Shanghai emerges out of a common belief in the indispensable value of higher education and in the special opportunities that can be created when the world's greatest cities join forces. This will be a great university and a great partnership."

In 2007, the INSEAD center opened in Abu Dhabi, UAE. In 2010, INSEAD's Abu Dhabi Center attained campus status, under the patronage of the Crown Prince of Abu Dhabi. The Middle East plays an increasingly critical role in the global business strategy of INSEAD, and it has launched open-enrolment programs in Abu Dhabi. Currently it has campuses in Europe (France), Asia (Singapore) and the Middle East (Abu Dhabi), a research center in Israel, and offices in America.

• Alliance and partners

In 2001, Wharton School and INSEAD launched an alliance to combine the resources of two schools, to build a compelling worldwide network, and to deliver global business education to executives across four dedicated campuses: INSEAD's in Fontainebleau (France), and Singapore and Wharton's US campuses in Philadelphia and San Francisco. INSEAD MBA students and PhD candidates have the chance to study on three continents through an alliance with the Wharton School and a multi-campus structure.

In 2006, INSEAD and The School of Economics and Management (SEM) at Tsinghua University, one of the best business schools in China, formed the TIEMBA, or the Tsinghua INSEAD Executive MBA. This is one of the premier English-language EMBA programs in mainland China. In 2008, Tsinghua and INSEAD signed a memorandum of understanding to strengthen the partnership in terms of faculty exchanges, research cooperation, and joint programs.

In France, INSEAD is an associated member of Sorbonne University, a French foundation for cooperation in higher education and research. Through this partnership, INSEAD obtains access to French educational resources.

Case Questions

1. How does INSEAD's operations strategy, particularly its facility location strategy, keep alignment with its mission and core values, characterized by the slogan "the business school for the world"?
2. In the facility location decision on the Asia campus, what was the strategic focus of INSEAD? Why did Chicago Booth make the same location decision, but Harvard and NYU go elsewhere in Asia?
3. In Europe, INSEAD chose to locate at Fontainebleau, a town, not the metropolis of Paris. In Asia, INSEAD chose Singapore, not larger Asian cities like Hong Kong, Shanghai, or Tokyo. In the Middle East, INSEAD chose Abu Dhabi, not Dubai. Which trade-offs did INSEAD need to make when choosing locations?
4. How should INSEAD cope with the coordination across borders to maintain its alliances and partnerships in Europe, Asia and North America?

(Product structure)

	Low volume, one of a kind	Low volume, multiple products	Higher volume, standardized product	Very high volume, commodity product
Jumbled flow	Job shop			
Disconnected line flow		Batch		
Connected line flow			Assembly line	
Continuous flow				Continuous

(Process structure)

Fig. 1.6 Hayes and Wheelwright product-process matrix

1.4   Basic Decisions in Global Operations Strategy

1.4.1   Structure Decisions

(1) Vertical integration

Vertical integration is a concept which was partly introduced by steel tycoon Andrew Carnegie in the nineteenth century. Contrary to horizontal integration, which refers to the consolidation of partner corporations to handle manufacturing processes for a target product, vertical integration refers to the degree to which a corporation controls its downstream suppliers and its upstream buyers. For example, Carnegie Steel controlled the mines where the iron ore was extracted, the coal mines that supplied the coal, the mills where the steel was made, the ship fleet that transported the iron ore and even the railroads that transported the coal to the factory.

Although vertical integration is effective in achieving economies of scale, it may lead to higher internal coordination costs, weaker motivation for good performance, and a rigid organizational structure. In global operations, some companies adopt vertical de-integration strategies, outsourcing manufacturing and service activities previously conducted in-house and focusing on their core value chain. Through a vertical de-integration strategy considering regional comparative advantages in terms of cost, quality or other factors, a corporation can transfer comparative advantage of locations to its competitive advantage.

(2) Manufacturing process

A corporation needs to make a decision between high volumes of homogeneous product and low volumes of differentiated product. Hayes and Wheelwright (1979a) present a product-process matrix to examine market-manufacturing congruence problem and to help manufacturing process decisions (see Fig. 1.6). The matrix consists of two dimensions, product structure and process structure.

The process structure dimension describes the process choice (job shop, batch, assembly line, and continuous flow) and process structure (jumbled flow, disconnected line flow, connected line flow, and continuous flow). The product structure describes the four stages of the product life cycle (low volume to high volume) and product structure (low to high standardization).

By Hayes and Wheelwright's (1979a) matrix relates process selection to product life cycle stage. In the early stage of a product's life cycle, a job shop may be appropriate to fulfill early demand and adjust design to fit customer requirements. When the product becomes mature, high volumes may necessitate an assembly line. In the declining phase, the batch process may be appropriate, when volumes fall and spare parts are needed. Furthermore, the application of this matrix has been extended beyond the product life cycle stage. By incorporating two dimensions into the strategic planning process of corporation, and relating process decisions more effectively to marketing opportunities, the matrix provides an effective method to facilitate winning competitive advantage.

(3) Facility design and planning

Facility design and planning is a set of strategic decisions involving irreversible and substantial investment. In particular, facility location problems (like plant location and headquarters location problems) and facility layout problems, which will influence manufacturing and service process in the long run, are vital to achieve competitive advantage.

Facility location is an active research topic in the fields of industrial engineering, economics, operations management, sociology, and geography. For global manufacturing, facility location is one of the most important factors to reduce cost or increase delivery speed. The manufacturing facility location problem considers the location of raw materials, markets, transportation, and local work force. It can be solved by quantitative methods, including exact methods like integer programming and dynamic programming, heuristics methods, like greedy heuristics and exchange heuristics, and qualitative methods, like the factor rating method. For global services, service facility location is a determinant to improve revenue and service quality. Typically service location problems involve traffic patterns, customer demographics, and demographics predicting the appropriate profitable location. However, boards' personal reasons and executive amenities are also very influential factors in the final decisions regarding facility location.

Facility layout is another long-run factor for global operations. An optimal warehouse layout design can reduce the traveling time of order pickers and improve productivity of order picking, the most important warehousing operation. The layout influences both productivity and flexibility of FMS (flexible manufacturing systems). The layout of stores like Walmart and Carrefour can influence the purchase intentions of customers. Unlike traditional retail stores which allow a consumer to navigate directly to any section, IKEA adopts a "one-way path" layout, steering shoppers away from the single entrance and driving them through different showrooms before granting access to the warehouse and checkout area. This layout can increase so-called "impulse buying".

(4) Factory capacity

It usually takes a long time to change the manufacturing capacity or service capacity of a corporation. Capacity refers to both the quantity and variety of products or services. There are three basic capacity strategies: lead capacity strategy, lag capacity strategy and match capacity strategy. The lead capacity strategy, a relatively risky option, increases capacity before demand actually increases, to achieve a competitive advantage in terms of lead times. Lag capacity strategy, a less risky option, builds capacity only after demand has occurred. Match capacity strategy tries to increase capacity in appropriate increments to match the increase in demand, although it is difficult to find an optimal increment.

1.4.2   Infrastructure Decisions

(1) Quality management

Hayes and Wheelwright (1984) list quality as one of the major areas in which a corporation can seek a competitive advantage in manufacturing. Quality strategy is beyond control and management technologies like statistical process control and DMAIC (design, measure, analysis, improve, control); it is more relevant in imposing long-run influence on business goals. For example, based on the existing quality improvement methodologies such as quality control, TQM (total quality management), and Zero Defects, Six Sigma is a quality strategy originally created by Motorola, seeking to improve the quality of process outputs by identifying and removing the causes of errors and minimizing variability in manufacturing processes, and to lay infrastructure for future development of low cost and high quality competencies.

Service quality is imperative to achieve a competitive advantage for service firms, and is important even for manufacturing corporations. Service quality is different from product quality. Fitzsimmons and Fitzsimmons (2008) introduce five dimensions of service quality: reliability, referring to service completed on time without errors; responsiveness, referring to prompt service delivery to customers; assurance, associated with the capacity of service staff to convey trust and confidence with courtesy; empathy, referring to understanding and serving customers with attention, approachability, and sensitivity; and tangibility associated with physical conditions showing tangible evidence of care and attention. The typical quality decision seeks to determine service level and focus along these five dimensions in a service package.

(2) Production and inventory planning

This is a huge decision set, and only a part of decisions in production and inventory planning can impose long-run strategic influence. One of the fundamental decisions is determination of a push or pull system. For example, JIT, a pull-system production strategy originally by Toyota Production System, can reduce work-in-process inventory and associated production and inventory costs, achieving advantages by continuously improving returns on investment, quality, and efficiency. Flexible manufacturing system, a manufacturing configuration able to adapt rapidly to changing demand, can help achieve competency in flexibility. Particularly in global operations settings, a decision over centralization versus decentralization of manufacturing or service will influence global manufacturing networks or global service systems.

(3) Work force

It is vital to formulate a global work force strategy to align both business strategy and employees' personal expectation. The advantage of global operations rests on the potential opportunities to utilize comparative advantages of human resources in different locations. With access to knowledge and skills in locations with work force quality or cost advantages, a global corporation can outperform peers in the same industry. The challenges rest in managing language skills and multicultural diversity in a global corporation. It is imperative for success to place emphasis on continuing education and lifelong learning via business conferences, online education, skills training, executive programs, and management seminars.

Case Example: Global Manufacturing of Volkswagen

The Volkswagen Group, headquartered in Wolfsburg, Germany, is one of the world's leading automobile manufacturers. As of 31 December 2011, Volkswagen operates 99 production plants in 18 European countries and further nine countries in the Americas, Asia and Africa. Around the world, nearly 501,956 employees produce about 34,500 vehicles or are involved in vehicle-related services each working day. The Volkswagen Group sells its vehicles in 153 countries. The competitive goal of Volkswagen is to offer attractive, safe and environmentally friendly vehicles and set world standards in their respective classes.

The product ranges from low-consumption to luxury vehicles. Volkswagen's passenger car business includes two brand groups: Audi and Volkswagen. Audi's brand group, with an emphasis on sporty values, consists of the Audi, Seat and Lamborghini brands. The Volkswagen brand group, designed for more classic values, consists of the Volkswagen, Škoda Auto, Bentley and Bugatti brands. Each brand retains differentiated products and operates as an independent unit (Fig. 1.7).

Volkswagen has developed alliances with some world-class suppliers, such as Metalurgica Romer SA. Outsourcing has been widely adopted by Volkswagen; it outsources auto components to India in huge quantities in order to lower its prices to become a competitive player. Recently Volkswagen has planned to reduce outsourcing to boost productivity. "We are increasingly thinking about insourcing. It is about engineering, about jobs in production and about making prototypes. We could also intensify in-house tool making. And we will certainly make more components ourselves," production head Jochem Heizmann told daily Braunschweiger Zeitung in an interview provided to Reuters.

Group Strategy 2018

The key element of our "Strategy 2018" is to position the Volkswagen Group as a global economic and environmental leader among automobile manufacturers. In 2018, the Volkswagen Group aims to be the most successful and fascinating auto-maker in the world. In order to achieve that, we have set ourselves four goals:

- Volkswagen intends to become a world leader by using intelligent innovations and technologies, while at the same time delivering customer satisfaction and quality.
- Over the long term, Volkswagen aims to increase unit sales to more than 10 million vehicles a year; it intends to capture an above-average share as the major growth markets develop.
- Volkswagen intends to increase its return on sales before tax to at least 8% in the long term in order to safeguard its solid financial position and ability to take action, even during difficult market periods.
- Volkswagen aims to become the top employer across all brands, companies and regions; it must do so in order to build a first-class team.

Source: Volkswagen Annual Report 2009 /2010

Fig. 1.7 Volkswagen "Strategy 2018"

Table 1.4 Examples of Volkswagen PL/PQ platform

Platform code	Product segments	Examples
PQ34	Small family cars/compact cars	Audi A3, Volkswagen Golf Mk4, Volkswagen Bora/Jetta, SEAT León, SEAT Toledo
PL45	Mid-size cars	Audi A4, Volkswagen Passat, Volkswagen Passat GP Lingyu
PL62	Full-size luxury cars	Audi A8, Bentley Continental Flying Spur, Bentley Continental GT/GTC, Volkswagen Phaeton

Volkswagen adopts a modular platform system to improve production efficiency and flexibility, thus increasing the group's profitability. An automobile platform is a shared set of common design and production activities to reduce the costs of product development and to further create new models on similar underpinnings. Table 1.4 shows several examples of the PL/PQ platform (P indicates a passenger car platform, Q indicates a transverse engine, L indicates a longitudinal engine).

In 2007, Volkswagen Group introduced a more flexible "modular component system" architecture on which to base future platforms, including the "modular transverse component system", for transverse-engined, small to medium-sized cars, the "modular longitudinal component system" for medium-sized and larger longitudinal engined models, and the "modular rear component system" for rear-engined city cars.

Platform selection is one of the vital decisions for the group. For example, there was tussling between Porsche and Audi over which brand would provide the platform for Volkswagen's future sports cars. After serious study and discussion, Volkswagen chose Porsche, not Audi, as the sports car platform for future models, including Audi, Lamborghini and Bentley.

Volkswagen pays particular attention to environmentally friendly vehicles and to setting new ecological standards in the area of vehicles, since this can leverage the group's strengths and systematically increase its competitive advantage.

In launching a large number of new models in Europe, China, and South America, quality management and control becomes an important infrastructure operating decision. Moreover, quality management and control faces challenges from growing product innovations. Volkswagen has made intensive efforts throughout the group to achieve both product and service quality.

Case Questions

1. How does global manufacturing fit the business strategy specified by Volkswagen's "Strategy 2018"?
2. What are the structural decisions in the global manufacturing of Volkswagen? Why did Volkswagen plan to reduce outsourcing?
3. What is the role of the modular platform system? Why is the decision on platform selection strategic? What is the influence of Volkswagen's decision to choosing Porsche, not Audi, as its sports car platform?
4. What are the infrastructure decisions in the global manufacturing of Volkswagen?
5. What are the integration decisions in the global manufacturing of Volkswagen?

1.5 Content Framework and Book Structure

1.5.1 Content Framework of Global Operations Strategy

This book presents a content framework of global operations strategy, shown in Fig. 1.8. Based on corporate strategy, global competition analysis, and global environment analysis, a corporation formulates a global business strategy. Global competition analysis is an assessment of the strengths and weaknesses of current and potential competitors worldwide, used to study competitors' objectives, assumptions, strategies, and capabilities, and to identify opportunities and threats. Global environment analysis can use the PESTEL model to examine political factors, economic factors, social factors, technological factors, environmental factors, and legal factors.

Global operations strategies (presented within the framework of dotted lines in Fig. 1.8) should keep alignment with the global business strategy. Some global operations strategies dealing with multi-business problems (e.g., an outsourcing

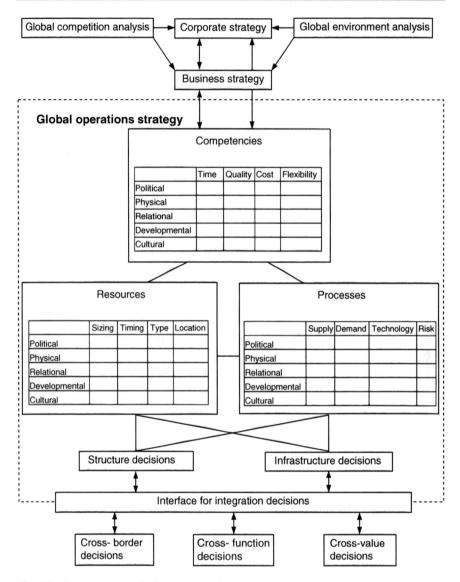

Fig. 1.8 Content framework of global operations strategy

decision for multiple products), involving substantial capital investment (e.g., a large scale manufacturing facility), or influencing long-term corporate development (e.g., a critical supplier or customer relationship) should also directly keep alignment with the corporate strategy. A global business strategy determines global competencies across borders, mainly measured by time, quality, cost, and flexibility competencies, among others.

To achieve competencies, a resource-based global operations strategy mainly considers capacity size, capacity time, resource types, and location problems across borders. A process-based global operations strategy mainly considers supply chain management, demand chain management or revenue management, technology management, and innovation across borders. Both resource and process problems may affect structure and infrastructure decisions.

A GOS (global operations strategy) must deal with interface practice including cross-border, cross-function, and cross-value decisions. Cross-border practice deals with decision across political, physical, relational, environment, cultural, and cultural separations. Cross-function practice considers integrative problems between operations and different functions, including marketing, finance, taxation, human resource, R&D, and IT management, among others. Cross-value practice considers decisions across economic, environmental, and social values. Furthermore, a GOS may deal with cross-business decisions. For example, Apple's outsourcing decision is relevant to its multiple products and businesses. Although a GOS may be relevant to cross-organization decisions, we have not used an independent chapter to present them since most cross-organization decisions are at the level of corporate strategy.

With such a content framework, the book is structured into three main parts: introduction, fundamentals, and practice. Within this structure the book consists of nine chapters. Each chapter consists of several sections. We provide a short case example for each section and a relatively long case for each chapter, with case questions to encourage critical reflection on the key issues in the associated chapter. We present chapter objectives at the beginning of each chapter. This design is used to maximize the clarity of the presentation of material via combining fundamentals and practice.

To facilitate the understanding, the book is structured into "triple triangles" (see Fig. 1.9). Triple triangles, representing respectively introduction (Part I), fundamentals (Part II), and practice (Part III), are interlinked and integrated into a large triangle representing global operations strategy.

Part I introduces global operations strategy through a "W-H-W triangle" or "3I" structure. We address the "what-problem" in this chapter, the "how-problem" in Chap. 2, and the "why-problem" in Chap. 3.

- Chapter 1 mainly answers the question: "what is GOS?" This chapter introduces basic concepts of global operations strategy, presents the evolving process of global operations strategy, addresses basic principles, and outlines basic decisions in global operations strategy.
- Chapter 2 introduces the modes of operational globalization, mainly answering the question "how are operations globalized?" This chapter studies the globalization of operations strategy and discusses basic globalization modes for both manufacturing and service operations.
- Chapter 3 introduces the rationale of operational globalization to help readers understand operational globalization, mainly addressing the question "why are operations globalized?" The chapter introduces the basic theories and

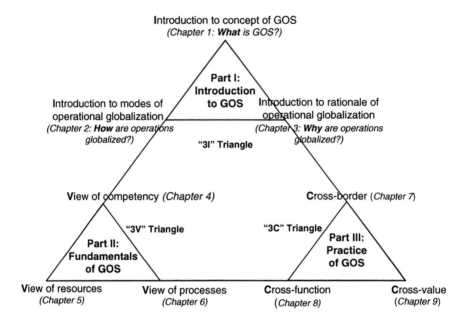

Fig. 1.9 Triple triangles book structure

frameworks of operational globalization analysis, explains drivers of operational globalization, identifies risks of global operations, and addresses the benefits of global operations.

Part II addresses the fundamentals of global operations strategy with a "3V" structure from three views. We address competency-based fundamentals in Chap. 4, resource-based fundamentals in Chap. 5, and process-based fundamentals in Chap. 6.

- Chapter 4 addresses competency-based views of global operations strategy. This is an extension of competency-based operations strategy in a setting of global operations.
- Chapter 5 presents resource-based views of global operations strategy. This chapter addresses resource size, capacity timing, resource type, and resource location problems.
- Chapter 6 studies process-based views of global operations strategy. This chapter includes global supply chain strategy, global revenue management strategy, global technology strategy, and global risk management strategy.

Part III discusses practice of global operations strategy through a "3C" structure. We address cross-border practice in Chap. 7, cross-function practice in Chap. 8, and cross-value practice in Chap. 9.

- Chapter 7 covers the implementation of global strategy across borders, including political separation, cultural separation, physical separation, developmental separation, and relational separation.

- Chapter 8 concerns integration issues between global operations and other functions, including marketing, finance, taxation, human resources management, and information management.
- Chapter 9 addresses cross-value global operations strategy and issues relevant to environmentally friendly, socially responsible, and sustainable global operations.

Case: Public Storage – Shurgard Warehouses

1. Introduction

   Self storage warehousing is a considerable industry in the US and a booming business in Europe and Asia. Self storage is a type of warehouse operations mode where customers store items themselves. There are two types of self storage: one is domestic self storage, the service objects of which are families or persons; another is business self storage, the service objects of which are companies and organizations.

   In the US, for example, the Self Storage Association (SSA, the official association representing this industry in the US) reported that while there were only 6,601 facilities at year-end 1984, the facility number rocketed to over 51,250 at year-end 2008. The SSA estimates that the industry had total sales in excess of $20 billion (USD) in 2008 in the US. In the European marketplace, according to the 2008 industry annual report of the Self Storage Association of UK (the official association representing this industry in the UK), the number of public storage warehouse facilities sharply increased by 117 % in Switzerland, 64 % in Denmark, 55 % in Sweden, 40 % in Portugal, 36 % in the Netherlands, 19 % in France and 17 % in Belgium from 2007 to 2008, within just a single year. Self storage is also rapidly developing in the rest of the world. For instance, the Self Storage Association of Australasia reports that there are over 1,100 self storage facilities and states that "self storage is one of the fastest growing industries in Australasia" (see selfstorage.com.au).

   The reasons behind this rapid growth rest on the self storage business model, which apparently fills a customer need. Self storage provides both private persons and small businesses with a temporary storage opportunity at a centrally located facility. Small rooms in a larger warehouse are rented out for a usually short period of time and can be operated by the renters themselves. One of the continual challenges for managers of such public storage warehouses is how to design facilities to improve their revenue.

   Public Storage, the world's largest self storage warehouse company, is an international corporation providing self storage warehousing services to both private and business customers. With decades of management experiences in cost control, this industry has been able to control the cost well. According to the SSA, at year-end 2008 the large self storage facilities employed "an average of 3.1 employees per facility" in the US. For example, a warehouse with about 5,000 m square rentable space only hires two workers per shift to run the facility. In traditional warehouses, labor is the main cost source.

2. Basic operations

The inner design of the warehouse is simple and relatively standardized. For instance, the height of all self storage warehouses we visited in the US is 8 ft. If the facility's floor height is higher than 8 ft, we find they even cover storage units and limit height to 8 ft to standardize the height and reduce service difference. Public Storage provides eight storage types for eight market segments. They classify the market segment by the types and sizes of customers' apartments. For example, for a family with a two-bedroom apartment, they offer a 10' × 10' storage unit, on the assumption that this is a sufficient size for the type of family's storage needs. Inner construction materials used by the self storage warehouse are cheap and flexible, and it is easy to assemble and disassemble a storage unit. With such materials, warehouses can update their inner layout.

A self storage warehouse includes heterogeneous storage types. Each storage type contains homogeneous storage units. Public Storage provides services to both family and business customers. In one of their warehouses in Chicago, there are only two laborers in a large warehouse, which implies relatively low costs. They adopt a "self storage" mode to achieve such low operation costs. In this type of warehouse, revenue rather than cost is the major concern, as is common in the public storage warehouse industry. Even a very large self storage warehouse in Philadelphia only assigns two workers per shift.

With the self storage operation mode, customers handle storage operations by themselves, without interference from warehouse personnel. Associated with self-service, the price of storage units is also dependant on the access difficulty. For example, the price of storage units on the group floor is usually higher since it is easier for self service. The price of first floor, with more difficulty of self-service, is lower. The prime objective for these public storage companies is to maximize the expected revenue at a stable cost level.

Customers can rent a storage unit for a certain period of time (measured in months). The monthly rent depends primarily on the storage unit's size and other properties, such as accessibility (situated on the ground floor, or on a higher floor; access from the street or only through an internal aisle) and required air conditioning of the room (heating or cooling). It may also depend on value-added services like extra security. Every month or quarter a new occupation plan is made.

For example, the occupation rate of a particular self storage warehouse in downtown Chicago is high in summer. This warehouse is near The University of Illinois at Chicago. Many faculty members and students will store their belongings here when not leasing a house, during the summer break. If the requested storage type is full, the warehouse will directly decline customers, and lose part of its revenue.

If an order is rejected by a warehouse, several alternatives are offered to the customer. In many cases the order is transferred to other Public Storage warehouses in the area. Other warehouses will adopt an upgrade operation.

Table 1.5 Public financial data before merger in 2005 (in $millions)

	PSA	Shurgard	Combined company	Percent
Revenue				
US	1,061	357	1,418	92 %
Europe	–	125	125	8 %
Total	1,061	482	1,543	100 %
NOI				
US	665	203	868	96 %
Europe	–	39	39	4 %
Total	665	242	907	100 %
Operations				
	1,501 facilities	624 facilities	2,125 facilities	
	37 states in USA	21 states in USA	38 states in USA	
	–	7 European countries	7 European countries	

For instance, in a warehouse in Philadelphia, if a requested storage type is fully occupied, the request will be upgraded to a higher class of storage with a larger area. The manager's decision depends on the expected revenue a customer can generate for the storage room, and depends on the current occupation of the warehouse. It is usually not possible to allocated currently occupied storage rooms for future demand, as customers can extend their contracts monthly.

Even for warehouses in the same companies and the same city, prices will differ. Their prices are highly dependent on geography. Prices are associated with occupation rate, real estate price, seasons and even weather. It is difficult for a market manager to price all the storage types at the same time, and pricing is considerably hard work for self storage warehouses.

A typical self storage warehouse dynamically updates its prices for each type of storage unit. It may adopt some heuristic algorithms to conduct pricing calculation. For example, a European warehouse updates prices by occupation rate. When the occupation rate of one storage type is higher, it will increase the price.

3. Public Storage and Shurgard merger

While Public Storage is the largest public storage company in USA, Shurgard is one of the largest in the European marketplace (Table 1.5). In 2005, Public Storage proposed to acquire Shurgard. "We believe that the combination of Public Storage and Shurgard will enhance our position as the premier self storage operator," said Ronald L. Havner, Jr., Chief Executive Officer of Public Storage.

Public Storage had approached Shurgard several times to discuss a potential merger and was repeatedly rejected. In July 2005, Public Storage proposed a stock-for-stock combination at a significant premium to market prices. After this proposal was rejected by the Shurgard board, Public Storage made its proposal public, and presented its case to the Shurgard shareholders though one-on-one meetings and through press releases and public statements. The resulting pressure and compelling logic led the Shurgard board to announce that it was studying strategic alternatives.

In 2006, Public Storage and Shurgard approved a merger agreement under which Public Storage would acquire Shurgard for approximately $5 billion. Public Storage would issue approximately 38.4 million shares of stock, assume about $1.8 million of debt, and redeem $136 million of Shurgard preferred stock. The transaction was slated to close by the end of the second quarter of 2006. Under the terms of the merger, each share of Shurgard common stock would be exchanged for 0.82 shares of Public Storage common stock. At closing, Shurgard shareholders would own approximately 23 % of the outstanding shares of the merged company.

The result was a combined total market capitalization of approximately $18 billion, with ownership interest in over 2,100 facilities in 38 states and seven European nations. Ronald L. Havner, Jr., president and chief executive officer of Public Storage, said, "The combination of Public Storage and Shurgard creates the largest self storage company in the world, with significant operating platforms in both the US and Europe, and enhances our prospects for continued growth and improved profitability."

David K. Grant, president and chief executive officer of Shurgard, said (see, e.g., allbusiness.com),"This merger represents a win-win situation for both Shurgard and Public Storage shareholders. A few months ago, we initiated a process to determine the best course of action for our company. After reviewing a number of strategic alternatives, it is clear that this transaction is the best option to create long-term value for our shareholders."

4. Global operations

Public Storage published a "Strategic Rationale" (see Fig. 1.10) to explain strategic benefits, objectives, and opportunities, including "operating synergies" to explain the benefits of M&A and "expanded growth opportunities" to explain how the growth opportunities become larger with a better platform. M&A undoubtedly plays a vital role in Public Storage's global operations. After acquiring Shurgard, M&A remained an important method of global expansion. During 2010, Public Storage acquired 42 facilities (2.7 million net rentable square feet). In January 2011, it acquired five facilities (386,000 net rentable square feet) in Nevada.

Although the self storage facilities may look different from outside, partially because some facilities were acquired from competitors, the storage units and service package are highly standardized in different countries in America and Europe. The pressure perceived by the managers mainly relates to global integration, not local responsiveness.

Public Storage adopted multi-site expansion, and exports its successful service package to another country without much modification. While even McDonald's takes account of cultural experiences, like German beer or Chinese breakfast, in local marketplaces, Public Storage almost entirely duplicates its original service package, perhaps with small variations such

---

Strategic Rationale

Operating Synergies

• **General & Administrative Costs**
– PSA: 2.0% of revenues vs. SHU 7.5% of revenues
– Eliminate redundancies in combined company's back office and executive infrastructure
– SOX compliance costs may be substantially reduced
• **Operating Costs**
– Opportunity to potentially increase operating margins
– Significant number of same markets (35) includes: Chicago, Dallas, Los Angeles, Minneapolis, San Francisco, and Seattle
– Sound financial systems which are scalable
– Economies of scale in media, call centers and supervisory personnel costs
– Potential to reduce duplicate expenses for Yellow Pages and management information systems
• **Revenues**
– Opportunity to generate higher revenues
– Participation in national media and promotional programs
– Ancillary businesses, e.g. tenant reinsurance, can be expanded

Expanded Growth Opportunities

• Largest self-storage owner/operator in world - Significant platforms in US and Europe suitable for continued expansion
• Financial strength to continue platform expansion
• Enhanced career opportunities for best people

Fig. 1.10 "Strategic rationale" of Public Storage after merger in 2006

as enhancing security, adding temperature control, or increasing accessibility in some regions.

Self storage industries also provide some value-added services, such as packages. But revenue from the value-added services is limited. In order to reduce cost, self storage industries adopt outsourcing operations to handle possible added service requests from customers. They usually outsource security services, transportation, and insurance to their business partners.

Case Questions

1. Use outcome/experience, Kellogg and Nie SP/SP, and Roth and van der Velde competitive service strategy frameworks to analyze the service operations of Public Storage.
2. Use the integration-responsiveness framework to study the global operations strategy of Public Storage.
3. Identify the structure, infrastructure, and integration decisions of global operations in Public Storage.
4. Study the "strategic rationale" of the Public Storage merger. What is the contribution of the Public Storage/Shurgard merger to Public Storage's global operations strategy?

References

Anderson, J. C., Cleveland, G., & Schroeder, R. G. (1989). Operations strategy: A literature review. *Journal of Operations Management, 8*(2), 133–158.

Bartlett, C. A., & Ghoshal, S. (1989). *Managing across borders: The transnational solution.* Boston: Harvard Business School Press.

Birkinshaw, J., Morrison, A., & Hulland, J. (1995). Structural and competitive determinants of a global integration strategy. *Strategic Management Journal, 16*(8), 637–655.

Buckley, P. J., & Ghauri, P. N. (2004). Globalization, economic geography and the strategy of multinational enterprises. *Journal of International Business Studies, 35*(2), 81–98.

Chandler, A. D. (1962). *Strategy and structures: Chapters in the history of the industrial enterprise.* Cambridge: MIT Press.

Chase, R. B. (1978). Where does the customer fit in a service operation? *Harvard Business Review, 56*(6), 137–142.

Chase, R. B., & Uday, M. A. (2007). A history of research in service operations: What's the big idea? *Journal of Operations Management, 25,* 375–386.

Cohen, M. A., & Lee, H. L. (1989). Resource deployment analysis of global manufacturing and distribution networks. *Journal of Manufacturing and Operations Management, 2,* 81–104.

Doz, Y., & Kosonen, M. (2008). *Fast strategy: How strategic agility will help you stay ahead of the game.* Harlow: Pearson Education.

Dunning, J. H. (1977). Trade, location of economic activity and the MNE: A search for an eclectic approach. In Bertil Ohlin, Per-Ove Hesselborn, & Per Magnus Wijkman (Eds.), *The international allocation of economic activity.* London: Macmillan.

Ettlie, J. E. (1998). R&D and global manufacturing performance. *Management Science, 44*(1), 1–11.

Ferdows, K., & De Meyer, A. (1990). Lasting improvements in manufacturing performance: In search of a new theory. *Journal of Operations Management, 9*(2), 168–184.

Fitzsimmons, J. A., & Fitzsimmons, M. J. (1994). *Service management for competitive advantage.* New York: McGraw-Hill.

Fitzsimmons, J. A., & Fitzsimmons, M. J. (2008). *Service management: Operations, strategy, information technology.* New York: McGraw-Hill.

Ghoshal, S. (1987). Global strategy: An organizing framework. *Strategic Management Journal, 8*(5), 425–440.

Hamel, G., & Prahalad, C. K. (1985). Do you really have a global strategy? *Harvard Business Review, 63*(4), July–August, 139–148.

Hayes, R. H., & Abernathy, W. I. (1980). Managing our way to economic decline. *Harvard Business Review,* July–August, 67–77.

Hayes, R. H., & Chase, R. B. (1992). Applying operations strategy to service firms. In T. A. Swartz, D. E. Bowen, & S. W. Brown (Eds.), *Advances in services marketing and management* (Vol. 1). Greenwich: JAI Press.

Hayes, R. H., & Schmenner, R. W. (1978). How should you organize manufacturing? *Harvard Business Review, 56*(1), 105–118.

Hayes, R. H., & Upton, D. M. (1998). Operations-based strategy. *California Management Review, 40*(4), 8–25.

Hayes, R. H., & Wheelwright, S. C. (1979a). Link manufacturing process and product life cycles. *Harvard Business Review,* January–February, 133–140.

Hayes, R. H., & Wheelwright, S. C. (1979b). The dynamics of process: Product life cycles. *Harvard Business Review,* March–April, 127–136.

Hayes, R. H., & Wheelwright, S. C. (1984). *Restoring our competitive edge: Competing through manufacturing.* New York: Wiley.

Hayes, R. H., Wheelwright, S., & Clark, K. (1980). *Dynamic manufacturing.* New York: The Free Press.

Hayes, R. H., Pisano, G. P., & Upton, D. M. (1996). *Strategic operations: Competing through capabilities*. New York: Free Press.

Hayes, R. H., Pisano, G. P., Upton, D. M., & Wheelwright, S. C. (2004). *Operations, strategy, and technology: Pursuing the competitive edge*. Indianapolis: Wiley.

Henderson, J., & Cool, K. (2003). Learning to time capacity expansions: An empirical analysis of the worldwide petrochemical industry, 1975–1995. *Strategic Management Journal, 24*(5), 393–413.

Herbert, T. T. (1984). Strategy and multinational organization structure: An inter organizational relationships perspective. *Academy of Management Review, 9*(2), 259–270.

Heskett, J. L. (1986). *Managing in the service economy*. Cambridge: Harvard Business School Press.

Hill, T. (2000). *Manufacturing strategy*. New York: Irwin/McGraw-Hill.

Hodder, J., & Jucker, J. (1985). International plant location under price and exchange rate uncertainty. *Engineering Costs and Production Economics, 9*, 225–229.

Hofer, C. W., & Schendel, D. (1978). *Strategy formulation: Analytical concepts*. St. Paul: West Publishing.

Hout, T., Porter, M. E., & Rudden, E. (1982). How global companies win out. *Harvard Business Review, 60*(5), September–October, 98–108.

Huchzermeier, A. (1991). *Global manufacturing strategy planning under exchange rate uncertainty*. Ph.D. thesis and working paper 91-02-01. Decision Sciences Department, the Wharton School, University of Pennsylvania, Philadelphia.

Huchzermeier, A., & Cohen, M. A. (1996). Valuing operational flexibility under exchange rate risk. *Operations Research, 44*(1), 100–113.

Jonsson, A., & Foss, N. J. (2011). International expansion through flexible replication: Learning from the internationalization experience of IKEA. *Journal of International Business Studies, 42*, 1079–1102.

Karabuk, S., & Wu, S. D. (2003). Coordinating strategic capacity planning in the semiconductor industry. *Operations Research, 51*(6), 839–849.

Karmarkar, U. S., & Pitbladdo, R. (1995). Service markets and competition. *Journal of Operations Management, 12*(3–4), 397–411.

Kazaz, B., Dada, M., & Moskowitz, H. (2005). Global production planning under exchange-rate uncertainty. *Management Science, 51*(7), 1101–1119.

Kellogg, D. L., & Nie, W. (1995). A framework for strategic service management. *Journal of Operations Management, 13*(4), 323–337.

Knight, G. A., & Cavusgil, S. T. (2004). Innovation, organizational capabilities, and the born-global firm. *Journal of International Business Studies, 35*(2), 124–141.

Kogut, B. (1985a). Designing global strategies: Comparative and competitive value-added chains. *Sloan Management Review, 26*(4), 15–28.

Kogut, B. (1985b). Designing global strategies: Profiting from operational flexibility. *Sloan Management Review, 27*(1), 27–38.

Kogut, B., & Kulatilaka, N. (1994). Operating flexibility, global manufacturing, and the option value of a multinational network. *Management Science, 40*(1), 123–139.

Kouvelis, P. (1999). Global sourcing strategies under exchange rate uncertainty. In S. Tayur, R. Ganeshan, & M. Magazine (Eds.), *Quantitative models for supply chain management* (pp. 625–667). Norwell: Kluwer Academic.

Levitt, T. (1983). The globalization of markets. *Harvard Business Review, 61*(3), May–June, 92–102.

Lovelock, C. H., & Yip, G. S. (1996). Developing global strategies for service business. *California Management Review, 38*(2), 64–86.

Lowe, T., Wendell, R., & Hu, G. (2002). Screening location strategies to reduce exchange rate risk. *European Journal of Operational Research, 136*, 573–590.

Martinez, J. I., & Jarillo, J. C. (1989). The evolution of research on coordination mechanisms in multinational corporations. *Journal of International Business Studies, 20*(3), 489–514.

McLaughlin, C. P., & Fitzsimmons, J. A. (1996). Strategies for globalizing service operations. *International Journal of Service Industry Management, 7*(4), 43–57.

Miller, J. G., & Roth, A. V. (1994). A taxonomy of manufacturing strategies. *Management Science, 40*(3), 285–304.

Porter, M. E. (1980). *Competitive strategy*. New York: Free Press.

Porter, M. E. (1985). *Competitive advantage*. New York: Free Press.

Porter, M. E. (1986). *Competition in global industries*. New York: Free Press.

Porter, M. E. (1987). From competitive advantage to corporate strategy. *Harvard Business Review, 65*(3), May–June, 43–59.

Porter, M. E. (1990/1998). *The competitive advantage of nations*. New York: Free Press.

Porter, M. E. (1991). Towards a dynamic theory of strategy. *Strategic Management Journal, 12* (Winter Special Issue), 95–117.

Porter, M. E. (1996). What is strategy. *Harvard Business Review, 74*(6), November–December, 61–78.

Porter, M. E., & Kramer, M. R. (2011). Creating shared value. *Harvard Business Review, 89*(1/2), 62–77.

Prasad, S., & Babbar, S. (2000). International operations management research. *Journal of Operations Management, 18*, 209–247.

Prokesch, S. (1995). Competing on customer service. *Harvard Business Review, 73*(6), 100–112.

Roth, A. V., & van der Velde, M. (1991). Operations as marketing: A competitive, service strategy. *Journal of Operations Management, 10*(3), 303–328.

Siferd, S. P., Benton, W. C., & Ritzman, L. P. (1992). Strategies for service systems. *European Journal of Operational Research, 56*, 291–303.

Skinner, W. (1969). Manufacturing – Missing link in corporate strategy. *Harvard Business Review, 47*(3), 136–145. May-Jun.

Skinner, W. (1974). The focused factory. *Harvard Business Review, 52*(3), 113–121. May-Jun.

Skinner, W. (1978). *Manufacturing in the corporate strategy*. New York: Wiley.

Skinner, W. (1985). *Manufacturing – The formidable competitive weapon*. New York: Wiley.

Slack, N., & Lewis, M. (2011). *Operations strategy* (3rd ed.). Harlow: FT Prentice Hall.

Thomas, D. R. E. (1978). Strategy is different in service businesses. *Harvard Business Review, 56*(4), July–August, 158–165.

Van Mieghem, J. A. (2008). *Operations strategy – Principles and practice*. Belmont: Dynamic Ideas.

Wheelwright, S. C. (1978). Reflecting corporate strategy in manufacturing decisions. *Business Horizons, 21*(1), 57–66.

Yip, G. S. (1992). *Total global strategy: Managing for worldwide competitive advantage*. New Jersey: Prentice Hall.

Yip, G. S. (2003). *Total global strategy II: Updated for the internet and service era*. New Jersey: Prentice Hall.

Young, S. T., & John, C. (1996). *Coordination*. Westport: Quorum Books.

Young, S. T., & Nie, W. (1996). *Managing global operations: Cultural and technical success factors*. Westport: Quorum Books.

Globalization of Operations

2

Chapter Objectives

- To introduce background knowledge about a firm's globalization.
- To study the globalization of operations strategy from three views (competency, resource, and processes) of operations strategy.
- To discuss the globalization of manufacturing and basic manufacturing globalization modes.
- To discuss the globalization of service operations and basic services globalization modes.

2.1 Globalization of a Firm

With the increasing interdependence of national economies and cross-border movement of products, labor, information, technology, and capital, firms are going global to pursue profits in global market (see, e.g., Ethier 1986). This section examines how a firm goes global and presents globalization approaches, stages, components, and directions. Although the content is in global strategy, we present it as a foundation for the following global operations strategy.

2.1.1 Globalization Approaches

A firm can go global through two types of globalization approaches. In the 1960s and 1970s, global strategy literature emphasized the market entry models, as MNEs were expanding from Western countries to new markets. In the 1980s and 1990s, the major problem became the configuration and coordination of value-chain activities to optimize competitive advantages, as many MNEs had entered new markets. This section focuses on market entry models, and we will visit the second type in Sects. 3.2.4, 3.2.6, and 3.2.7.

Y. Gong, *Global Operations Strategy*, Springer Texts in Business and Economics,
DOI 10.1007/978-3-642-36708-3_2, © Springer-Verlag Berlin Heidelberg 2013

"Buying versus building" is the basic decision in globalization, and acquisition and internal development are the primary globalization approaches (see Lee and Lieberman 2010; Yip 1982). Other approaches are interorganizational arrangements including joint venturing (Kim and Hwang 1992), licensing, and other partnerships. We present the following five approaches.

- Acquisition: A firm can enter market by acquiring an existing firm or a business unit. For example, Lenovo entered the US market by acquiring the personal computer unit of IBM.
- Internal development: A firm can enter a market organically through internal development and build wholly owned subsidiaries. For example, Microsoft built Microsoft Research Asia in Beijing.
- Joint venturing: A firm can enter a market by setting up a joint venture with another existing firm.
- Licensing: A firm can enter a market through a licensing agreement with other existing firms. Some global hotel chains and fast food chains will adopt this approach for going global.
- Partnership (excluding joint ventures and licensing): A firm can enter a market through a long-term supplier relationship. Huawei is selected as a preferred supplier and signs a global framework agreement with Vodafone. Airlines go global by building huge global alliances such as SkyTeam.

2.1.2 Globalization Stages

(1) Uppsala globalization stages
   Johanson and Vahlne (1977, 1990, 2006) maintain the "enterprise gradually increases its international involvement" (Johanson and Vahlne 1990, p. 11), and market entry is usually disturbed by the psychic distance, from differences in language, cultural, and political systems, with larger gaps between the firm and the markets than physical distance. By increasing its experience overseas, the firm acquires new knowledge and can gradually gain a stronger commitment to overseas markets. Assuming that internationalization is the consequence of a series of incremental decisions and the main obstacles are lack of knowledge and recourse, Johanson and Wiedersheim-Paul (1975) introduce the Uppsala internationalization model, and identify four sequential stages of the internationalization process:
   1. No regular export activities.
   2. Export via agents.
   3. Establishment of overseas sales subsidiary.
   4. Overseas production and manufacturing units.
   Johanson and Vahlne (1977, 1990) extend this model to a dynamic international model, assuming the market knowledge and market commitment affect both commitment decision and current activities, which in turn influence market knowledge and market commitment. Bradley (1995) thinks that foreign market entry strategies usually accord with the sequential stages of exporting, competitive alliances, acquisition, and foreign direct investment.

(2) The product lifecycle theory

Vernon (1966, 1971) presents a firm's internationalization process following the product lifecycle after observing that products were initially produced in the US, developed in other developed countries in their maturity phase, and finally serve developing countries. Vernon identified three stages:

1. New product. US firms are likely to be the first to develop new products with more flexibility in the introduction stage.
2. Maturing product. Firms try to achieve economies of scale through mass production with a degree of product standardization, and expand products in other developed countries.
3. Standardized product. Firms enter developing countries with standardized products.

(3) Other viewpoints on globalization stages

Many scholars (e.g., Andersen 1993) think that the stage internationalization model proposed in the 1960s and 1970s cannot explain the internationalization of many firms today. For example, different from Uppsala model, LVMH, a leading MNE in luxury products, does not globalize its manufacturing activities. Different from the Vernon theory, which presents one-way globalization from developed countries to developing countries, today's firms such as Tata, Lenovo, Haier, and Huawei are moving from emerging countries to developed countries.

The main opposition is from the "born global" theory (see Rennie 1993), arguing that many firms do not follow the incremental stage approach but start their international activities from their birth. The "born global" theory identifies two types of exporters: "domestic-based" firms and "born global" companies. The later ones are flexible, normally compete in niche markets, and move fast.

2.1.3 Globalization Components

Yip (2003) proposes the concept of the total global strategy, consisting of three separate components or stages.

1. Developing the core strategy. A firm may develop the core strategy in the home country, which is the basis of the organization's global competitive advantage.
2. Internationalizing the core strategy. A firm conducts the international expansion of activities and masters the basics of international business.
3. Globalizing the international strategy. A firm integrates the strategy across countries.

2.1.4 Globalization Directions

Figure 2.1 presents four possible internationalization directions. Simple directions from developed countries to developed ones or from developing countries to

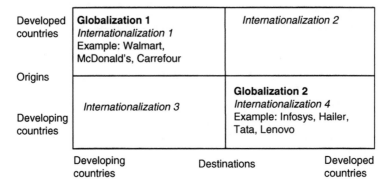

Fig. 2.1 Globalization direction

developing ones are not real globalization directions, which are supposed to include operations in both developed and developing countries. A firm's globalization may develop along multiple directions in different stages. For example, Coca-Cola first grew from developed countries to developed ones, then to developing ones. Huawei first grew from developing countries to developing ones, then to developed ones.

1. From developed countries to developing countries.

   Microsoft (US), IBM (US), Walmart (US), VW (Germany), Carrefour (France), and LV (France) grew from developed countries to developing countries. The advantages of these firms are in technology (e.g., Microsoft), advanced management experiences (e.g., Walmart and Carrefour), product quality (e.g., LV), and strong financial capacities (e.g., KFC). They enter developing countries for market, raw materials, labor, or to overcome trading barriers. They often meet challenges from legal (e.g., protection of intelligence property), political, social (e.g., poverty problem), and environmental systems (e.g., pollution).

2. From developing countries to developed countries.

   Infosys (India), Wipro (India), Cemex (Mexico), Haier (China), Lenovo (China), and Huawei (China) grew from developing countries to developed countries. The advantages of these firms are in low-cost resources or special natural resources. They enter developed countries mainly for market, technology, and talent, but often meet challenges from product quality, world-class service, technology, and international business knowledge.

Case Example: Globalization of Coca-Cola

Coca-Cola Company was a local company in Atlanta that was initially sold as a patented medicine. Now Coca-Cola Company is one of the largest MNEs in the world, and Coca-Cola sells a series of carbonated soft drinks sold in more than 200 countries (see Table 2.1), with more than 1.7 billion beverage servings sold each day.

The Coca-Cola products are globalized by increasing product mixes to respond to local customers throughout the world. The original version of

Table 2.1 Globalization of the Coca-Cola Company

Time	Location	Events
1886–1892	Atlanta	John Pemberton developed Coca-Cola and sold it at Jacob's Pharmacy in Atlanta, Georgia, as a patent medicine. Then Asa G. Candler secured rights to the business and became the company's first president
1893–1904	The US	In 1894, Joseph Biedenham became the first to put Coca-Cola in bottles. In 1899, three businessmen in Tennessee obtained exclusive rights to bottle Coca-Cola, and developed the Coca-Cola bottling system
1905–1918	8 countries	In 1916, the bottlers approved the unique contour bottle. The company entered Canada, Panama, Cuba, Puerto Rico, France, and others
1919–1940	53 countries	In 1919, Asa Candler sold the Coca-Cola company to the Woodruff family. In 1923, Robert Woodruff became the president and led the expansion of Coca-Cola overseas. In 1928 Coca-Cola supported the Amsterdam Olympics
1941–1959	120 countries	During World War II, the company grew rapidly and Coca-Cola was introduced to many countries and peoples for the first time
1960–1981	163 countries	The company expanded with product types (e.g., Sprite). The company's presence worldwide grew rapidly, and it entered China in 1978
1982–1989	165 countries	The company released Diet Coke and New Coke into global competition
1990–1999	Nearly 200 countries	The company expanded through acquisitions of brands like "Limca" in India and Cadbury Schweppes' beverage brands
2000-present	More than 200 countries	Coca-Cola is one of the most ubiquitous brands in the world. The Coca-Cola company becomes a symbol for the globalization of MNEs

Coca-Cola launched in 1886. In the process of globalization, the company launched Diet Coke in 1982, the caffeine-free version of Coca-Cola in 1983, Coca-Cola Cherry in 1985, Coca-Cola with Lemon in 2001, Coca-Cola Vanilla in 2002, and Coca-Cola Citra in 2006.

The production and distribution of Coca-Cola are globalized with a franchising operational mode. The Coca-Cola Company produces only concentrates, beverage bases, and syrups, which it sells to bottlers in the world. Bottlers, holding Coca-Cola franchises in specific geographical areas, produce the final drink by mixing the syrup with filtered water and sweeteners, and then carbonating. Then the bottling partners package, merchandise, and distribute the final branded beverages to customers and retailing partners, who then sell products to consumers.

The organization of Coca-Cola is globalized in two dimensions. Vertically, Coca-Cola is globalized along the supply chain and of relevance to the franchising system. The Coca-Cola supply chain comprises Coca-Cola Company and nearly 300 bottling partners worldwide. Horizontally, Coca-Cola is globalized in different regions, by building six operating groups – Eurasia, Africa, Europe, Latin America, North America, and the Pacific – and employing approximately 146,200 associates.

(Source: The Coca-Cola Company Heritage Timeline)

Case Questions

1. How did the Coca-Cola Company go global as a firm?
2. How did the Coca-Cola Company go global in terms of operations strategy (competency, resource, and process)?

2.2   Globalization of Operational Competencies, Resources, and Processes

2.2.1   Globalization of Operational Competencies

Globalization can enhance the operational competency of a firm by providing new conditions, reduce the competency of a firm by imposing new constrains, change the definition of a competency from the domestic market, and influence elements constituting a competency.

- Cost

    Globalization brings new cost challenges in transportation, tariff, tax, and duty. Globalized cost control needs to examine not only manufacturing cost, but also total landed cost and total cost of ownership in the global supply chain. Globalized cost competency is based on the low cost among not only domestic rivals, but also global competitors. Fortunately, globalization provides new processes like outsourcing, new resources like low-cost labor and raw materials, new technologies to reduce production cost, new facilities to reduce manufacturing and logistics costs, and new management skills such as tax-aligned supply chain management to reduce total landed cost.

- Flexibility

    Global flexibility refers to the ability to change manufacturing products and services to respond to fluctuations of global demand in the dimensions of both time and scope. On the one hand, a global operations strategy needs the construction of flexibility to exploit uncertainty over future changes (Kogut 1985). On the other hand, market heterogeneity and region differences impose higher requirement on scope flexibility of products and service.

    Globalization can lead to either product and service standardization in some fields such as medicine products, or increase willingness to manifest localized taste differences in other fields such as clothing and foods. Global companies can benefit from capabilities to respond to local taste differentiation, rather than simply overriding it in pursuit of economies of scale. With increasing international transfer, global flexibility in production diversity and service heterogeneity is used to leverage the demand differences among regions.

- Quality

  Global quality competency refers to maintaining a significantly high level of quality among competitive products or service worldwide. Globalization brings new challenges in quality. First, it is more difficult to achieve quality competency on a global scale since international competitors can easily enter any marketplace with the convenience of global transportation and global communication, and globalization is changing quality standards in different regions. Second, the globalization of some products like food and healthcare products poses risks for the safety and quality of ingredients. In a global environment, quality control is more important than before. Third, the globalization of quality reduces product heterogeneity for some products such as laptops and cameras, while goods can cross regions. However, in other cases, corporations seek to satisfy local taste and thereby reduce homogeneity for products such as foods. Finally, MNEs must consider more cross-value problems, and incorporate social and environmental values in global quality management.

- Time

  Globalization increases the difficulty to achieve time competency, considering longer shipping time and intercontinental physical distance between agents in a global supply chain, and longer manufacturing time from manufacturing configuration complexity, as well as the requirement to rapidly respond to local customers in different regions. The abilities to overcome these difficulties and to address competitiveness in speedy distinctiveness can help sustain a firm's strategic advantage in a dynamic environment. For example, Zara uses global operations systems to speed its design, manufacturing, and distribution process, to make the distinctiveness of fashion. Globalization influences time elements constituting the competency in fashion.

2.2.2 Globalization of Operational Resources

The resource-based view of global operations strategy is to tailor global real assets in a global environment. MNEs can use VRIO (valuable, rare, inimitable, and exploited by organization) resources to achieve competitive advantages. The resources are globalized in sizes, times, types, and locations.

The globalized capacity size decision needs to examine global demand, which is more difficult to forecast than local demand, study capacity structure problems across different regions, and investigate regional size problems considering local variables such as local cost, political environment, and tax system.

The global timing problem first reconsiders five generic capacity-timing strategies including leading, lagging, smooth, demand-chasing, hybrid timing, and follow-your-competitor strategies on a global scale. A leading strategy in one region may be a lagging strategy in another region. Second, timing drivers including demand growth forecasts, discount rate, scale economies, underage opportunity cost of lost sales, cost of capacity, and cost of holding inventory are different across regions. Third, the capacity-timing problem is linked with the time sequence of market entries in different regions.

It is more difficult for MNEs to improve resource flexibility in production input, production capacity, and production output, since the asset types and flexibility problem is globalized in the speed of changeovers and the breadth of activities across regions, and flexibility value drivers (e.g., economies of scale, risk mitigation, and real options) are redefined in a global setting.

Choosing an appropriate location for global manufacturing, global service, or global R&D is an important decision to reduce the cost, get access to markets, acquire knowledge, and recruit talents in GOS. For example, Chang'an Automobile, a Chinese company, is building research and development centers in Japan, Italy, Germany, and the United States to acquire technologies and marketing information. Louis Vuitton, the leading French luxury producer, chooses upscale areas in the largest cities to obtain access to high-end customers in Asia-Pacific regions.

2.2.3 Globalization of Operational Process

In the globalization of firms, operational processes like supply chain management, technology management, revenue management, and risk control are globalized.

The supply chain is globalized to meet dynamic needs of growing markets and new consumer segments, to balance risks caused by economic and political uncertainties, and to manage costs complexity. MNEs consider possibilities of global outsourcing, global distribution, global supply chain strategic alliance, and global coordination. Apple builds a complicated global supply chain, with the design in the US, components and parts purchasing in Korea and Japan, assembly in China, distribution in China and the US, and global retailing. Airbus had built a huge global supply chain network to produce different parts, components, and airplanes.

Revenue management companies use the global service chain, vertical integration, horizontal integration, and sector integration to provide global platforms for global revenue management. MNEs manage global revenue by dynamic pricing, dealing with global demand fluctuation and global capacity control in different regions. Particularly, global alliance (e.g., SkyTeam) revenue management has been a trend to optimize price and capacity control.

Product development and R&D processes are globalized, driven by market or technology factors across regions. Global product development strategy considers global manufacturability, different staff learning curves, customer heterogeneity, and product standardization versus localization to apply an open innovation paradigm and manage global R&D activities.

When going global, firms are exposed to more natural, economic, political, and social risks. MNEs can formulate a speculative strategy, hedge strategy, flexible strategy, and safety strategy to control its material flow risks, financial flow risks, and information flow risks. Firms are struggling to manage the complexities of global risks by coordinating global supply management, demand management, finance management, information management, and product management.

Case Example: Operational Globalization of Lenovo

In 1984, Liu Chuanzhi founded New Technology Developer Inc. in Beijing, then renamed it Legend in 1987. The company was incorporated in Hong Kong in 1988 and grew to be the largest domestic PC manufacturer in China in the 1990s. Realizing the limit of domestic market, Legend set globalization as the target in 2003. Chairman Liu Chuanzhi presented how Legend had made the decision about the globalization approach:

We recognized that there were two primary ways to globalize. One was to grow organically. We were aware, however, that this approach would involve a very long process. Another way was to expand through mergers and acquisition: this was, however, a very risky process. With the help of external advisers and consultants, we decided to adopt the second approach (Liu 2007, p. 574).

Since 2004 Legend carried out a "three-step globalization strategy." The first step to prepare for globalization was to change its name to Lenovo in 2004, as Legend had been registered overseas. Second, Lenovo acquired the former personal computer division of IBM (IBM PC) in 2005. The third step was to go global with Olympic Games in 2008. Today, Lenovo is the world's second-largest PC vendor, with more than 26,000 employees in more than 60 countries, serving customers in more than 160 countries (For the globalization timeline of lenovo, see Table 2.2).

• Globalization of competencies

In the 1980s, Lenovo only had cost competency and distribution capabilities to serve foreign PC companies. In the 1990s, Lenovo was the first company to introduce the home computer concept in China and grew into a national company with 27 % market share in the domestic market. Compared with foreign PCs, Lenovo's competency lies in its deep understanding of the domestic market and rapid response to local customer demand. After acquiring IBM PC, Lenovo established firm-specific competency in world-class cost control and operational efficiency.

• Globalization of resources

In the 1980s, Lenovo only had distribution resources to serve foreign PC companies. In the 1990s, Lenovo built manufacturing, R&D, and marketing resources in China and became the largest domestic PC producer. The milestone event to globalize the resource was to acquire IBM PC. After acquisition, Lenovo obtained a powerful global distribution and sales networks, absorbed and integrated important human resources and administration skills, acquired IBM's leading PC technologies, and got global brand recognition and an international customer base. In 2011 Lenovo set up a joint venture, "Lenovo NEC," with the Japanese company NEC to boost Lenovo's sales in Japan.

Lenovo has globalized its resources by building headquarters in Beijing and North Carolina, major research centers in Yokohama, Beijing, Shanghai, Shenzhen, and Morrisville, and manufacturing factories around the world in the US, Mexico, India, China, and Brazil.

Table 2.2 Globalization timeline of Lenovo

Time	Location	Events	Globalization of competencies	Globalization of resources	Globalization of process
1984	Beijing	Founded New Technology Developer Inc	Low-cost distribution in local market	Distribution of resources in local market	Distribution process for foreign PC
1987	Beijing	Renamed itself Legend	Low-cost distribution in China	Distribution of resources in China	A part of global outsourcing
1988	Hong Kong	Incorporated		Financial resource out of mainland China	
1990	China	Began marketing its own products	Building competitive advantages on a national scale	Built manufacturing, R&D, marketing resources on a national scale	Built national process networks
1991	Germany	Establishment of Legend Germany	Began to build competency in Europe	Began to globalize the resource	Began to globalize the process
2004	China	Renamed Lenovo		Prepared intangible resource	
2005	The US	Acquired the personal computer division of IBM	Began to build competency on a global scale	Obtained global distribution networks, and human resources and technologies	Globalized the supply chain, R&D management, risk control processes
2008	Beijing	Went global with Olympic Games		Built global reputation	
2011	Japan, Netherlands	Established a PC joint venture Lenovo NEC	Boosted Lenovo's sales competency in Japan	Marketing and channel resource in Japan	Distribution process in Japan
2012	Customers in 160 countries	Provided affordable, high-quality products with rapid response to local customers		Established headquarters in China and the US, research centers, and manufacturing factories around the world	A highly efficient global supply chain

- Globalization of processes

In the 1980s, the operational process of Lenovo, mainly just the distribution process, was a part of global sourcing, since it served foreign PC companies. In the 1990s, Lenovo built national processes in research and development, production, marketing, and service. After acquiring IBM PC, its processes became global. To avoid excessive reliance on original equipment manufacturers and keep costs low, Lenovo adopted vertical integration by integrating processes from design and manufacturing to distribution and sales.

Case Questions

1. In 2003, why did Legend plan to go global?
2. In acquisition versus internal development as modes of market entry, which mode did Lenovo mainly choose? Why did it not choose another entry mode?
3. Why did Lenovo prefer vertical integration in its global supply chain?

2.3   Globalization of Manufacturing Operations

2.3.1   Globalized Manufacturing and Key Operational Elements

The diminution of international trade regulations and free trade agreements facilitate global manufacturing. New communication and transportation technologies make global manufacturing networks more effective and efficient. Decreasing tariffs and taxes stimulate the development of global manufacturing. Overseas professional talents or low-cost raw materials drive global outsourcing. Facing global markets and competition, firms have globalized their manufacturing. Examples of global manufacturing include:

- Manufacturing plant implementation,
- Overseas facility construction,
- Global production line design, planning, and implementation,
- Overseas mechanical equipment design and construction,
- International globalization project management,
- Overseas manufacturing planning, supervision, and quality control,
- Offshore design,
- International purchasing and supply chain management, and
- Overseas product quality inspections.

Several operations elements are important for the success of global manufacturing: total landed cost, global quality control, global product planning, technology, workforces, and dependability.

(1) Total landed cost

When making decision in manufacturing globalization, particularly a decision on manufacturing locations, a firm should consider not only manufacturing cost, but total landed cost (TLC), the total end-to-end costs from inputs to product outputs with customers. TLC incorporates all the costs incurred in a supply chain to make the products available for customers, including manufacturing costs, transportation, inventory costs, trade costs, insurance, duties, and taxes, among others. TLC enables companies to capture both explicit and hidden costs associated with manufacturing relocation, revealing the true cost of global manufacturing activities like sourcing. The low cost competency of global manufacturing cannot be simply measured by manufacturing cost, but can by TLC.

(2) Global quality control

Globalization of quality control is driven by global quality standard, and standardized inputs have matured globalization processes. For example, ISO 9001 is the internationally recognized standard for the quality management of businesses. ISO 9001 is one of the standards in the ISO 9000 family, which applies to the processes that create and control the products an organization supplies and prescribes systematic control of activities to ensure that the needs of customers are met. Second, total quality management is no longer a functional integration in a company or a single region. The linkage is broader and encompasses one or multiple supply chains across country boundaries. Finally, manufacturing globalization can lead to risks in quality control.

(3) Global production planning

In global manufacturing, product planning is globalized. Different sources and location-specific comparative advantages can determine manufacturing locations of different components even for one product. Global production planning is complicated and will increase the difficulty of manufacturing management. Efficient information and communications system can improve the performance of global production planning.

(4) Global technology innovation

Global manufacturing needs continual innovation to sustain its competitive position in the future. While global manufacturing from developed countries to developing ones is typically supported by advanced technologies, global manufacturing from developing countries to developed ones may seek technological resources in global manufacturing.

(5) Global workforces

Globalization brings about the mobility of workers and job seekers across the world in a volume unprecedented in history. Global workforce management comprises several areas such as recruitment, selection, and formation processes, person-to-job assignation, pay systems and incentive policies, and job performance evaluation, considering both competitive and comparative advantages. One of the major challenges is to find the right skills in the labor forces and managers. Another important challenge rests on the definition of that human resource policy that aligns a firm's global operations.

Table 2.3 Examples of basic manufacturing globalization modes

	Outsourcing	Joint venture	Wholly owned
Resource seeking		TNK-BP, Chinalco Rio Tinto	Adidas factory in Indonesia, Lenovo purchased IBM PC, Huawei R&D center in India
Market seeking		Valin ArcelorMittal Automotive, Shanghai GM, Shanghai Volkswagen, Dongfeng Peugeot-Citroën Automobile	Toyota Motor Manufacturing in Texas, Haier manufacturing in the US, Airbus assembly plants Tianjin
Efficiency seeking	Apple outsources to Foxconn, Mattel outsources to China	GE Xianmen factory, Samsung joint ventures in China (e.g., Samsung Corning LCD factory)	Toyota Motor Manufacturing Texas
Asset seeking			Lenovo purchased IBM PC, Tata Steel acquired UK Corus, Tata Motors purchased Jaguar and Land Rover from Ford

2.3.2 Basic Manufacturing Globalization Modes

Manufacturing globalization modes can be classified along two dimensions: control levels and motivations. By the control level, there are three modes: wholly owned production units with the strongest control, joint venturing manufacturing units, and outsourcing with the least control on manufacturing activities. Based on the motivations of international production, Dunning and Lundan (2008) identify four modes of international manufacturing, resource seeking, market seeking, efficiency seeking, and asset seeking (see Table 2.3). These modes are not exclusive to each other, and a company may choose to develop global manufacturing with multiple motivations or multiple control levels to maximize its competitive edge. The reliability and coordination issues of these globalization modes require additional investments and resources.

- Resource seeking

A primary motivation for global manufacturing of a home-country firm is to gain access to certain resources in a foreign country, including natural resources (e.g., minerals and raw materials) or human resources like inexpensive or professional labor. In 2011 global miner Rio Tinto and Chinese aluminum producer Chinalco established a joint venture, "Chinalco Rio Tinto Exploration," to seek new mineral deposits in China. BP, the British oil giant, jointly with Alfa Access Renova built TNK-BP, a major vertically integrated Russian oil company headquartered in Moscow to seek oil resources in Russia and Ukraine.

A firm, particularly from developing countries, will try to acquire not natural resources, but technological capability, management expertise, and organization skills. For example, China-based Lenovo purchased the personal computer unit of IBM to acquire its technological capability, marketing resources, and management expertise.

- Market seeking

  A firm will adopt a market-seeking mode of global manufacturing when it chooses to produce its goods near a target market to understand the customers' needs and to adapt and tailor the product to respond to local demand changes. ArcelorMittal and the Valin Group built a downstream automotive steel joint venture, Valin ArcelorMittal Automotive (VAMA), to supply high-strength steels and value-added products for China's fast growing automotive market. Almost all leading Western automotive companies, including GM, Ford, BMW, PSA Peugeot Citroën, Benz, Volkswagen, and Fiat, have built joint ventures to seek market opportunities in China.

  Second, the global market brings higher requirements on product delivery and logistics, which has opened the door to global manufacturing networks, which could be a result of optimizing product delivery networks. For example, when the transportation distance of moving finished goods to the marketplace is long and both delivery accuracy and delivery time are influenced, the company may locate assembly plants near the market.

- Efficiency seeking

  A growing mode for global manufacturing is efficiency seeking to restructure a business's existing investments for achieving an efficient allocation of international economic activities. The mode takes advantage of different factor endowments, economic policies, institutional arrangement, and demand patterns to obtain benefits in product and factor prices, economics of scale, economics of scope, and risk controls.

  Global sourcing can be an efficiency-seeking mode to seek resource saving and improved efficiency by rationalizing the structure of global supply chain activities. Many firms offshore and outsource their manufacturing abroad to benefit from cost reductions and productivity improvement.

  Some countries offer an investment incentive program, consisting of tax breaks, grants, and subsidized land, to encourage economic development, which may attract global manufacturing. Efficiency-seeking global manufacturing can be attracted by specialized spatial clusters like science and industrial parks, and specific industrial areas like the "auto plant corridor" from Mexico City to Atlanta.

  For example, to attract Toyota Motors to build manufacturing facilities in Texas, the city of San Antonio paid for 2,600 acres of land and agreed to sell electricity to Toyota at a low price; the municipality also contributed to constructing a training center, the state of Texas provided funding for infrastructure development, and the federal government provided grants for training and transportation.

- Strategic asset seeking

  This mode is not just to seek cost and market benefits, but also to acquire strategic assets including physical assets and strategic human resources to enhance their ownership-specific advantages or weaken the advantages of

Table 2.4 BMW global manufacturing networks

Country	Plant (scale in the employee number; main manufacturing activities)
Germany	Berlin plant (1,900 employees; producing motorcycle parts and BMW automobile components), Dingolfing plant (18,600 employees; producing BMW vehicles, body shells for the Rolls-Royce Phantom, and BMW chassis components), Eisenach (235 employees; producing large metalworking tools), Landshut plant (3,000 employees; producing engine components), Leipzig plant (a new plant that will hire 800 employees; producing BMW automobiles), Munich plant (6,800 employees; producing BMW automobile, internal combustion engines, and high-performance power units), Regensburg plant (9,000 employees; producing BMW automobiles), Wackersdorf plant (2,000 at the Wackersdorf Innovation Estate, producing components for BMW)
Italia	Cassinetta plant (260 employees; producing Husqvarna Motorcycles)
UK	Hams Hall plant, near Birmingham (260 employees; manufacturing four-cylinder petrol engines for both BMW and MINI), Oxford plant (3,800 employees; producing MINI automobiles), Swindon plant (800 employees; producing steel pressings and complex sub-assemblies), Rolls-Royce Motor Cars and its Goodwood plant in West Sussex, England (about 1,000 employees; producing Rolls-Royce cars)
South Africa	Rosslyn plant (1,700 employees; producing BMW 3 Series Sedan)
China	Shenyang, a joint venture (3,000 employees; producing BMW 5, X1, and 3 Series long-wheelbase version)
USA	Spartanburg (7,000 employees; producing BMW X3 and X5 Sports Activity Vehicle and the X6 Sports Activity Coupe)
Austria	Steyr plant (3,600 employees; engine manufacturing)

competitors. For example, China-based Lenovo purchased the personal computer unit of IBM to enhance its ownership-specific advantages with physical assets and strategic human resources in the US. India-based Tata Motors purchased the high-class brands Jaguar and Land Rover from Ford Motors, and built Jaguar and Land Rover as a British multinational automotive company headquartered in Whitley, Coventry. As a wholly owned subsidiary of Tata Motors, the principal activity of Jaguar Land Rover is the development, manufacture, and sale of Jaguar and Land Rover vehicles. The motivation of Tata Motors' global production is not simple market seeking or efficiency seeking, but the long-run strategic development of Tata Motors.

Case Example: BMW Global Manufacturing

BMW built the first production plant in Munich in 1916. From a small company it became one of largest automobile producers in the world. The BMW Group manufactures and sells three car brands operating in the premium segments: BMW, MINI, and Rolls-Royce. The group has a strong market position in the motorcycle sector and operates a successful financial services business.

Currently, BMW produces cars and motorcycles in plants in Germany, the UK, the US, China, Italia, South Africa, and Austria (see Table 2.4). BMW adopts contract production with production a partner in Graz, Austria.

To respond to market demands around the world, and to enter markets with customs regulations governing the importation of complete automobiles, BMW manufactures automobiles from parts kits in assembly plants, called a "completely knocked down" (CKD) production process. The BMW Group uses CKD assembly to manufacture automobiles with partners in six locations including Thailand, Malaysia, Russia, Egypt, Indonesia, and India, and to manufacture motorcycles in Brazil.

Case Questions

1. Rolls-Royce has been a leading brand of luxury car. BMW acquired its assets and managed its manufacturing plants. What is this manufacturing globalization mode?
2. Shenyang plant is a joint venture between BMW and Brilliance China Automotive to product the BMW long-wheelbase version, only for the local market. What is this manufacturing globalization mode?
3. Which manufacturing globalization mode has been used in BMW's CKD assembly plants?
4. What are different advantages achieved by BMW through various global production modes of wholly owned plants from origin (e.g., Munich plant), wholly owned plants by acquisition (e.g., Rolls-Royce plant), joint venture (e.g., Shenyang plant), and contract production (Graz plant)?

2.4   Globalization of Service Operations

2.4.1   Global Services and Key Operational Elements

The development of telecommunications facilitates the globalization of the information-intensive service. Unbundling service components activates the movement of back-office service. Increasing demand and the distribution imbalance of service capacity cause the movement of high-quality professional service. The production globalization increases the global delivery of relevant services such as design, project management, quality controls, management strategic consulting, and accounting. With the globalization of market and competition, firms are globalizing their services. Examples of global service include:

- Global hotel service by hotel chains and hotel agencies,
- Global tourism service by tourism agencies and theme parks,
- Global travel service by global railroad system and airline alliances,
- Global management consulting and strategic planning,
- Global accounting service,
- Offshoring hospital,
- International project management,
- Quality evaluation and audit,
- Risk analysis and management,

- Global investment advice and financial service,
- Global IT service such as enterprise resource planning consulting, and
- International supplier selection and assessments.

Chase (1978), Collier (1985), and Haywood-Farmer (1988) identify the critical operational elements in service operations: customer contact, customization, cultural adaptation, and labor intensity. McLaughlin (1992) and MacLaughlin and Fitzsimmons (1996) propose more elements including telecommunications, the potential for unbundling service components, teamwork, and reengineering opportunities. Based on these studies, the key operational elements for service globalization are:

(1) Customization

Global service needs to respond to the customized demand of local regions in a global reach. Global restaurants will change the menu to suit local tastes. Global hotel chains will change room layout, room service, and foods to provide customized service.

(2) Cultural adaptation

Service companies have to decide whether to adapt their initial service package to the local culture. Disney Hong Kong incorporated Chinese cultural elements, speaking in Cantonese, English, and Mandarin, and increased the Chinese New Year celebration show. Overseas service organizations need to consider adapting to local culture when hiring local employees. With about 99.9 % employees being local Chinese, KFC China adapted to local Chinese culture and tried to be a part of Chinese society. Unlike Disney's American theme parks, Disney Paris aimed more for permanent employees than seasonal and temporary part-time employees.

(3) Information intensity

Telecommunication technologies such as the Internet facilitate the diffusion of information, and have helped with the globalization of services. With the development of new telecommunication technologies, physical distance becomes less important and new service modes such as foreign call centers became possible. Once information is digitized, it becomes instantaneously accessible for customers all over the world. This stimulates the development of informant-intensive services.

(4) Service unbundling

Service can be viewed as a dichotomy between the front office to contact customers and the back office to complete additional processing (Chase 1978), the dichotomy of which increases the possibility of service globalization by relocating back office service. With advanced communication systems, service companies can unbundle services and focus their operations strategy on core services while outsourcing back office services to other sites.

(5) Labor intensity

Labor intensity influences the globalization of service. Firms outsource labor-intensive service like information processing and routing software development to low-cost sites to reduce cost or to labor-intensive locations to acquire trained talent.

(6) Service innovation

Service globalization is often accompanied or even driven by service innovation, including but not limited to service product innovation, service processes innovation, and service organizations innovation. The Metro, a leading Germany-based retailer, uses radio frequency identification (RFID) to provide a new service mode, "future store," for catering to customer needs better and making the shopping experiences easier. Global banks like HSBC and BNP Paribus use new automaton technologies to provide self-service, globalizing its customer contact at a low cost.

2.4.2   Basic Service Globalization Modes

The difference between the manufacturing globalization mode and service globalization mode is of relevance to the inseparability of service supplier and customers in service. By the interaction between service suppliers and customers, we identified six service globalization modes of four movement types.

(1) Movement of service

- When the service market is characterized by a number of routine services or relatively standard service, a firm will globalize its service through the movement of the service organization to the customer's countries by multisite expansion, based on the duplication of the key success elements of the service worldwide. For example, Pizza Hut, Starbucks, and KFC build retail chains throughout the world by means of multisite expansion.
- When service needs a high level of customization, a firm will globalize its service through the movement of the service organization to the customer's countries by either joint venturing or using wholly owned subsidiaries to provide tailor-made service. The firm may change service organizations and service packages to fit local tastes. For example, Huawei, a telecom equipment maker, builds joint innovation centers for its large customers to provide a tailor-made technology consulting service.
- The third mode is through the movement of individual service staff or a service team to the customer's countries. A management-consulting firm may not establish a subsidiary in a country, but may send a consultant team to provide service to a foreign firm. A firm of large-scale machine equipment may send a technical expert to its customers to help with maintenance and repair.

(2) Movement of customers

- The fourth mode is through the movement of customers to the place the service is delivered. For example, in a "hub and spoke" airline system, the customers are attracted from different regions to a hub, and then take a long-distance flight from a hub to another hub. Disneyland (Paris and Orlando), Europa Park (Germany), Efteling (Netherlands), Macau Fisherman's Wharf (Macau), and other theme parks attract customers from foreign countries.

(3) No physical movement
  • The fifth mode is through cross-border communication between service providers and consumers. A global service firm can divide its activities into front-desk and back-office services, and then organize a global outsourcing strategy. For example, a firm can outsource the back-office service like call centers to India, and consumers can obtain service by communication.
(4) Movement of both customers and service
  • Some global service companies, instead of targeting local customers, are trying to chase their clients overseas. For example, a French restaurant in China focuses its offer on attracting French customers living as expatriates.

Case Example: KFC Global Service

We take KFC China as an example to introduce the service globalization of KFC, since it adopts a similar operational mode in other regions. The first KFC restaurant opened in Beijing in 1987, and expanded to more than 3,800 stores in 800 cities or towns by 2012, with one new restaurant opening a day. KFC is managed by Yum Brands, an American fast food company, and entered China through a multisite expansion strategy. Yum creates its own distribution company and sources with local suppliers with uniform quality standards. At the store level, Yum makes sure that the service's quality is consistent and trains employees based on uniform standards.

KFC first operated through joint ventures and franchises because of the government restrictions, but since 1992, most restaurants have become company-owned units. Its ownership strategy aims to:
  • Unify its quality standards through the country,
  • Set centralized purchasing systems,
  • Focus on brand building and consistent communication strategy, and
  • Offer a consistent and high-quality service.

From the beginning, KFC had tried to build a fast-food chain "rooted in China, be part of China." Of its 300,000 employees, 99.9 % are local Chinese. KFC had also built local supply chain networks and purchased more than 90 % of food materials from 570 suppliers in China. While maintaining its classic foods like original recipe chicken, colonel's crispy strips, and hot wings, KFC has offered a special menu to suit Chinese tastes and styles of eating, and developed about 150 new foods including rice items, egg tarts, Chinese doughnuts, and soy milk drinks to respond to local demand.

Case Questions

1. What is the service globalization mode of KFC? Why did KFC not use other service globalization modes?
2. How has KFC responded to local demand in the process of global expansion?

Fig. 2.2 The domestic contracts versus foreign contracts of Huawei (in US$ billion)

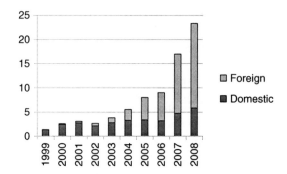

Case: Globalization of Huawei

1. Introduction

   Huawei Technologies Co. Ltd, a multinational networking and telecommunications equipment and services company headquartered in Shenzhen, China, is the largest telecommunications equipment maker in the world in terms of revenue in 2012, overtaking all its competitors, including Ericsson, Alcatel-Lucent, Nokia Siemens Networks, and ZTE.

   The past 25 years have witnessed the rapid growth and globalization of Huawei (see Fig. 2.2). In 2011, Huawei achieved revenue of $32 billion by selling products and services to customers in more than 140 countries, including 45 of the world's 50 largest telecoms operators. Huawei Technologies was one of six telecom industry companies included in "The World's Most Respected 200 Companies" list by *Forbes* magazine in 2007, and was in the list of "The World's Most Influential Companies" by *Business Week* in 2008.

2. Globalization stages

   Using the Yip globalization component theory, we identify the following three stages for Huawei globalization. Table 2.5 presents the relevant timeline.

   • 1987–1997: Domestic development

   Established in Shenzhen originally as a sales agent of Private Branch Exchange, it switched to targeting rural markets in 1987, and Huawei expanded into metropolitan areas of China in 1998. Huawei established a core competency of low cost, based on its strong R&D capabilities in its home country.

   • 1997–2004: Internationalization

   In 1997, Huawei obtained its first overseas contract for network products with Hutchison Whampoa in Hong Kong, which is a milestone to show when Huawei entered the stage of internationalization. In 1999, Huawei opened an R&D center in Bangalore, India. Then Huawei entered developed countries and established R&D centers in Europe and the US. In 2004, its milestone contract with Dutch operator Telfort was a symbol of the success of internationalization.

Table 2.5 Timeline of Huawei globalization

Time	Location	Events	M&A	Joint venture	Internal develop
1987	Shenzhen	Established originally as a sales agent			
1990	Shenzhen	Embarked on independent research and commercialization of PBX technologies			
1997	Hong Kong	Obtained its first overseas contract			
1997	Russia	Set up a joint venture Beto-Huawei with Russian Beto Konzern and Russia Telecom		+	
1998	Algeria	Established an office in Africa			+
1999	India	Established R&D center in Bangalore, India			+
1999	Brazil	Established the first office in Latin America			+
2000	Sweden	Established R&D center in Stockholm, Sweden			+
2001	US	Establishes four R&D centers in the US			+
2001	US	Established North American headquarters in Texas			+
2003	US/CN	Established joint venture with 3Com		+	
2004	Germany	Established joint venture TD Tech with Siemens		+	
2004	Netherlands	Achieved milestone contract win Dutch operator Telfort			
2005		International contract orders exceed domestic sales			
2005	UK	Selected as a preferred supplier and signed global framework agreement with Vodafone			
2005	UK	Selected as a preferred supplier by British Telecom			
2006	Shanghai	Established joint R&D center with Motorola		+	
2007	UK	Established joint venture with Global Marine		+	
2007	US	Failed in acquiring American company 3Com	−		
2007	Chengdu	Established joint venture with Symantec		+	
2008	Australia	Developed a mobile innovation center with Optus		+	
2010	Belgium	Acquired Belgian chipmaker M4S	+		
2010	US	Failed in acquiring American software supplier 2Wire	−		
2010	US	Failed in acquiring Motorola's mobile network infrastructure unit	−		
2011	US	Failed in acquiring 3Leaf Systems	−		
2011	Hong Kong	Acquired Symantec's shares in Huawei Symantec at USD 530 million	+		

+ success, − fail, *otherwise* not applicable

(*Source*: Huawei milestones)

Huawei overseas organization					
Europe	**North American**	**Asia-Pacific** (Excluding China)	**Africa**	**Middle East**	**Latin America**
-2 regional offices (Düsseldorf and Warsaw) -10 R&D centers -9 training centers -2 logistic centers	- Headquarters in Plano, Texas -8 regional offices -9 R&D centers	-4 regional headquarters -20 representative offices -2 R&D centers -6 training centers	-4 regional headquarters -20 representative offices -2 R&D centers - 6 training centers	-Headquarters in Bahrain -Offices across 10 countries	-Headquarters in Mexico City -19 regional offices -3 software R&D centers -3 training centers

Fig. 2.3 Huawei organic growth

- 2005–2012: Globalization
  In 2005, international contract orders exceeded domestic contracts, which shows that Huawei entered the stage of internationalization. At this stage, Huawei took an integrated method to globalize its core competency across both developed and developing countries.

3. Globalization direction
   Different from Haier (for Haier, see the case example in Sect. 3.2), Huawei avoided Western Europe and the US and chose locations with less competition. Huawei called this strategy "surrounding the cities with rural areas," which means developing a rural market first and then the urban market, and comes from successful experiences in its previous domestic development.

   It set up a joint venture with Russian Beto Konzern and Russia Telecom in 1997. After getting the first order in Russia in 2000, the business of Huawei in Russian market grew quickly. After 2000, Huawei extended its marketplace to Southeastern Asia, the Middle East, and Africa. In 2001, Huawei began to sell products in the Western Europe market, including German, France, Spain, and the UK, through the local agents. Then Huawei established R&D centers in Europe and the US.

4. Globalization approaches
   From Table 2.5, we can observe that Huawei had first used internal development from 1997 to 2001, and then joint venture from 2002 to 2008. It tried to use acquisition from 2007 to 2011, but was not successful. This timeline roughly fits Bradley's three stages theory, arguing that foreign market entry usually follows three stages: exporting, competitive alliances, and acquisition (Bradley 1995).

   - Organic growth
   The globalization of Huawei relies on its organic growth. Huawei had built subsidiaries in seven regions including China and six overseas regions, a number of region offers, R&D centers, training centers, logistics centers, technical assistance centers, outsourcing factories, and multi-language call centers (see Fig. 2.3). A vice president heads each of regional headquarters. The regional offices are organized by product lines with technical support departments, and two departments of client relations and business development.

- Joint venture and partnerships

Huawei goes global via a number of partnerships. In 2003, Huawei and 3Com Corporation formed a joint venture company, 3Com-Huawei, for data networking products. Huawei set up a joint venture with Siemens in 2005, a Shanghai-based joint R&D center with Motorola in 2006, a joint venture company with American security firm Symantec in 2007, and a joint venture with a UK-based marine engineering company in 2008.

- M&A

Although Huawei had tried to acquire overseas assets, M&A is not a main approach for Huawei to go global, partially because of political barriers and the defense sensitivity of telecommunication technologies. The most famous example is the 3Com acquisition. In 2007 Huawei, in conjunction with Bain Capital, failed in acquiring leading American computer network infrastructure products manufacturer 3Com, a company making anti-hacking computer software for the US military, after the Committee on Foreign Investment in the US examined the national security risks of the deal. For a similar security reason, Huawei failed in acquiring American software supplier 2Wire in 2010, Motorola's mobile network infrastructure unit in 2010, and American Technology Company 3Leaf Systems in 2011.

Huawei had acquired M4S, Belgian wireless Internet equipment maker Option's wholly owned semiconductor company. But the influence is not significant because the acquisition scale is just approximately eight million EUR.

In 2012, a US congressional panel warned that Huawei posed a security threat to the US. Huawei denied the accusations in front of the panel in September 2012. Huawei Vice President William Plummer said the accusations were "dangerous political distractions." China's Foreign Ministry urged the US to "set aside prejudices" about Huawei.

5. Operational globalization: competency, resources, and processes

Compared with its competitors, Huawei maintains cost and price advantages when it has gone global. Another competency is the rapid response to local customers with global reach. The high diligence, core enterprise culture of Huawei helps build the competency of rapid response in the global market. Deng Tao, vice president of Huawei, said: "After receiving feedback from customers, while the responses of other companies are relatively slow, Huawei usually works overtime with extreme diligence and responds to customers rapidly."

This competency is confirmed by its large clients. In 2001, when Huawei contacted Neuf, a French telecom operator, Neuf did not trust this newcomer. But after Huawei rapidly completed telecom networks construction in two French cities including Lyon in less than three months, Huawei got the contract from Neuf to build a network throughout France. Michel Paulin, CEO of Neuf, said: "This project helps us achieve the competency of speed. Previously the

French market was dominated by France Telecom, but now we have become its rival. Why? Because we move faster. Of course, our price is lower, based on Huawei equipment."

In 2004, Huawei, competing with Ericsson, the number one telecom equipment maker at that time, obtained the first significant contract in Europe valued at more than $25 million USD from Dutch operator Telfort. Van de Wiel, CTO of Telfort commented on the competency of Huawei: "People may think Huawei obtained this contract by low cost. We actually appreciate its fast response."

We take R&D as the example to explain the globalization of resources, as R&D is critical for a high-tech company and Huawei's globalization level of R&D is high. As of December 2010, Huawei employed more than 110,000 persons, 51,000 of whom are based outside China, and around 46 % of whom are engaged in research and development. Huawei operates a global network of 20 R&D facilities in the following locations:

- Bangalore, India, focusing on software.
- Moscow, Russia, focusing on wireless algorithm, application, and software.
- Dallas, USA, focusing on ASIC technologies and wireless algorithm.
- Ottawa, Canada, focusing on wire-line, wireless, optical, and IP networking.
- Munich, Germany, focusing on an all-IP network, core network, and high-speed transmission.
- Paris, France, focusing on telecom standard GSM-R.
- Milan, Italy, focusing on microwave.

Huawei's R&D globalization follows three modes. Since 1999, it has built R&D centers in India and Russia to acquire talent. Since 2000, it has built R&D centers in the US and Europe to acquire knowledge and technology and to understand the market. In addition, Huawei has established more than 20 innovation centers, jointly with large customers, focusing on developing tailored solutions.

We use a management consulting project about business processes, "IT Strategy and Planning" by Huawei and IBM Consulting, to study the globalization of its processes. Beginning in 1998, Huawei and IBM started a consulting project together with 50 IBM consultants to improve and transform business processes to learn IBM experiences in business processes transformation. In five years, Huawei invested about $50 million to improve internal business processes. "IT Strategy and Planning" is a project to design and plan a business processes and IT support system, consisting of eight items such as integrated product development and integrated supply chain.

Previously, Huawei mainly reduced costs in manufacturing, but when implementing "IT Strategy and Planning" project it realized the importance of optimizing business processes and minimizing the cost in the whole supply chain, including purchasing, manufacturing, logistics, and customer service. "IT Strategy and Planning" is an example of Stage 2 (internationalizing the core strategy) in the Yip globalization component theory. Through this project, Huawei enhanced its competency of low cost, mastered the know-how of international business, and laid a foundation for globalization.

6. Operational globalization: manufacturing and service

In manufacturing globalization, Huawei chooses to manufacture in domestic locations, and then export its branded products to foreign locations. Although Huawei built some outsourcing factories (e.g., Hungary-Pecs, Hungary-Komarom), the scale is not large. Compared with Haier, with a high level of manufacturing globalization to localize its products, the level of manufacturing globalization is lower in Huawei. Domestic manufacturing reduces the cost since labor and operational cost is low in China.

Compared with the low level of manufacturing globalization, service is highly globalized. Taking Huawei service in Europe as an example, it has built two technical assistance centers (UK, Romania), nine training centers (France, the UK, Germany, Italy, The Netherlands, Spain, Belgium, Poland, and the Czech Republic), four network operation centers (Romania, Spain, Switzerland, and Italy), two logistic centers (The Netherlands and Hungary), two regional spare parts centers, 41 country-level spare parts centers, and multi-languages call centers. It also has more than 320 certified service partners.

Case Questions

1. Compare the approaches of global expansion (M&A, partnerships, and organic growth) for Lenovo and Huawei. Why do they use different globalization approaches? (Hints: Lee and Lieberman 2010, p. 143)
2. Compare the globalization direction (see Fig. 2.1) for Haier and Huawei at their early stage (for Haier, see the case example in Sect. 3.2). Why do they choose different globalization directions at their early stage (or component 2 in the Yip globalization component system)?
3. Analyze the globalization stages of Huawei. Did Huawei follow the Uppsala internationalization stages? Did Huawei follow the Yip globalization component system?
4. Compare the manufacturing globalization of Haier and Huawei (for Haier, see the case example in Sect. 3.2). Why did they choose different global operations strategies for manufacturing globalization?
5. Summarize the globalization modes of R&D activities in Huawei.
6. Study the influence of the political separation on the global growth of Huawei.

References

Andersen, O. (1993). On the internationalization process of firms: A critical analysis. *Journal of International Business Studies, 24*(2), 209–231.

Bradley, F. (1995). *International marketing strategy*. New York: Prentice Hall.

Chase, R. B. (1978). Where does the customer fit in a service operation? *Harvard Business Review, 56*, 37–42.

Collier, D. A. (1985). *Service management: The automation of services.* Reston: Reston Publishing.

Dunning, J. H., & Lundan, S. M. (2008). *Multinational enterprises and the global economy.* Cheltenham: Edward Elgar Publishing.

Ethier, W. J. (1986). The multinational firm. *Quarterly Journal of Economics, 101*(4), 805–834.

Haywood-Farmer, J. (1988). A conceptual model of service quality. *International Journal of Operations and Production Management, 8*(6), 19–29.

Johanson, J., & Vahlne, J.-E. (1977). The internationalization process of the firm – A model of knowledge development and increasing foreign market commitment. *Journal of International Business Studies, 8*(1), 23–32.

Johanson, J., & Vahlne, J.-E. (1990). The mechanism of internationalization. *International Marketing Review, 7*(4), 11–24.

Johanson, J., & Vahlne, J.-E. (2006). Commitment and opportunity development in the internationalization process: A note on the Uppsala internationalization process model. *Management International Review, 46*(2), 165–178.

Johanson, J., & Wiedersheim-Paul, F. (1975). The internationalization of the firm: Four Swedish cases. *Journal of Management Studies, 12*(3), 305–322.

Kim, W. C., & Hwang, P. (1992). Global strategy and multinationals' entry mode choice. *Journal of International Business Studies, 23*(1), 29–53.

Kogut, B. (1985). Designing global strategies: Profiting from operational flexibility. *Sloan Management Review, 27*(1), 27–38.

Lee, G. K., & Lieberman, M. B. (2010). Acquisition vs. internal development as modes of market entry. *Strategic Management Journal, 31*, 140–158.

Liu, C. Z. (2007). Lenovo: An example of globalization of Chinese enterprises. *Journal of International Business Studies, 38*(4), 573–577.

McLaughlin, C. P. (1992). International service operations. *Operations Management Association Review, 9*(2), 22–30.

McLaughlin, C. P., & Fitzsimmons, J. A. (1996). Strategies for globalizing service operations. *International Journal of Service Industry Management, 7*(4), 43–57.

Rennie, M. W. (1993). Born global. *The McKinsey Quarterly, 4*, 43–52.

Vernon, R. (1966). International investment and international trade in the product cycle. *Quarterly Journal of Economics, 80*(2), 190–207.

Vernon, R. (1971). *Sovereignty at bay: The multinational spread of US enterprises.* New York: Basic Books.

Yip, G. S. (1982). Diversification entry: Internal development vs. acquisition. *Strategic Management Journal, 3*(4), 331–345.

Yip, G. S. (2003). *Total global strategy II: Updated for the internet and service era.* Upper Saddle River: Prentice Hall.

Rationale Behind Operational Globalization

3

Chapter Objectives

- To introduce the global strategy theories relevant to operational globalization analysis.
- To present the primary global strategy frameworks relevant to operational globalization analysis.
- To explain the drivers of operational globalization.
- To address the benefits of operational globalization.
- To identify the risks of global operations.

3.1 Basic Theories

This section presents the global strategy theories relevant to operational globalization analyses (see Table 3.1). While research on global strategy is voluminous and a comprehensive review is beyond the scope of this book, we mainly present a subset of global strategies as a foundation of global operations.

These theories explain why a firm goes global from different views. Eclectic theory states that a firm goes global to achieve ownership, location, and internalization advantages. Transaction cost theory (TCT) states that a firm goes global to minimize transaction costs. The competitive advantage of nations (CAN) theory argues that a firm in a particular industry goes global to build firm-specific competitive advantages with the characteristics, cultures, and resources of different nations. The resource-based view (RBV) focuses on the rents from scarce firm-specific resources. Competency theory focuses on achieving competencies as a source of sustained competitive advantage.

These theories can work as a foundation of operational globalization analysis or influence global operations strategy.

Table 3.1 Basic theories for global strategic analyses and their influence on operational globalization analysis

Theories of global or international strategies	Representative works	Main viewpoints	Application or influence at the operational level
Eclectic theory	Dunning (1977, 1988)	Ownership, location, and internalization advantages influence a firm's globalization	Location strategy, global manufacturing
TCT	Anderson and Gatigon (1986), Erramilli and Rao (1993), Klein et al. (1990)	Transaction cost minimization is the decision criteria in classical TCT. Modified TCT considers non-transaction cost benefits	Vertical integration, outsourcing decisions, global manufacturing networks, global supply chain management, global service
CAN	Porter (1990)	A firm can utilize the characteristics and indigenous resources of different nations as a source to achieve competitive advantage in the global market	Competency-based global operations strategy, global value chain
Learning theories (experiential and organizational learning)	Johanson and Vahlne (1977, 2009), Kogut and Zander (1993)	Knowledge development and learning are fundamental to a firm's internationalization. "Firm are social communities that serve as efficient mechanisms for the creation and transformation of knowledge into economically rewarded products and services" (Kogut and Zander 1993, p. 623)	Internationalization process, technology management, information management, production
RBV theory	Penrose (1959), Prahalad and Bettis (1986)	Competitive advantage relies on the firm's idiosyncratic and VRIO resources rather than the economic profits from product market positioning	Resource-based global operations strategy
Core competency theory	Sanchez et al. (1996), Prahalad and Hamel (1990), Hamel and Prahalad (1994)	A core competency with potential access to a wide variety of markets, contribution to the perceived customer benefits, and difficulty to imitate can lead to sustainable competitive advantage. Instead of competing in existing industries, a firm competing for the future targets opportunity share rather than market share	Competency-based global operations strategy. Improvement and innovation

Theory	References	Description	Application
Interorganizational network theory	Powell (1990), Hamel (1991), Nohria and Eccles (1992), Powell et al. (1996)	Firms can be involved in interorganizational relationships to acquire knowledge and skills, access technologies, enter new markets, benefit from economies of scale, and share risks to compete effectively	Global manufacturing networks, global supply chain networks, global revenue management (e.g., airline alliance), cooperation research
Strategic groups, theory based on industry organization	Hunt (1972), Thomas and Venkatraman (1988)	Within a strategic group, firms with similar asset configurations will set the same strategic objectives to achieve similar performances	Benchmarking, performance evaluation, operational competency
Cognitive communities theory based on psychology	Porac et al. (1989, 1995), Spender (1989)	In an industry, managers can construct competitive groups from shared cognition	Production process, categorization process, product type, production technology
Real options theory	Kogut and Kulatilaka (1994)	Study operating flexibility and global manufacturing by the option value of a multinational network	Global competencies such as flexibility, global resource such as manufacturing networks, risk management

- Global competency
  CAN, core competency, real options theories can guide competency-based global operations strategy. Core competency theory provides direct guidelines for competency-based global operations strategy. According to the competing for future theory (Hamel and Prahalad 1994), a firm competing for the future can obtain competency in a nascent market using improvement and technology innovation to gain opportunity share. Real options theory can be used to achieve global flexibility.
- Global resources
  Eclectic theory, RBV, CAN, and real options theories influence resource-based global operations strategy. Based on international trade theory, RBV, and TCT, eclectic theory presents a multi-theoretical approach for resource decisions including location decisions. RBV provides direct guidelines for resource-based global operations strategy. CAN theory points out that a firm can utilize the indigenous resources of nations as a source to win competitive advantage. Real options theories can be used to manage global manufacturing networks.
- Global processes
  CAN, TCT, core competency, network theory, real options, and learning theories influence process-based global operations strategy. According to CAN theory, a firm can optimize the global value chain by utilizing the resource advantages of different nations to achieve competitive advantage in the global market. Strategic groups theory can work as a foundation for benchmarking in an industry and for evaluating operational performance. According to cognitive communities theory, managers can share cognition in operational elements including production processes, product types, and production technology. According to interorganizational network theory, firms can join or develop interorganizational relationships and networks (e.g., alliances, cooperative joint ventures, equity sharing agreements, cooperative research pacts) to design global manufacturing networks, build global supply chain networks, improve global revenue management, and achieve cooperation research. TCT examines the core dimensions of the transaction including specific assets, the frequency of economic exchange, and the uncertainty of resource exchanges to aid decisions on vertical integration, outsourcing decisions, global manufacturing networks, and global supply chain management with the objective of transaction cost minimization. Real options theories can be used to improve global risk management and supply chain management. Learning theories influence global technology management and information management.

Case Example: PSA Peugeot Citroën

The manufacturing of PSA Peugeot Citroën, the largest French multinational manufacturer of automobiles and motorcycles, is globalized in not only developed countries but also in emerging countries (see Table 3.2).

The operational globalization of PSA fully utilizes the indigenous resources of different nations as sources to achieve competitive advantage. It utilizes

Table 3.2 Globalization timeline of PSA

Time	Location	Events
1810	France	Peugeot launched metallurgy business
1976	France	The PSA Peugeot Citroën Group is created by the merger of Citroën S.A. and Peugeot S.A
1978	UK, France, Spain, USA	Acquired Chrysler Europe
1992	China	Set up a joint venture DCAC with Dongfeng Motors to assemble Citroën models
1998	Argentina	Acquired Sevel Argentina
2001	Brazil	Started Porto Real production plant in Brazil
2002	China	Created a joint venture DPCA with Dongfeng Motors to expand cooperative production of Peugeot and Citroën models
2006	Slovakia	Inaugurated new production plant in Travna
2005	Czech Republic	Set up a joint venture factory "Toyota Peugeot Citroën" with Toyota to manufacture Toyota, Peugeot, and Citroën cars
2008	Russia	Started a joint venture Kaluga plant with Mitsubishi to manufacture cars
2010	China	Started a joint venture with the China Changan Automobile Group
2011	Germany, France	Started a new hybrid technologies joint venture with BMW
2012	France, USA	Built a long-term global strategic alliance with GM

financial and technology resources in France, R&D resources in Germany (e.g., joint venture with BMW), technology resources in the US (e.g., Chrysler acquisition, the alliance with GM), and low-cost resources in Argentina (e.g., Sevel Argentina Acquisition), Brazil (e.g., Porto Real production plant), China (e.g., joint venture with Dongfeng Motors), Slovakia (e.g., Travna plant), and the Czech Republic (e.g., Toyota Peugeot Citroën plant). PSA has also developed its market presence in fast-growing emerging countries such as Brazil, China, and Russia.

PSA globalizes operations in three ways: internal organic growth, joint ventures, and strategic alliances. It has built wide interorganizational relationships to achieve competitive advantage. It has also established a long-term global strategic alliance with GM to benefit from economies of scale by platform sharing and common purchasing, a joint venture with BMW to generate and acquire new hybrid technologies, joint ventures with Dongfeng Motors to enter new markets, and joint ventures with Toyota and Mitsubishi to share risks.

PSA and its partners GM, BMW, Toyota, and Mitsubishi have similar asset configurations and they have made similar strategic moves, such as entering the Chinese market in the 1980s or 1990s. They can thus be regarded as a "strategic group" that features leading automobile manufacturers with substantial investment in the Chinese market. In 1985, when PSA built "Guangzhou Peugeot", the Chinese market was small. Since 2010, China has become the largest automobile market (according to Bloomberg). This "strategic group" has benefited from market growth.

Case Questions

1. Use "eclectic theory" to explain the globalization of PSA.
2. Use "the competitive advantage of nations theory" to study the globalization of PSA.
3. Use "interorganizational network theory" to study the globalization of PSA.
4. Use "strategic groups" theory to study the globalization of PSA.
5. Compare PSA, VW (see Sect. 1.4), and BMW (see Sect. 2.3) in terms of manufacturing globalization.

3.2   Basic Frameworks

In this section, we present the primary frameworks of global strategic analysis by the sequence of publishing time. As global strategic analysis is a huge field, we introduce only those frameworks of relevance to operational globalization analysis. These frameworks can be classified into four levels of analysis:

- The industry level. For example, Porter's five forces framework assesses industry attractiveness.
- The location level. Porter's diamond framework studies competitive advantages afforded by a location with four dimensions.
- The firm level. Dunning's OLI framework summarizes the sustainable competitive advantage of a firm from internationalization.
- The activity level. Porter's configuration-coordination framework studies value chain globalization with two dimensions, namely configuration and coordination. Prahalad and Doz's integration-responsiveness framework assesses activities along the dimensions of global integration and local responsiveness. Bartlett and Ghoshal's globalization-localization framework provides a view of how firms respond to the forces of globalization and localization.

3.2.1   Dunning's OLI Framework

Dunning (1977) provides a fruitful way to study multinational enterprises (MNEs) and this work has inspired many applications in global operations such as global sourcing and global service. Therefore, we present Dunning's OLI framework as a foundation of global operations strategy. OLI stands for Ownership, Location, and Internalization, the three advantages that influence a firm's decision to become an MNE (see Fig. 3.1). The three advantages are:

- Ownership advantages refer to the specific advantages (e.g., products, designs, patents, trade secrets, and resources) used to overcome operational costs in a foreign country. These are used to answer the question of why some firms go abroad but not others.

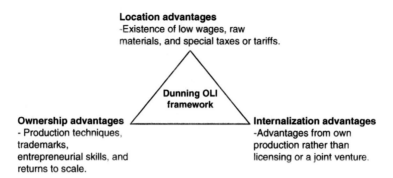

Location advantages
-Existence of low wages, raw materials, and special taxes or tariffs.

Dunning OLI framework

Ownership advantages
- Production techniques, trademarks, entrepreneurial skills, and returns to scale.

Internalization advantages
-Advantages from own production rather than licensing or a joint venture.

Fig. 3.1 OLI triad framework

- Location advantages refer to cheap input factors, transport costs, and trade barriers. These are used to address the question of where an MNE chooses to locate.
- Internalization advantages influence a firm's decision to operate in a foreign country. They relate to the trade-off between the benefits of a wholly owned subsidiary and the advantages of other entry modes such as exports, licensing, or joint ventures.

3.2.2 Porter's Five Forces Framework

Based on industrial organization economics, Porter (1979) proposes a five forces framework for industry analysis and business strategy and develops five forces that determine the competitive intensity and attractiveness of an industry. The attractiveness of an industry refers to overall industry profitability. If the combination of five forces acts to decrease overall profitability, the industry is "unattractive". These five competitive forces are:
- Threat of new entrants,
- Threat of substitute products and services,
- Intense rivalry among existing players,
- Bargaining power of suppliers, and
- Bargaining power of customers.

Porter's five forces framework argues that to compete for profits, a firm should consider not only established industry rivals, but also four competitive forces: "customers", "suppliers", "potential entrants", and "substitute products and services" (see Fig. 3.2). The extended industry rivalry resulting from five forces defines an industry's structure and shapes the competitive strategy.

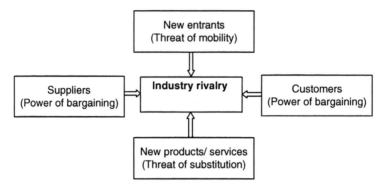

Fig. 3.2 Porter's five forces framework

	(Comparative advantages of countries)	
	No advantage	Advantage
(Competitive **No advantage** advantage of firms)		I
Advantage	II	III

Fig. 3.3 Kogut's international competition modes

3.2.3   Kogut's Comparative and Competitive Advantage Framework

Kogut (1985) studies the difference between location-specific comparative advantage and firm-specific competitive advantage and puts forward a key concept of "comparative advantage-based competitive advantage", particularly useful in global operations, including global value chains.

Kogut (1985) states that the design of global strategies is based on "the interplay between the comparative advantage of countries and competitive advantages of firms". Figure 3.3 shows Kogut's three modes for global competition. Competition mode I is mainly related to comparative advantages among countries. Competition mode II rests on differences in the chain of comparative advantages among firms. Competition mode III is of relevance to the interplay between competitive and comparative advantages along a value-added chain.

3.2.4   Porter's Configuration-Coordination Framework

Porter (1986) states that to deal effectively with global competition, a firm must choose a value chain configuration, determine how and where activities are performed, and consider the coordination problem to decide if activities should be shared among operational units. The value chain is a system of discrete activities

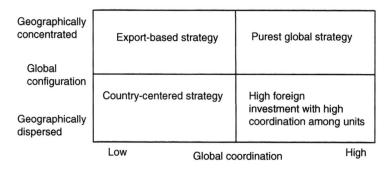

Fig. 3.4 Porter's configuration-coordination framework

conducted to do business. Its activities include primary activities such as inbound logistics, operations, outbound logistics, marketing and sales, service, and support activities such as firm infrastructure, human resource management, technology development, and procurement.

Porter (1986) develops a framework to address how firms can gain competitive advantage in their value chains through two dimensions: configuration and coordination. Global configuration refers to where and in how many places the firm's value chain activities are located worldwide. Global coordination refers to how and to what extent similar value chain activities are coordinated with each other across countries to maximize the firm's competitive edge.

Figure 3.4 presents Porter's configuration-coordination framework. Global configuration options range from the concentrated option, referring to performing a value chain activity in one location and serving foreign locations from it, to the dispersed option, referring to performing value chain activities in dispersed countries. Coordination options range from none to high. Figure 3.4 presents four global strategies. The "purest" global strategy is to concentrate value chain activities in one country and serve the world from this home base.

Porter's configuration-coordination framework can be applied in the following fields of global operations strategy (see Porter 1986, p. 18):

- Global production. Its configuration issues include the location of production facilities for components and end products, while its coordination issues include the networking of international plants, transferring of process technology, and production of know-how among plants.
- Global service. The configuration issues include the location of service organization, while its coordination issues include the similarity of service, service standards, and procedures worldwide.
- Global technology development. Its configuration issues include the number and location of R&D centers, while its coordination issues include interchanging among dispersed R&D centers, product development to respond to local markets, and product introduction sequence in the world.

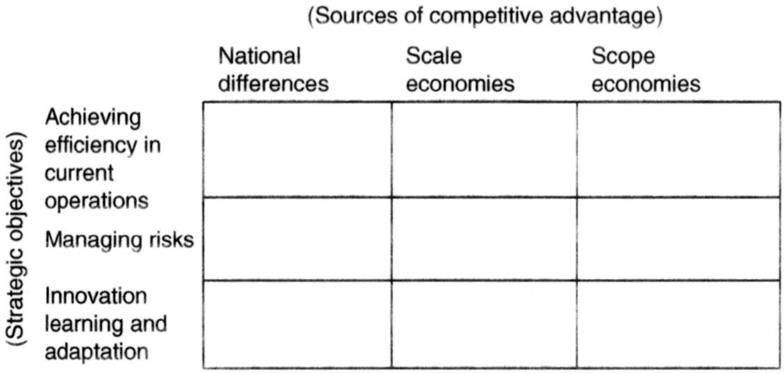

(Sources of competitive advantage)

	National differences	Scale economies	Scope economies
Achieving efficiency in current operations			
Managing risks			
Innovation learning and adaptation			

(Strategic objectives)

Fig. 3.5 Ghoshal's global strategy framework

3.2.5 Ghoshal's Means-Ends Framework

Ghoshal (1987) presents a conceptual framework for global strategy (see Fig. 3.5) and introduces a map for research on global strategy. The goals or "ends" can be classified into three categories: achieving efficiency in current operations, managing risks, and innovation learning and adaptation. Ghoshal (1987) points out that an MNE has three "means" (sources of competitive advantage): national differences, scale economies, and scope economies. First, the comparative advantage of a location is one of the most important sources of competitive advantages in global operations. Although different nations have different factor endowments, the realization of benefits from these factor endowments is not natural but via appropriate corporate strategies. Second, scale economies have been used as a competitive tool for a long time. Third, scope economies can help a firm share physical assets, including facilities and equipment, share external relations with suppliers, customers, distributors, and government, and share learning and knowledge.

3.2.6 Prahalad and Doz's Integration-Responsiveness Framework

The integration-responsiveness framework is an important tool for examining operations strategy in a global context (see, e.g., Prahalad and Doz 1987; Bartlett and Ghoshal 1989; Roth and Morrison 1990). Roth and Morrison (1990) empirically analyze the integration-responsiveness framework in global industries. Prahalad and Doz (1987) propose the following three strategies (Fig. 3.6):

1. Global integration

   If the pressure of global integration is perceived, this strategy will be adopted to highlight global coordination. Roth and Morrison (1990) point out that this strategy is characterized by intense competition with both domestic and global competitors.

Fig. 3.6 Prahalad and Doz's integration-responsiveness strategy framework

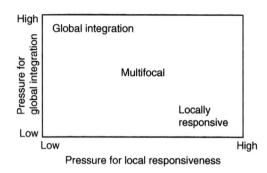

2. Local responsiveness

   In this strategy, local responsiveness will be emphasized if industry pressures are predominantly perceived at the domestic level. Roth and Morrison (1990) characterize this strategy by a high level of customer service needed and variable factor costs across locations.

3. Multifocal

   When both local responsiveness and global integration are perceived as important, a "multifocal" strategy will be used to respond to both dimensions (Prahalad and Doz 1987). While this strategy is characterized by intense competition and the presence of global competitors, little standardization of product exists (Roth and Morrison 1990).

3.2.7 Bartlett and Ghoshal's Globalization-Localization Framework

Based on the integration-responsiveness strategy framework, Bartlett and Ghoshal (1987) further elaborate on the globalization-localization framework. This framework analyzes in depth a firm's strategic position in the global environment, and has high practical values for managing different businesses, functions, and markets.

Figure 3.7 shows the globalization-localization framework. The vertical axis represents globalization level. A higher globalization level means a higher level of global integration and a higher level of central coordination. The horizontal axis represents the level of localization and national differentiation.

In Fig. 3.7, the left-hand diagram labeled "business" demonstrates the strategic positions of different businesses in a firm. For example, business 3 needs more global integration than business 4 and higher localization than businesses 1, 2, and 4. The middle diagram labeled "function" demonstrates the strategic positions of the different functions of business 3. For example, the "marketing" function needs to consider localization and national differentiation more than research. The right-hand diagram labeled "geography" demonstrates the strategic positions of different countries for marketing functions in this firm. For example, countries 1 and 2 are critical markets for the firm, so its marketing function will consider higher localization and higher global coordination.

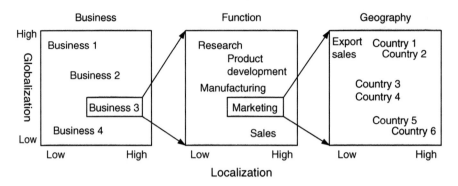

Fig. 3.7 Bartlett and Ghoshal's globalization-localization framework

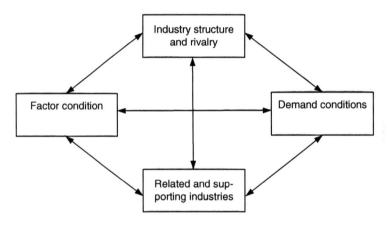

Fig. 3.8 Porter's diamond framework

3.2.8   Porter's Diamond Framework of Nation Advantage

Porter (1990) studies the determinants of international competitiveness and summarizes nation advantage with a "diamond", including four dimensions (see Fig. 3.8). The diamond framework states that a firm needs to utilize the components of its home country diamond to achieve sustainable competitive advantage.

Although this "diamond" is the most popular framework to study operations in a location considering CAN, debate about the "diamond" is fierce. Rugman and D'Cruz (1993) think that Porter's single diamond model works for large economies but needs to be adapted for smaller countries. They propose a "double diamond" model to explain international competitiveness in Canada with access to the US market through the free trade agreement.

Table 3.3 The world's five largest beauty manufacturers (ranked by 2011 sales volume)

Rank	Company	Representative brands	HQ, country	Sales (USD Billion)
1	L'Oreal	L'Oreal Paris, Maybelline New York, Lancôme, Biotherm, Vichy	Clichy, France	28.33
2	Procter & Gamble	Pantene, Head & Shoulders, Clairol, Herbal Essences, Rejoice	Cincinnati, US	20.7
3	Unilever	Impulse, Degree, Dove, Lux, Pond's, Suave, Clear, Mods, Vaseline	London UK/ Rotterdam, NL	18.58
4	Estée Lauder	Estée Lauder, Aramis, Clinique, Prescriptives	New York, US	9.44
5	Shiseido	Shiseido, Clé de Peau Beauté	Tokyo, Japan	8.53

(*Source:* WWD Beauty Inc's Top 100, August 10, 2012)

Case Example: L'Oreal

L'Oreal Group, headquartered in France, is the world's largest cosmetics and beauty Company, with 68,900 employees managing 27 global brands across 130 countries in 2012. L'Oreal consists of three major groups, namely Cosmetics, The Body Shop, and the dermatology branch, as well as a joint venture Galderma Laboratories with Nestlé. The Cosmetics group contributes over 90 % of its revenue.

• Industry

Competition is fierce in the cosmetics and beauty industry. In particular, the bargaining power of global customers is strong in the consumer products division. In the global beauty market, new trends such as the aging population in developed countries, aspiring consumers in emerging markets, growing demand for male beauty products, and increasing ethnic groups bring about serious threats of demand fluctuation and new product substitution. Thus, the group invested €721 million into cosmetic and dermatological research and filed 613 patents in 2011 to achieve product innovation and to sell the "science of beauty" worldwide.

L'Oreal's main rivals are P&G, Unilever, Estee Lauder, and Shiseido (see Table 3.3), all of which have strong financial, operational, and marketing capacities, particularly in their home countries. L'Oreal meets higher competition pressure from P&G and Estee Lauder in the US, from Unilever in Europe, and from Shiseido in Asia. In the hair care category, the biggest revenue generator of L'Oreal, its main rival is P&G. In the consumer division, its rivals are P&G and Unilever. In the luxury division, it competes with LVMH and Estee Lauder.

Table 3.4 L'Oreal divisions and brands in 2012

Division	Representative brands	Acquisition/own brand	Origin
Luxury products	Lancôme	Acquired in 1965	Europe
	Biotherm	Acquired in 1969	Europe
	Helena Rubinstein	Acquired in 1988	US
	Ralph Lauren Fragrances	Acquired in 1984	US
	Kiehl's	Acquired in 2000	US
	Yue-Sai	Acquired in 2004	Asia
Consumer products	L'Oreal	Own brand since 1907	Europe
	Garnier	Acquired in 1964	Europe
	CCB Paris	Own brand since 1987	Europe
	Maybelline New York	Acquired in 1996	US
	Mininurse	Acquired in 2003	Asia
	Essie	Acquired in 2010	US
Professional products	L'Oreal Professional	Own brand since 1907	Europe
	Kérastase	Own brand since 1965	Europe
	Redken	Acquired in 1993	US
	Matrix	Acquired in 2000	US
	PureOlogy	Acquired in 2007	US
Active cosmetics	Vichy	Acquired in 1980	Europe
	La Roche-Posay	Acquired in 1989	Europe
	SkinCeuticals	Acquired in 2005	US
Naturally oriented segment	The Body Shop	Acquired in 2006	Europe

- Globalization

While internal development is one way for globalization, acquisition has also played an important role in the globalization of L'Oreal (see "Acquisition/Own brand" column in Table 3.4). Acquisition is an approach to obtaining access to the local markets in the US and Asia. For example, the acquisition of Maybelline New York helped L'Oreal respond to local customers in the US, while its acquisition of Yue-Sai helped it understand local demand in Asia. After acquiring Chinese skincare brand Mininurse in 2003, L'Oreal made the following comments:

This acquisition is an outstanding opportunity to speed up our growth in the Chinese market. It is a major step forward in L'Oreal development in a market which is strategically important for the group (Lindsay Owen-Jones, CEO, L'Oreal, 2003, see loreal.com).

The globalization level of operations is high. Its manufacturing is globalized with 41 factories around the world and 5.8 billion units manufactured in 2011. Its R&D is globalized with 3,676 employees of 60 different nationalities working in 30 disciplines. The group made 100 active cooperation agreements with leading academic and research institutions.

- Localization

L'Oreal develops global brands in four divisions: luxury products, consumer products, professional products, and active cosmetics (see Table 3.3) and has an independent unit The Body Shop for the natural segment. Each division builds its own marketing team for individual brands. Regional teams further reach local customers.

L'Oreal develops "geocosmetics" to address the specific demand of local customers. For example, it has established a research institute in Chicago and a research center in Shanghai to understand local customers. The L'Oreal Shanghai center has developed more than 300 products for Chinese consumers. To adapt global products to local markets, L'Oreal has built 19 research centers in five regional hubs as well as 16 evaluation centers and 50 scientific and regulatory departments across the world. It emphasizes the localization of manufacturing and its production policy is "local manufacturing", to set the number of units produced in each region proportional to their contribution to turnover.

Case Questions

1. Use Porter's five forces framework to analyze the industrial environment of L'Oreal.
2. Use Porter's diamond framework to analyze the nation advantage of France, the home of L'Oreal.
3. Use Porter's configuration-coordination framework to analyze L'Oreal. Which global strategy (among the four strategies in this framework) is used by L'Oreal?
4. Use Kogut's comparative-competitive advantage framework to analyze the value chain of L'Oreal.
5. Use Bartlett and Ghoshal's globalization-localization framework to analyze the L'Oreal group. Read Unilever's case to assess the original application of this framework (see Bartlett and Ghoshal 1987, Fig. 1). These two firms are competing in several common markets. What is the difference between Unilever and L'Oreal in the globalization-localization framework?

3.3 Drivers

3.3.1 Drivers for Global Manufacturing

Yip (2002) presents four groups of globalization drivers at an industry level. We present the drivers of the global manufacturing of a firm at an operational level (see Fig. 3.9).

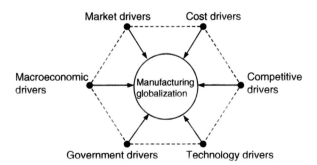

Fig. 3.9 Manufacturing globalization drivers

(1) Market drivers
Market drivers such as increasing demand in emerging countries, changing market structure and segmentation in developed countries, and growing global channels are changing global manufacturing. For example, BMW has built manufacturing plants in China to access the Chinese market.

(2) Cost drivers
As cost pressures become higher, firms continue to move manufacturing activities to access low cost resources or reduce costs by reconfiguring global manufacturing systems. For example, the iPhone is designed and marketed by Apple, but its hardware parts are produced in South Korea (application processor in Samsung), Japan (Flash memory, display module, and touch screen in Toshiba), and Germany (camera module, GPS receiver in Infineon). At the final production stage, Foxconn, a Taiwanese company, assembles all the iPhone components and exports the final product to the US and other countries. According to this production pattern, Apple has reduced the total landed cost of the iPhone.

(3) Competitive drivers
Manufacturing globalization can be driven by new competitive marketplaces, transferring from local competitors to global competitors, and strategically competitive objectives. Most leading automobile firms from Europe, the US, and Japan manufacture in China, the largest automobile marketplace, in order to compete with their rivals. European automobile manufactures, currently taking the largest market share in China, can use the profits obtained in the Chinese market to support competition in other marketplaces where Japanese and US automobile makers dominate.

(4) Technology drivers
Manufacturing globalization can be driven by access to manufacturing technology, technology diffusion, technology sharing, global R&D activities, and the advancement of logistics and communication technologies. In September 2012, Wuhan Steel, a leading Chinese steelmaker, signed a deal to acquire German giant ThyssenKrupp's subsidiary "Tailored Blanks Unit", a world-class leader in "laser-welded" technology, critical for automotive steel manufacturing. Wuhan Steel purchased the manufacturer to acquire its "laser-welded" technology and develop high-end automotive steel manufacturing.

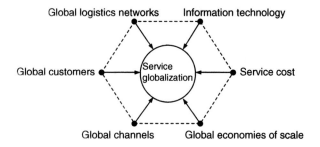

Fig. 3.10 Service globalization drivers

(5) Government drivers

Government drivers include bilateral and regional free trade agreements (e.g., the North American Free Trade Agreement), privatization of state-dominated economies, reduction of tariff barriers, creation of export processing zones, and establishment of special economic zones (e.g., Shenzhen SEZ in China, Mumbai SEZ in India, 16 federal economic zones in Russia).

(6) Macroeconomic drivers

Macroeconomic drivers such as the reduction in interest rates, fluctuation in exchange rates, fluctuation in inflation rates, reduction in unemployment rates, and difference in tax systems can influence global manufacturing. A firm may build manufacturing facilities in foreign locations with low interest rates to facilitate investment, exploit low unemployment rates to hire labor, use low tax rates to reduce costs, and benefit from high economic growth rates to access potential markets.

3.3.2 Drivers for Global Service

Drivers for global service differ from those of global manufacturing. Based on Lovelock and Yip (1996), who identify eight drivers for service businesses at an industry level, this section presents several of the drivers relevant to service operations for a firm (Fig. 3.10).

(1) Global logistics networks

Global logistics networks can improve customer convenience and reduce costs in service globalization type 1 "movement of service", type 2 "movement of customers", and type 4 "movement of both" (see Sect. 2.4.2). Without advanced global logistics networks, global service modes such as the "hub and spoke" airline service cannot be implemented.

(2) Information technology

Information technology is the critical driver in service globalization type 3 "no physical movement" (see Sect. 2.4.2). Information technologies make information-intensive (such as financial services, business services, health care, and education) or information-based services feasible, while technological features enable globalization to proceed at low costs. For example, online education provides low-cost global services and resources for adults, children, parents, and teachers. Without information technologies, this global service would never be realized.

(3) Service cost

These drivers are of relevance to service outsourcing to seek low labor costs, or global service modes to seek low-cost service products. Wipro, an Indian firm headquartered in Bangalore, uses its 130,000 employees to provide world-class outsourcing services in HR, tax transactions service, information-based services, and business processing services.

(4) Global economies of scale

When one country is not large enough to allow the optimal scale of a firm, a firm may seek global economies of scale. For example, even the US market is still small to achieve the optimal scale for Public Storage, and so the firm goes global to pursue optimal scale. The global service of McDonald's is partially driven by pursuing optimal global economies of scale. With standardizing service processes, global service providers enter multiple markets to increase scale. For example, Starbucks has entered multiple countries with different drinking cultures. By maintaining a relatively standard service process, it has achieved global economies of scale and accelerated profitable global growth.

(5) Global channels

The formulation of global distribution helps services go global. For example, with the support of global distribution, Starbucks has developed a "hub and spoke" geographic expansion strategy by firstly selecting a large city to serve as a "hub", with teams of professionals. Once the construction of the hub has been completed, additional stores are opened in surrounding "spoke" areas in the region. Furthermore, the electronic channel plays a critical role in the globalization of information-based services. For example, financial consulting sectors can deliver time-sensitive services via the Internet to global customers.

(6) Global customers

The tastes of some customers are globalized, namely they are standardized and simplified by a certain global service. These global customers further drive the globalization of service. Starbucks stores offer a choice of regular or decaffeinated coffee beverages, a broad selection of Italian-style espresso drinks, a wide selection of fresh-roasted whole-bean coffees, and a selection of fresh pastries and other food items. These products and services simplify the array of services and make a group of global customers. Starbucks can thereby pursue these global customers when they travel or move.

3.3.3   Drivers for Sustainable Global Operations

Socially responsible operations involve the consideration of a broad set of stakeholders that goes beyond shareholders. Many business leaders and entrepreneurs are committed to serving stakeholders that range from consumers to suppliers and from employees to external constituencies. Their motivation is primarily driven by the "triple bottom line" (profits, planet, and people) as follows:

(1) Profit driven

Products or services provided by socially and environmentally friendly companies are likely to be preferred by consumers or regulators. Consequently, these companies may be able to earn a higher profit by selling higher quantities at a higher price to offset any increase in costs.

(2) Planet driven

Business leaders are committed to ensuring sustainable resources for future generations, especially because there is only "one planet" with finite resources and rapidly growing consumption in developed as well as developing countries.

(3) People driven

MNEs recognize that to succeed in emerging markets, they need to alleviate poverty by creating businesses or jobs, by educating the poor to increase productivity, and by developing new ways to use natural resources in a sustainable manner.

Case Example: Haier Goes Global

• Globalization process

Haier has been the number one white goods manufacturer in China since 2001. Haier was a small refrigerator factory in Qingdao in 1984, but its founder and CEO Zhang Ruimin transformed it to a leading refrigerator manufacturer worldwide (according to Euromonitor) and started a globalization process (see Table 3.5).

• Pressure from local market

Competition in the Chinese refrigerator market is fierce. In 1989, there were more than 100 refrigerator producers, but only 20 survived in 1996. Its major domestic rival Kelon has an advantage in several market segments. After China joined the World Trade Organization in 2001, foreign entrants further increased the pressure. Siemens, GE (General Electric), Sony, LG, Samsung, and Whirlpool were taking market share from Chinese brands. It was necessary for Haier to seek new markets to increase revenue.

• Revenue growth from the international marketplace

The international marketplace brought about revenue growth for Haier. Total revenue grew from 16.8 billion RMB in 1998 to 150.9 billion RMB in 2011. Overseas revenue (including two parts: exports from China, overseas made and sold) increased from 3 % of total revenue in 1998 to 27.5 % of total revenue in 2010.

• Knowledge acquirement

An important reason for going global for Haier is to acquire market and technology knowledge. Haier's global strategy is to "firstly focus on difficult markets" such as the US, Europe, and Japan. By entering the US market, Haier learned the marketing knowledge of US customers. CEO Zhang Ruimin stated (Yatsko 1996):

Only by entering the international market can we know what our competitors are doing and can we raise our competitive edge. Otherwise, we will lose the China market to foreigners.

Table 3.5 Globalization process of Haier

Year	Globalization events
1984	Zhang Ruimin began to lead the Qingdao General Refrigerator Factory
1990	Haier passed the US UL Certification and started Haier's globalization
1994	Entered the US market
1999	Built alliance with Indian appliance firm Fedder Lloyd to jointly produce refrigerators in India
2000	Haier Europe began to coordinate sales in European countries
2000	Built a production facility in the US at Camden, South Carolina
2001	Haier America moved its New York headquarters to Broadway
2002	Production facilities were built in Pakistan
2003	Built production facilities in Jordan
2010	Haier surpassed Whirlpool as the world's top refrigerator producer in terms of brand market share (according to Euromonitor, accessed in 2011)

- Brand reputation

Another benefit of going global and "firstly focus[ing] on difficult markets" is building its brand when Haier sells in the US and Europe. When other Chinese manufacturers export products with an OEM (original equipment manufacturer) brand, Haier pays the cost to build an independent brand overseas. When Haier arrives in developing countries, customers already know Haier when they travel or stay in developed countries. Good sales records in the US and Europe also help build reputation in its local market of China.

Case Questions

1. What are the drivers (using drivers' definition in this section) for the globalization of Haier?
2. Why did Haier "firstly focus on difficult markets"?
3. What are the benefits for Haier from globalization?

3.4   Benefits

This section studies the benefits of operational globalization for a firm. Figure 3.11 presents the main benefits of operational globalization. A firm's operational globalization can bring multiple benefits.

3.4.1   Growth

Operational globalization can boost growth in two aspects. The first one is by entering new markets for potential growth. LVMH enters emerging markets to increase revenue. Huawei enters developed countries to increase market share in the

Fig. 3.11 Benefits of operational globalization

telecommunication equipment market. The second aspect of growth is increasing revenue, market size, and market share in existing markets. Apple improves its profits in existing markets by operational globalization such as outsourcing.

3.4.2 Cost Reduction

By operational globalization, a company can acquire labor or raw material resources to gain cost competency, realize economies of scale, realize economies of scope, and develop a broader range of products and services to reduce total supply chain costs in design, manufacturing, and distribution costs.

3.4.3 Knowledge Generation and Acquisition

With operational globalization, a firm can generate and acquire location-specific marketing knowledge and general knowledge such as technologies and management expertise. A firm can learn local knowledge from local suppliers, customers, competitors, foreign research centers, local professional talents, and knowledge workers. A firm moving from emerging countries to developed countries can learn advanced technologies and world-class management skills.

3.4.4 Competitive Leverage

Operational globalization provides competitive leverage to attack rivals or defend positions. A firm can have more options in terms of locations, technologies, human resources, and business processes to attack or counterattack.

3.4.5 Customer Satisfaction

Operational globalization improves customer satisfaction in three ways. First, it can increase access to local customers. By understanding local demand, a firm can improve customer satisfaction. Second, operational globalization can reduce the distance to local customers and improve customer satisfaction by shortening response time. Third, global availability by manufacturing globalization and global serviceability by service globalization can improve the customer satisfaction of global business travelers and tourists.

3.4.6 Social and Environmental Value Creation

Globalization offers new environments and social opportunities to MNEs. A firm can create "shared value", identify potential markets and opportunities, reduce operational risks, reduce operational costs, identify value-based new products and markets, and gain value-based competitive advantage. Thereby some global operations strategies consider value elements. A value-based global operations strategy can bring the following benefits to firms:

(1) Reputation

Companies such as the Body Shop, Ben & Jerry's, and Patagonia have distinguished themselves through long-term commitment to a value-based strategy and by building a global reputation among customers and other stakeholders. This improves company or brand image and brings about new revenue sources.

(2) Moral appeal

Companies have a duty to be good citizens. A value-based global operations strategy can help companies achieve business success and honor ethical values by considering people, communities, and the environment. This improves employee satisfaction, morale, and retention and enhances stakeholder relations. It also opens up new opportunities to collaborate, develop products, and keep stakeholders happy and confident.

(3) Sustainability

A value-based global operations strategy can help companies develop sustainably in the long-term. Sustainability improves economic value by reducing operating costs and optimizing lifecycle economic performance.

(4) Global license to operate

Global operations occur in different social and political environments. For companies that depend on government permits (e.g., the chemical industry, which is environmentally hazardous), it is critical to gain a "license" to do business in specific communities. A value-based global operations strategy can help companies conduct constructive dialogue with governments, regulators, local citizens, and pressure groups.

(5) Inspiring innovations

A value-based global operations strategy inspires two kinds of innovations. The first is product, service, and market innovation. The company will innovate to develop value-based products or services to meet new market demand on a global scale. Second, the company will formulate business models or process innovation to achieve value-based competency to improve both economic and social value. For example, VisionSpring formulates innovative business models to create channels for delivering low-cost eyeglasses in developing countries.

Table 3.6 Globalization timeline of Louis Vuitton

Time	Location	Events
1854	Paris	Vuitton founded French fashion house Louis Vuitton
1885	London	Set up its first overseas store on Oxford Street
1893	Chicago	Exhibited products at the World's Fair
1913	Paris	Set up the Louis Vuitton Building on the Champs-Elysees
1978	Tokyo and Osaka	Set up its first stores in Japan
1983	Taipei	Opened a store
1984	Seoul	Opened a store
1987	Paris	Created LVMH with Moët & Chandon and Hennessy
1992	Beijing	Established its first Chinese location at the Palace Hotel
2003	Moscow	Opened a store in Russia
2003	New Delhi	Opened a store in India
2004	New York, São Paulo, Mexico City, Cancun, Johannesburg, Shanghai	Celebrated its 150th anniversary and inaugurated a series of stores
2011	Singapore	Established first "Island Maison" in Southeast Asia

Case Example: Louis Vuitton

LVMH, the world's largest luxury goods conglomerate headquartered in Paris, was formed as a merger of Louis Vuitton, champagne producer Moët & Chandon, and the cognac manufacturer Hennessy. Christian Dior is the main holding company of LVMH, owning 42.36 % of its shares. Louis Vuitton is a leading international fashion house that has been named the world's most valuable luxury brand.

Louis Vuitton's globalization mode is of relevance to features of luxury products. Previously, its products were sold in department stores. To reduce counterfeiting products and improve brand reputation, its products are now primarily available at authentic Louis Vuitton boutiques in upscale shopping districts or inside luxury department stores. Table 3.6 shows Louis Vuitton's globalization focuses on marketing, brand, and sales. It has established a number of its own stores in the world. In order to globalize, Louis Vuitton achieves sustainable development, increases market share and revenue, obtains access to customers, improves global availability, and acquires local market knowledge.

Louis Vuitton's manufacturing is internationalized, but not globalized, mainly limited to a few European countries. It produces leather goods collections in workshops located in France, Spain, and the US, footwear and ready-to-wear collections in France and Italy, watches in timepiece workshops in Switzerland, jewelry collections in France, Italy, and Switzerland, and sunglasses in France and Italy.

Table 3.7 Recent disasters

Natural risks	Examples	Influence on operations
Earthquakes	Japan earthquakes; March 11, 2011	Influence global supply chains in the electronic, steel, and automobile industries
Volcanic eruptions	Eyjafjallajökull, Iceland; April 14, 2010	Influence the global airline industry, then railroad and ocean shipping when transportation flow went to other modes
Hurricane	Katrina storm, USA; August 2005	Influence oil supply chain in the Gulf of Mexico and the forestry supply chain in Mississippi
Drought	France drought; 2011	Influence the global agricultural supply chain

Case Questions

1. What are the benefits of globalization for Louis Vuitton?
2. What is the difference between manufacturing globalization and marketing globalization in Louis Vuitton? Why has it made such a distinction?
3. Compare L'Oreal and Louis Vuitton in terms of globalization (hints: acquisition and internal growth, globalization stages, operational globalization and marketing globalization, drivers, and benefits, among others)?

3.5   Risks

3.5.1   Natural Risks

Natural risks such as earthquakes, volcanic eruptions, and hurricanes can lead to social, economic, and environmental losses, and affect the infrastructure and structural decisions of a firm's operations strategy (for recent examples, see Table 3.7). The severity of these effects depends on the types of natural risks, the social and economic situation of the affected area, the area's relevance to the global supply chain, and the relief and restoration capacity of governments and NGOs.

3.5.2   Economic Risks

Economic risks, manifested in lower revenue or higher costs than expected, refer to the possibility that an economic factor would negatively affect firm performance.

The first risk of global operations is from foreign exchange risks, referring to the risk that a business's financial performance or strategic position would be affected by fluctuations in the exchange rates between currencies. Second, macroeconomic fluctuations can influence global operations. For example, launching a capital-intensive manufacturing project immediately before or during a recession carries a great deal of economic risks. Third, economic policy uncertainties can lead to risks. A central bank may unexpectedly raise interest rates or the legislature may raise taxes, resulting in economic risks affecting a global manufacturing project that needs substantial investment.

3.5.3 Political Risks

The interconnection of markets across various political systems, the growing reliance on global service and global manufacturing, and the deterioration of global security all contribute to the increasing awareness that political risk plays a critical role in global operations. Political risk normally refers to the probability of suffering losses for MNEs by political forces and events (see Kobrin 1979). Broadly speaking, it includes two parts, namely the uncertainties triggered by the actions of the government or organizations in the host country and the restrictions or sanctions on the outward investment made by the home country. Political risks can be divided into six categories:

- Political violence including war, separatism, terrorism, revolution, insurrection, civil unrest, and extremist movements.
- Governmental expropriation or confiscation of assets, especially in countries with dictatorial systems.
- Breach of contract by the government.
- Non-honoring of government guarantees.
- Inconvertibility of foreign currency or the inability to repatriate funds.
- Business interruption. A typical interruption is the restriction on FDI outflows in home countries.

It is important to estimate and evaluate political risks in the host nation before entering. In countries with high protectionism and intervention, the probabilities of expropriation and breaches of contract are high. A host nation that has an imperfect legal system and weak intellectual property rights is likely to infringe the interests of MNEs and break its contract promises. Instead of an evaluation and avoid strategy, a firm can choose the option of political risk insurance.

3.5.4 Social, Ethical, and Environmental Risks

When operating in new markets with different social and ethical backgrounds, a firm will be exposed to larger social and ethical risks, which it rarely meets in the domestic market. Nike faced consumer boycotts when the *New York Times* reported that its Indonesian supplier abused workers in the 1990s. Even just outsourcing to another country without directly manufacturing can lead to such risks for a firm. Although Apple had not directly hired manufacturing workers in China, it was criticized for a sweatshop problem since several employees of its supplier Foxconn committed suicide owing to the poor work conditions and salary issues in the 2010s.

Operational globalization can expose a firm to larger environmental risks. Nestlé, one of the largest producers of bottled water, was attacked for its waste of freshwater. Shell's sinking of the Brent Spar, an obsolete oil rig in the North Sea, led to Greenpeace protests in 1995.

Case Example: Japanese Earthquake and the Global Supply Chain

On 11th March 2011, an earthquake with an intensity of 9.0 on the Richter scale hit Japan, destroying infrastructure including ports, plants, and railways and damaging manufacturing in industries including electronics, steel, and automobile parts where Japan is a major supplier. The aftermath of the Japanese earthquake caused logistical disruptions and supply shortages, and foreign companies needed to reexamine the robustness of their supply chains.

Apple is one such company that is facing shortages of the lithium-polymer batteries used in its iPod and iPad lines, as its Japanese supplier has been forced to shut its facilities after the earthquake. Furthermore, at least five components of the iPad 2 were sourced from Japanese suppliers, including the NAND flash from Toshiba, dynamic random access memory made by Elpida Memory, electronic compass from AKM Semiconductor, the touch screen overlay glass from Asahi Glass, and the system battery from Apple Japan. These suppliers have encountered difficulties in raw materials supply, distribution, shipping, facilities damage, and employee absences, which have led to shortages. These shortages have influenced Apple's global supply chain and finally its customers.

Case Questions

1. How did the earthquake influence the global supply chain?
2. How should Apple change its operation strategy in order to avoid a shortage of components?

Case: Foxconn and Apple

• Background of Foxconn

Foxconn Technology Group, well known as a main manufacturer of Apple's iPhone and iPad, is a multinational company that specializes in electronics manufacturing. This Taiwan-based company was founded in 1974, under the name of Hon Hai Precision Industry Company Ltd. Foxconn makes products for Apple, HP, Motorola, Sony, IBM, Nokia, Intel, LG, Cisco, Samsung, and Dell, and helps their global operations.

Foxconn is in a special but huge industry called EMS (Electronics Manufacturing Services). EMS providers mainly make products for OEMs, which design and distribute the products using their own brand names. The business model for the EMS industry is to specialize in large economies of scale in manufacturing and raw materials procurement. Foxconn, which has

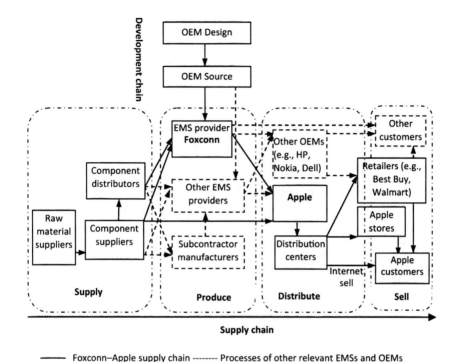

— Foxconn–Apple supply chain -------- Processes of other relevant EMSs and OEMs

Fig. 3.12 Supply chains of Foxconn

more than a million (as of 31 December 2011) employees, is the largest MNE in the EMS industry.

• Supply chain of Apple

Apple is a US MNE that designs and markets consumer electronics, computer software, and personal computers. Apple outsources manufacturing to Foxconn and other EMS providers. Some EMS providers may outsource to other subcontractors. Apple also directly buys from component suppliers. Apple network stores are the main advantage of the Apple distribution system. Apple also uses the distribution channels of AT&T, Best Buy, and Walmart to reach millions of customers. By building strategic alliances with other companies such as HP (which sells a co-branded form of the iPod), Apple can sell and distribute its products. Its direct online store is another increasingly important distribution channel (Fig. 3.12).

• Suicides at Foxconn

In the pursuit of "Total Cost Advantage", the Foxconn business model is called "eCMMS" (e-enabled Components, Modules, Moves, and Services). This is a one-stop shopping business model that integrates mechanical, electric, and optical capabilities. It covers solutions ranging from molding, tooling, mechanical parts, components, modules, system assembly, design, manufacturing, maintenance, and logistics. The competency of Foxconn is price and cost, based on low labor cost. In the EMS market, OEMs can earn gross profit margins of 50–60 %, but contract manufacturers only have small margins.

Owing to high price pressure from OEMs, some EMS employees may receive inappropriate treatment including overtime, low salaries, and bad working conditions. By the end of 2010, the total number of attempted suicides reached 17 with only three survivors. Many of them jumped from Foxconn's high buildings. However, Foxconn claimed the suicide rate of Foxconn employees was lower than the average suicide rate in China.

• Responses and countermeasures

In mainland China, the suicides arose wide debates and discussion. In Hong Kong, a nonprofit organization SACOM (Students and Scholars against Corporate Misbehavior) demanded a boycott of relevant products. In Taiwan, labor unions organized protests against "sweatshops".

Apple sent executives to review the operations at Foxconn and sent experts to investigate the suicide events. However, it has not addressed the issue of low price and thereby low wages. Foxconn promised to do anything possible to stop these tragedies and took the following substantial measures:

• Required employees to sign a "no suicide" pledge,
• Installed suicide-prevention netting,
• Increased salaries,
• Introduced sociologist and psychiatrist services,
• Improved working conditions, and
• Moved from Southern China (relatively rich region in China) to other places such as Henan that has even lower labor costs.

(*Source: Foxconn CSR report 2011*)

Case Questions

1. Use Porter's five forces framework (see Sect. 3.2) to study the EMS industry.
2. What are the drivers, risks, and benefits for Apple to outsource to Foxconn?
3. What are the drivers, risks, and benefits of global operations for Foxconn?
4. What is the responsibility of Apple for these suicides? What is the responsibility of Foxconn for these suicides? Any suggestions for their global operations?

References

Anderson, E., & Gatigon, H. (1986). Modes of entry: A transaction cost analysis and propositions. *Journal of International Business Studies, 17*(3), 1–26.
Bartlett, C. A., & Ghoshal, S. (1987). *Managing across borders: The transnational solution.* Boston: Harvard Business School Press.

Dunning, J. H. (1977). Trade, location of economic activity and the MNE: A search for an eclectic approach. In Bertil Ohlin, Per-Ove Hesselborn, & Per Magnus Wijkman (Eds.), *The international allocation of economic activity*. London: Macmillan.

Dunning, J. H. (1988). The electric paradigm of international production: A restatement and some possible extensions. *Journal of International Business Studies, 19*(1), 1–31.

Erramilli, M. K., & Rao, C. P. (1993). Service firms' international entry mode choice: A modified transaction-cost analysis approach. *Journal of Marketing, 57*(3), 19–38.

Ghoshal, S. (1987). Global strategy: an organizing framework. *Strategic Management Journal, 8* (5), 425–440.

Hamel, G. (1991). Competition for competence and interpartner learning within international strategic alliances. *Strategic Management Journal, 12*, 83–103.

Hamel, G., & Prahalad, C. K. (1994). *Competing for the future*. Boston: Harvard Business School Press.

Hunt, M. S. (1972). *Competition in the major home appliance industry*. Doctoral dissertation, Harvard University, Boston.

Johanson, J., & Vahlne, J.-E. (1977). The internationalization process of the firm – A model of knowledge development and increasing foreign market commitments. *Journal of International Business Studies, 8*(1), 23–32.

Johanson, J., & Vahlne, J.-E. (2009). The Uppsala internationalization process model revisited: From liability of foreignness to liability of outsidership. *Journal of International Business Studies, 40*, 1411–1431.

Klein, S., Frazier, G., & Roth, V. J. (1990). A transaction cost analysis models of channel integration in international markets. *Journal of Marketing Research, 27*(2), 196–208.

Kobrin, S. J. (1979). Political risks: A review and reconsideration. *Journal of International Business Study, 10*(1), 67–72.

Kogut, B. (1985). Designing global strategies: Comparative and competitive value-added chains. *Sloan Management Review, 26*(4), 15–28.

Kogut, B., & Kulatilaka, N. (1994). Operating flexibility, global manufacturing, and the option value of a multinational network. *Management Science, 40*(1), 123–139.

Kogut, B., & Zander, U. (1993). Knowledge of the firm and evolutionary theory of the multinational corporation. *Journal of International Business Studies, 24*(4), 625–645.

Lovelock, C., & Yip, G. (1996). Developing global strategies for service businesses. *California Management Review, 38*(2), 64–86.

Nohria, N., & Eccles, B. (1992). *Networks and organizations*. Boston: Harvard Business School Press.

Penrose, E. (1959). *The theory of the growth of the firm*. London: Oxford University Press.

Porac, J., Thomas, H., & Baden-Fuller, C. (1989). Competitive groups as cognitive communities: The case of Scottish knitwear manufacturers. *Journal of Management Studies, 26*, 397–416.

Porac, J., Thomas, H., Wilson, F., Paton, D., & Kanler, A. (1995). Rivalry and the industry model of Scottish knitwear producers. *Administrative Science Quarterly, 40*, 203–227.

Porter, M. E. (1979). How competitive forces shape strategy. *Harvard Business Review, 57*(2), 137–145.

Porter, M. E. (1986). Changing patterns of international competition. *California Management Review, 28*, 9–40.

Porter, M. E. (1990). *Competitive advantage of nations*. New York: The Free Press.

Powell, W. (1990). Neither market nor hierarchy: Network forms of organization. In L. L. Cummings & B. Staw (Eds.), *Research in organizational behavior* (Vol. 12, pp. 295–336). Greenwich: JAI Press.

Powell, W., Koput, K., & Smith-Doerr, L. (1996). Interorganizational collaboration and the locus of innovation: Networks of learning in biotechnology. *Administrative Science Quarterly, 41*, 116–145.

Prahalad, C. K., & Bettis, R. (1986). The dominant logic: A new linkage between diversity and performance. *Strategic Management Journal, 1*, 485–501.

Prahalad, C. K., & Doz, Y. L. (1987). *The multinational mission: Balancing local demands and global vision*. New York: The Free Press.

Prahalad, C. K., & Hamel, G. (1990). The core competence of the corporation. *Harvard Business Review, 68*, May-June, 79–91.

Roth, K., & Morrison, A. (1990). An empirical analysis of the integration-responsiveness framework in global industries. *Journal of International Business Studies, 21*(4), 541–564.

Rugman, A., D'Cruz, J. (1993). The "double-diamond" model of international competitiveness. *Management International Review, 33*(special issue 2), 17–40.

Sanchez, R., Heene, A., & Thomas, H. (Eds.). (1996). *Dynamics of competence based competition*. Oxford: Elsevier.

Spender, J. C. (1989). *Industry recipes: An enquiry into the nature and sources of managerial judgment*. New York: Blackwell.

Thomas, H., & Venkatraman, N. (1988). Research on strategic groups: Progress and prognosis. *Journal of Management Studies, 25*, 537–555.

Yatsko, P. (1996). To service and the profits: A Chinese fridge-maker wows customers with service. *Far Eastern Economic Review, 17*, 47–50.

Yip, G. (2002). *Total global strategy II*. New Jersey: Prentice Hall.

Part II

Fundamentals of Global Operations Strategy

Part Objectives

Figure II shows the position of Part II in the whole book. The objectives of Part II are:
- To address three views of global operations strategy: competency-based, resource-based, and process-based GOS.
- To introduce concepts and the evolution of operational competencies and discuss approaches to achieving competencies.
- To introduce RBV and discuss resource-based decisions including resource size, type, location and dynamic capacity problems in a global environment.
- To introduce global supply chain strategy, global revenue management strategy, global technology strategy, and global risk management strategy (Fig. II).

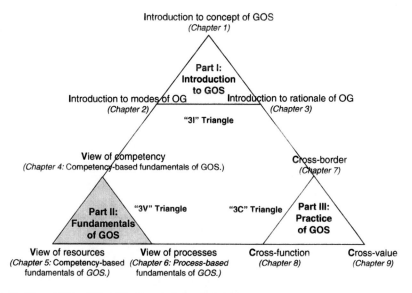

Fig. II The position of Part II in the whole book structure

Competency-Based Fundamentals

4

Chapter Objectives

- To introduce the evolution of operational competencies.
- To present a competency-based view of global operations strategy.
- To introduce concepts of global operational competencies, including time-, quality-, cost-, flexibility- and value-based competencies.
- To discuss the roles of competencies in global operations strategy.
- To address approaches to achieving competencies.

4.1 Introduction to Operational Competencies

Building from the work of Stalk (1988), who presented the evolution of operational competencies from cost- to time-based competencies, and including quality competency as understood in the 1980s and more recent trends from the 2000s, Table 4.1 presents a brief history of competencies. The evolution of operational competencies has been accompanied through the continuing process of globalization. When a firm goes global, it expands and penetrates more markets. New market demands drive the firm to adopt various competencies.

Prior to the 1960s, the common operational competency was cost and economies of scale represented the main approaches to achieving cost competency. Andrew Carnegie (1835–1919) increased the scale available to his operations by vertically integrating iron and coal mines, steel production and other steel-related operations to become the most efficient steel producer in the world. Another representative thought is the famous quote by Henry Ford, the founder of the Ford Motors, "You can have any color you want as long as it is black". Ford applied assembly line manufacturing to the mass production of affordable automobiles.

Y. Gong, *Global Operations Strategy*, Springer Texts in Business and Economics,
DOI 10.1007/978-3-642-36708-3_4, © Springer-Verlag Berlin Heidelberg 2013

Table 4.1 Evolution of competencies in history

Time	Competency	Examples
Pre-1960s	Cost	Carnegie and scale, Ford assembly-line production
Mid-1960s	Productivity and cost (focused factories)	SKF (Swedish ball bearing factory)
1970s	Flexibility	Honda-Yamaha variety war, GM
1980s	Quality	Ford-GM quality competition, Martin, Toyota
1990s	Time	Toyota, Dell, Honda, Citicorp, AT&T, GE, HP
2000s	VBC	Nestlé, Walmart, GE, Google, IBM

In the middle of the 1960s, responding to a "productivity crisis", Japanese manufacturers identified a new source of competitive advantage – the focused factory, which produced goods either made nowhere else or which targeted a high-volume market segment. Western manufacturers such as the Swedish ball-bearing factory SKF adopted Japanese strategies and focused each factory on products best suited to the particular factory. Skinner (1974) summarized these strategies and proposed the concept of "focused factories", which suggested that manufacturers focus each plant on a limited, concise, manageable set of products, technologies, volumes, and markets, and that they structure their basic manufacturing policies and support services to focus on a specific manufacturing task.

By the early 1920s, Ford – in selling his Model T for $290 – had built an unbeatable dominance in low-cost automobile manufacturing. Alfred Sloan, realizing this fact, made creative use of product varieties and market segment strategy – exemplified by the maxim, "a car for every purse and purpose" – by positioning Chevrolet at the low end of the market to attack Ford and Cadillac at the high end of the growing automobile market. In the 1970s, flexible factories and strategies focused on product variety became popular, highlighted in particular by the so-called "variety wars" of the late 1970s and early 1980s, a business war fought between Honda and Yamaha in the motorcycle market. In 18 months, Honda introduced 113 motorcycle models, and in the process devastated Yamaha.

In the 1980s, quality became a popular operational competency, although it had been considered as a success element for long time. In explaining quality management, Philip Crosby famously wrote, "Quality is free". This realization contributed to Crosby's decision to initiate a "zero defects" program at the Martin Company. The increase in quality competency was associated with increased competition between Ford and GM in the 1980s. In 1981, Ford's sales were falling, which led the company to recruit a quality management guru, W. Edwards Deming, to assist the company in improving the quality of its products. Donald Petersen, then Chairman of Ford, said, "We are moving toward building a quality culture at Ford and the many changes that have been taking place here have their roots directly in Deming's teachings." In 1986, Ford's earnings exceeded those of its rival GM for the first time since the 1920s.

Stalk (1988) introduced the concept of "time-based competition" and argued that a firm's competitive advantage lay in its ability to rapidly deliver products or services. By the 1990s, many firms had adopted time-based operations strategies, including Toyota, Honda, Citicorp, AT&T, GE and HP. Dell used an on-time-delivery (OTD) strategy, a cornerstone of operations strategy, which promised product shipment within five days of receiving the order and two-day delivery.

In the 2000s, firms emphasized social and environmental values in global manufacturing and service. Going beyond corporate social responsibility (CSR), Porter introduced the concept of "creating shared value" (CSV), which sought to link social and economic values, exert a larger influence without the limitations of a CSR budget and achieve value-based competency (VBC). Many companies, including GE, Google, IBM and Nestlé, have since sought to implement a global operations strategy to aid in their pursuit of VBC.

In Table 4.1, the time division is not absolute, but it does show the relative periods during which a particular competency has received the majority of corporate attention. Flexibility competency, for instance, was adopted by GM in 1924, was an increasingly popular application in the 1970s, and is still developing new forms and modes. Section 4.4.2 presents the history of quality management, which was commonplace in the 1980s, but has a long history of development, from ancient civilization to the present. For further readings, see Bowen and Jones (1986), Dibrell et al. (2005), Ettlie and Penner-Hahn (1994), Gupta and Goyal (1989), Prahalad and Hamel (1990), and Rich and Hines (1997).

Case Example: Toyota

Toyota, a leading Japanese multinational automaker, occupies a special place in the history of operations strategy and has played an important role in the evolution of operational competency due to its landmark management innovations while also contributing to both the theoretical and practical sides of operations strategy. We present the evolution of Toyota's operations strategy as follows.

• Jidoka

In 1902, Sakichi Toyoda, founder of Toyota, invented a loom which would stop automatically if one of the threads snapped. Sakichi's invention reduced defects and raised revenues, since a loom would not go on producing imperfect fabric and using up thread after a problem had occurred.

The principle of designing equipment to stop automatically and call attention to a problem in an immediate manner was central to Jidoka, an early quality control method. When a problem occurred, the equipment stopped immediately, preventing defective products from being produced. This method highlighted and visualized problems. The core philosophy, "Quality must be built in during the manufacturing process!", allowed Jidoka to build from a quality foundation for just-in-time production.

• Just in time (JIT) production

In the 1930s, Sakichi's son Kiichiro Toyoda laid the groundwork for JIT production and coined the term "just in time". JIT production was again proposed and implemented by vice president Taiichi Ohno, who had been inspired by observations of supermarket operations made in the 1950s.

JIT referred to the practice of making "only what is needed, when it is needed, and in the amount needed". With a core philosophy which regarded inventory as waste, JIT reduced in-process inventory and costs by "Kanban" (Kanban cards or electronic kanban systems) between different points in the process, which informed the manufacturing system of the appropriate time at which to fabricate the next part. JIT could improve return-on-investment, quality and efficiency, and save warehouse space and help to limit costs.

• Toyota Production System (TPS)

Based on Jidoka and JIT, Taiichi Ohno, Shigeo Shingo and Eiji Toyoda developed TPS during the period 1948–1975. Steeped in the philosophy which sought "the complete elimination of all waste", TPS made vehicles "in the quickest and most efficient way, in order to deliver the vehicles as quickly as possible". While activities, connections and production flows in a Toyota factory were rigid, its operations were flexible and adaptable.

Spear and Bowen (1999) identified the "DNA" of TPS, which consisted of "four rules", including three rules of design which showed how Toyota organized all of its operations as experiments, and one rule of improvement which described how Toyota taught the scientific method to its workers.

• Lean manufacturing

In the 1990s, lean manufacturing as a management philosophy was derived mostly from TPS. The objectives of lean manufacturing were to reduce time, to reduce total costs by producing only to meet customer demand, to improve quality, and most importantly to eliminate waste, which was defined as any activity that consumed time, resources or space but did not add value to the end product or service. Toyota identified seven types of wastes (muda): (1) overproduction; (2) waiting, time on hand; (3) unnecessary transport or conveyance; (4) over-processing or incorrect processing; (5) excessive inventory; (6) motion; and (7) defects.

Lean manufacturing could be achieved by either of two different methods. A firm could use tools such as Value Stream Mapping to identify and eliminate waste. Once the waste has been eliminated, quality will be seen to have improved while production time and costs will have been reduced. The second approach sought to improve the smoothness with which the work proceeded and to eliminate unevenness and variance which existed through the application of the system and of techniques such as Kanban.

• The Toyota Way, 2001

In 2001, Toyota summarized its philosophy, principles, values and manufacturing ideals in "The Toyota Way 2001", a document which was organized into four sections: (1) long-term philosophy, (2) the right process will produce the right results, (3) add value to the organization by developing your people, and (4) the continuous solving of root problems drives organizational learning (Ohno 1988; Ohno and Mito 1988; Spear and Bowen 1999).

1. How has Toyota contributed to the historic development of operations strategy?
2. What are the competencies to which Jidoka, JIT, TPS, lean manufacturing and the Toyota way, respectively, contribute?
3. In January 2010, Toyota suspended US sales of several car and truck models to fix sticking gas pedals; as part of this course of action, Toyota recalled 2.3 million vehicles. How do you view new challenges of global quality risk facing Toyota?

4.2   Cost Competency

4.2.1   Concept of Cost Competency

In both the manufacturing and service sectors, cost competence has been identified as a core competency for some time. Some companies use a defensive, cost-based strategy to survive and win market share; others use an aggressive, cost-leadership strategy to achieve growth and build leadership in the global marketplace.

A defensive cost-based strategy is achieved by maintaining low prices to attract price-sensitive customers in the targeted market segment, or via the low price-performance ratio, which refers to a product's ability to deliver performance while charging a lower price. Generally speaking, products or services with a higher price-performance ratio are more competitive. To succeed at market by offering the lowest price while still achieving profitability and a high return on investment, a firm must be able to operate at lower costs than its rivals. A local restaurant, for example, can attract price-sensitive customers by offering a limited menu, rapid table turnover and by employing a low-wage staff.

An aggressive cost-leadership strategy provides products and services at the lowest price, tries to win the largest market share, uses costs and price as strategic weapons with which to attack rivals and builds dominance in the global market-place. Prior to 2009, laws in France essentially forbade retailers from price competition. Carrefour was therefore forced to pursue a quality-based strategy. When the pricing laws were subsequently loosened, Carrefour found it was not as competitive as it had been. After Lars Olofsson became chief executive, in January 2009, Carrefour restored its low-price strategy in hypermarkets as a means of combating discounters. Whereas Carrefour stores previously had banners which bore the slogan "quality for all", most in-store advertising now focuses on "the lowest price". Carrefour has used low cost to win cost leadership in the global marketplace.

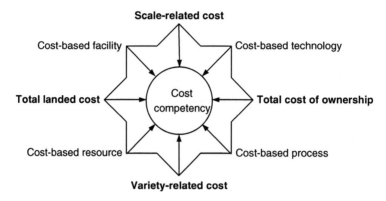

Fig. 4.1 Approaches to achieving cost competency

4.2.2 Approaches to the Achievement of Cost Competence

A cost-based GOS can work to reduce four categories of costs. In a factory, manufacturing costs include both scale-related cost and variety-related cost. For more complicated manufacturing systems, and for manufacturing networks in global operations, a cost-based GOS can cut both the total landed cost (TLC) and the total cost of ownership (TCO). A firm can apply cost-based technology, a cost-based process, cost-based labor and raw materials and cost-based facilities to achieve cost competency (Fig. 4.1).

(1) Scale-related cost

The most common approach to cost reduction is to reduce scale-related costs in early manufacturing systems, as Ford did by introducing mass production. When production volume increases, scale-related costs will decline. A firm can use mass manufacturing and assembly lines to reduce scale-related cost.

(2) Variety-related cost

When product variety increases, setup, changeover, material handling, inventory and overhead costs will all increase. Flexible manufacturing systems (FMS), for instance, can use the flexibility of machines as well as routing flexibility to reduce variety-related cost.

(3) Total landed cost

TLC is the total cost, from input to end product. A global logistics system or global supply chain should act to reduce TLC and not just the manufacturing cost. TLC is mainly used to inform production-location sourcing decisions.

(4) Total cost of ownership

TCO includes all of the costs associated with buying and owning an asset across an equipment or product lifecycle. TCO includes all of the costs which are included in TLC as well as post-purchase costs such as maintenance, repairs and training. A firm which uses primarily TCO in their decision-making processes will do so to inform their capital expenditures, materials purchasing and supplier selection.

(5) Cost-based technology

Technological innovation might enable a company to offer a cheaper product in a global manufacturing context. Mitsubishi Electric uses robots to reduce the production costs in the various industries. Technology can help in eliminating repetitive or wasteful steps in delivering services, as well. Information technology, for instance, has been used to reduce the cost of post-sale services.

(6) Cost-based process

MNEs can restructure production and service processes to reduce costs. Deloitte uses a "tax-aligned supply chain", for example, and KPMG uses a system of "tax-efficient supply chain management" to restructure global supply chains to achieve tax reductions. A firm can use production and service outsourcing to reduce their labor and purchasing costs. Dell, Zara and Benetton each use a strategy of late customization to postpone product differentiation, which acts to reduce the variety-related cost.

(7) Cost-based resources

A firm may try to: obtain access to low-cost labor and raw materials; establish plants in locations which offer a clear cost advantage (e.g., Foxconn established factories in China to take advantage of the available low-cost labor); hire immigrant labor (e.g., construction companies in Dubai having long hired workers from South Asia); set up purchasing centers in locations with low prices for finished products (e.g., Carrefour and Walmart having set up purchasing centers in China); and, build purchasing subsidiaries in locations known to be rich in raw materials (e.g., steel companies establishing purchasing subsidiaries in Brazil and Australia to purchase iron ore).

(8) Cost-based facilities

Cost-based facilities are of relevance to facility resources, facility planning processes, facility logistics and manufacturing technologies. Walmart built cross-docking distribution centers to reduce their logistics costs and LTC. Fashion and clothing companies have built Automated Storage/Retrieval Systems (AS/RS) in an effort to reduce both scale-related cost and variety-related cost in warehouse operations. Foxconn built a large-scale electronics manufacturing town, capable of housing more than 300,000 workers while also accommodating a number of assembly lines, to reduce scale-related cost in Shenzhen, China.

Case Example: Ryanair Airline

Ryanair, an Irish low-cost airline founded in 1985 by the Ryan family and headquartered at Dublin Airport, is an airline which operates over 1,500 flights per day from 51 bases on 1,500 low-fare routes across 28 countries, connecting over 168 destinations. In 1990, Ryanair built a cost-based GOS which focused on a "low fares, high frequency formula", making it Europe's first low-fare airline – copying the Southwest Airlines low-fare model – after the airline had amassed losses of £20 million trying to compete with British Airways and Aer Lingus.

Using IT, Ryanair has been able to improve its operational processes by reducing distribution costs, and now sells more than 95 % of all its seats through its online booking system. Its prices start at a very low level, and rise as seats are filled. Passengers receive an email with their travel details and booking reference number, which has helped the company reduce the costs associated with issuing, distributing, processing and reconciling the millions of tickets it has sold over the last few decades.

In 1992, Ryanair restructured airline networks by cutting its route network from 19 to 6 routes and increasing the frequencies and lowering fares on those remaining routes. The restructuring lead to a 45 % increase in traffic, as passengers responded positively to the lower fares and the more frequent service. Ryanair had previously launched many low-fare flights during non-peak times to utilize idle resources.

Ryanair ceased offering free drinks and expensive meals on board in order to reduce their cost. Passengers can purchase food and refreshments on board. Previously, Ryanair did not sell pre-assigned seats and passengers were allowed to sit wherever they chose, which helped Ryanair speed up passenger boarding. Beginning in 2012, Ryanair has offered priority boarding – for a fee of €4, which allows passengers to board early – and pre-assigned seats – for €10, and restricted to seats in row 1 (front of the plane), row 2 (near the front, for quicker disembarkation) and rows 16 and 17 (over the wing and with extra legroom).

Ryanair actively seeks aircraft with extra-wide doors, which allows the flight and ground crew to get passengers on and off the plane more quickly, thereby helping the airline reduce its turnaround times. It has even considered removing toilets to make way for more seats. Ryanair prints its in-flight magazine on thinner paper, cut the amount of ice it brings on board, and reduced the weight of its seats and carts. Ryanair uses less-crowded, smaller European airports and the secondary airports in many capital cities to limit the landing charges to which it is exposed.

(*Source: Ryanair annual report 2012*)

Case Questions

1. Why did Ryanair decide to implement a low-cost strategy?
2. What are the benefits to being a low-fare airline?
3. Which approach (see Fig. 4.1) has Ryanair used to achieve cost competency?

4.3   Flexibility Competency

4.3.1   Concepts of Flexibility and Flexibility Competency

4.3.1.1 Definition

Flexibility is a competency which is associated with uncertainties and risks, and with an ability to respond and conform to new environments. Upton (1994) has defined flexibility as "the ability to change or react with little penalty in time, effort,

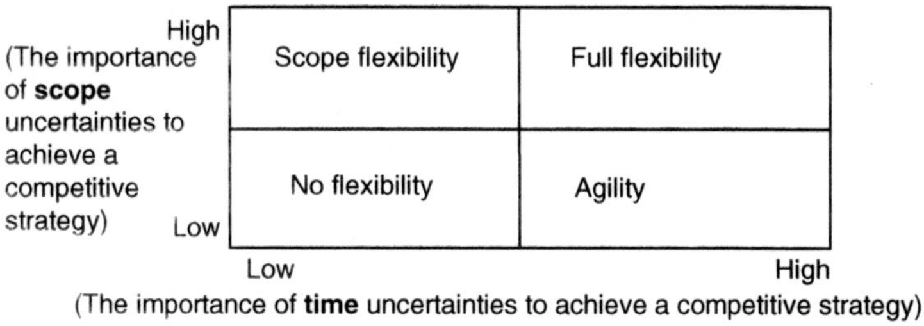

High (The importance of **scope** uncertainties to achieve a competitive strategy) Low	Scope flexibility	Full flexibility
	No flexibility	Agility

Low   High

(The importance of **time** uncertainties to achieve a competitive strategy)

Fig. 4.2 Scope and time flexibility

cost or performance" (p. 73), and thinks flexibility can be characterized by three major attributes: dimensions, time horizon and elements.

The changes in the global environment and to global risks have made flexibility one of the competencies that firms must deal with. Globalization increases exchange-rate risks, political risks and global customer heterogeneity risks, and imposes new requirements on flexibility competency. Furthermore, globalization has influenced the scope (e.g., product scope) and time (e.g., increasing delivery time due to global transportation networks as opposed to regional logistics) of flexibility, in addition to having affected the difficulty of handling flexibility on a global scale. On the other hand, globalization has provided more methods (e.g., increasing operational flexibility under exchange-rate risks or considering global tax system differences), resources (e.g., increasing the number of suppliers available) and processes (e.g., manufacturing and design out-scouring) with which to deliver flexibility competency.

4.3.1.2 The Dimension of Flexibility

1. Hierarchical classification

   A simple classification of flexibility can be made according to a hierarchy: flexibility in an individual machine or server, flexibility in manufacturing workshop or service units, flexibility in a manufacturing plant or service system and flexibility in a multi-plant manufacturing system or multiple-facility service system.

2. Scope and time dimensions

   Scope and time are simple but widely-applied dimensions of flexibility. Scope flexibility is a competency in an environment with uncertainties of product mix or product scope, and it allows a firm to adapt to a changing demand mix. Time flexibility, or agility (the more common term), is a competency which allows firms to rapidly shift their focus between activities. Full flexibility covers both scope flexibility and agility.

   Figure 4.2 shows how to tailor the appropriate type of flexibility to accommodate different business strategies. If uncertainties of the product or service scope are large and the importance of the scope is high in order to achieve a competitive strategy, a firm can choose scope flexibility. If uncertainties of time are large and the importance of time is high in order to achieve a competitive

Table 4.2 A sample of Gerwin's flexibility dimensions in a global environment

Uncertainties	Strategic objectives	Flexibility dimension
Global customer preference difference in products	Diversity of products	Mix
Length of product life-cycles in global competition	Global R&D competition and product innovation	Changeover
Local product features	Responsiveness to local customers	Modification

strategy, a firm can opt for agility, the flexibility along the time dimension. When both scope and time uncertainties are important, a firm can implement a full-flexibility operations strategy.

3. Gerwin's dimensions

Gerwin (1993) identified seven dimensions of flexibility: mix, changeover, modification, volume, rerouting, material and responsiveness. One advantage of Gerwin's dimensions is the ability to show the linkage of flexibility with uncertainties and strategic objectives (Table 4.2), with great convenience in the application. Facing uncertainties due to global customer differences, for example, BMW sets as its strategic objective product diversity, with mix flexibility an operations strategy meant to allow it to deliver a range of products to satisfy its customers in Europe, Asia and America. Facing competition from global rivals like Apple and Nokia, Samsung sets as its strategic objective innovation on mobile phones, and changeover flexibility is an operations strategy which has helped Samsung survive in the global mobile-phone market. When Pizza Hut enters different markets, it will often modify its fast-food products to better respond to the tastes of local markets. This is modification flexibility.

4. D'Souza and Williams' dimensions

D'Souza and Williams (2000) presented a four-dimension taxonomy of flexibility which views manufacturing flexibility dimensions across two generalized categories: "externally-driven flexibility", focused on meeting the market needs of the firm; and "internally-driven flexibility", focused on the operational activities of the firm (Table 4.3). Each dimension of manufacturing flexibility consists of two elements: range and mobility.

4.3.2 Framework of Flexibility Competency

Figure 4.3 presents a framework of flexibility competency and demonstrates the relationship among uncertainties in the global environment, business strategy, required flexibility competency, flexibility delivery and performance measurement.

- Uncertainties in the global environment

  The relationship between operations strategy and flexibility has traditionally been understood in terms of environmental variability (Riley and Lockwood 1997). An operations strategy is meant to be able to react to the changes which affect competition which arise as a result of new industrial and social trends. An MNE in an environment full of international competitors encounters

Table 4.3 D'Souza and Williams' flexibility dimensions

Category	Type	Description
Externally-driven flexibility	Volume flexibility	The ability to change the level of output
	Variety flexibility	The ability to produce a range of products and services, and to introduce new products and service
Internally-driven flexibility	Process flexibility	The ability to adjust to and accommodate changes in the manufacturing and service process
	Materials handling	The ability to effectively deliver materials to the appropriate stages of the manufacturing process

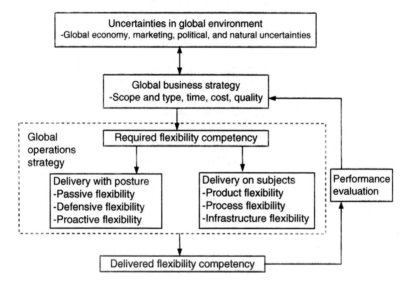

Fig. 4.3 Framework of flexibility competency

uncertainties and risks as well as tremendous potentials. As a consequence, operational flexibility can be regarded as the firm's option to respond to uncertainties such as government policies, competitors' decisions or the arrival of new technologies (Kogut and Kulatilaka 1994). Global economic, marketing, political and natural uncertainties will influence business strategy and the formulation of required flexibility.

• Global business strategy

A firm will formulate its global business strategy based on its understanding of the surrounding uncertainties. The global business strategy will evaluate scope and type, time, cost and quality, all of which are associated with the required flexibility competency. Firms' business strategy positions are based on their understandings of customers' needs, customers' accessibility or the variety of a company's product or services (Porter 1996). Among them, variety-based strategic positioning, informed by a specific set of products or services, could lead to operational flexibility in scope (Fig. 4.3).

- Required flexibility competency
  The scope flexibility competence of a firm is focused on efforts to produce a subset of an industry's products or services which customers perceive as exceptional values. A strategy based on variety competition chooses a unique mix of products or services which allows the firm to differentiate itself from its rivals. In order for a GOS to succeed, the firm will first need to formulate the required flexibility competency in both scope and time. An effective GOS can rely on operational flexibility to identify potential opportunities and capture features of the changing environment in the global context.
- Flexibility delivery
  A firm can deliver flexibility with different postures – e.g., passive, defensive and proactive flexibility operations strategies – or on different subjects – e.g., product flexibility, process flexibility and infrastructure flexibility.
- Performance measurement and feedback
  There is a close interrelationship between business strategy, manufacturing flexibility and organizational performance (Gupta and Somers 1996). A GOS will deliver a certain level of flexibility. When the level of flexibility delivered in every dimension supports the operations strategy to be implemented, it will be seen to positively affect operational performance (Spina et al. 1996); otherwise, it will not support the operations strategy. We therefore need to conduct a performance evaluation and compare the required and delivered flexibilities; alternatively, we could conduct a discrepancy analysis between the required and actual flexibilities (Gerwin 1993). The performance evaluation function provides feedback on business strategy, which will dynamically update understandings of the required flexibility competency.

4.3.3   Delivering Flexibility

4.3.3.1 Passive, Defensive and Proactive Flexibility Operations Strategies

- Passive flexibility strategy
  A firm may consider flexibility to be less important, which may lead them to seek a reduction to their product flexibility or process flexibility so that the firm may realize its competitive strategy. A passive flexibility strategy is not always a negative strategy, as it could still be a smart operations strategy. Apple, for example, has adopted a passive strategy in regards to its product flexibility. The color options of the iPhone are limited to black and white. As compared with other cell phone makers, which offer multiple color options, Apple has made a conscious effort to reduce the number of types and to keep its products "simple".
- Defensive flexibility strategy
  A defensive flexibility strategy is an adaptive response undertaken after observing environmental uncertainties. Some clothing companies, for example, will design, modify, produce and deliver new clothing styles only after they have

been able to collect information at fashion shows and from competitors' stores in the brief period prior. This is a defensive flexibility strategy which allows for a response to up-to-date marketing information.

- Proactive flexibility strategy

  While maintaining a defensive strategy for some of its products, the clothing-maker Zara also designs a portion of its lines as new styles, which are delivered to market in seasonal fashion shows. Zara then sells these new styles in Zara stores within a period of weeks. Some new styles may be successful, others may fail. This is a proactive flexibility strategy designed to handle market uncertainties.

  Another proactive strategy is to hold some new modes and product types in reserve. While IT companies such as Intel, Nokia and IBM might sell some models of their electronic products, they typically will develop, design and release a set of newer models, future products or conceptual products to be held in reserve. A similar process can be observed among automobile companies like Volkswagen, Ford and Peugeot. This is another proactive flexibility strategy, meant to handle potential market change.

4.3.3.2 Processes, Product and Infrastructure Flexibility

Flexibility can be classified as process, products and infrastructure flexibilities (Lau 1999; Noori and Radford 1995; Upton 1995):

- Processes flexibility

  Process flexibility refers to the capability to fabricate different types of products in the same plant, at the same time (Graves and Tomlin 2003; Jordan and Graves 1995). The most commonly used approaches to achieving this end are resource sharing, resource substitution, transshipment, postponed differentiation and mass customization. One of the most influential theories in process flexibility is Jordan and Graves' (J-G) principles on the benefits of process flexibility, which assert that, "(1) Limited flexibility, configured in the right way, yields most of the benefits of total flexibility. (2) Limited flexibility has the greatest benefits when configured to chain products and plants together to the greatest extent possible." (Jordan and Graves 1995, p. 577).

  To explain limited flexibility in the right way with regards to chain configuration, Fig. 4.4 presents flexibility as a bi-partite graph, and shows four possible configurations: (1) dedicated network, (2) pair partial flexibility, (3) J-G complete chain partial flexibility, and (4) total flexibility. In configuration 3, all products and plants are in a single closed chain, which means that the products and plants are all connected by product assignment decisions. Jordan and Graves (1995) have demonstrated that the J-G complete chain (configuration 3) outperforms configurations 1 and 2, and is nearly as valuable as configuration 4 in terms of expected throughput, although configuration 3 requires far fewer links than does configuration 4.

- Product flexibility

  Production systems usually evolve as products progress through their life cycles. In a global economy with more new products being introduced by global

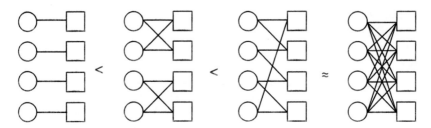

1. Dedicated   2.Partial flexibility (pairs) 3.Partial flexibility (complete chain) 4.Total flexibility

Note: ○denotes product; □denotes plant; a link denotes the plant can make the product.

Fig. 4.4 J-G flexibility configuration (Based on Jordan and Graves 1995)

competitors, the product life cycles have tended to become shorter. MNEs have therefore needed more flexible operations strategies to accompany the more frequent development and introduction of new products. We will present further elements of product flexibility in Chap. 5.

- Infrastructure flexibility
  A firm can deliver flexibility by infrastructure subjects. Lau (1999) presented the following five subjects: workforce autonomy (e.g., the level of empowerment of workers in the decision-making process), communication (e.g., the level of access which exists between senior managers and line workers), interdepartmental relationships (e.g., the relationship between the manufacturing, supply, marketing, design and finance departments within a company), supplier flexibility (e.g., the level of flexibility of the major suppliers in terms of adjusting production volumes and types) and technology (e.g., the use of group technology for process design). Another infrastructure is flexible production and inventory planning, in which production planning might be based on a flexible manufacturing system, such as a manufacturing configuration able to rapidly adapt to changing demands, which can help the firm achieve flexibility competency.

Case Example: Mass Customization in Starbucks

Starbucks provides different kinds of coffee with various flavors, and has leveraged mass customization principles to allow the consumer to create their own beverage according to their tastes. A Starbucks store in Lyon, France, provides a standard menu as well as a "create your perfect beverage" program to its customers (Table 4.4).

Customers can "create" their beverages, or customize their beverages, for example by choosing the size, temperature and mix of their favorite flavors, or by choosing cream to make it light, or by adding an extra short of espresso. Figure 4.5 diagrams the options thereby made available to Starbucks' customers.

Table 4.4   A part of the menu in a Starbucks in Lyon, France

Series	Beverages
Chocolate beverages	Chocolat Viennois Signature, Chocolat Viennois Classic
Espresso beverages	Espresso Macchiato, Espresso con Panna, Caffè Americano, Capuccino, Caffè Latte, Vanilla Latte, Caramel Machiato, Mocha, White Mocha
Frappuccino blended beverages	Mocha Frappuccino, Java Chip, Strawberries and Crème, Vanilla, Caramel, Mangue Passion, Raspberry

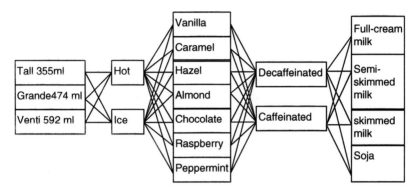

Fig. 4.5   Options of the "create your perfect beverages" program

Case Questions

1. By analyzing the menu, do you think Starbucks Lyon uses mass customization in the menu design? Why does Starbucks use mass customization?
2. By analyzing the "create your perfect beverage" program, do you think Starbucks Lyon uses mass customization in the program? Why? What are the advantages of this program?
3. Starbucks claims that their "Frappuccino blended beverages are completely customizable". Do you agree with this claim? Why?

4.4   Quality Competency

4.4.1   Concepts of Quality and Quality Competency

The Gucci family has traditionally emphasized the importance of quality with its well-known motto, "Quality is remembered long after the price is forgotten". Quality is the ability of a product or service to consistently meet customer expectations. The American National Standards Institute (ANSI) and the American Society for Quality (ASQ) have both defined quality as, "The totality of features

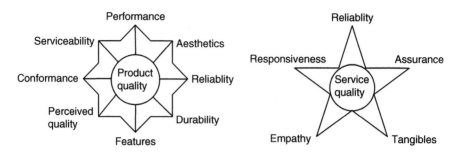

Fig. 4.6 Garvin product quality dimensions and RATER service quality dimensions

and characteristics of a product or service on its ability to satisfy given needs".
Quality as a concept encompasses both product quality and service quality. We
present hear Garvin's classic product quality dimension system and RATER service
quality dimension system.

Garvin (1987) described product quality as including eight dimensions
(Fig. 4.6): performance (product's primary characteristics), aesthetics (product's
appearance, feel, smell, sound or taste), reliability (consistency of the product's
performance), durability (time until the product will need to be replaced), special
features (additional characteristics), perceived quality (indirect evaluation, similar
to reputation), conformance (the degree to which a product conforms to customer's
expectations), and serviceability (service after sale). A firm does not need to pursue
all eight of Garvin's dimensions simultaneously.

The dominant dimension system of service quality is the RATER model
(Zeithaml et al. 1990), originally called SERVQUAL, which measured ten aspects
of service quality – reliability, responsiveness, competence, access, courtesy, communication, credibility, security, understanding the customer and tangibles – with
the basic assumption that customers will be able to evaluate a firm's service quality
by comparing their perceptions with their expectations. The authors refined the
model to the acronym RATER, deciding to include reliability (ability to provide the
promised service consistently, accurately and on time), assurance (the knowledge,
skills and credibility of the staff and their ability to use their expertise to inspire
trust and confidence on the part of the customer), tangibles (the physical evidence of
the service), empathy (ability to treat customers as individuals) and responsiveness
(ability to provide quick, high-quality service to customers).

A firm is said to have achieved quality competency if the firm can use product or
service quality to satisfy customer demand, distinguish its products and services
from those offered by competitors, and build a competitive advantage over its
rivals. Quality competency is customer dependent, beginning with the careful
assessment of customer demand, and is progressively expanded upon through
value-chain activities throughout the product's life-cycle.

4.4.2 Evolution of Quality Management

Compared with the management of other operational competencies, the evolution of quality management has been more influential, with successive generations of "quality philosophies" arising from past quality management perspectives, quality inspection beginning with the industrial revolution, statistical quality control beginning in the 1920s, total quality management beginning in the 1970s, up to modern interpretations such as Six Sigma, the Malcolm Baldrige National Quality Award (MBNQA) framework commonly applied in the US, and the European Foundation for Quality Management (EFQM) model commonly applied in Europe.

Simple quality control and standardization efforts can be traced as far back as the ancient civilizations of Babylon and Egypt. Early, large-scale, standardized manufacturing techniques, verified by rigorous modern archaeological technology, have been observed in weaponry manufacture in the Qin Empire (221–206 B.C.) of ancient China. The system made standard armaments for approximately one million infantrymen, 10,000 cavalry, and 1,000 chariots. The parts used in manufacturing crossbows were interchangeable, with an error tolerance of less than 1 mm; four product series' of arrowheads were standardized, with an error tolerance of less than 0.15 mm; swords used standardized surfaces and coating technologies. Without modern machining tools, the empire used strict quality laws and a manufacturing administration system to control product design, raw materials, production processes and workers. The empire used a "name engraving" information management system to control quality: the names of workers and supervisors, along with the time and place of manufacture, were engraved on products so that the quality control system could track each item in the case of quality failure, which could lead to harsh punishment.

During the Industrial Revolution, craftsman regularly checked product quality, and companies began to use quality inspection to produce large numbers of goods of similar quality. In 1798, Eli Whitney built a firearms factory near New Haven, Connecticut, at which he applied the principle of interchangeable parts manufacture in assembly lines to make muskets. Frederick Taylor, "the father of scientific management", laid a further foundation for quality management by including standardization and adopting improved practices.

In the 1920s, quality control efforts began to include statistical theory. Walter Shewhart proposed the first quality control chart in 1924, a landmark event in modern quality management. Developed by Deming, Dodge and Romig, the theory of statistical quality control (SQC) soon came to be applied in practice.

In 1946, Deming was invited to assist in rebuilding Japanese industry. He gave SQC seminars to Japanese industry. With the help of quality gurus like Joseph Juran and Armand Feigenbaum, Deming's SQC practices developed rapidly in Japanese plants in the 1940s and throughout the 1950s. In 1948, Taguchi began to study experiment design and put forward the Taguchi Method. Japanese companies established a national advantage in quality and quality management philosophy in the 1960s. The 1960s also saw the introduction of Zero Defects programs in US industry. During this same period, Japanese and American manufacturers and American quality gurus laid the foundations for the coming TQM.

In 1969, the first international conference on quality control was held in Tokyo. It was at this conference that Feigenbaum first used the term "total quality". Quality management then evolved from SQC, a statistical- and engineering-based approach, to total quality management (TQM), a "management approach to long-term success through customer satisfaction" (ASQ), which was based on total organizational involvement and continuous quality improvement, with customer satisfaction as its driving force. TQM had been developed by quality leaders like Crosby, Deming, Feigenbaum, Ishikawa and Juran. The primary elements of TQM included: a focus on the customer, total employee involvement, a process-centered approach to manufacturing and quality control, integrated systems, a strategic and systematic approach, continual improvement, fact-based decision making and open lines of communication.

In 1979, the British Standard (BS) 5750 for quality systems was published and, in 1983, the National Quality Campaign was launched based on BS5750. Then ISO 9000 has become the internationally recognized standard for quality management systems and has helped to initiate the globalizing process of TQM.

The 1980s were a key developmental period for quality management: TQM continued to mature and gained wide acceptance throughout the world; ISO established the first quality standard; new quality management models and frameworks like Six Sigma, MBNQA and EFQM were developed. In 1988, MBNQA was established by the US Congress and EFQM was established in Europe. The MBNQA process previously had been a valuable assessment tool, and many US companies had used the performance excellence criteria for self-assessment. In Europe, EFQM and the British Quality Foundation (BQF) promoted a "business excellence" model. In 1989, Motorola adopted Six Sigma, with a focus on process improvement and an emphasis on achieving a significant business impact.

Since the 1980s, quality management has faced new challenges as a result of ongoing economic and operational globalization, the IT boom, increasing global quality risks and continually evolving management philosophies pertaining to sustainable development.

4.4.3   Quality Competence in a Global Environment

In a global environment, a quality-based operations strategy should consider the following factors:

- Vertical complexity

  MNEs need to apply TQM not only within the organization, but also to the global supply chain. To achieve global business excellence, quality management seeks to leverage the vertical opportunities created by upstream activities associated with suppliers and the downstream activities linked with customers. Whereas previously quality competency was achieved in a competitive context of "firm versus firm", today's quality is achieved in an environment of "supply chain versus supply chain".

- Horizontal complexity

  Since quality depends on customers' perceptions, customers in different locales do not expect the same things from a given product or a service. A quality-centric GOS should involve not only different functions within the firm, but also ought to build a cross-organizational quality management system able to deal with governments, standards organizations, ethics-focused pressure groups, the media, various stakeholders, suppliers, global logistics providers, service carriers, retailers, and customer-advocacy organizations.
- Global quality standards

  In a global environment, a firm must conform to global quality standards in order to build global quality competency. The ISO 9000 series has long been accepted as a quality standard by both manufacturing and service companies worldwide. With more concerns surrounding social and environmental problems, the adoption of ISO 14000 (for occupational health and safety and environmental management) has been important to quality management activities.
- Global quality risks

  In recent years, global quality problems such as Mattel toxic toys (2007), Sony overheat batteries (2008), Peanut Corporation of America's contaminated peanut butter (2009), Toyota recalls for a power window problem (2012) show MNEs and consumers are vulnerable to quality risks in global operations. Product quality is easier to control in house, and may lose control if the company resorts to suppliers worldwide or use outsourcing in global manufacture. Successful GOS should be able to mitigate global quality risks.
- Global information system

  Global information system can closely integrate suppliers, manufacturers and customers to provide MNEs quality-based competency. Enterprise resource planning (ERP) and other management information systems are integrating with TQM and global supply chain management (SCM) to improve product quality. Web services and digital markets are integrating businesses with global customers to improve service quality.
- Continuous improvement processes

  In a global environment, a quality management system can be expected to be met by a more dynamic environment, one in which customer demands fluctuate and the changing competitive landscape may feature newcomers, substitute products, the improvement of competitors and dynamic political and macroeconomic conditions. A quality system therefore must evaluate the dynamics and continuously make improvements to meet any new changes.

4.4.4 Quality-Based Global Operations Strategy

The new global challenges to quality management presented in the previous section have led firms to look beyond TQM and develop quality-based global operations strategies (QGOS) which feature:

Table 4.5 Comparison of quality management systems

		Statistical quality control (SQC)	Total quality management (TQM)	Quality-based global operations strategy (QGOS)
V	R&D	Low relevance	Cross-functional integration	Cross-border global R&D networks
	Purchasing	Moderate relevance	Cross-functional integration	Cross-border purchasing, global supply management
	Production	High relevance	High priority, cross-functional integration	Cross-border production networks, high risks
	Distribution	Low relevance	High priority, cross-functional integration	Cross-border, cross-organization logistics
	Marketing	Irrelevant	High priority, cross-functional integration	Globalization and localization, cross-value concerns
	Post-sales service	Irrelevant	Cross-functional corporate integration	Cross-value concerns
H	Cross-function	Within production function	Cross R&D, purchasing, production, distribution, marketing and service	Cross-function with larger operation complexity
	Cross-border	Irrelevant	Cross physical separation and cultural separation	Cross political separation, cultural separation, physical separation, developmental separation and relational separation
	Cross-organization	Irrelevant	Cross standard organizations, suppliers, service carriers, and retailers	Cross government, standards organizations, ethics pressure groups, media, stakeholders, suppliers, global logistics providers, service carriers, retailers and customer-advocacy organizations
	Cross-value	Economic value	Economic value and limited social value	Cross economic, social and environmental values

A consistent integrated pattern of decisions across borders, functions, organizations and values, determining continuous improvement process, product or service quality dimensions and employee involvement level of a manufacturing or service system to satisfy global intermediate and final customer demand and achieve global quality competency alignment with business strategy.

By incorporating many of the basic principles of TQM, QGOS has been able to develop both vertically, in global supply chains, and horizontally, across borders, functions, organizations and values (Table 4.5).

4.4.4.1 Vertical Development

Ross (1997), Robinson and Malhotra (2005) and Foster (2008) have each proposed the concept of supply chain quality management (SCQM), which is based on the integration and coordination of SCM and TQM. Robinson and Malhotra's definition of SCQM is:

> The formal co-ordination and integration of business processes involving all partner organisations in the supply channel to measure, analyse, and continually improve products, services, and processes in order to create value and achieve satisfaction of intermediate and final customers in the marketplace. (Robinson and Malhotra 2005, p. 319)

In QGOS, the application of SCQM is extended to a global environment.

- R&D

  In QGOS, global R&D activities can improve design quality, by including or excluding features in a product or service, with the end result that they improve conformance quality and enhance global customer satisfaction. The quality of the relationships which exist within the supply chain have a positive impact on product design quality (Fynes et al. 2005), and a firm can therefore achieve quality competency by improving their supply chain relationships.

- Purchasing

  A SQC team checks the quality dimensions of the raw materials, components and parts after purchasing. While purchasing in countries with low costs can help firms build their cost competency, doing so may bring with it additional maintenance and quality costs. Since purchasing practices can exert substantial influence on product and service quality, a QGOS should select appropriate global suppliers, effectively manage long-term purchasing contracts, monitor the performance of suppliers and seek to manage cross-border relationships with suppliers to improve the quality of their production inputs.

- Production

  In QGOS, global manufacturing can help build quality by promoting conformance to the design, but the firm will be exposed to global manufacturing risks. Mattel, for example, was recently forced to recall 1.5 million Fisher-Price toys made in foreign plants, due to the paint with lead harmful for children, from the paint supplier of a foreign contracted manufacturer.

- Distribution

  Global distribution can build quality by facilitating OTD, providing the right product in good shape on time and without error, which will build quality across a firm's responsiveness and serviceability dimensions. The complexity associated with distribution goes beyond local quality management, however, when cross-border transportation is also taken into account. QGOS may require a third-party logistics provider and cross-organizational operations.

- Marketing

  QGOS should consider the globalization of marketing efforts and the localization of its products as a means of improving the performance, aesthetic, special features, perceived quality, conformance and serviceability dimensions of its product, in addition to studying cross-value customer concerns to enhance the assurance, empathy and responsiveness dimensions of service quality.

- Service after sales

  In a global environment even regular services such as installation and maintenance become complicated. A QGOS should cross borders, functions, organizations and values to improve the perceived quality, conformance and serviceability dimensions of product quality, while also attempting to enhance the assurance, empathy and responsiveness dimensions of service quality.

4.4.4.2 Horizontal Development

Kim and Chang (1995) proposed a concept of global quality management which extended TQM to a broader cross-organizational and cross-country scope. In recent years, social and environmental values have received increased attention in the global operations of MNEs. This book emphasizes cross-border operations which, as a category, include more dimensions than do cross-country operations. In a QGOS, we extend TQM to a system which is able to cross borders, functions, organizations and values.

- Cross-border marketplaces

  Local customers may have different product tastes and service perceptions. A QGOS should cross political separation, cultural separation, physical separation, developmental separation and relational separation to improve the performance, aesthetic, special features, perceived quality, conformance, serviceability and responsiveness quality dimensions through product globalization and localization. HSBC, for example, achieved service quality competency by adopting a strategy which sought to position the institution as "the world's local bank".

- Cross-value quality concerns

  To achieve global quality competency, a firm should consider different values in making the decision to expand their operations to a global basis. Increasing numbers of ethics groups have come to regard the social and environmental impacts of a product as part of its value or service quality. A QGOS should consider both CSR and environmental concerns.

- Cross-functional quality control process

  In global operations, design, marketing and manufacturing subsidiaries can be located in foreign locations. A firm may use inter-organizational relationships like joint ventures and licensing agreements to manage its design, marketing and manufacturing activities worldwide. While a TQM uses multiple functions to control quality, cross-functional operations are more complex in a QGOS.

- Cross-organizational quality management system

  A QGOS not only involves different functions within the firm, but also must build a cross-organizational quality management system to deal with governments, standards organizations, ethics pressure groups, media, stakeholders, suppliers, global logistics providers, service carriers, retailers and customer-advocacy organizations.

Case Example: Quality Excellence in Bosch

The Bosch Group, with more than 300,000 employees, generated sales of 51.5 billion Euros in fiscal year 2011. It is a multinational engineering and electronics company comprised of approximately 350 subsidiaries and regional companies based in some 60 countries. The company was originally established in Stuttgart in 1886, as a "workshop for precision mechanics and electrical engineering", and is to this day a respected German manufacturer well-known for its excellent quality. Almost all Bosch plants are ISO 9001 accredited, a quality-standard certificate, and ISO 14001, a standard certificate in environmental protection.

The Bosch Bamberg Plant, a leading manufacturing site for components used in gasoline and diesel fuel-injection systems, as well as sensors and spark plugs for the automotive technology sector, has won the "EFQM Excellence Award 2012", a reputable quality management award. Bosch Bamberg impressed the judges with its employees' active commitment to achieving corporate goals:

The executive management of the Bosch plant in Bamberg act as role models. They lead by example, and through the many approaches they use to involve their associates in the deployment of their strategy (Marc Amblard, chief executive officer of EFQM, 2012).

This was further confirmed by the Bamberg plant's managers:

We owe our outstanding performance to the commitment of our associates. They are ultimately responsible for Bosch's lasting success (Franz Hauber, plant manager, 2012).

Bosch uses cross-functional systems, including a quality management department, and considers the entire supply chain – from the suppliers to its international customers – in its efforts to achieve quality excellence. Its quality principles are:

- Customer satisfaction. Bosch tries to satisfy customers' expectations through the quality of its products and services.
- Employee involvement. Quality is the employees' responsibility and goal.
- Knowledge and compliance. The quality management system is based on requirements stipulated by international standards, informed by customer expectations and the company's specialized knowledge. Knowledge and compliance is therefore the foundation of quality management.
- Continuous improvement. Bosch emphasizes efforts to continuously improve their quality management.
- Preventive quality assurance. Bosch systematically implements preventive quality assurance measures to eliminate the root causes of errors.
- Supplier management. Bosch requires that its global suppliers live up to the same high standards of quality they have themselves adopted.
  (*Source: Bosch Press Release, 10 October 2012*)

Case Questions

1. What is the role of "employee involvement" in Bosch's quality management system?
2. Is Bosch's quality system a TQM system?

3. Which challenges of quality management will Bosch encounter in global marketplaces? Can Bosch's quality principles effectively deal with these global challenges?

4.5   Time Competency

4.5.1   Concept of Time Competency

Stalk (1988) introduced time-based competency (TBC) as "the next source of competitive advantage". Time-based competency argues that a firm's competitive advantage lies in its ability to rapidly deliver services or products, and presents the need to reduce the time cycle involved with each stage of production included in the delivery of a service or a product, which means shortening the time required for product design, new product introduction, raw materials purchasing, parts and components production, assembly, distribution, marketing and sales. A number of firms have since implemented TBC initiatives, including Toyota, Honda, Citicorp, AT&T, GE, HP, ABB, Seven-11, Federal Express and Domino's Pizza.

Time-based competency, with customer responsiveness as a critical measure, can lead to a combination of production efficiencies and customer service improvement. Time-based competency can be accomplished by introducing market-oriented methods to manufacturing companies, and implementing cross-functional integration between a company's design, manufacturing and marketing arms. Time-based competency can lead to operational and financial benefits which include:
- Improved customer satisfaction and customer loyalty,
- Improved productivity,
- Reduced costs,
- Increased market share, and
- Increased revenue and profit.

4.5.2   Time-Based Global Operations Strategy

Stalk and Hout (1990) presented a time-based competitive strategy and further pointed out how time-based competition reshapes global markets. A time-based GOS compresses time across all processes included in production and global service delivery, improves local customer responsiveness and achieves rapid new production introductions.

Figure 4.7 depicts the basic elements of a time-based GOS and the approaches necessary to achieve TBC. The primary elements are time-based organization, time-based business process reengineering (BPR), time-based factories and time-based new product development (NPD). To achieve TBC, firms can use vertical integration, logistics time compression, IT applications and white-collar JIT, if applicable.

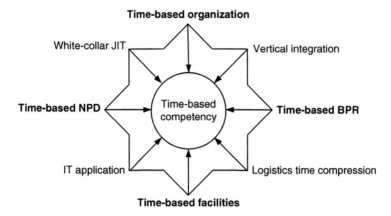

Fig. 4.7 Approaches to achieving time-based competency

(1) Time-based organization

Time-based organization is the foundation required to achieve TBC. Firms can build a flat management structure which is able to make decisions rapidly. Organizational restructuring can empower employees to make decisions and share more information with their fellow employees; both actions will contribute to the building of a rapid-response team.

(2) Vertical integration

A firm can consider three varieties of vertical integration – upstream vertical integration, downstream vertical integration and balanced (encompassing both upstream and downstream) vertical integration – to achieve TBC. While balanced vertical integration can lead to high costs, a firm can use partial vertical integration, backward (upstream) vertical integration to control its subsidiaries that produce inputs or forward (downstream) vertical integration to control its distribution centers and retailers to improve response time. To achieve TBC, Zara uses vertical integration to improve the control and coordination of its design, manufacturing, distribution and sales departments.

(3) Time-based business process reengineering

Firms can identify, evaluate and redesign workflows and processes to achieve time competency via BPR. Banking and insurance companies, for example, identify bureaucratic redundancies, eliminate non-value-adding activities and require that customers deal with some paperwork on their own to increase time competency and customer satisfaction. A successful time-based BPR should be able to:

- Eliminate non-value-adding activities and processes;
- Shorten value-adding activities and processes; and
- Improve the coordination of value-added activities and processes.

(4) Time compression in logistics

A direct method by which to achieve TBC is to compress time in logistics and in supply chains. DHL, UPS, Federal Express and TNT all seek to reduce the total transportation and logistics time in order to achieve time-based delivery. Apparel and fashion industry companies reduce the cycle time of their supply chains to achieve a competitive advantage.

(5) Time-based facilities

Stalk (1988) proposed the concept of time-based factories with optimal facility layout and planning to reduce the average throughput time of products. Different from traditional factories organized by process technology centers, time-based factories are organized by products. The manufacturing activities for a product are put in close proximity to one another, to minimize the handling of materials and the manufacturing time of the finished product and its components. Other types of facilities, like cross-docking distribution centers, can also be utilized to achieve TBC.

(6) Information technology application

Information technology is critical to efforts focused on gaining TBC. First, firms use communications technologies to acquire new market information and rapidly respond to fluctuations in global demand. Walmart, for instance, uses a satellite-based communications system to collect information from their global network of customers. Second, firms use communications technologies to reduce trading and business time. Levi Strauss, for instance, have used electronic data interchanges (EDI) to speed trading time. Third, IT provides a platform from which to create new business modes, such as e-commerce, which enable reductions in the response time to customers. Finally, firms use IT to share information spontaneously with employees, and to create fast response times within the firm.

(7) White-collar JIT

Time-based competition can be applied in white-collar activities like new policy applications in insurance companies, consumer loans in commercial banks and patient billing in hospitals. Blackburn (1992) found that the percentage of time devoted to value-adding activities is often less than 5 %, while more than 95 % of time is devoted to white-collar activities. Blackburn (1992) proposed that JIT systems could work in office settings as well as in manufacturing facilities.

(8) Time-based new product development

A firm can achieve TBC by reducing the cycle time of NPD. The traditional method seeks to improve project management by optimizing the scheduling of various NPD activities. A second method forgoes centrally-controlled optimization efforts, with the target firm instead empowering researchers to conduct new projects meant to rapidly respond to market opportunities. A third method utilizes cross-functional integration between R&D functions and marketing, manufacturing and distribution. HP used the concept of "stretch objectives", referring to its efforts to reduce all of its product failure rates to one-tenth their previous values over a 10-year period, to integrate its functions and reduce NPD time.

Case Example: Time-Based Competency of Zara

Zara, a Spanish clothing and accessories retailer and the flagship store of the Inditex group, is famous for its TBC, best exemplified by its cycle time of just two weeks from NPD to the time the product arrives in stores; this is compared with a six-month industry average. The label is also well-regarded for its ability to launch approximately 10,000 new designs in a given year.

• Time-based NPD

Zara's products are characterized by a large number of styles and a low quantity produced per style. Time-based NPD begins at the market research stage, during which information is collected from stores, streets, university campuses and entertainment centers to allow their designers to observe fashion trends. Sales reports compiled by sales associates and store managers provide detailed information on local demand. More than 200 designers develop 1,000 new styles every month, an average of one–two styles per week per designer.

• Time-based facilities

Zara builds its factory in La Coruña and improves it to act as a JIT-based production and distribution facility, which enables the company to reduce the throughput time of its materials handling, manufacturing and distribution to its global network of stores. Once receiving a new design, for example, the factory uses high-tech robots to cut the appropriate fabrics, and then distributes the cut pieces to networks of small workshops for assembly. With a set of instructions, the workshops can sew the pieces and quickly complete production. Zara's two world-class logistics centers – Zara Logistica in Arteixo and Plataforma Europa in Zaragoza, both of which receive articles from their own factories or outside suppliers and rapidly ship them to stores – are critical for TBC.

• Time-based BPR

Zara improves its business processes in order to achieve TBC, for example by using postponements to achieve both flexibility and time competency. Zara forecasts and designs products based on the kind and amount of fabric it had available, since raw material errors are less serious than are errors in finished products. Zara purchases semi-processed or un-colored fabric and then dyes it just prior to the selling seasons. Zara has also deployed a process based on operations research models to determine each inventory shipment from its two central warehouses to its 1,500 stores worldwide.

• Time-based organization

Zara's organization is well-fit to its time-based GOS. One example of this can be seen in Zara's efforts to build flexible cross-functional teams which include designers, market specialists and production planners working in the same design space, so that each is available to examine designs, check resources and develop prototypes in short periods of time. The team can thus produce a sample rapidly, since fabrics and trims are readily available in the company's warehouses, and the resultant prototypes can thus gain quick approval.

- Information technology

Zara first and foremost uses IT to collect information on consumer demand; designers are then able to use the database to acquire real-time information. Second, Zara applies information systems management techniques to better manage its production processes and inventory. Third, Zara uses a warehouse management system, barcode technology and automated tracking systems to reduce the sorting time in its distribution centers.

- Time compression in logistics

Zara achieves TBC by directly compressing time in its logistics and supply chains. Its warehouses in Spain reduce the operational time included in order picking, sorting and packing. Its logistics centers supply merchandise to stores twice a week. Zara ships products from a central warehouse to stores in the European market by truck, coordinating the time zones of the destinations to reduce inventory and time; air freight is used to ship products outside of Europe. Although it is more expensive, air shipping brings greater value from a TBC perspective. Stores in Europe can receive orders in 24 h, the US in 48 h.

- Vertical integration

Zara achieves TBC in part through partial vertical integration. With controls in place for the design, manufacture, distribution and sale of its products, its coordination mechanism is efficient and can respond far more quickly than can any outsourcing system. Zara produces fashionable articles of clothing and apparel – more than 50 % of the products sold as the Zara brand – at company-owned factories, only outsourcing clothes with a longer shelf life to lower-cost suppliers.

Case Questions

1. How has Zara achieved its TBC?
2. Why did Zara try to achieve TBC? What are the benefits?
3. What are disadvantages of a time-based GOS for Zara?

4.6   Value-Based Competency

4.6.1   Concept of Value-Based Competency

Global operations strategies increasingly deal with not only economic value, but also environmental and social values, through such value-based global practices as "environmentally friendly operations", "green operations", "socially responsible operations", and "sustainable operations". A sustainable GOS tries to achieve a sustainable balance between three pillars – people, planet and profit.

Companies previously thought making any contribution to social value would bring about cost pressure, and therefore argued that a company needed to make a trade-off between its social contributions and the value of its business. Instead of regarding business success and societal development as a zero-sum game, Porter and Kramer (2006, 2011) went beyond this trade-off and proposed the so-called CSV framework, which sought to link competitive advantage and CSR. CSV is not just about philanthropy, social responsibility or environmental protection, but is rather a new means of achieving competencies.

Value-based competency is of relevance to globalization since values differ across countries. The same manufacturing and service operations will have different social consequences in different contexts. Production of the same chemical product, for example, may contribute to poverty reduction in China but environmental pollution in the US. Value-based competency will therefore be seen to have different definitions across regions.

4.6.2   Approaches to Achieve Value-Based Competency

A firm can achieve VBC through the creation of new products, services, processes, business models, even organizations, or through some combination of VBC and other competencies.

4.6.2.1 Creating a Unique VBC

- Product and service innovation
  Value-based product innovation helped ensure that the Toyota Prius, the hybrid electric/gasoline vehicle, was able to contribute environmental benefits while also giving Toyota a competitive advantage over other car manufacturers. Value-based service innovation allowed Crédit Agricole, a leading bank in France, to differentiate itself from its competitors by offering its customers responsible products, supporting forms of agriculture which respect the environment, financing renewable energy and offering socially responsible investment solutions.
- Process innovation
  A firm can achieve VBC through process innovation. Michelin used a closed-loop supply chain and reverse logistics to achieve VBC. Green facilities adopt the process of reusing material handling equipment and recycling materials, including packaging and packing material, to achieve VBC.
- Business model innovation
  This is a somewhat unique form of VBC. Business model innovation helped VisionSpring create channels for the delivery of low-cost eyeglasses, in the process establishing a unique competency to reduce poverty and generate opportunities in the developing world through the sale of affordable eyeglasses.
- Social organization innovation
  The Grameen Bank has built a unique competency in the banking service sector by providing small loans to the impoverished and to women. This competency is different from the competencies discussed above, like time and cost. Kiva, an organization headquartered in San Francisco (and not the Kiva system discussed in Sect. 4.7), works with microfinance institutions on five continents to provide

loans to people without access to traditional banking systems, and has built a unique competency by allowing individuals to borrow as little as $25 to help create opportunities around the world.

4.6.2.2 Combining VBC and Other Competencies

- Combining value-based competency and quality competency.
  While a fundamental operations model innovation is difficult for most companies to achieve, a company can combine VBC and quality competency, since many customers have begun to connect social and environmental values with the product or service quality companies already offer their customers. Carrefour and other supermarkets, for example, provide Bio-milk, sourced from healthy cows, or some low-lactose, non-fat, dry milk products. Customers in Europe buy lighters which have child safety features. Elements of value, including health and safety, are increasingly regarded as a part of quality.
- Combining value-based competency and cost competency.
  Value-based global operation practices can help companies reduce their costs. DuPont has saved over a billion dollars, for example, by adopting environmentally friendly energy use operations. Green logistics and reverse logistics can reduce the overall costs associated with the product life cycle.
- Combining value-based competency and flexibility competency.
  A firm can combine VBC with product variety. L'Oreal did this by acquiring The Body Shop, enabling it to provide a variety of ethical beauty products to satisfy ethically-sensitive customers. Starbucks and Nestlé have provided fair-trade coffee to achieve VBC while also increasing the product variety they are able to offer their customers.

Case Example: Grameen Bank–Bank for the Poor

The Grameen (meaning "rural" or "village" in the Bengali language) Bank is a community development bank which provides small loans to the impoverished. In 1976, Professor Muhammad Yunus launched a research project to design a credit delivery system able to provide banking services to the rural poor. In 1983, the project was transformed into an independent bank by government legislation. The organization and its founder, Muhammad Yunus, were jointly awarded the Nobel Peace Prize in 2006.

Grameen Bank is owned by the impoverished borrowers of the bank, the majority of which are women. The borrowers own 95 % of the bank, with the remaining 5 % owned by the Government of Bangladesh. As of 2011, the bank's total number of borrowers is 8.35 million, having grown from 3.12 million members in 2003; 96 % of those are women today. The bank has a total staff of 22,124 employees working in 2,565 branches covering 81,379 villages, having grown from 43,681 villages serviced as of 2003.

From its inception, the total amount of loans disbursed by Grameen Bank is US $11.35 billion, US $10.11 billion of which has been repaid. The loan recovery rate is 96.67 %. The total revenue generated by Grameen Bank in 2010 was US \$252.05 million.

The operational processes of Grameen Bank feature a group-based credit approach which utilizes peer pressure within the group. This pressure ensures that borrowers exhibit strict discipline, which in turn helps ensure repayment.

The bank provides housing loans for the poor, micro-enterprise loans, scholarships (for the high-performing children of past Grameen borrowers, with a priority on female children), education loans and telephones (both indirectly, by providing loans to 457,953 borrowers to buy mobile phones, and directly, by offering telecommunication services). The bank accepts deposits, and Grameen Bank finances 100 % of its outstanding loans from its deposits. The bank also runs a "Grameen network", including about 30 independent companies in development-oriented businesses including textiles, telephone and energy companies.

The work of Grameen Bank in Bangladesh has recently begun to expand to a global context. The Grameen Foundation not only provides micro-loans in the US, but also supports micro-finance institutions worldwide with loan guarantees, training and technology transfers in the Asia-Pacific region (China, East Timor, India, Indonesia, Lebanon, Pakistan, the Philippines, Saudi Arabia and Yemen), the Americas (Bolivia, the Dominican Republic, El Salvador, Haiti, Honduras, Mexico, Peru and the USA) and Africa (Cameroon, Egypt, Ethiopia, Ghana, Morocco, Nigeria, Rwanda, Tunisia and Uganda).

(*Source: Grameen Bank at a glance, October, 2011*)

Case Questions

1. What is the unique competency of Grameen Bank?
2. How does Grameen Bank's unique competency influence its operations in terms of resource and process?

4.7 Other Competencies

Time, price, quality and flexibility are the most common competencies. Certain other competencies exist as well, usually specific to a given industry or environment.

4.7.1 Revenue

In "revenue management industries" (e.g., airlines, hotels, car rentals, public storage warehousing, theaters and sporting events), revenue – not cost – is the primary competency a firm will pursue.

In 1978, PEOPLExpress was a rapidly rising company with competencies in achieving both low costs and low prices. Its rival, American Airlines (AA), found that its planes were flying only half-filled, which meant that AA was producing some number of seats at a cost approaching zero. In this scenario, the revenue competency was more important than the cost competency since the cost was regarded as zero. American Airlines built a revenue management system to act as a competitive weapon, eventually beating PEOPLExpress. Both AA and PEOPLExpress admitted that successful revenue management was the primary factor which allowed AA to emerge as the winner in their competition.

4.7.2   Scalability

Scalability is an increasingly popular competency associated with capacity investment in dynamic environments, and refers to the ability of a system or process to handle growing marketing demand with low scale-related costs, or to the ability of a system or process to be expanded or enlarged to accommodate that growth, or to an underlying business model which retains the potential for growth.

The concept of scalability was originally developed in facilities investment and management. Retailers previously may have adopted the approach by investing millions in order fulfillment, with the attendant risks of reaching over-capacity during periods of reduced demand. New mobile order-fulfilling systems can use robots (which cost only €5,000–10,000) to first build out a small capacity and then increase the number of robots in response to increased demand.

The capacity investment of public storage is easily scalable. A public storage warehouse can build fewer storage units during an initial phase of operation and then increase the number of storage units to meet growing demand with low costs, since its units are modular. David Grant, president and CEO of Shurgard, has said: "There are very few real estate asset classes that are as scalable as self storage and none that benefits as much from economies of scale." (allbusiness.com)

4.7.3   Ubiquity

To provide global customers with timely and high-quality services covering all regions, telecommunications companies in particular have focused on ubiquity as a competency. To support global service, Huawei tried to achieve ubiquitous interconnectivity in order to push its service to every destination country by building a Wide-Area Network (WAN) which covers the entire world, and then integrating all of its dedicated line resources into its WAN. To support the ubiquity of its global operations, Huawei has also built its own enterprise network, which serves over 90,000 employees and 200,000 terminals at more than 100 branches, 22 regional offices, 17 R&D centers and 36 training facilities in more than 100 countries and regions.

In other industries, ubiquity can be just as important a competency. The Coca-Cola Company, for instance, claims that Coca-Cola is the most ubiquitous brand in the world. Each day, people in 200 countries around the world drink some 1.2 billion 8-oz servings of the cola.

Case Example: Kiva Systems and Amazon

Kiva Systems, a hi-tech company financed by Bain Capital Ventures, makes mobile order fulfillment systems using robots for warehouses, which help companies build competitive scalability strategies. Staples, Walgreens, GAP and Toys "R" Us have all adopted the Kiva material handling system.

Online retailers are thus challenged to forecast dynamic demand to determine the appropriate warehouse capacity. Online retailers had previously adopted carousel systems and AS/RSs (which require investments on the order of several millions Euros) to fulfill their orders. Were the market demand to either grow or shrink, this investment may result in either overcapacity or shortage. To enable warehouses and fulfillment operations to accommodate changing market demands, Kiva invented a mobile order-fulfillment system which uses robots to fill orders. The system allowed online retailers to build out a Kiva system with fewer robots in the initial stage, increasing the number of robots as demand increased, thereby avoiding the huge initial investments and wasted capacity of non-scalable carousel systems and AS/RSs.

Amazon had roughly 65 fulfillment centers at which the retailer stored products and filled orders worldwide, which utilized a range of alternative warehouse technologies until 2012, when Amazon acquired Kiva for an acquisition price of $775 million. If Amazon had not acquired Kiva, with this cash Amazon could buy a number of robots without distracting from core business. However, Amazon perhaps tries to build a strategic advantage over other online retailing rivals with this acquisition.

Case Questions

1. What are the competencies of the Kiva system?
2. What are benefits of these competencies? Why has Amazon decided to acquire Kiva?

Case: Samsung Versus Apple Battle

1. Samsung and Apple's battlefields
   Samsung Electronics, the world's largest IT company as measured by 2011 revenues, is a subsidiary of Samsung Group, a South Korean multinational conglomerate. Its product range is large and includes mobile phones (the world's largest mobile phone maker), semiconductor chips (the second-largest manufacturer, after Intel), televisions (the largest television

manufacturer), Liquid-crystal display (LCD) panels (the largest manufacturer), memory chips (with the largest market share of any manufacturer), and tablet computers.

Apple, named as the most-admired company in the world from 2008 to 2012 by Fortune magazine, is a leading American multinational corporation that designs and sells consumer electronics, computer software and personal computers.

In recent years, these two companies have been competing in several business battlefields. First, the smartphone space is perhaps the fiercest marketplace in which the two companies compete. While Samsung has made millions of its Galaxy phones, powered by Google's Android operating system, Apple has sold millions of its iPhones. In the first quarter of 2012, Samsung had bested Nokia, the previous number one in the global mobile phone market, and had also bested Apple in the smartphone market. Second, the two companies compete in the tablet computer space, albeit with less competition. The sales figures for Apple's iPads are still far larger than those for Samsung's Android-based Galaxy tablets. Third, Samsung has begun to build a standard Samsung user interface even though it uses Google's operating system, and these efforts are now being seen as a threat to Apple's software. Apple, meanwhile, is exploring the potential of entering the television market and other fields which Samsung has traditionally dominated.

2. Competency battle

   Samsung and Apple have built different competencies (Table 4.6). First, the price of Samsung's offerings is typically lower, not just for customers but for service carriers, as well. Although the current situation is safe for Apple, since they operate in different market segments, Samsung can compete more effectively on price in the future if it uses its revenues from the lower-end market to subsidize the R&D of its higher-end products. Second, Samsung offers a wider variety of phones than does Apple, which takes "simplicity" as a core philosophy in providing fewer options to the market. Third, generally speaking, the perceived quality of Apple is regarded as being higher. Finally, while Apple would often make its fans wait for new products during Steve Jobs' time as CEO, the speed with which Samsung is able to deliver products to market is greatly improved due to their in-house manufacturing and the stronger control the possess over their supply chain. The speed with which Apple realized the global launch of the iPhone 5, however, astounded observers in 2012, as new CEO Tim Cook took on the unglamorous task of global supply chain management.

3. Value chain battle

   Samsung versus Apple is a competition not between two companies, but between two supply chains. Figure 4.8 shows the primary supply chains for the Samsung Galaxy phone and the Apple iPhone, respectively. Note that the supply chains are dynamic and their supply chain networks may be more complicated than is represented in Fig. 4.8.

Table 4.6 Competencies of Samsung and Apple

Category	Items	Samsung	Apple	Winner
Competency	Cost	Low price	Accessible-affluent price	Samsung
	Flexibility	A wide variety of phones with a wide array of features at a wide array of price points	Intentionally fewer options to keep focus on simplicity	Samsung
	Quality	High quality allows the successful capturing of low-end customers and leaves potential for upgrades	High primary performance, focus on aesthetics, special features, perceived quality, conformance and serviceability	Apple
	Time	Delivery on time, strong supply chain management	iPhone fans often wait	Samsung
Value chain activities	Software design	Relies on Google's Android operating system	iOS; applications available through proprietary app store	Apple
	Hardware design	"Crisis of design"	Hardware leader for all six generations of iPhone	Apple
	Components	Made in-house by Samsung	From Samsung, LG, and Japan Display; often at risk of supply shortage	Samsung
	Assembly	Samsung-operated assembly plant allows for risks to be controlled	Outsourced to Foxconn, introducing risks and various ethical concerns	Samsung
	Distribution and channels	Charges low subsidies to all carriers, to deliver the most phones	Charges high subsidies to limited number of carriers, to make the most profit	S/A
	Customers	Far broader customer base which expands beyond mobile devices	High loyalty of Apple fans	S/A

- Software design

Apple has maintained its status as the technology and innovation leader in the market. In terms of software design, the Apple iPhone uses a mobile operating system, iOS, which has a 23 % share of all smartphone operating system units sold in the first quarter of 2012; Apple does not license iOS for installation on non-Apple hardware. Apple is strong in software and Apple's App Store contained more than 700,000 iOS-compatible applications as of September 12, 2012. The Samsung Galaxy relies primarily on Google's Android operating system, which has the largest market share of any smartphone operating system.

- Hardware design

Apple is the hardware leader for all six generations of its iPhone. The GSM iPhone created the original design which has persisted through all subsequent models. The iPhone design follows the Apple style philosophy of uniqueness and simplicity. In order to retain the feature of having only a single "home" button, for example, the newer iterations of the iPhone have a sleep button at the top, volume buttons on the side and have removed the physical keyboard.

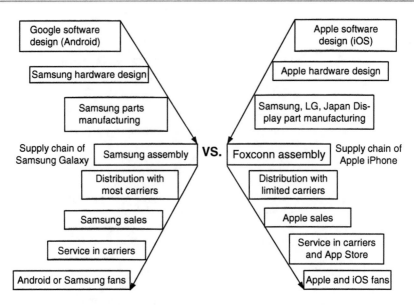

Fig. 4.8 "X" comparison framework for supply chains of Samsung Galaxy and Apple iPhone

Apple added 3G cellular network capabilities with the iPhone 3G, added a faster, more powerful processor and a higher-resolution camera with the iPhone 3GS, a higher-resolution "retina display" with the iPhone 4, an 8-megapixel camera, dual-core processor and "Siri" natural language voice-control system with the iPhone 4S, and the new A6 processor as well as a 4-in. "retina display" with the iPhone 5.

The Galaxy is predominantly plastic and offers customers two colors, Marble White and Titanium Gray. Surrounding the edges and the rounded corners is a chromed bezel. Its rivals and IT reviewers claim Samsung is adopting a "plastic design philosophy". During a lawsuit heard in 2012, Apple's attorneys introduced a Samsung internal memo since released to the public in which the president of Samsung Mobile, JK Shin, expressed outrage that Samsung was suffering from a "crisis of design", and told designers "not to create a plastic feeling and instead create a metallic feel".

• Manufacturing

Hi-tech parts in the mobile phone industry often become bottlenecks in the supply chain, and parts manufacturing can be a company's most important strategic activity. In 2012, for example, Apple was unable to keep up with iPhone 5 orders and customers were forced to wait months because Apple's suppliers had difficulties producing two components for the iPhone 5: the in-cell display screen and the long-term evolution (LTE) chip. The screen is produced by Apple's long-term partner, Korea's LG Display, as well as by Japan Display. Apple also contracted with Sharp, Japan's largest manufacturer of LCDs, but even Sharp failed to produce the screens at a sufficient pace prior to the launch of the iPhone 5. These parts require such high levels of technology that suppliers think it unfeasible to produce enough on time. Prior to 2012, the bottleneck of parts manufacturing was even more serious when Apple released the iPhone 4 under Steve Jobs, who placed a greater emphasis on design and marketing than on supply chain management.

Samsung, with its in-house parts manufacturing capacity, possesses a clear strategic advantage in this regard. The parts used in the Samsung Galaxy S III, for example, from the screen to the quad-core processor to the RAM to the NAND flash memory, are all made in-house. In component manufacturing, Samsung takes advantage of the fact that it is a primary supplier of chips, displays and flash memory to Apple. This is also the reason that Samsung can make smartphones at lower costs. With the iPhone 5, Apple has made attempts to contract with other component suppliers to avoid operational risks.

Apple outsources iPhone assembly to Foxconn in China. After several workers committed suicide at Foxconn's facility, Apple has been exposed to ethics risks in recent years. The Fair Labor Association (FLA) has identified issues with the work conditions at Foxconn, including excess overtime and low wages. Foxconn has agreed with the FLA to reduce employees' work time and increase pay. Samsung has its own assembly plants in Korea and China, which allow it to control outsourcing risks.

- Marketing and service

The marketing strategies of Apple and Samsung are different: while Apple focuses on generating the most profit, Samsung ships the most phones in an effort to win the largest share of the still-growing smartphone market. Apple's strategy revolves around the high subsidies it charges to carriers who wish to offer the iPhone and allow it to achieve astonishing margins of 49–58 % on iPhone sales from 2010 to 2012. Apple can maintain these high carrier subsidies and high margins only if consumer demand for the iPhone remains strong.

While carriers of the iPhone are limited (e.g., at first limited to only AT&T, then Sprint, then Verizon in the US), Samsung makes a point of selling the Galaxy on all major carriers, including US regional carriers. Samsung has generally been willing to cut the price it charges carriers, which allows the company to maintain good working relationships with the service carriers. This is critical to allowing Samsung to build marketing channels through which they can compete with Apple. The strategic focus of Samsung is on the cumulative volume of sales, not the margins.

- Customers

Due to its long-term success and reputation, Apple has earned highly loyal fans, many of whom are willing to wait in long queues for new products, while Samsung can only conduct promotional activities to attract customers. Samsung has the advantage of a far broader customer base, however, and can attract customers from all areas of consumer electronics since it makes a huge range of products, including HDTVs, DVRs and Blu-ray disc players, laptops, camcorders and refrigerators. Furthermore, Samsung can draw in customers from other markets of the Samsung Group, which includes Samsung Heavy Industries (the world's leading shipbuilder), Samsung Engineering and Samsung Life Insurance.

4. Lawsuit battle
   Since the spring of 2011, when Apple began litigating against Samsung in patent infringement suits, Apple and Samsung Electronics have been locked in a series of lawsuits pertaining to their smartphone and tablet computer design and the related patents. The mobile device patent wars highlight the fierce competition in the global consumer mobile communications market. As of July 2012, the two companies were still embroiled in more than 50 lawsuits worldwide. While Apple won recent cases in the US, Samsung won in South Korea and Japan. In Europe, the lawsuit battle is more complicated and fiercer, and neither company has registered a complete victory in either the German, Dutch, French or British courts.

Case Questions

1. Is quality the most important competency of Apple? If yes, how has Apple achieved it?
2. What is Samsung's most important competency? How does it achieve it?
3. What is the competitive advantage offered by Apple's supply chain?
4. What is the primary competitive advantage of Samsung's supply chain? In its supply chain, what is the most important activity in strategic leverage?
5. Are the lawsuits filed by both companies being used as strategic weapons?
6. Optional question: Using the "smile curve" (see Chap. 6), analyze these two supply chains.

References

Blackburn, J. D. (1992). Time-based competition: White-collar activities. *Business Horizons, 35*(4), 96–101.

Bowen, D. E., & Jones, G. R. (1986). Transaction cost analysis of service organization-customer exchange. *The Academy of Management Review, 11*(2), 428–441.

D'Souza, D. E., & Williams, F. P. (2000). Toward a taxonomy of manufacturing flexibility dimensions. *Journal of Operations Management, 18*(5), 577–593.

Dibrell, C., Davis, P. S., & Danskin, P. (2005). The influence of internationalization on time-based competition. *Management International Review, 45*(2), 173–195.

Ettlie, J. E., & Penner-Hahn, J. D. (1994). Flexibility ratios and manufacturing strategy. *Management Science, 40*(11), 1444–1454.

Foster, S. T., Jr. (2008). Towards an understanding of supply chain quality management. *Journal of Operations Management, 26*(4), 461–467.

Fynes, B., Voss, C., & de Burca, S. (2005). The impact of supply chain relationship quality on quality performance. *International Journal of Production Economics, 96*(3), 339–354.

Garvin, D. A. (1987). Competing on the eight dimensions of quality. *Harvard Business Review, 65*(6), 101–109.

Gerwin, D. (1993). Manufacturing flexibility: A strategic perspective. *Management Science, 39*(4), 395–410.

Graves, S. C., & Tomlin, B. T. (2003). Process flexibility in supply chains. *Management Science, 49*(7), 907–919.

Gupta, Y. P., & Goyal, S. (1989). Flexibility of manufacturing systems: Concepts and measurements. *European Journal of Operational Research, 43*(2), 119–135.

Gupta, Y. P., & Somers, T. M. (1996). Business strategy, manufacturing flexibility, and organizational performance relationships: A path analysis approach. *Production and Operations Management, 5*(3), 204–233.

Jordan, W. C., & Graves, S. C. (1995). Principles on the benefits of manufacturing process flexibility. *Management Science, 41*(4), 577–594.

Kim, K. Y., & Chang, D. R. (1995). Global quality management: A research focus. *Decision Science, 26*(5), 561–568.

Kogut, B., & Kulatilaka, N. (1994). Operating flexibility, global manufacturing, and the option value of a multinational network. *Management Science, 40*(1), 123–139.

Lau, R. S. M. (1999). Critical factors for achieving manufacturing flexibility. *International Journal of Operations and Production Management, 19*(3), 328–341.

Noori, H., & Radford, R. (1995). *Production and operations management: Total quality and responsiveness.* New York: McGraw-Hill.

Ohno, T. (1988). *Toyota production system: Beyond large-scale production.* Cambridge: Productivity Press.

Ohno, T., & Mito, S. (1988). *Just-in-time for today and tomorrow.* Cambridge: Productivity Press.

Porter, M. E. (1996). What is strategy. *Harvard Business Review, 74*(6), 61–78.

Porter, M. E., & Kramer, M. R. (2006). Strategy and society: The link between competitive advantage and corporate social responsibility. *Harvard Business Review, 84*(12), 78–92.

Porter, M. E., & Kramer, M. R. (2011). Creating shared value. *Harvard Business Review, 89*(1/2), 62–77.

Prahalad, C. K., & Hamel, G. (1990). The core competence of the corporation. *Harvard Business Review, 68*(3), 79–91.

Rich, N., & Hines, P. (1997). Supply-chain management and time-based competition: The role of the supplier association. *International Journal of Physical Distribution and Logistics Management, 27*(3/4), 210–225.

Riley, M., & Lockwood, A. (1997). Strategies and measurement for workforce flexibility: An application of functional flexibility in a service setting. *International Journal of Operations and Production Management, 17*(4), 413–419.

Robinson, C. J., & Malhotra, M. K. (2005). Defining the concept of supply chain quality management and its relevance to academic and industrial practice. *International Journal of Production Economics, 96*(3), 315–337.

Ross, D. F. (1997). *Competing through supply chain management: Creating market-winning strategies through supply chain partnerships.* Boston: Kluwer.

Skinner, W. (1974). The focused factory. *Harvard Business Review, 52*(3), 113–121.

Spear, S., & Bowen, H. K. (1999). Decoding the DNA of the Toyota production system. *Harvard Business Review, 77*(5), 97–106.

Spina, G., Bartezzaghi, E., Bert, A., Cagliano, R., Draaijer, D., & Boer, H. (1996). Strategically flexible production: The multi-focused manufacturing paradigm. *International Journal of Operations and Production Management, 16*(11), 20–41.

Stalk, G., Jr. (1988). Time – The next source of competitive advantage. *Harvard Business Review, 66*, 41–51.

Stalk, G., Jr., & Hout, T. M. (1990). *Competing against time: How time-based competition is reshaping global markets*. New York: Free Press.

Upton, D. M. (1994). The management of manufacturing flexibility. *California Management Review, 36*(2), 72–89.

Upton, D. M. (1995). What really makes factories flexible? *Harvard Business Review, 73*(4), 74–84.

Zeithaml, V. A., Parasuraman, A., & Berry, L. L. (1990). *Delivering quality service: Balancing customer perceptions and expectations*. New York: Free Press.

Resource-Based Fundamentals

5

Chapter Objectives

- To address the resource-based view (RBV) of global operations strategy.
- To introduce global resource size management.
- To study global resource type problems and operational flexibility.
- To introduce global location strategy.
- To present global dynamic capacity management.

5.1 Introduction to Resource-Based Global Operations Strategy

5.1.1 Introduction to Resources of a Firm

A firm typically has two groups of resources: tangible and intangible (see Table 5.1). There are physical, financial, and human tangible resources. Intangible resources can be classified into two groups: people-dependent and people-independent resources (Hall 1993).

An appropriate bundle of resources can create competitive advantage. Carrefour, for example, possesses a range of resources that yield competitive advantages in global retailing. Superior performance will therefore be based on developing a competitively distinct set of resources and deploying them in a well-conceived operations strategy. We present main theories on resource and competitive advantage as follows.

Y. Gong, *Global Operations Strategy*, Springer Texts in Business and Economics, DOI 10.1007/978-3-642-36708-3_5, © Springer-Verlag Berlin Heidelberg 2013

Table 5.1 Classification of the resources in a firm

Group	Type	Examples
Tangible	Physical	Plant, office, equipment, warehouse, vehicles
	Financial	Cash, securities
	Human	Managers, engineers, workers
Intangible (Hall 1993)	People-dependent	Reputation, personal and organizational networks, perception of quality, ability to learn, know-how of employees, suppliers, and distributors
	People-independent	Databases, contracts and licenses, trade secrets, intellectual property rights

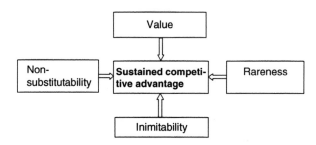

Fig. 5.1 Barney's resource-based theory

5.1.2   Resource and Competitive Advantage

5.1.2.1 Barney's VRIO Framework

When a firm is implementing a value-creating strategy, if any current and potential competitors have not simultaneously implemented this strategy, then Barney (1991) thinks the firm has competitive advantage. If other firms are unable to duplicate the benefits of this strategy, then Barney (1991) thinks the firm has a sustained competitive advantage. In order to hold a sustained competitive advantage, a resource should have four attributes (see Fig. 5.1).

To obtain competitive advantage, a resource should have at least two attributes. First, the resource must be "valuable" in seizing an opportunity for a firm, neutralizing threats, or shielding the firm against the threat. Second, the resource must be "rare" in the current and potential competition.

To further get a sustained competitive advantage, the relevant resources firstly must be "non-imitable" or "costly to imitate", namely competitors cannot acquire or accumulate resources with the desired attributes. Then, the relevant resources must be "non-substitutable" or "costly to substitute", namely competitors cannot access the resources to implement the same strategy.

Barney and Hesterly (2010) further develop the VRIO framework, a renowned tool in practice. Compared with Barney (1991), they change the fourth question to a question about organization to examine whether the firm is organized, ready, and able to exploit the resource. Table 5.2 shows how to apply the VRIO framework.

Table 5.2 VRIO framework (Barney and Hesterly 2010)

Valuable?	Rare?	Inimitable?	Exploited by organization?	Competitive implications	Firm performance
No	–	–	No	Competitive disadvantage	Below average
Yes	No	–	Yes	Competitive parity	Average
Yes	Yes	No	Yes	Temporary competitive advantage	Above average
Yes	Yes	Yes	Yes	Sustained competitive advantage	Persistently above average

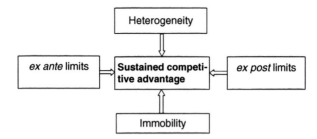

Fig. 5.2 Peteraf's resource-based theory

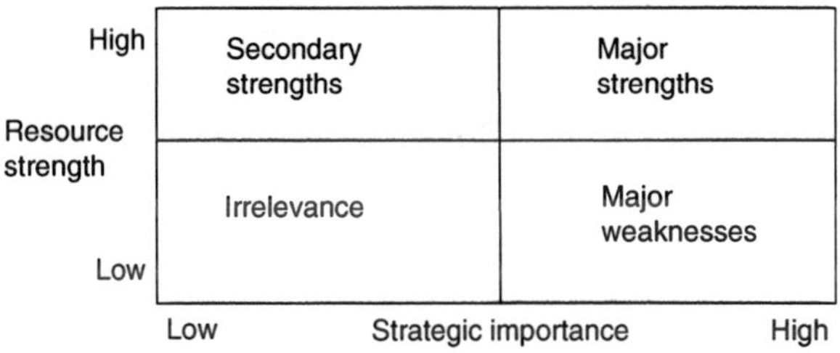

Fig. 5.3 Resource strength–strategic importance matrix (Based on Grant 2009)

A firm can examine each question and assess the competitive and economic implications through the different possibilities and outcomes.

5.1.2.2 Peteraf's Framework
Peteraf (1993) argues that to gain a sustained competitive advantage all of the following four conditions must be met (see Fig. 5.2). The first condition is the heterogeneity of resources, under which condition a firm may generate a differential profit. The remaining three are "ex ante limits" to competition, "ex post limits" to competition, and resource immobility.

5.1.2.3 Resource Strength–Strategic Importance Matrix
Figure 5.3 presents a "resource strength–strategic importance" matrix, which is based on Grant (2009), to determine the operations strategy of resources to gain

Table 5.3 Comparison of relevant strategic frameworks

Frameworks	Representative works	Main viewpoints
Competitive forces	Porter (1980)	The essence of competitive strategy formulation is to relate a company to its environment
		Five industry-level forces (entry barriers, threat of substitution, bargaining power of buyers, bargaining power of suppliers, and rivalry among industry incumbents) determine the inherent profit potential of an industry or sub-segment of an industry
Strategic conflict	Shapiro (1989)	Employs game theory to study competitive interactions between rival firms
		Explains how a firm can influence the behavior and actions of rivals and its environment
RBV	Chandler (1966), Teece (1980), Wernerfelt (1984), Barney (1991)	Focuses on the rents from scarce firm-specific resources rather than the economic profits from product market positioning
		Competitive advantage relies on the firm's idiosyncratic and VRIO resources

competitive advantage. A process to describe, appraise, and analyze this resource strength–strategic importance matrix is as follows:

1. Identify and describe the resources and strategies.
2. Appraise each resource's strength and strategic importance.
3. Identify the strategic position using the "resource strength–strategic importance" matrix in Fig. 5.3.
4. Develop and keep investing into the major strengths. Improve the major weaknesses to shift them to strengths or adopt an outsourcing strategy.

5.1.3   RBV of Strategic Management

The RBV of the firm (see Chandler 1966; Teece 1980, 1982; Wernerfelt 1984; Collis and Montgomery 1995; Barney 1991; Peteraf 1993; Teece et al. 1997; Hoopes et al. 2003) is an important stream in strategy management. There are different viewpoints to explain how to obtain competitive advantages. Table 5.3 compares RBV and two competing frameworks, namely "competitive forces" and "strategic conflict".

RBV maintains that firms are heterogeneous in terms of resources or endowments. In addition, resource endowments are more or less sticky. RBV does not focus on the economic profits from product market positioning or on the influence on the behavior of rivals, but rather focuses on the rents from scarce firm-specific resources. In RBV, competitive advantage relies on the firm's idiosyncratic and VRIO resources.

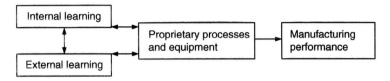

Fig. 5.4 Schroeder, Bates, and Junttila's RBV manufacturing strategy model

5.1.4 Resource-Based Global Operations Strategy

RBV considers two types of resources: (1) resources that can be acquired in factor market or external systems and (2) resources developed inside the firm. If the resource is non-imitable, resources can be employed to contribute positively to performance and confer competitive advantage. RBV is an important research topic at the levels of business strategy and corporate strategy (or "firm level" in the RBV literature). This chapter will not focus on RBV corporate strategy and business strategy, but on RBV operations strategy.

Schroeder et al. (2002) propose a resource-based model of manufacturing strategy (see Fig. 5.4). In this model, internal learning means learning within the organization, for example, the training of multifunctional employees and incorporating employee suggestions. Schroeder et al. (2002) define external learning as interorganizational learning via problem solving with customers and suppliers. Their model argues that internal and external learning in manufacturing facilities leads to unique proprietary processes and equipment, good manufacturing performance, and thus competitive advantage since the resources are not available to competitors in the factor market.

Although this section mainly introduces RBV, which has substantially influenced operations strategy, "RBV-based operations strategy" is a subset of "resource-based operations strategy". Even for firms taking views of "competitive forces" and "strategic conflict", their corporate strategies still need the support of an aligned operations strategy consisting of the resource part. Resource-based global operations strategy is the long-term plan for developing and optimizing global resources, and involves decisions on sizing, types, and locations as well as dynamic decisions on real assets or resources. In the remainder of this chapter, we introduce these four decisions.

Case Example: Best Buy

In 2011, US electronics firm Best Buy, the world's largest consumer electronics retailer, closed all nine of its branded stores in China after five years in the market and switched its focus to a local retailing chain (5 Star) it acquired several years ago. In the Chinese market, its main competitors are Gome and Suning, which are much larger than Best Buy in the local market in terms of both sales and facility size. Table 5.4 shows tangible and intangible resources of Best Buy in China.

Table 5.4 Resources of Best Buy in China

Categories	Resources	Comments
Tangible	Large stores	Not rare in China
	Good quality products with wide ranges	Chinese customers care about price
	Locations	Its competitors have strong networks to get better or similar locations
	Layout and category management	Cost-to-imitate is low
	136 appliance stores of 5 Star in eight provinces	Competitors even have larger stores
Intangible	Brand equity, generic brands	The reputation is high in the US, but Best Buy is not well known in China
	Pre-sales and after-sales services	Not rare. Cost-to-imitate and cost-to-substitute are low
	Know-how of employees, suppliers, and distributors	Shortage of some know-how of local suppliers and distributors
	Centricity philosophy	Neither rare nor a completely new idea. Competitors also care about customers
	Personal and organizational networks	Competitors Gome and Suning build better local networks
	Contracts and trade secrets	Unfamiliar with the trade secrets of successful local retailers

Tangible resources

Opened in 2007, Best Buy's first store in Shanghai was the largest Best Buy store in the world. Best Buy opened eight other big stores – all in downtown areas of large cities such as Beijing and Shanghai. It focused on building large flagship stores, like in the US, rather than smaller, conveniently located retail outlets. However, because of traffic congestion and a lack of parking, Chinese consumers often prefer shopping close to their homes.

With these giant stores, Best Buy was able to offer a wide range of high-quality products. However, while Chinese customers are more sensitive to price, the prices in Best Buy are relatively higher compared with other competitors in China, even for identical products. Although Best Buy is good at retailing layouts and category management, which is convenient for customers, many local retailers imitated its layout and category management.

In 2006, Best Buy acquired 5 Star, China's fourth-largest appliance chain, and had 136 appliance stores at the time. The 5 Star brand has been in the market considerably longer and is a brand Chinese recognize.

Intangible resources

Best Buy is famous in the US and the brand is well established. Through this reputation, it has developed relationships with international suppliers such as Toshiba, Sony, and Dell. However, Best Buy is not well known to Chinese and it has a shortage of networks with local governments, suppliers, and distributors.

In the Chinese electronics retailing industry, managers identify two contract and operations modes. In the first, termed "Chinese mode", an electronics retailer divides its retailing space into different zones and rents these zones to different electronics producers. These electronics producers send salespeople to promote the products in their zones. The electronics retailer charges a relatively high "retailing space occupying fee" and can postpone the payment to electronics producers. This is a contract favorable to retailers not producers. By contrast, under the "Best Buy mode", Best Buy purchases and sells products alone. This is a fair contract, but the operational cost is much higher.

In 2001, Best Buy implemented a concept called "centricity", which means looking at an enterprise through the lens of customers rather than producers. Best Buy offered excellent pre-sales and after-sales services. Vendors provided customers with useful advice in the store because of their qualifications and skills.

Case Questions

1. Evaluate Best Buy's resources using the VRIO framework.
2. Analyze Best Buy's resources using the resource strength–strategic importance matrix.
3. Appraise the dynamic capacity strategy of Best Buy, particularly its three key decisions: (i) started own-branded Best Buy stores, (ii) acquired local chain 5 Star, and (iii) closed all nine of its branded stores in 2011.
4. Best Buy plans to return to China and continue its "dual brand strategy" (branded Best Buy and 5 Star) for different customer segments. What suggestions would you make for its resource-based operations strategy?

5.2   Global Resource Size Management

5.2.1   Introduction to Resource Size Problems

Global resource sizing problems determine the capacity level by considering key trade-offs between the cost of global excess capacity and the opportunity cost of global capacity shortage; thus, they can be of substantial importance to the future of an MNE. For example, Apple was struggling to respond to the demand for its iPad 2 since its supply chain had capacity problems. This capacity issue resulted in delays and lost sales, as many competitors released similar products such as Samsung's Galaxy Tab and Blackberry's Playbook. As a consequence, Apple and its major supplier Foxconn jointly announced that a new plant in Brazil would start assembling iPads in addition to its plants in China from December 2011.

The opportunity cost of capacity shortages can be mitigated by such capacity expansion as well as by tactical countermeasures such as raising prices, putting customers on a waiting list, building inventory in advance, or subcontracting.

The cost of excess capacity can be alleviated by contracting capacity as well as by countermeasures such as sales promotions.

5.2.2 Capacity Size Problem in a Global Environment

5.2.2.1 Sizing Problem in a Global Business Environment

In a global environment, the capacity size problem is influenced by the complexity of the business environment, uncertainty of global industrial structures, dynamics of the global supply chain, and diversity of the business culture. Environmental complexity refers to the extent to which environmental factors in a host country are diverse and heterogeneous. Structural uncertainty involves the volatility and variability of the industrial environment or related market structure. The dynamics of the global supply chain refers to fluctuations in supply prices, production costs, supply chain structure, and technology innovation in global supply chains. Business cultural specificity refers to the unique characteristics of a host country's business culture relative to international standards.

5.2.2.2 Sizing Problem in the Global Political Environment

Global companies in different industries or locations are often treated differently by central or local governments. Before joining the WTO, the Chinese government enforced strict and detailed regulations on capacity size (e.g., store size, number of stores in a city) and capacity expansion for foreign retailing companies. Therefore, the capacity size decisions made by Carrefour and Walmart should consider not only economic objectives but also political feasibility.

There are regulatory differences between central and regional governments. This volatility or restriction varies across industries or regions within a foreign emerging market. For instance, a global company in Hong Kong may face a more open business atmosphere and a more liberal regulatory environment compared with its venture in Beijing.

5.2.2.3 Sizing Problem in Global Risks and Uncertainties

The impact of environmental dynamics on subsidiary operations is generally enduring and fundamental. Uncertainties and risks embodied in contextual environments are usually difficult to control. To reduce risks, global firms may adjust their economic exposure to environmental uncertainty or manipulate resource commitments, primarily by manipulating capacity deployment. For example, many companies examine the global capacity problem with exchange rate uncertainties. Kazaz et al. (2005) introduce such a case: A global electronics manufacturer makes a quarterly aggregate plan to determine how much to manufacture of each product in each plan to maximize expected profit, subject to exchange rate risks.

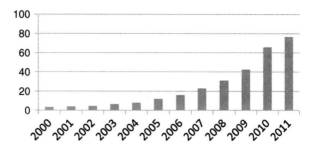

Fig. 5.5 Accomplished shipbuilding output in China (unit: million deadweight tonnages) (*Source: CANSI*)

5.2.2.4 Sizing Problem in Global Tax Systems

Different to the capacity size problem at a national scale, the tax problem is critical in global capacity planning including decisions on capacity size. Pricewaterhou-seCoopers calls a global capacity strategy that considers the transfer price as "production capacity management (PCM) and transfer pricing economics" (PwC 2007) and argues that an alignment between PCM and tax considerations can bring benefits to MNEs. The following tax factors influence decisions on facility' size:

1. Intercompany contract. When MNEs build new facilities, they must establish and optimize intercompany contracts. This will restructure global capacity planning and influence the size of new facilities.
2. Global transfer pricing policy. PCM restructuring should keep the alignment with transfer pricing economics. For example, an MNE may increase capacity size in lower-cost countries and reduce capacity size in higher-cost countries. Such aligned PCM restructuring can enhance the transparency of global operations, improve the predictability of global output, and increase the profitability of global value chains.
3. Global tax and legal systems. When designing global manufacturing and service networks, a manager needs to consider global tax and legal systems, including customs duty, local tax treatment, grant availability, restrictions imposed by favorable tax regimes, local control rules to foreign company, and international tax treaties.

Case Example: Shipbuilding Overcapacity Crisis

1. Crazy investment and shipbuilding booming
   According to CANSI (China Association of the National Shipbuilding Industry), in 2011 China edged out South Korea to become the world's largest shipbuilder in terms of accomplished shipbuilding output. In the first half of 2010, China's shipbuilding capacity, the number of new orders, and the volume of backlog orders accounted for about 41 %, 46 %, and 38 % of the world market, respectively. Figure 5.5 shows the boom in shipbuilding in the past decade in China. This boom is from two drivers, government and private investors.

   Under central government guidance, China has poured money into developing its shipbuilding and maritime logistics sectors, deeming them crucial for the nation's development. China aims to nearly double its annual ship

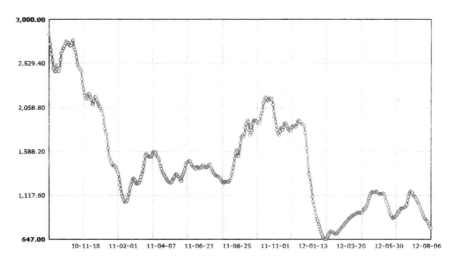

Fig. 5.6 Baltic Dry Index in recent years

sales to $190 billion by 2015. Another driver is private investment. From 2004 to 2010, as China's imports and exports both grew continually, domestic shipowners were in urgent need to increase transportation capacity and optimize fleet structure, which had thus provided the domestic shipbuilding industry with enormous space for growth. Effective market demand is of critical importance to the development of the shipbuilding industry. A number of private investors rushed into the shipbuilding industry, including Zhang Zhirong, a real estate tycoon, who made a sensation by building Rongsheng Group, the largest private shipyard in China.

2. Decreasing demand

   Figure 5.6 shows the Baltic Dry Index, a shipping and trade index created by the London-based Baltic Exchange that measures changes in the cost to transport raw materials. This index can give shipbuilding investors insights into global supply and demand trends in shipping. Figure 5.6 also shows the likely future economic contraction, since the index has fallen in the past two years.

   Shipbuilding is typically a cyclical industry disturbed by overcapacity every few years. According to CANSI, Chinese firms received shipbuilding orders for 35.22 million deadweight tonnages during 2011. This is a decline of 51.9 % on 2010, which continues into 2012. Notably, about 30 % of Chinese shipbuilders received no orders at all in January 2012, relying instead on their backlog orders.

3. Serious overcapacity and industry crisis

   Chinese shipyards are facing difficulties such as the lack of new orders, delivery setbacks, price drops, a tightened ship financing market, increases in production costs, decreases in profit, and a stagnant global shipping market. Chinese shipbuilders are jumping into cut-throat competition to snatch lower-priced orders. Many shipyards located in China's major

Table 5.5 Chinese shipyards face massive bankruptcies in 2011 and 2012

Time	Shipbuilder	Situation
10/2011	Ningbo Hengfu Shipyard Group	Went bankrupt
10/2011	Blue Sky Shipbuilding Group	Went bankrupt
02/2012	Zhejiang Dongfang Shipbuilding Company	Financial crisis, Chairman ran away
03/2012	Jiangsu Nantong Huigang Shipyard	Financial crisis
04/2012	Dalian Oriental Shipyard	Went bankrupt
06/2012	Zhejiang Jingang Shipyard	Went bankrupt
07/2012	Rongsheng Group, the largest private shipyard in China	Financial crisis

shipbuilding complexes are facing a bankruptcy crisis with no orders (see Table 5.5). In May 2012, Zhejiang Jingang Shipbuilding, the largest private-owned shipyard in Taizhou, Zhejiang, filed for bankruptcy.

Case Questions

1. How did this overcapacity happen?
2. From this case, what do you learn to determine capacity size when considering global risks and uncertainties?

5.3 Global Resource Type Management

5.3.1 Introduction to Resource Type Problems

The resource type problem is to configure the set of resources and capabilities to achieve global competitive advantages. The resource type strategy is one of the main parts of operations strategy.

Based on the concepts of "strategic flexibility" (i.e., the ability to respond to various demands in a dynamic competitive environment) and RBV, Sanchez (1995) develops a concept of "resource flexibility", which can be characterized by three dimensions:

- Range: a resource can be applied to a range of alternative objectives or subjects. For example, it can be used to develop, produce, distribute, and ship a range of different products.
- Cost: the low cost of efforts to switch from one use of a resource to an alternative use.
- Time: the shorter time of switching from one use of a resource to an alternative use.

We particularly consider flexibility problems in a global environment. Global operational flexibility is a firm's competency to respond to environmental fluctuations by "shifting factors of production within a multinational network of subsidiaries" (Tang and Tikoo 1999, p. 749). In a global setting, flexibility may cost

Fig. 5.7 Trade-off between
flexibility and cost

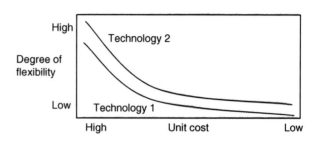

more and its benefits are difficult to measure, value, and convey. Cost flexibility is
one of the main trade-offs in operational flexibility. As pointed out by Van
Mieghem (1998) and Fine and Freund (1990), although resource flexibility provides
firms with a hedge against demand uncertainties and responds to a variety of future
demand outcomes, it increases cost compared with dedicated resources.

We now present resource flexibility in different stages of production: production
input, production capacity (including single facility and networks), and production
output (product flexibility).

5.3.2 Resource Flexibility in Production Input

In the input part of production, a critical type of flexibility is material flexibility
(Gerwin 1993), which is the ability to handle unexpected uncertainties in production input and can improve product quality and increase productivity. There are two
dimensions of material flexibility: the scope of materials and the time to make an
adjustment. For example, when a type of material is in shortage, an MNE can find
another to replace the material. This flexibility is not only in raw materials, but also
in upstream activities or products such as critical components, parts, and semi-
finished products.

Whereas material flexibility is a tangible resource, input flexibility is an intangible resource. The first type of flexibility is suppliers themselves, as it depends on
suppliers' capacities to respond to changing demand from downstream producers.
The second type is based on the relationship between a producer and its upstream
suppliers, which can establish contract flexibility or build flexible relationships into
the delivery of input flexibility. For example, Sun Microsystems used a quantity
flexibility contract in its workstation component purchasing department, while
Toyota, IBM, HP, and Compaq have established flexibility contracts with their
upstream producers (Tsay 1999).

5.3.3 Resource Flexibility in Production Capacity: Single Facility

Flexible production resources allow a firm to be more adaptable to demand fluctuation. The main trade-off in production capacity flexibility is between operational
flexibility and cost (see Fig. 5.7). Usually, a firm incurs a higher cost to build a more

High
Degree of flexibility
Low
Low
Degree of automation
High

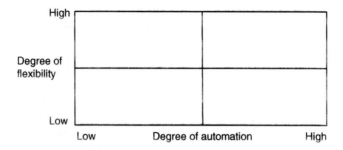

Fig. 5.8 Degree of flexibility and automation

High
Breadth (number of foreign countries)
Low
Type IV (higher flexibility, greater ERC)
Type I (no significant difference)
Type III (no significant difference)
Type II (lower flexibility, smaller ERC)
Low
High
Depth (number of subsidiaries per foreign country)

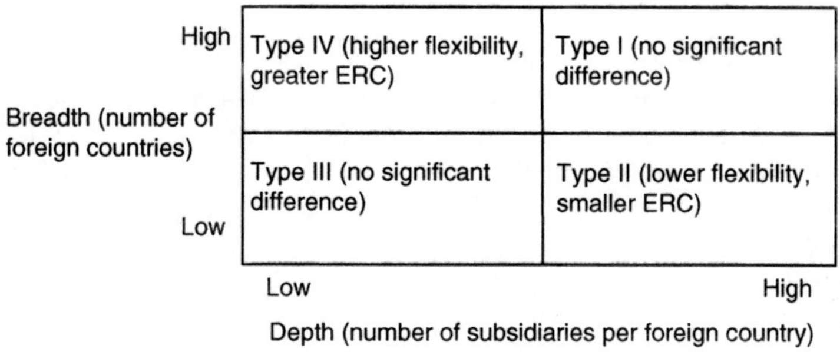

Fig. 5.9 Tang and Tikoo's classification of multinational networks

flexible production resource. Technology innovation can fundamentally change the trade-off curve between operational flexibility and cost. Some flexible manufacturing systems can improve resource flexibility while reducing or maintaining the cost level.

Another trade-off in production capacity flexibility is between human resources and capital assets. For example, a common decision is determining how to configure a firm's resources and capabilities according to the degree of flexibility vs. degree of automation matrix (see Fig. 5.8). A firm needs to identify an appropriate strategic point between flexibility and automation by considering economies of scale, operations flexibility, and risk mitigation.

5.3.4 Resource Flexibility in Production Capacity: Networks

Tang and Tikoo (1999) use the geographic breath (the number of foreign countries where subsidiaries are located) and depth (the number of subsidiaries per foreign country) of a firm's multinational network as indicators of operational flexibility. A firm enhances operational flexibility by building subsidiaries in more foreign countries and diminishes it by deepening its global networks.

Operational flexibility influences performance as measured by the ERC (earnings response coefficient), namely the stock price's response to earnings changes. The ERC is used to measure the extent to which investors revise their expectations on future earnings based on current information. Figure 5.9 presents a classification

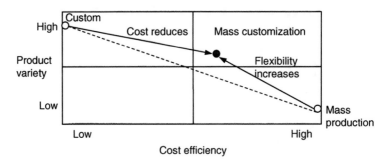

Fig. 5.10 Mass customization

of multinational networks. Generally speaking, the breadth of the network is associated with a greater ERC and the depth is associated with a smaller ERC. For type II firms with lower flexibility, the ERC is smaller. For type IV firms with higher flexibility, the ERC is larger. Tang and Tikoo (1999) thus conclude that if MNEs build broad and less concentrated networks, they obtain operational flexibility.

5.3.5 Product Flexibility

Product flexibility refers to the capacity to deliver a variety of products to meet fluctuations in customer demand and consists of two elements: scope and time.

5.3.5.1 Scope Aspect of Product Flexibility
The scope aspect of product flexibility can be measured with the size of parts produced by the manufacturing system without adding major capital equipment, the number of different part types or range of sizes and shapes that the system can produce without major setups, or the number of new parts introduced per year.

It is a classic operational problem to deliver an appropriate product mix to meet customer demand. Mass customization is a way to trade off the variety demand for customers and cost efficiency for product suppliers (see Fig. 5.10). Its flexibility is higher than mass production and production cost is lower than custom production. With the development of Internet business, mass customization is widely applied in businesses such as watches, eyeglasses, color paints, and laptops. Conventional businesses such as automobiles, coffee (e.g., Starbucks), and insurance companies also implement mass customization strategies.

5.3.5.2 Time Aspect of Product Flexibility
The time aspect of product flexibility can be measured by the time and cost required to introduce new products. In order to accommodate mass customization for meeting increasing customization requirements, firms such as Dell can change supply chain structures to implement an operations strategy called postponement,

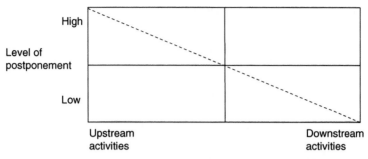

Fig. 5.11   Van Hoek's postponement application framework

which includes "time postponement" (i.e., postponing the delivery of the products until after customer orders arrive) and "form postponement" (i.e., delaying the differentiation of products until later operational stages) (see Su et al. 2005; van Hoek 2001). In an environment of global operations, such a postponement strategy will be influenced by production location, international logistics, transportation costs, and customs tariffs (see Choi et al. 2012).

The best-known case of postponement is HP (Lee et al. 1993). HP postpones the final assembly of its DeskJet printers to local distribution centers, ships the products in a semi-finished state to a downstream facility where final customization occurs, and the regional distribution centers can localize printers in a make-to-stock fashion.

By implementing postponement, firms can customize and localize products according to customer demand and the local environment. Van Hoek (2001) presents a postponement application framework (see Fig. 5.11). If the postponement of downstream activities such as packaging and shipping can handle customer demand fluctuation, firms will choose a low level of postponement. If the postponement of upstream activities such as sourcing fabrication is needed to handle customer demand fluctuation, firms will just choose a high level of postponement. For example, Dell uses a high level of postponement by delaying every operation in its supply chain and applying this approach to every order.

Case Example: Apple Versus Dell Laptops

Dell provides a large range of options to its customers. It provides at least five laptop series: Vostro with a focus on "value and support", Latitude with a focus on "best in class performance", Inspiron with a focus on "style and entertainment", XPS with a focus on "stylish and productive", and Dell Precision with a focus on "mobile advanced applications". It also provides products to five different customer segments: "home", "small and home office", "small and medium business", "education, government and healthcare", and "large enterprise".

Table 5.6 Comparison of Apple and Dell laptops

	Apple		Dell				
	MacBook Air	MacBook Pro	Vostro	Latitude	Inspiron	XPS	Precision
Screen size (inch)	11, 13	13, 15	13.3, 14, 15.6, 17.3	13.3, 14, 15.6	14, 15, 15.6, 17.3	14, 15, 15.6, 17.3	15.6, 17.3

However, Apple mainly provides two series, namely MacBook Air and MacBook Pro laptops. Within one series, the number of product types is also smaller compared with other laptop providers (see Table 5.6) in terms of screen size, processor, memory, hard drive, and other product features.

Case Questions

1. Complete Table 5.6 and compare Apple and Dell in terms of processor, memory, hard drive, and other product features.
2. Why does Apple provide fewer product types? What is the advantage of this strategy?
3. Why does Dell design more product types? Can Dell use the same strategy as Apple (i.e., provide fewer product types)?

5.4   Global Location Strategy

5.4.1   Introduction to Global Location Strategy

Location theory was first introduced by Weber (1909), who located a warehouse to minimize the total distance between the warehouse and spatially distributed customers. Location becomes even more important in a global environment and the right location is a key element to the success of an MNE, since it can support firm-specific ownership advantages and internalization advantages in the process of globalization (e.g., the OLI framework in Dunning 1977). A global location strategy is a plan to determine the optimal location for a company by identifying its strategic objectives and searching for locations to achieve them. This is part of operations strategy and must be aligned with corporate strategy and business goals.

Location decisions can be made at different levels: business strategy, operations strategy, and operations management. It is relatively difficult to completely separate location problems at different levels. In this section, while we mainly present operations strategy in this regard, we also briefly introduce the business strategy and operations management levels as follows.

1. At the level of corporate strategy and business strategy, we briefly introduce Dunning's (1977) OLI theory in Sect. 5.4.2.

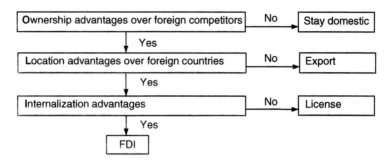

Fig. 5.12 Decision process based on OLI framework

2. At the level of operations strategy, we present several types of location strategies: manufacturing location strategy, service location strategy, R&D location strategy, and sustainable location strategy.
3. At the level of operations management, we recommend classical reviews Brandeau and Chiu (1989) and Revelle and Laporte (1996), which present the main approaches and models to handle location problems.

5.4.2 OLI Framework and Dunning's Location Theory

The OLI (Ownership-Location-Internalization) framework or "eclectic" approach (see Chap. 1) was developed by Dunning (1977). Dunning's OLI is a dominant theoretical framework to explain the incentives for MNEs to go overseas, the organizational forms of MNEs, an MNE's location choices, and the decision between foreign direct investment and its alternatives, such as international trade, licensing, and outsourcing. The framework is widely applied in a decision process of global operations (see Fig. 5.12), including location decisions.

5.4.3 Location Strategy in Global Manufacturing

5.4.3.1 Location in a Factory Manufacturing System or a Single Firm
Location strategy can serve a single factory manufacturing system or a single firm. We present location strategy from different perspectives.
1. Basically, location strategy can be a part of a manufacturing company's global production capacity planning, which is a set of decisions that operations managers must periodically make and consists of two parts: (1) the size and type of capacity to be installed in production plants and warehouses in each period and (2) the locations of plants and warehouses.
2. From an RBV, location can be a VRIO resource for a manufacturing company and thus provides a source of competitive advantage. For example, Foxconn, the world's largest manufacturer of electronic components, typically chooses locations where it can get strong support from the local government and thereby

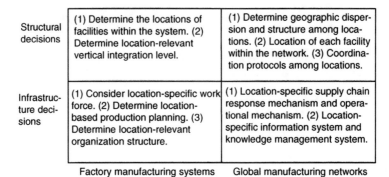

Structural decisions	(1) Determine the locations of facilities within the system. (2) Determine location-relevant vertical integration level.	(1) Determine geographic dispersion and structure among locations. (2) Location of each facility within the network. (3) Coordination protocols among locations.
Infrastructure decisions	(1) Consider location-specific work force. (2) Determine location-based production planning. (3) Determine location-relevant organization structure.	(1) Location-specific supply chain response mechanism and operational mechanism. (2) Location-specific information system and knowledge management system.
	Factory manufacturing systems	Global manufacturing networks

Fig. 5.13 Location strategies: factory manufacturing systems vs. global manufacturing networks

access cheap labor and land. These locations are valuable since they are low cost, rare since not all manufacturers can get them, difficult to be imitated by other foreign manufacturers, and developed by the organization. The location, as a VRIO resource, helps Foxconn build the competitive advantage of low cost.

3. In terms of the OLI framework, we further consider specific location strategies in a global environment. Dunning (1998) thinks more attention should be paid to the importance of location since it influences the global competitiveness of a firm. Location strategy can support internalization advantages and ownership advantages in the OLI triad.

5.4.3.2 Location in a Global Manufacturing Network

Firms establish global manufacturing networks to seek markets, efficiency, strategic assets, or resources. In such a context, location strategy is formulated for global manufacturing networks, which consider multiple locations and non-linear structures as opposed to a single factory manufacturing system with either a single location or a simple linear structure.

Figure 5.13 compares the location strategies of global manufacturing networks and factory manufacturing systems in terms of structural and infrastructure decisions. The classical decisions (see the left column in Fig. 5.13) about factory manufacturing systems are from Hayes and Wheelwright (1984). The location strategies of global manufacturing networks particularly consider (1) decisions on geographic dispersion and structure (e.g., hub and spoke structure or circle structure, location of headquarters, and location of the central warehouse) among locations by understanding customer distribution and market opportunities, raw materials and product cost differences, and transportation system and (2) coordination protocols among locations including vertical coordination among supply chain locations and horizontal coordination.

5.4.3.3 Location in Global Sourcing

Global sourcing refers to decisions on production and procurement locations. By operating in different locations, MNEs obtain firm-specific competitive advantages

		(Location)	
		Domestic	Foreign
(Ownership)	Internal	Integrated domestic firm	Wholly owned subsidiary, foreign direct investment.
	External	Domestic sourcing	Foreign sourcing

Fig. 5.14 OLI-based global sourcing model

and location-specific comparative advantages. We study global sourcing from different perspectives.

1. From the viewpoint of the OLI framework, an MNE can obtain firm-specific ownership advantages by considering internal sourcing vs. external sourcing and location advantages by researching domestic vs. foreign sourcing. Figure 5.14 shows a matrix to help sourcing decisions. For example, if a firm has firm-specific ownership advantages in external sourcing and location advantages in a foreign location, it may consider foreign sourcing.
2. From the viewpoint of international economics, Antras and Helpman (2004) propose a classical international trade equilibrium model for global sourcing to show how firms choose between production at home and abroad and between keeping production within the firm and outsourcing it to a subcontractor.
3. From the viewpoint of transaction cost analysis (Anderson and Gatignon 1986; Klein et al. 1990), optimal location portfolios can minimize transaction costs among locations. Such an analysis can be used to identify the determinants of a global sourcing system and help "make or buy" decisions in global sourcing.

5.4.3.4 Locations in Global Value Chains
With deepening or widening global value chains, location strategy becomes more critical to an MNE's global competitive advantage (Dunning 1998). In a global value chain, a location portfolio needs to consider the following factors:
- Location attractions such as tax policy or industry policy,
- Distribution of labor, land, finance capital, and natural resources,
- Local market structure and customer differences,
- Spatial transaction costs in the global value chain,
- Geographical dispersion of created assets such as intellectual capital, organizational expertise, entrepreneurship, and interactive learning,
- The difficulty of coordinating global value chain activities,
- The benefits of forging alliances with foreign firms,
- The knowledge spillover at locations and the influence of knowledge spillover on value creation, and
- Human infrastructure, macroeconomic environment, and institutional differences among locations and countries.

		(Location)	
		Domestic sourcing	Foreign sourcing
(Service types)	Core service	More suitable.	Possibly, but it may negatively influence core competency.
	Supplementary service	Possibly, but it may reduce operational flexibility.	More suitable.

Fig. 5.15 Location decisions in global service operations

5.4.4 Location Strategy in Global Service Operations

Service businesses are going global to remain close to their customers and targeted market segments and sourcing their service activities globally (Murray and Kotabe 1999). Therefore, the location strategy becomes critical for service firms.

5.4.4.1 Location Decisions: Core Service Versus Supplementary Service

When considering the location problem in service businesses, firms typically distinguish between core and supplementary services. For example, for a hotel, the accommodation is the core service. However, a hotel may also provide supplementary services such as picking up guests from the airport, booking a train ticket, and making reservations at a local theater.

Typically, a service firm will provide its core service by itself or through domestic sourcing. If a firm outsources its core service to foreign locations, it risks negatively influencing its core competency (see Fig. 5.15). On the contrary, if a service firm provides a supplementary service internally, it risks a reduction in operational flexibility.

5.4.4.2 Location Decisions: Public Service Versus Private Service

At the operational level, location problems are often formulated as a spatial resource allocation paradigm, where one or multiple servers work for a spatially distributed set of demands. The objective is to locate servers or to design their response districts to optimize spatially dependent objectives such as minimizing service response time, minimizing travel time and cost, and maximizing the total revenue of networks by maximizing covered demand. In this paradigm, we classify the application into public and private applications (see Table 5.7).

In public services, typical research considers public service systems (e.g., policy and fire departments, taxicab fleets, outpatient clinics, ambulances) that dispatch vehicles from fixed facility locations and finds that (1) the location of the facilities and (2) the design of their response districts minimize average response time in the face of spatially distributed demand patterns (see Larson and Stevenson 1972).

In private services, typical research considers the locations of providers. For example, Psaraftis et al. (1986) study the problem of locating appropriate cleanup capability to respond to oil spills and allocating such providers in locations that have a high potential for oil spills. Another type of research focuses on customer

Table 5.7 Global service locations problems in the spatial resource allocation paradigm

	Application (examples)	Reference (examples)	Basic problems
Public services	Urban services	Larson and Stevenson (1972)	Considering urban service systems, this problem finds that location of the facilities and design of their response districts minimize average response time
	Emergency services	Fitzsimmons (1973)	This research may be used to find the deployment of ambulances that minimizes mean response time
Private services	Bank branches	Hopmans (1986)	This paper studies the distribution of customer accounts across branches, considering the attraction of branches and a distance decay function
	Oil spill cleanup providers	Psaraftis et al. (1986)	The paper studies the problem of locating cleanup providers to respond to oil spills

spatial distribution. To plan and design the branch network of Rabobank Group, Hopmans (1986) develops a spatial interaction model for the distribution of current Rabobank customer accounts over branches, considering the attraction of branches and a distance decay function.

5.4.4.3 RBV for the Location Problem in Global Services

According to RBV, location can be a VRIO service resource and provide a source of competitive advantage. For example, the Apple Retail Store is a self-owned chain of retail stores for computers and consumer electronics. The locations of 378 Apple stores worldwide are typically in downtown areas of metropolises, close to customers. In particular, Apple has built flagship stores in high-profile locations in metropolises such as Paris, London, Chicago, Shanghai, Tokyo, Hong Kong, Amsterdam, Barcelona, Beijing, Munich, and Sydney. The largest Apple store is on Fifth Avenue, New York. Each Apple store is designed to satisfy the needs of the location and the regulatory authorities. Location is a VRIO resource that is used to provide unique services and establish competitive advantage for the firm.

5.4.5 Location Strategy in Global R&D

5.4.5.1 Locations of Global R&D Units

Before determining the locations of global technology activities, it is important to identify the objectives of R&D sites. Kummerle (1997) categorizes R&D sites into two types by their main objectives (see Table 5.8).

One type of R&D is termed "home-based augmenting", which aims to extract knowledge from local competitors and universities around the world. In such cases, information flows from foreign laboratories to a centralized lab unit in the home country are of essential importance. Kuemmerle (1997) argues that some of the key determinants for the location of global R&D units of the "home-based augmenting"

Table 5.8 Types of R&D locations (Kummerle 1997)

Types	Objectives	Information flow
Home based-augmenting sites	To extract knowledge from competitors and the local scientific community	From foreign laboratories to a centralized lab unit in the home country
Home-based exploiting sites	To commercialize knowledge	From the central lab at home to foreign laboratories

Fig. 5.16 Geographic distribution–quality innovation relation (Lahiri 2010)

kind are the availability of technological resources and the strength of intellectual property protection offered.

By contrast, "home-based exploiting" is established to hold up manufacturing facilities in foreign countries or to adapt standard products to demand (Kuemmerle 1996). Information flows from the central lab at home to foreign laboratories around the world are of key significance here. The locations of these kinds of R&D facilities are around important markets and manufacturing facilities so that new products can be rapidly commercialized.

5.4.5.2 Geographic Distribution–Innovation Quality Relation

Lahiri (2010) presents the relation between geographical distribution and innovation quality. The curve follows an inverse U-shape (see Fig. 5.16). Quality of innovation increases with geographical distribution (see the beginning part of the curve in Fig. 5.16) until it peaks, immediately followed by an inflection point. Then, coordination costs between facilities and additional costs linked with risk avoiding make the innovation not worth the investment in large distributed R&D activities. This theory is useful to determine the level of geographic distribution and number of R&D locations.

5.4.6   Location Strategy in Sustainable Global Operations

Sustainable global operations provide a completely new way of viewing location strategy. Such operations are important for location strategy since they provide new application backgrounds.

5.4.6.1 Selecting Environmentally Friendly Locations

First, facility location and manufacturing network must consider environmental problems. Shougang Group, one of largest steel manufacturing groups in China, moved away from Beijing before the 2008 Olympic Games as steel manufacturing seriously affected the environment in Beijing. Likewise, residents in Hong Kong protested against the location selection of the Dayawan nuclear station for environment reasons.

Second, considering rising energy use and carbon emissions from transportation, environmentally friendly strategies have more place in procurement, long distance distribution, and highly dispersed production. For example, Olam, headquartered in Singapore, is a processor of agricultural products and food, sourcing 20 products in 65 countries. It opened local processing plants in Africa to reduce shipping costs and carbon emissions from Africa to other countries.

5.4.6.2 Selecting Locations for Social Value

Many companies choose to operate in developing regions to help local development. For example, VisionSpring chooses locations in the developing world to sell affordable eyeglasses, while the Grameen Bank chooses rural areas and villages to provide small loans to the impoverished and women.

5.4.6.3 Developing Local Social Value

Sustainable global operations strategies consider building local communities and contributing to local cluster development by developing local suppliers, boosting local transportation services, and improving the local business environment. For example, Nestlé built new agricultural and logistics firms in coffee regions to improve location production and development.

Case Example: IBM

IBM, driven by the growing global connectedness of economies, enterprises, and societies, is building global research, service, and production networks. In the process of globalization, its locations are changing to capture the new global opportunities appearing in foreign markets.

As IBM conducts R&D and sells products and services on a global scale, its location strategy considers factors such as new talent bases, centers for shared services and production facilities, proximity to markets, languages spoken, culture and the political environment, and low costs. Table 5.9 shows several IBM research locations, which are either in world-class science and technology areas (San Jose, Haifa, and Dublin) and talent bases (Beijing, Delhi, and Bangalore) or in valuable marketplaces (Europe and China).

IBM used to mostly be located in developed countries but now follows emerging markets. For example, IBM offices have recently been set up in Bangalore, Buenos Aires, Krakow, and Shanghai. Location strategy is closely associated with the outsourcing strategy of IBM. In recent years, it has been offshoring jobs from North America and Europe to developing countries.

Table 5.9 Locations of IBM research centers

Established time	Location	Focus
1955	Almaden, San Jose, CA, the US	Computer science, database, user interface, web software, storage systems software and technology, physical sciences, materials science, nanotechnology, life sciences, services research
1961	Watson, NY and MA, the US	Computer science, database, data mining, business intelligence, user interface, storage systems software, materials science, nanotechnology, life sciences, services research, mathematics
1956	Zurich, Switzerland	Nanoscience and technology, semiconductor technology, IT security and privacy, business optimization, services research
1972	Haifa, Israel	Healthcare and life sciences, cloud computing and virtualization, information retrieval, business transformation
1995	Beijing, China	Business integration and transformation, information and knowledge management
1998	Delhi and Bangalore, India	Speech technologies, pervasive computing, e-governance, information management, e-commerce, life sciences
2010	Dublin, Ireland	Smarter Cities, intelligent urban and environmental systems, real-time systems for sustainable energy

IBM builds a vast global network of service delivery, with 200,000 service employees worldwide and nearly 80,000 in India. Its lower costs of labor and capital give the company a strategic advantage compared with firms operating only in higher-cost countries.

Case Questions

1. Why did IBM choose to relocate jobs to developing countries?
2. Discuss the R&D location strategy of IBM.
3. What are the advantages and disadvantages of the location strategy of IBM's global network of service delivery?

5.5   Global Dynamic Capacity Management

5.5.1   Introduction to Global Dynamic Capacity Management

Global dynamic capacity management examines the evolution of capacity over time on a global scale. Dynamic capabilities can renew competences to achieve congruence with the changing business environment (Teece et al. 1997). The dynamic capabilities theory extends RBV by addressing how VRIO resources can be refreshed in changing environments (Ambrosini and Bowma 2009).

At the level of operations strategy, global dynamic capacity management handles operational problems such as the capacity timing and capacity expansion

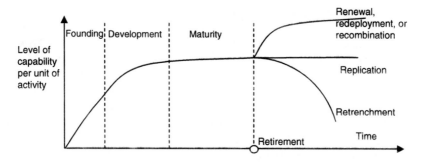

Fig. 5.17 An example of Helfat and Peteraf's (2003) capability lifecycle

problems. The capacity timing problem refers to a decision about time when a company should increase or reduce resources. The capacity expansion and contraction problem refers to decisions on resource sizes, locations, and types over a finite or infinite horizon with uncertain demand.

5.5.2 Dynamic Capacity and Capability Lifecycles

It is crucial to understand the capability lifecycle before deciding on dynamic capabilities. Helfat and Peteraf (2003) propose the concept of the capability lifecycle, which describes a general pattern and trajectory, to characterize the evolution of capabilities over time. There are differences between the capability lifecycle and the product lifecycle, since capabilities may support multiple products, and a capability may pass through multiple stages before decline.

Figure 5.17 shows an example (not all firms follow the same curve and trajectory) of Helfat and Peteraf's (2003) capability lifecycle, which includes the following stages:

1. Founding stage. In this stage, a firm begins to create a capability for its strategic objective.
2. Development stage. By comparing alternatives and combined with accumulation over time, a firm develops capabilities to keep alignment with corporate and business strategy.
3. Maturity stage. In this stage, capability maintenance is an important activity.
4. Branches. The factors from either within or outside the firm can change the current trajectory of capabilities development and may lead to one or several types among the following six capability branches: renewal, redeployment, recombination, replication, retrenchment, and retirement.

5.5.3 Dynamic Capacity Models

In previous sections, most of the discussed problems are static over time. Dynamic capacity problems consider decisions over time. A dynamic capacity model is used to solve capacity expansion problems (for classical surveys, see Manne 1967; Luss 1982). To improve its competitive position, a firm may consider capacity expansion while also trying to avoid overcapacity, typically given a pattern of demand over time, and the main objective is to minimize the expected cost in the expansion process. The major decisions include:
1. Optimal capacity sizes over time,
2. Optimal capacity types over time,
3. Optimal capacity expansion locations over time.

Global operations are particularly associated with the location factor in different regions and countries, and we classify the problems into one-region, two-region, and multi-region problems (we use term "region" following Fong and Srinivasan 1981). The installed capacity may have an infinite or a finite economic life. We summarize the models in Table 5.10.

Case Example: Yahoo and Google

Yahoo was founded in 1994, and was a pioneer in the Internet business. At that time, when there were few competitors, it was easy to reach a significant amount of users. In the mid-1990s, most Internet companies thought searching was only a way to bring in users, and just one of the many services that surfers would use on a website. Yahoo did not regard search engines as the most important strategic resource.

Google started in 1996 as a research project. At first glance, it was difficult to compete with Yahoo, which was well-established. One of Google's principles is "do only one thing and do it well". Unlike Yahoo's multiple service areas, Google focused on its search engine business.

An Internet firm Overture changed all Internet business by selling the rights to the keywords of a web search on a cost-per-click basis. In 2000, Google learned from the Overture business model and began to sell advertisement associated with search keywords. Google patented its Internet search technology and improved search performance.

Although Yahoo entered the Internet market early, it did not invest in patentable technology for search engines. Yahoo mainly outsourced its search business to other companies. In 2001, Yahoo search was powered by Inktomi and then powered by Google. After realizing the importance of the search business, Yahoo bought Inktomi in 2002, bought Overture in 2003, and then dumped Google and powered itself in 2004 (see Fig. 5.18).

According to Netmarketshare's data in 2012, the market share of Google is 86 % and the second player Yahoo only 7 % in the search engine business. While Yahoo obtained advantages by being a pioneer in the Internet business, Google became the final winner.

Table 5.10 Dynamic capacity models

	Horizon	Reference	Basic problem
One region	Infinite horizon	Manne (1961)	This research uses a diffusion process to show that the expected discounted cost and optimal expansion sizes over an infinite horizon increase when the uncertainty of demand increases
	Finite horizon	Wagner and Whitin (1958), Zangwill (1968, 1969)	Considering expansion cost and the holding cost of excess capacity, the objective is to find the expansion policy to minimize the total discounted costs in the finite horizon. The problem can be formulated as a dynamic programming problem or be applied by a network flow approach to solve
Two regions	Infinite horizon	Manne (1967), Erlenkotter (1967)	The capacity in one location can be used to satisfy demand in another location. Considering transportation and capacity expansion costs, the problem can use integer programming or dynamic programming to find the expansion policy
	Finite horizon	Fong and Rao (1975), Luss (1979)	The problem can use network flow representation or dynamic programming to find the expansion policy within a finite horizon
Multiple regions	Infinite horizon	Erlenkotter (1975)	With a continuous time scale and infinite horizon, this research uses incomplete dynamic programming to solve a problem with linear demand
	Finite horizon	Fong and Srinivasan (1981)	With a discrete time scale and finite horizon, this research determines a facility expansion schedule, including the location, timing, and size of facilities planning over time, with the objective to minimize the discounted cost

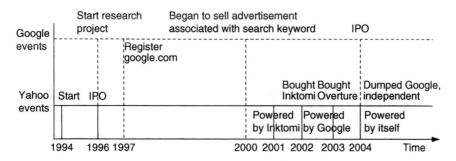

Fig. 5.18 Dynamic events: Google vs. Yahoo

Case Questions

1. While Google has always regarded its search engine as a core capability, before 2004 Yahoo outsourced its search business. Evaluate the outsourcing strategy of Yahoo.
2. Yahoo bought Inktomi in 2002 and Overture in 2003. Yahoo search was powered by Inktomi in 2001, then Google, and itself (see Fig. 5.18). Discuss the dynamic resource strategy of Yahoo.
3. Evaluate the timing strategy of Yahoo in the search business.
4. Inktomi, Overture, Yahoo, and Google use different search engines. Discuss the capability lifecycles of each.

Case: Carrefour Expansion in China

Carrefour is the first foreign retailer to operate in China. When the Chinese government had only partially opened the retail sector in 1995, Carrefour entered China with a joint venture in which it held the majority share. The first hypermarket was opened in Beijing.

At that time, joint ventures had to be approved by the central government in China, and only three outlets could be opened in each of the approved cities. Carrefour convinced local governments that it would create employment opportunities in their regions, generate taxes for the governments, and help in the development of the regions, expanding its operations quickly into different cities.

In 2001, the State Economic and Trade Commission carried out an investigation into Carrefour's expansion. Carrefour was accused of not respecting the government's stipulations regarding the ownership stake in retail joint ventures and the number of stores in each city, and was ordered to suspend expansion in the country.

Carrefour tried to persuade the central government to believe its expansion was beneficial to the country. After months of work, the company was allowed to continue its expansion. Carrefour formed one holding company for each of its local subsidiaries and transferred a stake of its ownership in its three hypermarkets to two local partners.

After China joined the WTO, these restrictions on the number of outlets that foreign retailers could operate per city were lifted and foreign retailers were allowed to have 100 % ownership. Carrefour began to invest to acquire complete ownership of its Chinese stores. Since then, Carrefour has maintained solid growth (see Table 5.11). As of June 2012, Carrefour China had 208 hypermarkets in 64 Chinese cities, employing more than 58,000 people. For Carrefour, China is one of its most profitable countries.

In terms of both market share and sales, Carrefour is more successful than all of its foreign rivals including Walmart in China. As the first world-class retailer

Table 5.11   Carrefour expansion in China

Time	Event
1995	Carrefour started its first hypermarket in mainland China
1996	Entered Shanghai and Shenzhen
2002	Built headquarters of global purchasing in Shanghai
2003	Carrefour opened its first discounter store (Diya discounter)
2004	Carrefour introduced the supermarket format (Champion supermarket)
The end of 2004	The restrictions on foreign retailers were lifted and Carrefour invested to acquire complete ownership of its Chinese stores
2007	Built online shopping website
2012	By June 2012, Carrefour China had opened 208 hypermarkets

Table 5.12   Comparison of Carrefour and Walmart in China

	Carrefour	Walmart
Expansion method	Primarily organic expansion	Acquisition and organic expansion
Retailing format	Hypermarket, discounter, and supermarket	Focus on hypermarket
Product variety	More local responsive to different regions	More unified variety across regions
Logistics strategy	Decentralized logistics systems	Nationwide distribution networks based on centralized distribution center

in China, Carrefour introduced advanced operational experiences, administration systems, and retailing skills to local retailers. Domestic retail managers call Carrefour the "retailing Godfather in China".

Table 5.12 compares Carrefour and Walmart. Basically, the advantage of Carrefour is its local responsiveness to different regions in China and its understanding of the social, cultural and economic differences among Chinese. To achieve local responsiveness and create internal heterogeneity, Carrefour adopted a decentralized management structure where each store operates with a degree of freedom, multiple formats including hypermarkets, discounters, and supermarkets provide for different Chinese customers, and decentralized logistics systems support local responsiveness.

In the process of expansion, Carrefour highlights the importance of location strategy. Its principles on location are as follows.

- Carrefour principle. If possible, it always tries to be located at a *carrefour* (crossroad in French).
- Eight kilometer radius principle. Carrefour chooses the location based on the purchasing power of the people within eight kilometer bus ride.
- Independent investigation principle. Before opening new stores, it sends two independent investigation companies to conduct a detailed study of the store location to assess the purchasing potential and habits of local people.

- Flexible principle. Usually, Carrefour only occupies two floors of a business complex. It can be located on the underground floor and fourth and fifth floors, although it prefers the first and second floors.

Case Questions

1. What are the drivers for Carrefour to enter and expand in China?
2. How did Carrefour choose locations to set up its stores?
3. What problems did Carrefour meet in its early expansion in China?
4. Why is Carrefour more successful than its foreign rivals?

References

Ambrosini, V., & Bowma, C. (2009). What are dynamic capabilities and are they a useful construct in strategic management? *International Journal of Management Reviews, 11*(1), 29–49.

Anderson, E., & Gatignon, H. (1986). Modes of foreign entry: A transaction cost analysis and propositions. *Journal of International Business Studies, 17*, 1–26.

Antras, P., & Helpman, E. (2004). Global sourcing. *Journal of Political Economy, 112*(3), 552–580.

Barney, J. B. (1991). Firm resources and sustained competitive advantage. *Journal of Management, 17*, 99–120.

Barney, J. B., & Hesterly, W. S. (2010). VRIO framework. In *Strategic management and competitive advantage* (pp. 68–86). New Jersey: Pearson.

Brandeau, M. L., & Chiu, S. S. (1989). An overview of representative problems in location research. *Management Science, 35*(6), 645–674.

Chandler, A. D., Jr. (1966). *Strategy and structure*. New York: Doubleday/Anchor Books Edition.

Choi, K., Narasimhanb, R., & Kim, S. W. (2012). Postponement strategy for international transfer of products in a global supply chain: A system dynamics examination. *Journal of Operations Management, 30*, 167–179.

Collis, D., & Montgomery, C. A. (1995). Competing on resources: Strategy in the 1990s. *Harvard Business Review, 73*, 118–128.

Dunning, J. H. (1977). Trade, location of economic activity and the MNE: A search for an eclectic approach. In B. Ohlin, P.-O. Hesselborn, & P. M. Wijkman (Eds.), *The international allocation of economic activity*. London: Macmillan.

Dunning, J. H. (1998). Location and the multinational enterprise: A neglected factor? *Journal of International Business Studies, 29*, 45–66.

Erlenkotter, D. (1967). Two producing areas dynamic programming solutions. In A. S. Manne (Ed.), *Investments for capacity expansion: Size, location and time-phasing* (pp. 210–227). Cambridge: MIT Press.

Erlenkotter, D. (1975). Capacity planning for large multi-location systems: Approximate and incomplete dynamic programming approach. *Management Science, 22*, 274–285.

Fine, C. H., & Freund, R. M. (1990). Optimal investment in product-flexible manufacturing capacity. *Management Science, 36*, 449–466.

Fitzsimmons, J. A. (1973). A method for emergency ambulance deployment. *Management Science, 19*, 627–636.

Fong, C. O., & Rao, M. R. (1975). Capacity expansion with two producing regions and concave costs. *Management Science, 22*, 331–339.

Fong, C. O., & Srinivasan, V. (1981). The multiregion dynamic capacity expansion problem, Part I and II. *Operations Research, 29*(4), 787–816.

Gerwin, D. (1993). Manufacturing flexibility: A strategic perspective. *Management Science, 39*(4), 395–410.

Grant, R. M. (2009). Contemporary strategy analysis. Hoboken: Wiley.

Hall, R. (1993). A framework linking intangible resources and capabilities to sustainable competitive advantage. *Strategic Management Journal, 14*(8), 607–618.

Hayes, R. H., & Wheelwright, S. C. (1984). *Restoring our competitive edge: Competing through manufacturing*. New York: Wiley.

Helfat, C. E., & Peteraf, M. A. (2003). The dynamic resource-based view: Capability lifecycles. *Strategic Management Journal, 24*(10), 997–1010. Special issue: why is there a resource-based view? toward a theory of competitive heterogeneity.

Hoopes, D. G., Madsen, T. L., & Walker, G. (2003). Guest editors' introduction to the special issue: Why is there a resource-based view? Toward a theory of competitive heterogeneity. *Strategic Management Journal, 24*, 889–902.

Hopmans, A. C. M. (1986). A spatial interaction model for branch bank accounts. *European Journal of Operational Research, 27*, 242–250.

Kazaz, B., Dada, M., & Moskowitz, H. (2005). Global production planning under exchange-rate uncertainty. *Management Science, 51*(7), 1101–1119.

Klein, S., Frazier, G. L., Roth, V. J. (1990). A transaction cost analysis model of channel integration in international markets. *Journal of Marketing Research, 27*(2), 196–208.

Kummerle, W. (1997). Building effective R&D capabilities abroad. *Harvard Business Review, 75*(2), 61–70.

Lahiri, N. (2010). Geographic distribution of R&D activity: How does it affect innovation quality? *The Academy of Management Journal, 53*(5), 1194–1209.

Larson, R. C., & Stevenson, K. A. (1972). On insensitivities in urban redistricting and facility location. *Operations Research, 20*, 595–612.

Lee, H. L., Billington, C., & Carter, B. (1993). Hewlett Packard gains control of inventory and service through design for localization. *Interfaces, 23*(4), 1–11.

Luss, H. (1979). A capacity expansion model for two facility types. *Naval Research Logistics Quarterly, 26*, 291–303.

Luss, H. (1982). Operations research and capacity expansion problems: A survey. *Operations Research, 30*(5), 907–947.

Manne, A. S. (1961). Capacity expansion and probabilistic growth. *Econometrica, 29*, 632–649.

Manne, A. S. (Ed.). (1967). *Investments for capacity expansion: Size, location and time-phasing*. Cambridge: MIT Press.

Murray, J. Y., & Kotabe, M. (1999). Sourcing strategies of U.S. service companies: A modified transaction-cost analysis. *Strategic Management Journal, 20*(9), 791–809.

Peteraf, M. A. (1993). The cornerstones of competitive advantage: A resource-based view. *Strategic Management Journal, 14*, 179–191.

Porter, M. E. (1980). *Competitive strategy*. New York: Free Press.

PricewaterhouseCoopers PwC. (2007). Production capacity management in the automotive industry: A taxing issue.

Psaraftis, H. N., Tharakan, G. G., & Ceder, A. (1986). Optimal response to oil spills: The strategic decision case. *Operations Research, 34*, 203–217.

Revelle, C. S., & Laporte, G. (1996). The plant location problem: New models and research prospects. *Operations Research, 44*(6), 864–874.

Sanchez, R. (1995). Strategic flexibility in product competition. *Strategic Management Journal, 16*, 135–159. Special Issue: Technological Transformation and the New Competitive Landscape.

Schroeder, R. G., Bates, K. A., & Junttila, M. A. (2002). A resource-based view of manufacturing strategy and the relationship to manufacturing performance. *Strategic Management Journal, 23*(2), 105–117.

Shapiro, C. (1989). The theory of business strategy. *The RAND Journal of Economics, 20*(1), 125–137.

Su, J. C. P., Chang, Y.-L., & Ferguson, M. (2005). Evaluation of postponement structures to accommodate mass customization. *Journal of Operations Management, 23*, 305–318.

Tang, C. Y., & Tikoo, S. (1999). Operational flexibility and market valuation of earnings. *Strategic Management Journal, 20*(8), 749–761.

Teece, D. J. (1980). Economics of scope and the scope of the enterprise. *Journal of Economic Behavior and Organization, 1*, 223–247.

Teece, D. J. (1982). Towards an economic theory of the multiproduct firm. *Journal of Economic Behavior and Organization, 3*, 39–63.

Teece, D. J., Pisano, G., & Shuen, A. (1997). Dynamic capabilities and strategic management. *Strategic Management Journal, 18*(7), 509–533.

Tsay, A. A. (1999). The quantity flexibility contract and supplier-customer incentives. *Management Science, 45*(10), 1339–1358.

Van Hoek, R. I. (2001). The rediscovery of postponement a literature review and directions for research. *Journal of Operations Management, 19*(2), 161–184.

Van Mieghem, J. A. (1998). Investment strategies for flexible resources. *Management Science, 44*(8), 1071–1078.

Wagner, H. M., & Whitin, T. M. (1958). Dynamic version of the economic lot size model. *Management Science, 5*, 89–96.

Weber, A. (1909) Uber den Standort der Industrien, 1909; translated as Alfred Weber's theory of the location of industries, University of Chicago, 1929.

Wernerfelt, B. (1984). A resource-based view of the firm. *Strategic Management Journal, 5*, 171–180.

Zangwill, W. I. (1968). Minimum concave cost flows in certain networks. *Management Science, 14*, 429–450.

Zangwill, W. I. (1969). A backlogging model and a multi-echelon model of a dynamic economic lot size production system-a network approach. *Management Science, 15*, 506–527.

Process-Based Fundamentals

6

- To introduce concepts of global business process, business process design, business process reengineering, business process management, to present a process-based view of GOS, and to introduce the primary processes of GOS.
- To discuss global supply chain strategy, including its concepts, global sourcing strategy, global internal supply chain strategy, global distribution strategy, global supply chain coordination, global supply chain strategic alliances, and global sustainable supply chain strategy.
- To introduce concepts of global revenue management strategy, present its globally evolving process, and discuss strategies for global revenue management.
- To discuss global technology strategy, including its concepts, global product development strategy, R&D internationalization modes, global R&D coordination and communication, global R&D sourcing strategy, and technology strategies for global sustainable operations.
- To discuss global risk management strategy, including its concepts, basic operational strategies, basic approaches and the operational risk management framework.

6.1 Introduction to Process-Based Global Operations Strategy

6.1.1 Introduction to Global Business Processes

"Processes are structured, recurrent activities that transform inputs into outputs" (Van Mieghem 2008, p. 10). Davenport and Short (1990) define process as a set of logically related tasks performed to achieve a specific business outcome. Processes

Y. Gong, *Global Operations Strategy*, Springer Texts in Business and Economics, DOI 10.1007/978-3-642-36708-3_6, © Springer-Verlag Berlin Heidelberg 2013

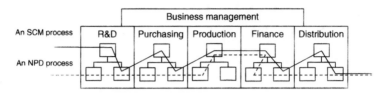

Fig. 6.1 Business process versus functional department views

can be divided into "operationally oriented process" related to products and
customers and "management oriented process" dealing with obtaining and
coordinating resources. Anupindi et al. (2012) present five elements of a process:

- Inputs and outputs,
- Flow units,
- Activity networks and buffers,
- Resources, and
- Information structure.

Most MNEs are structured into functional departments dedicated to performing
specific functions and staffed with professional personnel in specific functions.
Business processes go across these functional departments, require different skills,
and involve different talents. For example, while SCM and NPD processes go
through several internal departments, a customer may only see processes not
functions (see Fig. 6.1).

The process-based view (PBV) regards a firm as an activity network or a set of
processes to transform inputs into outputs. Global business process is a global
cross-functional and result-oriented activity network for MNEs to create values
with global material flows, cash flows and information flows. For an MNE, the
primary global operational processes are global supply chain processes, global
revenue management processes, global technology management processes, and
global risk management processes. For further readings, see (Bartlett and Ghoshal
1986; Cheng and Bolon 1993; Dunning 1995; Ghoshal 1986; Hayes et al. 2004;
Kleindorfer and Van Wassenhove 2004 Kuemmerle 1996; Lahiri 2010; Laseter
1998; Pearce 1989; Pearce 1991; Porter 1990; Vernon 1966).

6.1.2   Business Process Design

Business process design (BPD) is the method by which a firm understands and
defines the business activities to support and sustain development. The process
design includes the design of a manufacturing or service process network for
producing quality goods and services for the targeted markets or customers.
Business process design typically occurs as an early phase in projects, and BPD
activities can range from the evolutionary to the radical.

Loch (1998) builds a conceptual framework of BPD (see Fig. 6.2). The first step
of BPD is "specification" which is based on "processing network paradigm"
(Harrison 1997). Loch (1998) proposes the following basic elements in specification of an business process.

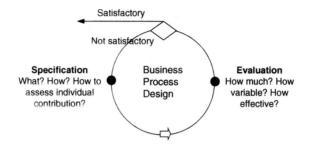

Fig. 6.2   Loch's framework of business process design

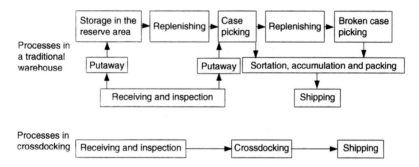

Fig. 6.3   Crossdocking: the use of modern information technology to radically redesign warehouse operational process

- Jobs. They are the entities (e.g., orders, projects, and transactions) made up of tasks and flows through a process.
- Tasks. They are activities or operations.
- Precedence constraints. Tasks are connected by precedence relations.
- Resources. They are operational units to execute the tasks.
- Flow management protocols. Protocols specify the route, sequence, rules for resources to execute tasks, and may be based on system status information such as the location of jobs, the product information, and logistics capacity status.
- Incentives. A manager needs a system of assessing individual contributions for long-term development.

Figure 6.3 presents process networks for a traditional warehouse and a crossdock by Harrison and Loch's conceptual framework. In this example, jobs are customer orders from suppliers to stores, tasks are depicted by the box, and precedence constraints are denoted by arrows. These three elements describe what the process should complete. A warehouse use resources, warehousing flow management protocols, and warehouse system status information to determine how to perform warehousing activities.

The second step of BPD is to evaluate resource consumption rate and utilization, the variability on performance, and the effectiveness in terms of response time, cost, quality and service levels. The BPD could be a repeated cycle until the evaluation shows the process performance is satisfactory.

6.1.3 Business Process Reengineering

Business Process Reengineering (BPR) is fundamental management thinking about radical redesign of a business process to obtain dramatic and sustained improvements in business performance. Hammer (1990) defines reengineering as "the use of modern information technology to radically redesign business process". Hammer and Champy (1993) propose the concept of BPR and point out two distinct elements of BPR:

- Reintegration of industrial work, reversing the trend of specialization and division of labor from industrial revolution, and
- Radical change, different from incremental or evolutionary process improvement.

Figure 6.2 uses crossdocking as an example to explain the use of modern information technology to radically redesign warehouse operational process. Crossdocking managers identify a non-value-added activity, storage, in traditional warehouses, and redesign the activity network with abilities to unload goods from incoming vehicles, sort the goods, and load these goods directly to outbound trucks, trailers, or rail cars, with little or no storage in crossdocking (Bartholdi and Gue 2004). This BPR is supported by the application of IT. For example, Walmart implements crossdocking through an advanced satellite telecommunication network, which can send point of sale (POS) data directly to 4,000 vendors and sales information to Walmart headquarters and distribution centers. Cross-docking can streamline the supply chain process, reduce warehousing costs, decrease inventory, and speed the distribution to customers.

A typical process reengineering life cycle includes six stages (Guha et al. 1993):

- Envisioning a reengineering project through securing commitment from senior management, identifying reengineering opportunities, identifying enabling technologies, and aligning with competitive strategy,
- Getting started through building the reengineering team and setting performance goals,
- Diagnosing process pathologies,
- Redesigning by exploring alternative designs, designing new processes, designing the human resources, building prototypes, and selecting an IT platform,
- Reorganizing activities through IT platform, and
- Measuring the configured process.

6.1.4 Business Process Management

Not all companies are suitable to implement radical BPR. Increasing companies adopted the concept of business process management (BPM), which could be

Fig. 6.4 The steps of BPM

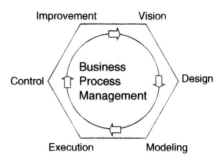

radical or evolutionary, dependent on their competitive strategies and environments. BPR activities can be grouped into six steps: vision, design, modeling, execution, control, and improvement (Fig. 6.4).

- Vision. BPM firstly builds process management vision based on competitive strategy.
- Design. Process design encompasses the identification of existing processes and the design of new processes.
- Modeling. Modeling conducts the theoretical design and introduces combinations of variables.
- Execution. A firm can execute BPM by developing or purchasing an application or using a combination of software and human power.
- Control. A firm needs to collect status information and statistic data on the performance for one or more processes.
- Improvement. Evolutionary process improvement includes optimizing existing process framework, identifying bottlenecks, finding improvement opportunities. When evolutionary improvement cannot lead to desired outputs and performance, the firm can reengineer the entire business process.

6.1.5   Global Business Processes and Competencies

Resource-based view studies who or what provide competitive advantages and process-based view studies how to provide competitive advantages. By global operational process management, a firm can improve operational performance of processes in three process flow dimensions: flow time, flow rate, and inventory (Anupindi et al. 2012), and can further achieve operational competencies:

- Global process cost. A firm can reduce the total cost in input processes such as purchasing, transforming processes such as manufacturing and service, and output processes such as shipping.
- Global process flow time. A firm can reduce the total throughput time by decreasing flow time in each process or optimizing the process structure.
- Global process flexibility. Global process management can make contribution to time or variety flexibility of a firm.

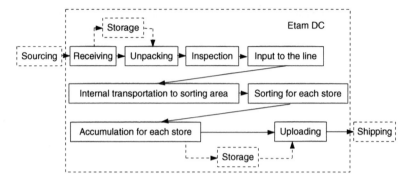

Fig. 6.5 Operational processes in Etam DC

- Global process quality. Total quality management can be combined with all processes to make quality products or deliver quality service.
- Global process revenue. By increasing the added value associated with each process, a firm can increase global process revenue.
- Global process social and environmental values. An MNE can achieve social and environmental values in global processes such as purchasing, manufacturing, packaging, and shipping.

Case Example: Etam Distribution Center

The Etam Group (www.etamgroep.nl) is a Dutch clothing company, with its headquarters and distribution center (DC) in Zoetermeer, the Netherlands. The Etam Group includes two retailers, Miss Etam and Promiss, and a service company, with 185 stores and 2,400 employees.

In garment industry, the rapid response towards fashion trends is the key to its success. To speed distribution and improve warehousing productivity, Etam builds an advanced DC of clothing with a surface 36,000 m^2 in three floors. Its Zoetermeer complex facility integrates a modern DC, the planning departments, goods administration, and quality assurance to improve operational efficiency. This DC has discarded processes in traditional clothing warehouses and taken the advantage of automation systems, barcode systems, clothing hanging systems, and WMS (Warehouse Management System), to make a fundamental process improvement (see Fig. 6.5). Etam has moved from a push distribution process by supplying stores with predetermined bulk allocations of garments, to a pull process started by stores' garment reorder request to replenish their inventories.

The inputs of warehousing process are products from different suppliers by trucks. Traditional warehouses handle clothing with packages, but Etam DC handles clothing in a hanging status. With WMS, Etam can know the location of individual article in each SKU (stock keeping unit) at any time, which is helpful to reduce order picking and sorting time. After quality and quantity inspection and checking that the specification of the garments matches the barcoded tag, hanging garments are transferred to trolleys suspended from the monorail and manually guided to appropriate stock locations. DC uses automatic sorting equipment to sort all incoming goods, and accumulate goods in the channel dedicated to each store. In the garment industry, shipping unit is called a "hanging set" including different garments. The hanging sets are then transferred to the despatch area for bagging, and computer system will calculate the precise quantity of standard protective garment shipping bags for each shipment. Finally hanging sets are loaded to road transport vehicles and shipped to each store.

DC can deliver goods in the same evening or the next morning, the turnaround time of orders is less than 24 hours. The productivity is high and each day DC can deliver 140,000 pieces. Coordinated with quality control department, DC has taken preventive steps to monitor quality in warehousing processes.

(Note: Multi-media teaching material available for this case)

Case Questions

1. Identify and analyze warehousing process' five elements (Anupindi et al. 2012) for Etam DC.
2. How has Etam DC used processes to achieve competencies?

6.2 Global Supply Chain Strategy

6.2.1 Introduction to Global Supply Chain Strategy

6.2.1.1 Concept

Supply chains have been expanding beyond borders with increasing competitive pressures, reducing trade barriers, advances in transportation and communication technologies, and the emergence of new marketplaces. In the process of globalization, supply chains encounter risks like currency exchange rate variability, economic and political instability, and changes in the regulatory environment. These benefits and risks from the globalization process bring new resources and constraints for supply chain strategy, which requires the development of a systematic concept of a "global supply chain strategy". We define global supply chain strategy (GSCS) as

> A consistent pattern of structural, infrastructural, and integration strategic decisions in a global competitive environment, considering benefits and risks of global operations and incorporating information, material, and cash flows between suppliers and end customers, to determine the role of each supply chain entity and process of the global supply chain system to achieve a set of competencies aligned with business strategy.

GSCS makes strategic decisions including locations and the structure of global manufacturing and warehousing facilities, making versus buying of products, modes of distribution from manufacturing plants to customers, supply chain coordination modes, approaches to supply chain integration, supply chain organizational relationships, and sustainable issues.

6.2.1.2 Taxonomy

Global supply chain strategy (GSCS) can be classified with different perspectives:

- Upstream versus downstream

  GSCS includes global sourcing strategies mainly handling upstream supply chain activities with a focus on suppliers, and global distribution strategy mainly handling downstream supply chain activities with a focus on distribution and customers. GSCS includes three supply chain macro processes: supplier relationship management (SRM) dealing with the interface between the MNE and its suppliers; internal supply chain management (ISCM) internal to the MNE; and customer relationship management (CRM) dealing with the interface between the MNE and its customers.

- Operational competency

  In a global environment, a firm mainly needs to choose between a "low cost global supply chain" to reduce total landed cost and a "responsive global supply chain" to improve customer satisfaction. Some firms use mass customization and postponement to build a "flexible global supply chain". For timely and flexible satisfaction of customer demand, firms can build an "agile global supply chain".

- Push versus pull

  An MNE can establish a "push-based GSCS" including speculative processes initiated in anticipation of customer orders or forecasted demand, or a "pull-based GSCS" including reactive processes in response to customer orders. Some MNEs use a "push-pull GSCS" consisting of both push processes linked with raw material suppliers and pull processes linked with end customers, and need to identify the push/pull boundary, that is, the interface between push-based and pull-based stages.

- Process cycle

  A GSCS includes five stages: supplier, manufacturer, distributor, retailer, and customer, and determines decisions in four cycle processes performing at the interface between two successive stages: the procurement cycle between suppliers and manufacturers, the manufacturing cycle between manufacturers and distributors, the replenishment cycle between distributors and retailers, and the customer order cycle between retailers and customers.

- Production versus marketing

  An MNE can build a production-based GSCS, determining manufacturing strategies among make-to-order, make-to-stock and assemble-to-order, timing strategies including postponement vs. speculation, and manufacturing processes including job shop vs. flow shop. A marketing-based GSCS, or "global demand chain management", thinks that demand fulfillment should remain aligned with demand creation, considers purchasing behavior and market segmentation, and determines products including functional vs. innovative products (see Fisher 1997).

- Organization

  From the organization structure's viewpoint, a firm can build a flat supply chain, supply chain networks, or a multi-tier supply chain. From the ownership's viewpoint, a firm can consider wholly owned subsidiaries, joint venture subsidiaries for some supply chain activities, interorganizational partnerships, or arm's-length transaction relationships.

- Contracts
  From the financial and legal viewpoint, an MNE considers various supply chain contracts for strategic components including buy-back, revenue-sharing, quantity flexibility, and sales rebate contracts, and contracts for non-strategic components including long-term contracts, flexibility contracts, spot purchase, and portfolio contracts.

6.2.2   Global Sourcing Strategies

The "purchasing" department previously served as clerical support for the business units, with the primary function of sending suppliers their purchases. In the 1980s, many companies began to consider outside suppliers and used a "sourcing strategy", linking purchasing with other functions. In the 1990s companies used cross-functional "global sourcing strategies" to cut costs during the process of globalization.

Global sourcing strategies are upstream or supplier-side strategies, and should consider downstream strategies, global distribution strategies to establish a balanced overall supply chain. Global sourcing manages the logistics to serve specific production units for a particular market, and serve components suppliers for specific production, and integrate R&D, manufacturing, purchasing, and marketing. Global sourcing strategy is intended to determine appropriate supply relationships for supply chain activities, including strategic decisions on "insourcing versus outsourcing", "make versus buy", "domestic versus offshore sourcing", and strategic supplier relation management.

- Insourcing versus outsourcing
  While insourcing is a global supply chain strategy with an internal relationship, outsourcing uses an external organization to supply. A company seeks outsourcing for two reasons: dependency for capacity, where the company can make products but chooses to extend its capacity through a supplier, and dependency for knowledge, where the company has no skills to make the products. The decomposable items are more suitable for outsourcing because of easy outsourcing implementation. Fine and Whitney (1996) see the outsourcing decision as depending on whether one seeks knowledge or capacity and whether the item is easily decomposed (see Fig. 6.6).

- Domestic sourcing versus offshore sourcing
  From a locational point of view, an MNE can purchase parts and finished products domestically, called "domestic sourcing" or from abroad, called "offshore sourcing". A firm uses a global sourcing strategy to exploit both its own and its suppliers' competitive advantage and its location's comparative advantage in the global marketplace.

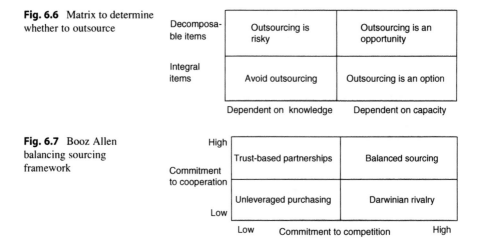

Fig. 6.6 Matrix to determine whether to outsource

Fig. 6.7 Booz Allen balancing sourcing framework

- Cooperation versus competition

  Tim Laseter wrote the book "Balanced Sourcing: Cooperation and Competition in Supplier Relationships" while a Vice President at Booz Allen in 1998 to establish the "balanced sourcing" concept and describe a methodology for developing cooperative relationships with suppliers and simultaneously achieving the required cost savings (see Fig. 6.7).

  Some supply chains focus only on cooperation but overlook competitive pricing, and this approach without aggressive motivation leads to stagnation in the supply base and "trust-based partnerships" that do not provide a clear incentive to drive improvement and deliver optimal results. Other supply chains focus only on competitive pricing but overlook cooperation and concern with supplier profitability, leaving suppliers in a "Darwinian rivalry". A few companies just regard sourcing as purchasing processing by clerks or expediters, leading to "unleveraged purchasing".

  Booz Allen suggested that "balanced sourcing", which fully leverages supplier capabilities, including a reasonable profit for suppliers and lowering the cost for buyers, drives improvement at both customer and supplier levels, and targets long-term sourcing relationships.

6.2.3 Global Internal Supply Chain Strategy

Internal supply chains (ISC) focus on operations internal to the MNE, including all internal processes involved in designing, producing, and distributing for customer orders. An ISC can go global with organic growth when building internal subsidiaries worldwide. A global internal supply chain strategy is the basis of the global supply chain strategy.

6.2.3.1 Globalization of Manufacturing

There are different theories to explain the globalization of manufacturing. Based on the OLI framework, Ethier (1986) explains and predicts the emergence of MNEs

Fig. 6.8 Ethier's theory of manufacturing globalization

Information asymmetry	Risky	Profitable
Information symmetry	Feasible	Unnecessary if no other consideration
	Stay domestic	Go global

due to internalization advantages, and presents a global manufacturing equilibrium model for a vertically integrated firm with three stages of production: research, upstream production and downstream production (see Fig. 6.8). Ethier's theory focuses on the relation between the uncertainty of research outcomes and incentives to internalize. Due to information asymmetry preventing verification of research efforts and products, research and upstream firms often choose to internalize their downstream operations.

6.2.3.2 Global Supply Chain Networks

The design of global supply chain networks has a long-term influence on the performance of a global supply chain and considers the following decision problems:

- Strategic role of facilities in global supply chain
  An MNE should specify the strategic role of each facility and determine the supply chain configuration. For example, Haier built manufacturing facilities to acquire marketing and administration knowledge in the US, created strategic leverage for the future, and won competitive advantage over rivals.
- Manufacturing and warehousing facility location
  Facilities require large and irreversible investment, and the selection of their location is critical for global supply chain strategy. Considering the marketplace, cost factors, the transportation situation, tariff duties, currency exchange rates, corporate income tax, workforce availability, and the industrial environment of locations, appropriate facility location can help build various global supply chains: cost-efficient, responsive, agile or lean.
- Capacity allocation and networks structure
  Allocation of appropriate capacity to a facility can avoid both over- and under-capacity at that facility. Centralization versus decentralization is another major decision in capacity allocation. While a centralized warehousing or manufacturing facility system can reduce scale-related cost and pool risks, a decentralized system can respond rapidly to the local markets. A global supply chain network should determine localization versus standardization of locations, and decide to what extent the processes at various locations should be different. While a localized design can improve customer satisfaction, standardization can improve productivity, achieve economies of scale, and build a capacity pool to achieve flexibility.

- The market served by each facility
  A global ISC strategy determines the marketplace served by each facility, considering scale and the variety a facility can provide. A facility also needs to examine the distance to the market and improve its responsiveness.
- The supply required to feed each facility
  A global ISC strategy considers the raw material and component suppliers to feed a manufacturing facility and feed finished products to a warehousing facility. An optimal supply allocation can improve the cost, responsiveness, and flexibility competencies of a facility.

6.2.4 Global Distribution Strategies

After manufacturing, an MNE needs to formulate a global distribution strategy to store and transport the products to end customers. While most MNEs choose warehousing as their global distribution strategy, an increasing number of MNEs are considering newer strategies like cross-docking and direct shipping.

- Warehousing
  Although some firms propagandize their "zero inventory" strategy, most manufacturing firms need inventory and warehouses to better the supply to customer demand, consolidate products, pool inventory risks, reduce transportation costs and time, and provide value-added processing. Warehousing is a traditional distribution strategy in which goods are received by warehouses and stored in tanks, pallet racks or on shelves, then moved on to retailers.
    An important decision is about centralized versus decentralized warehousing. With a centralized distribution system, an MNE can achieve risk pooling and low cost, but will suffer from a long lead time from the distribution center to customers. A decentralized system will have a high cost but short lead time. While Walmart has built two large-scale centralized distribution centers in China, Carrefour China has built many decentralized distribution centers to rapidly respond to local customers in different regions.
- Cross-docking
  Cross-docking (just in time distribution) is a relatively new distribution facility in which incoming shipments are sorted, consolidated with other products and transferred directly to outgoing trailers without intermediate storage or order picking. For example, Walmart uses cross-docking to distribute fast-moving products, perishable products, large-volume products, or high-value products in the US.
- Direct shipping
  Following a direct shipment strategy, an MNE ships goods directly from the manufacturer to the end-users without storing them in warehouses. This strategy is mainly for difficult-to-handle products, non-assortment products, customers with large volume demand, and products with a very short life cycle.

Fig. 6.9 The Stan Shih smiling curve in the global supply chain

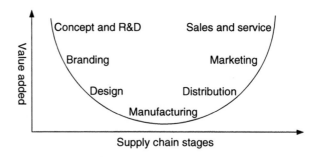

6.2.5 Global Supply Chain Coordination

6.2.5.1 Smiling Curve Effect

In the 1990s, Stan Shih, the founder of Acer, an IT company headquartered in Taiwan, proposed the concept of the "smiling curve", an illustration of the value-added potentials of different supply chain stages in the IT industry (see Fig. 6.9). He observed that firms can create higher values at the end of the value chain than at the middle. Based on this concept, Acer has retreated from manufacturing, and focused on services, R&D and brands. Many global supply chains including the Apple-Foxconn supply chain have verified the "smiling curve": while Apple enjoys high profits from design and branding, Foxconn gets a small part of the profits from assembly manufacturing. Although the concept has been used to identify high value-added supply chain activities in other industries, we should point out that the "smiling curve" is not rigorously verified, and it is unclear if the "smiling curve" can be applied in various manufacturing industries.

Based on the double smile curves of two competing supply chains, we can use an "X"-shape framework to study the competition between two supply chains (for an example, see Fig. 6.10), and identify the main competitive advantage and bottleneck of each supply chain and design strategic leverage weapons.

The smiling curve effect highlights the value imbalance and fairness issues of supply chain entities. This imbalance increases the difficulty of global supply chain coordination. For example, the sources of Mattel's quality risks and Apple's ethical risks are not from themselves but in assembly manufacturing. However, with lower value-added and profits, assembly manufacturers have neither much motivation nor the financial resources to improve quality or deliver social and environmental values in line with designers' expectations.

6.2.5.2 Bullwhip Effect

The bullwhip effect (see Forrester 1961; Lee et al. 1997a, b) refers to the variance of order increases as they move from customers to suppliers (see Fig. 6.11). The bullwhip effect highlights the information distortion in the supply chain, which will be enlarged in a global environment since information processing is more complicated and it is more difficult to achieve information visibility and accuracy on a global scale.

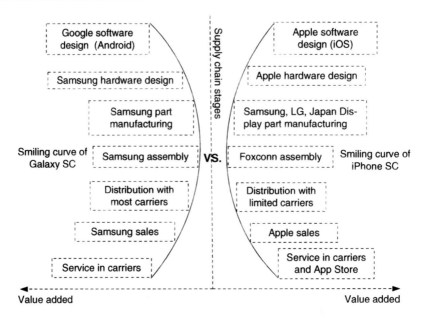

Fig. 6.10 Supply chain competition "X" framework based on double smiling curves

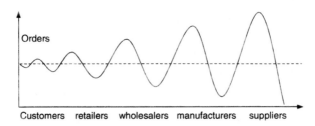

Fig. 6.11 Bullwhip effect

6.2.5.3 Approaches to Achieving Global Supply Chain Coordination

With the smiling curve effect and the bullwhip effect, it is difficult to achieve coordination for a global supply chain without value balance and information sharing. To achieve global coordination, supply chain systems can take the following actions:

- Balancing the value and profits of supply chain entities,
- Improving information visibility and accuracy,
- Establishing strategic interorganizational partnerships,
- Improving long-term supply chain contracts,
- Coordinating the competitive goals of supply chain entities.

6.2.6 Global Supply Chain Strategic Alliances

A firm can perform the supply chain function by internal activities with available internal resources and processes, acquisition if willing to make the commitment, or arm's-length transactions, the short-term arrangement between suppliers and buyers. However, in a global environment with greater uncertainties and a global marketplace requiring more expertise and resources, internal activities and arm's-length transactions may not be sufficient to achieve a long-term strategic advantage, and acquisition may be too costly. Firms will build global strategic alliances, long-term interorganizational partnerships to share risks and benefits. We present several typical global supply chain strategic alliances, most of which are vertical alliances, with just a few horizontal alliances.

- Continuous replenishment
  In this information-sharing alliance between retailers and suppliers, the retailers send information like POS data to suppliers, who then prepare an optimal shipment and send it to retailers after a specified interval to maintain an optimal inventory position.
- Vendor-managed inventory (VMI)
  The suppliers, not the retailers, determine inventory levels and inventory policies in a VMI alliance to provide a mutually beneficial relationship where both sides will be able to more smoothly and accurately control the availability and flow of goods. This practice was first implemented by Walmart and P&G in the 1980s. Walmart shared demand information with P&G, then the supplier P&G delivered products to Walmart automatically.
- Third-party logistics (3PL)
  A firm can build a 3PL alliance with an outside logistics provider to perform logistics and distribution activities. A 3PL alliance is a long-term interorganizational partnership with multiple functions. For example, "Kuehne+Nagel" has established a 3PL alliance with Airbus, and "Kuehne+Nagel" have built a new aviation logistics hub in Montoir-de-Bretagne in Western France, designed to handle the entire production logistics of Airbus' manufacturing plants at Nantes and Saint-Nazaire.
- Distributor integration (DI)
  Manufacturers can build a DI alliance with distributors to share knowledge of markets and customers. A DI alliance can build a large pool of inventory to reduce inventory cost and risks, and improve customer satisfaction.
- Horizontal strategic alliances
  Suppliers can build horizontal strategic alliances for mutual needs including negotiation, information, and a common approach to the market. Buyers can build horizontal strategic alliances to increase their negotiating power. For example, global steel manufacturers build horizontal alliances to increase negotiation power and coordinate their steel manufacturing capacities, and iron ore suppliers build alliances to increase the iron ore price.

6.2.7 Global Sustainable Supply Chain Strategy

Value-based practice such as "environmentally friendly operations", "green operations", "socially responsible operations", and "sustainable operations" are influencing today's global supply chain management. Global sustainable supply chain strategy is a supply chain strategy to consider not only economic value, but also environmental and social values. Global sustainable supply chain strategy is operating across several sectors, including nonprofits, academics, governments, suppliers, consumers and investors, to accelerate sustainable innovation, turning from sustainability as a cost and risk reduction measure to an opportunity for business growth, developing systems for continuous improvement, and improving transparency in operations and the supply chain.

1. Sustainable procurement

   Sustainable purchasing considers fair trade products (e.g., Nestlé), direct farm sourcing (e.g., Walmart) and local sourcing (e.g., Walmart, Nestlé) to link economic value and social value. To help poor small- and medium-sized suppliers, Walmart and Nestlé consider smaller candidates in their supplier selection. By sharing technology, helping suppliers to build socially responsible goals, and providing financial aid, sustainable purchasing improves supplier quality and productivity.

2. Sustainable manufacturing

   For environmental value, sustainable manufacturing redesigns the manufacturing process to reduce waste of water, energy and raw materials. For social value, a sustainable manufacturing program redesigns operations for older workers in societies that are ageing, and uses ergonomics technology or medical knowledge to improve working conditions. For example, Johnson & Johnson helps employees to stop smoking to save on health care costs. GE is going to start paying its employees to quit smoking. About 20 % of the GE workforce smokes, and the company estimates that it spends tens of millions of dollars each year on smoking-related illnesses. Effective from January 2012, a tobacco surcharge has applied to employees using tobacco in GE.

3. Sustainable distribution

   For environmental value, Internet-based distribution like Google Books, Kindle and iTunes can reduce paper and plastic consumption. DHL is running a "GoGreen" program to achieve environmental value. For social value, Walmart provides logistics equipment to help small- and medium-sized suppliers without financial and logistics capabilities. To overcome logistical challenges for service supply chains in emerging markets, "Riders for health", a social enterprise, is working to make sure health workers in Africa have access to reliable transportation so they can reach isolated people with health care.

4. Sustainable retailing

   Sustainable retailing incorporates sustainability into retailing operations, workforce engagement, and connection to consumers and communities. Retailers are redesigning packaging, facility layout, and product labeling to achieve sustainable goals. The "Whole Foods Market" is starting a color-coded sustainability rating program for wild-caught seafood, and the system's green, yellow and red ratings make it easy for customers to make decisions. Green ratings indicate a species is relatively abundant and is caught in sustainable ways, and other colors mean there are concerns about either overfishing or fishing methods.

Case Example: Global Supply Chain of H&M

H&M, a group headquartered in Stockholm, designs and retails a range of fashionable apparel, cosmetics, footwear and accessories for men, women, children and teenagers through its stores, online stores, and catalogue sales. In 2012, H&M has almost 2,600 stores across 47 markets. H&M is well known for its cheap but chic fashion strategy, with a business concept "to give the customer unbeatable value by offering fashion and quality at the best price".

By visiting trade fairs, talking with fashion media, meeting trend forecasters, and visiting H&M stores, H&M collects demand information for the design. Approximately 140 in-house designers work with pattern designers and buyers to create a large range of products, with a core to balance between fashion, quality and the best price.

H&M does not own any factories, and outsources production to 700 independent suppliers through its 16 local production offices in Asia and Europe. For example, one important H&M supplier is the TL silk factory in Hangzhou city, China. With an area of 6,000 m^2, the factory has advanced silk weaving equipment mainly for production of high-grade silk jacquard fabrics and jacquard scarves.

H&M does not own any stores, but rents store space from landlords. The merchandise is subsequently transported by sea, rail, road or air to distribution centers located in sales markets. After unpacking and allocating, the goods are then distributed directly to the stores or to central regional replenishment centers. For instance, a central warehouse in Hamburg in Germany collects all apparel from various locations and distributes locally to distribution centers across countries. Stores do not build safety stocks, but are replenished from central warehouses by a request for replenishment once a product is sold. While physical stores are the main sales channel, H&M is developing online sales to make itself more accessible.

H&M is developing a sustainable supply chain of design, manufacturing and distribution. In 2010 H&M became the number one user of organic cotton worldwide. H&M tries to make products with added sustainability value to conscious customers, chooses and rewards responsible partners, inspires others to reduce total CO_2 emissions, reduces waste by 3R (reduce, reuse, recycle), use natural resources responsibly, and contributes to the development of the communities where it operates.

(*Source: H&M annual reports 2000–2012*)

Case Questions

1. Study H&M's global supply chain strategy using the GSCS taxonomy (see Sect. 6.2.1).
2. What is the relationship between the global supply chain strategy and its business strategy of pursuing "cheap but chic fashion"?

6.3   Global Revenue Management Strategy

6.3.1   Introduction to Global Revenue Management Strategy

6.3.1.1 Globally Evolving Process of Revenue Management

In 1978, the US congress passed the Airline Deregulation Act, and then the US Civil Aviation Board decided to loosen controls on airline prices which were previously strictly regulated. This is generally regarded as the catalyst for revenue management. Taking this chance, low-cost and low-fare airlines like PeoplExpress rapidly expanded due to their ability to charge less than "Super Saver Fares", a program of the major airline company, AA.

Under the pressure of competition, AA invested millions in the next generation capability DINAMO (Dynamic Inventory Optimization and Maintenance Optimizer), and announced its "Ultimate Super Saver Fares" in 1985 that were priced lower than the PeoplExpress. The main difference between "Ultimate Super Saver Fares" and PeoplExpress policy is:

* While PeoplExpress put no restriction on discount fares, AA put restrictions on discount fares and asked customers for a booking lead time of at least two weeks before departure and a stay at their destination over a Saturday night.
* While PeoplExpress allowed all seats to be sold at low fares, AA restricted the number of discount seats on each flight.

These are the earliest RM techniques. The pioneer of RM, Robert Crandall, former Chairman and CEO of AA, called the new discipline "yield management". Finally, PeoplExpress failed in the game and AA won victory. On the reason for the results of the competition, Robert Crandall made one of the most famous comments in the history of RM: "Yield management is the single most important technical development in transportation management since we entered the era of deregulation." The same view was taken by his rival Donald Burr, CEO of PeoplExpress: "We did a lot of things right. But we didn't get our hands around yield management and automation issues."

This was generally regarded as the origin of revenue management. Then RM began its development on a global scale (see Table 6.1), and expanded from the US to other countries. British Airways, KLM, and Lufthansa were among the first airlines in Europe to use yield management approaches.

Marriott International was the pioneer outside the airlines to apply "yield management", and began to call the practice "revenue management", since "yield" was not relevant for hotels. Marriott built a revenue management organization, invested in an automated revenue management system, and built a Demand Forecast System to forecast demand and manage an inventory of hotel rooms. From the airline industry, the concept of revenue management has spread to other industries, such as car rental, hotel bookings, restaurants, casinos, insurance and telecommunications. Since airlines and hotel industries are essentially linked with global travel, revenue management was globalized from the early stages.

Then RM developed from business-to-consumer (B2C) mode to business-to-business (B2C) mode in the early 1990s. This development was led by UPS, which

Table 6.1 Globally evolving process of revenue management

Time	Progress	Representative organizations	Event description
1978	Catalyst for RM	US Civil Aviation Board	Congress passed Airline Deregulation Act of 1978. US Civil Aviation Board decided to loosen controls on airline prices
1985	Birth of the term "yield management"	American Airlines	AA invested in DINAMO and announced "Ultimate Super Saver Fares" program in 1985. PeoplExpress failed in the competition
1980s–1990s	From US to Europe	British Airways, KLM, Lufthansa	These were among the first in Europe to use yield management approaches
1980s–1990s	From airlines to other industries	Marriott International	Birth of the term "revenue management". Marriott and others began to build automated revenue management system for hotel industry
Early 1990s	From B2C to B2B	UPS	UPS built a "Target Pricing" system to forecast the outcomes of bidding at different net prices and search for a suitable discounting level
1990s	From perishable to non-perishable	Ford Motor	Ford Motor segmented customers, measured the price-responsiveness of segments, and created a differentiated price structure
1990s–2000s	From corporation RM to alliance RM	Star Alliance, SkyTeam and Oneworld	"Alliance revenue management" was developing to synchronize decision-making to maximize revenue across the alliance networks
1990s–2000s	From developed to developing countries	China Southern, Xiamen Airline	China Southern adopted PROS 5 Revenue management system. Xiamen Airline developed an RM system

needed to negotiate annual service rates with large customers. UPS built a Target Pricing system to forecast the outcomes of bidding at different net prices and the search for a suitable discounting level.

In the 1990s, RM developed from the pricing of perishable to non-perishable products. In order to maximize revenue from its vehicles, Ford Motor used RM to segment customers into micro-markets, measured the price-responsiveness of different segments, and created a differentiated price structure.

In 1997, the Star Alliance was established as a truly global airline alliance to offer customers convenient worldwide reach and a smoother travel experience. Since then, "alliance revenue management" has been developing to synchronize the decision-making of members to maximize revenue across alliance networks. "Alliance revenue management" has also developed in the hotel, car rentals and other industries.

In the 2000s or earlier, RM evolved from developed countries to developing ones. For example, in 2001, China Southern adopted the PROS 5 Revenue

Fig. 6.12 Three levels of
revenue management
decisions (Phillips 2005)

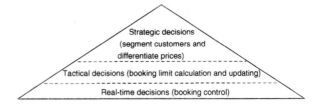

management system provided by a US company, PROS Revenue Management.
Then in 2003, China Eastern and Air China adopted the same system. In 2004,
Xiamen Airline developed its own RM system.

6.3.1.2 Concepts of Global Revenue Management

Generally speaking, revenue management is used to sell the right products to the
right customer at the right time for the right price. Unlike supply chain management, revenue management deals with the demand side of an operation system, to
design, plan and evaluate processes to understand, anticipate and influence consumer behavior in order to maximize revenue or profits.

Revenue management is characterized by three levels of decisions (Phillips
2005, see Fig. 6.12). At strategic level, a firm annually or quarterly identifies
customer segments and differentiates prices. At a tactical level, a firm weekly or
daily computes booking limits, which are controls to limit the amount of capacity
that can be sold to a special customer segment. A firm makes a real-time decision to
determine whether to accept a booking request.

Globalization brings challenges to revenue management. Some firms traditionally using revenue management go global and build a global service chain. Airlines
and hotels achieve horizontal coordination and integration by building global
alliances. With the help of information platforms, airlines and hotels vertically
integrate and coordinate. Firms traditionally using revenue management are developing sector coordination among travel-relevant sectors like airlines, hotels, and car
rentals. While globalization improves market penetration, service delivery, and
global coverage, it increases the complexity of coordinating prices, booking and
ticketing, scheduling and frequent flyer program exchanges. The main challenges
that globalization brings to revenue management are:

- It is more difficult to understand, anticipate and influence global consumer
  behavior considering cultural, economic, and political differences between
  customers.
- It is more complicated to manage the capacity and optimize the availability of
  services or products considering vertical, horizontal, and sector coordination
  among revenue management companies.
- It is harder to price services or products with increasing the number of consumer
  segments worldwide.
- It is more complicated to set and achieve revenue objectives since there is a need
  to consider the revenue allocation within alliances and between partners.

Based on the introduction to basic revenue management and discussion of its global environment, we define global revenue management strategy as follows:

A process-based operations strategy to identify customer segments by understanding, anticipating and influencing global consumer behavior with consideration of consumers' global heterogeneity, to control the availability of services or products on a global scale, and to price services or products in different consumer segments with the objectives of maximizing the expected revenues of a corporation or to optimize revenue allocation within a revenue alliance.

Unlike supply chain management, which can be applicable in many industries, revenue management is distinguished by the conditions in which it can be applied. (see Talluri and Van Ryzin 2004; Phillips 2005). Phillips (2005) defines "revenue management industries" as industries meeting these conditions and "revenue management companies" as companies that use booking controls and fare classes.

6.3.1.3 Basic Methods of Revenue Management

Revenue management companies use two basic methods to handle problems in revenue management, which are still fundamental for global revenue management although in a global environment.

- Price-based RM
  Revenue management companies use four price control methods: traditional fixed pricing, supplier-led pricing or dynamic pricing, consumer-led pricing, and value-led dynamic pricing.

  In supplier-led pricing, revenue management companies make use of dynamic pricing in applications like style-goods markdown pricing, discount airline pricing, and consumer-packaged goods promotions. Revenue management companies use various dynamic pricing techniques like single-product dynamic pricing, multiproduct multiresource pricing, and finite-population pricing.

  In consumer-led pricing, auctions are widely adopted by revenue management industries. There are four types of auction for selling a single object: open ascending auction (English auction), open descending auction (Dutch auction), seal-bid first-price auction and sealed-bid second-price auction (Vickrey auction). Revenue management companies also use multiunit auctions for selling multiple objects, and combinatorial auctions for selling several products simultaneously. Revenue management companies also employ other methods like reverse auctions, trading exchanges, and price matching.

- Quantity-based RM
  Quantity-based RM approaches consider four types of controls: booking limit, protection control, bid price control and displacement cost. Revenue management companies use static or dynamic models to manage single resource capacity, and network capacity control to manage multiple resources. With constrained capacity, revenue management companies apply overbooking techniques to sell more units than they can actually provide.

Table 6.2 Organization modes of global service chains

	Control of codified asset	Control of organizational routines	Daily management	Control of physical assets
Full ownership	++	++	++	++
Partial ownership	++	+	+	+
Management contracts	++	+	+	
Franchise contracts	++	+		

Notes: ++ strong control, + control, otherwise: no control

6.3.2   Strategies for Global Revenue Management

We first present the global service chain, the strategy used by a single corporation, then discuss strategies for multiple corporations: vertical integration, horizontal integration, and sector integration. These are approaches adopted by typical industries to provide conditions for improving and optimizing price-based and quantity-based revenue management on a global scale.

6.3.2.1 Global RM by Global Service Chain

When hotels, airlines, and restaurant companies enter global marketplaces, they build global service chains to achieve effective control while ensuring sufficient responsiveness to local market conditions. Then they can apply both price-based and quantity-based revenue management techniques on a global scale.

Global service chains can be organized through full or partial ownership, management contracts, and franchise contracts (see Table 6.2). They usually use multiple controls and combine different advantages. In the full ownership and joint venture modes, the chain can control (in the case of full ownership) or influence (in the case of a joint venture) all aspects. In the management contract mode, the service chain is responsible for daily management, but cannot control physical assets which are controlled by the owner. In the franchise contract mode, the service chain can control neither daily management nor physical assets, which are managed by the owners. In any case, a service chain needs to control codified assets (e.g., brands). For example, Hilton Worldwide owns, manages, or franchises a portfolio of ten brands including Waldorf Astoria Hotels and Resorts, Conrad Hotels & Resorts, Hilton Hotels & Resorts, and Embassy Suites Hotels. Hilton brands encompass huge global hotel chains with 3,800 hotels with over 630,000 rooms in 88 countries.

6.3.2.2 Global RM by Horizontal Integration

It is a new trend to combine global revenue management with horizontal coordination or even closer horizontal integration. In particular, alliances bring global opportunities and challenges to revenue management, and "alliance revenue management" is an emerging direction of revenue management on a global scale (see Vinod 2005).

Table 6.3 The influence of an airline alliance on strategies

	Impact on business strategy	Impact on operations strategy
Advantages	Achieving strategic leverage, improving profitability	Generating revenue growth and cost savings, enhanced asset utilization, improving customer delivery
Disadvantages	Reducing competition, brand equity risk, restrictions in strategic direction	Pressure on prices, restrictions in options of operations strategy, reduced flexibility of operations

- Global airline alliances

  Airline alliances are one of the most dramatic changes in recent global revenue management. An airline alliance refers to the collaboration between two or more airlines while retaining their independence during the course of the relationship. Unlike vertical integration, the alliances have provided airlines with successful horizontal integration of airline businesses by consolidating financial and operational strengths and mitigating growing global risks.

  Transporting over 60 % of the world's scheduled passenger traffic, the airline industry is now dominated by three alliances: Star Alliance, Skyteam and Oneworld. The types of member links include cost sharing ventures, asset pools, pro rata agreements, codesharing, feeders, marketing alliances, joint ventures and equity stakes.

  In regard to business strategies, alliances provide significant advantages to members being able to leverage their resource by generating more revenue from the same invested resource (see Table 6.3). This leverage is achieved by integrated scheduling and pricing, utilizing other members' facilities at airports, optimizing load management and information sharing. It also brings disadvantages including brand equity risk, reduced competition, and restrictions in strategic direction.

  Regarding global operations strategy, alliances provide a range of advantages including generating revenue growth and cost savings, leading to improved profitability, and improving customer delivery. However, these bring pressure on prices, restrictions in the options for operations strategy (e.g., marketing segments, levels of service), reduce the flexibility of operations (e.g., scheduling tie-ups, pricing flexibility and ancillary revenue measures freedom). Alliances improve revenue management through the
  - Integration of route networks,
  - Integrated scheduling and pricing,
  - Combining of market presence,
  - Improved resource utilization,
  - Sharing of customer service facilities,
  - Improved marketing communications, and
  - FFP (frequent flyer program) coverage.

  Alliances improve global revenue management particularly by delivering customers and driving customer demand. Alliances encourage passengers to stay within their members' earnings boundaries more often and for longer, by expanding the coverage of passenger benefits such that passengers are able to improve personal scheduling, enjoy smoother connections, and reduce layover times. Alliances give frequent fliers greater opportunities to earn and redeem miles, contribute to elite and priority status and provide more lounge access.

- Global hotel alliance
  The hospitality industry has also built a number of alliances. For example, the "global hotel alliance" (GHA) is a collection of 14 luxury regional hotel brands with 300 hotels, palaces and resorts in 52 countries around the world. An important RM tool of GHA is "GHA Discovery", a loyalty program rewarding travelers with "local experiences" to offer members access to a large selection of adventures not easily available to the general public, since GHA believes that rewarding members with memorable experiences is more valuable than collecting points. GHA Discovery also provides general hotel benefits such as complimentary Internet, early check-in, late check-out, upgrades, and guaranteed availability.

6.3.2.3 Global RM by Vertical Integration

From the beginning, global revenue management is vertically integrated with distribution and central reservation systems via information systems to manage sales and inventory. The information platform and information integration play an important role in vertical integration, which provides conditions for global optimization of revenue management.

Figure 6.13 presents the global information integration of revenue management, particularly in the airline industry environment. The revenue management system interfaces with the global reservation system. The global reservation system is linked with the following three distribution channels.

- Global distribution systems. These are global computerized reservation networks used as a common point of access for reserving airline seats, hotel rooms, and other travel-related items by travel agents, online reservation sites, and corporations. The premier global distribution systems are Sabre, Galileo, Amadeus and Worldspan, typically owned and operated as joint ventures by major airlines, car rental companies, or hotel groups. Global distribution systems need travel agents serving as an additional layer between airlines and customers.
- Home websites. Home websites can bypass the commissions and fees of global distribution systems. For example, customers can make reservations directly through the home website of Air France.
- Third-party websites. This channel can bypass travel agent commissions, and includes famous sites like Expedia, Orbitz, and Priceline. Via the Internet, they provide a cost advantage by selling directly to customers.

6.3.2.4 Global RM by Sector Integration

Global RM is developing sector coordination and integration. In the airline industry, sector coordination and integration are mainly conducted among travel-relevant sectors. For example, FlyingBlue is the loyalty program of Air France and KLM.

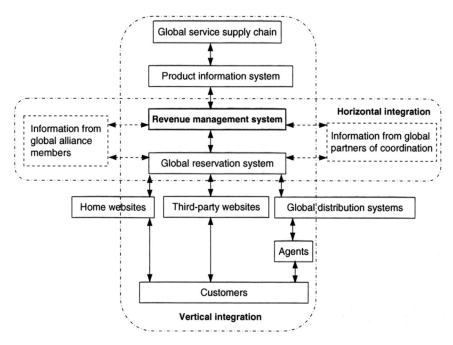

Fig. 6.13 Global RM integration by information platform

It cooperates with American Express, and provides a "Flying Blue – American Express" card to help customers earn reward tickets, enjoy frequent flyer benefits, and additional financial benefits.

The hospitality industry is actively participating in sector coordination and integration to improve revenue management. Global hotel alliances build partnership with airline programs including FlyingBlue (Air France/KLM), Mileage Club (All Nippon Airways), Executive Club (British Airways), and car rental programs including Avis Rent-a-Car and Sixt Rent-a-Car. HHonors builds numerous partnerships with airlines, credit cards, car rental, and retailers, and provides hundreds of ways to earn points on everyday purchases, and to earn discounts. HHonors are even linked with charities such that customers can make donations easily (see Fig. 6.14). All of these can change and influence customer behavior and improve RM.

Case Example: SkyTeam Alliance

SkyTeam, the second largest airline alliance, based in Amsterdam, was formed in 2000 and is made up of 15 member airlines (see Fig. 6.15) and several future members (with * in Fig. 6.15). SkyTeam is a global network with 926 destinations in 173 countries, 490 lounges, a mainline fleet of 2,431, 399,469 employees, and 151 million frequent flyer members all over the world.

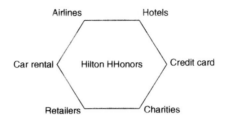

Fig. 6.14 Sector integration of HHonors

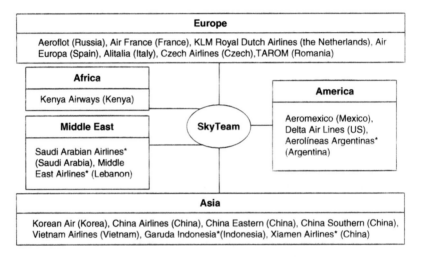

Fig. 6.15 Skyteam's global members

Members of SkyTeam benefit from the alliance by gaining greater brand recognition, improving their market positioning, increasing their reach to new destinations, enhancing customer service and cost savings and knowledge-sharing. The alliance helps members to maximize airport facility utilization by co-location of check-in and ticketing areas, reduction of ground handling costs through shared staff and equipment, and optimization of lounge facilities. SkyTeam can provide the following better service to customers:

- Global coverage. With 15 member airlines, the SkyTeam network offers customers more destinations and more connections from the best hubs in the world.
- Frequent flyer benefits. Customers can earn and redeem miles with all 15 member airlines. With "elite" status, customers can enjoy priority check-in, preferred seating and lounge access.
- Lounge access. SkyTeam member airlines provide customers with over 465 lounges worldwide.

- Travel passes to simplify global travel. With "SkyTeam Go Passes", customers can take advantage of global networks and enjoy more flexibility and savings during travels.
- Corporate solutions. "SkyTeam Global Corporate Contracts" go beyond a standard loyalty program in meeting companies' travel requirements, providing cost savings and a vast network of travel needs. SkyTeam can help streamline the process of event travel with "SkyTeam Global Meetings" with discounted fares and reward tickets.
  (*Source: SkyTeam fact sheet 2012*)

Case Questions

1. What are the benefits of the SkyTeam alliance for its members, and for its customers?
2. How does SkyTeam improve the global revenue management of its members?
3. Which RM techniques (quantity-based and price-based) has SkyTeam used?

6.4   Global Technology Strategy

6.4.1   Introduction to Global Technology Strategy

6.4.1.1 Concept of Global Technology Strategy

Generally speaking, a technology strategy is "a firm's approach to the development and use of technology" (Porter 1985, p. 176). Porter sees the main decisions in technology strategy as: types of technology to develop, strategic position of technological leadership or followership, and role of technology licensing.

Technology is a critical element for economic development and human development, and can influence not only the competitive advantage of a firm and a business, but also the development of an industry (Porter 1985) and even a nation. Thereby technology strategy is a huge field, including the following different levels.

- Industry technology strategy, as a part of industry strategy.
- Corporate technology strategy, as a part of corporate strategy.
- Business technology strategy, as a part of business strategy.
- Operational technology strategy, as a part of operations strategy, including process-based operational technology strategy and resource-based operational technology strategy.

This book does not intend to cover all levels of technology strategies, but just the operational level of technology strategy. For classic readings of technology strategy at other levels, we recommend Buegelman et al. (1995), Porter (1985) and Tushman and Anderson (1997). At the operational level of technology strategy, technology strategy also includes resource-based and process-based technology strategy. We present aspects of resource-based technology strategy in Chap. 5, and address process-based technology strategy, particularly new product development (NPD) and R&D activities at operational or project levels, in this chapter. This book focuses on global technology strategy at the operational level, and presents a definition:

> Global technology strategy is a consistent pattern of structural, infrastructural, and integration decisions about developing and using technology to achieve a set of optimal competencies alignment with business strategy in a global competitive environment.

6.4.1.2 R&D Globalization

While manufacturing globalization began with cost-seeking, NPD globalization began with resource-seeking in the 1970s. "The pioneers of R&D internationalization are high-tech companies operating in small markets and with little R&D resources in their home country" (Gassmann and von Zedtwitz 1999, p. 231). Swiss, Dutch and Belgian companies are among the earliest to carry out a large part of R&D activities outside their home. For example, pioneers of R&D internationalization include ABB and Novartis in Switzerland, Philips in the Netherlands, and Ericsson in Sweden.

In the 1980s and 1990s, with the development of the Internet, software product development went global to gain access to low-cost resources, since software applications were available to make the software product digital, and the Internet allowed this digital product to be instantaneously portable worldwide. With the development of technologies like computer-aided design (CAD) and computer-aided engineering (CAE), manufacturing companies built digital product development processes for resource portability and started global product development.

Global technology management makes the following contributions to MNC's global growth: While some firms may perform R&D activities in locations with lower costs, others go global from lower cost-seeking to technological expertise-seeking, for know-how, knowledge, and technical talent. Increasing numbers of firms perform R&D activities in foreign locations for marketing reasons, to understand local demand or rapidly respond to fluctuations in demand. Moreover, by establishing networks of R&D subsidiaries, the company can achieve greater flexibility in coordination between its various research facilities. Finally, some firms globalize technology management to achieve competitive leverage over rivals, for example, by building R&D networks excelling at commercializing products at a competitive speed in foreign markets in order to attack rivals. However, globalization brings risks for global technology strategy. For example, by involving more actors in the R&D process, the firm is more exposed to potential losses of crucial knowledge and risks from the protection of intellectual property rights.

Fig. 6.16 Eppinger and
Chitkara's GPD modes

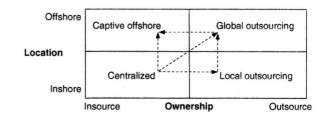

6.4.2 Global Product Development (GPD) Strategies

6.4.2.1 GPD and GPD Strategy

New products can be the nexus of competition for MNEs in the global marketplace, and NPD is a potential source of competitive advantage (for a classical literature review and a survey of product development, see Brown and Eisenhardt (1995) and Ulrich and Eppinger (1995)). In the dynamic global marketplace, NPD is a critical process for success, survival, adaptation, and renewal of an organization (Brown and Eisenhardt 1995).

Subramaniam et al. (1998) and Graber (1996) have studied global product development processes. Considering both multi-national research in earlier literature, and simultaneous product development, Eppinger and Chitkara (2006) propose a concept of global product development (GPD), and characterize GPD as

> A single, coordinated product development operation that includes distributed teams in more than one country utilizing a fully digital and connected collaborative product development process. This may include third parties that provide engineering or design capacity, or it may be an entirely captive, company-owned operation. (Eppinger and Chitkara 2006, p. 23)

While traditional product development uses co-location of cross-functional teams, Eppinger and Chitkara (2006) see GPD adopting globally distributed teams, and a collaborative development process facilitated by a fully digital PD system in multiple geographic locations. Figure 6.16 presents four GPD modes including "centralized PD", "captive offshore", "local outsourcing" and "global outsourcing", with arrows to show the potential direction of growth. While the centralized mode develops products within the organization at onshore locations, local outsourcing considers on-site contractors in NPD activities. While captive offshoring owns an NPD operation in a foreign location and has the commitment to establish a captive center, the global outsourcing mode uses foreign contractors to undertake basic NPD tasks.

Based on the GPD concept, GPD strategy is "a consistent pattern of structural, infrastructural, and integration decisions to determine the GPD process, to achieve competitive advantage, or for the success, survival, adaptation, and renewal of MNEs". GPD strategy includes decisions on the following processes:

- Global idea generation,
- Global idea screening,
- Concept development and testing,

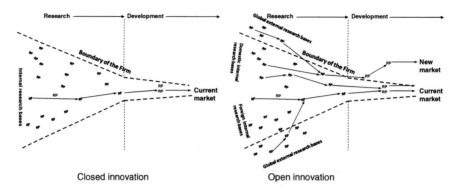

Fig. 6.17 Closed versus open innovation processes in a global environment

- Global business analysis,
- Prototype and Beta testing,
- Global market testing,
- Technical implementation,
- Global commercialization, and
- Global new product pricing.

6.4.2.2 GPD Strategy and Open Innovation Model

If the NPD process is essentially internal, product innovation is limited, since researchers have the same background, the NPD process is linear, and the firm boundaries are impermeable (Fig. 6.17). Consequently, a new concept product may not fit market needs or manufacturing capabilities, leading to possible economic losses. However, if the firm boundaries are made permeable so that information can be exchanged more easily, an "open innovation model" can be implemented. Realizing the drawbacks of "closed innovation", the earlier paradigm where innovation was closed to outside ideas and technologies, Chesbrough (2003, 2006) proposes the "open innovation" paradigm, enabling companies to develop products from internal and external ideas, and increase the chances of NPD success and the quality of innovation.

The "open innovation" paradigm distinguishes innovative processes as either "research", performing initial analysis and design tasks, or "development", constructing the product. In contrast to closed innovation, which closes organizational boundaries to external organizations, the open innovation process benefits from external organizations, which can participate in the NPD (Chesbrough 2003, 2006).

The "open innovation" paradigm is important for global NPD strategy and encourages firms to open boundaries and go global to source external knowledge and effectively generate new knowledge. Chesbrough (2003) provides the following guidelines: A firm needs to develop new products with talent inside and outside the organization, since not all the necessary talent is found inside. A firm can beat the competition if it makes the best use of internal and external ideas. While external R&D can create significant value, internal R&D is needed to make part

Fig. 6.18 Von Zedtwitz and Grassman's R&D internationalization archetypes

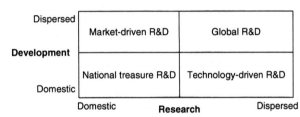

of the contribution to that value. Instead of completely profiting from original research, a firm should profit from others' use of its intellectual properties, and the firm should buy others' intellectual properties to advance its own business model.

6.4.3 R&D Internationalization Modes

Kuemmerle (1997) proposes classic R&D globalization modes. While some R&D activities go global in a "home-base augmenting" mode to absorb knowledge from global scientific communities, generate new knowledge, and transfer it to the home R&D site, others use a "home-base exploiting" mode to commercialize knowledge by transferring it from the home base to the R&D site abroad for local manufacturing and marketing.

Based on the Kuemmerle modes, von Zedtwitz and Gassmann (2002) define four archetypes of R&D internationalization (see Fig. 6.18):

- National treasure R&D, where both research and development are performed domestically.
- Technology-driven R&D, where development is domestic and research is dispersed.
- Market-driven R&D, where research is domestic and development is dispersed.
- Global R&D, where both research and development are dispersed.

Companies would normally start from "national treasure" and then proceed either through "technology-driven" or "market-driven" to "global R&D".

From another viewpoint, Chiesa (2000) thinks R&D activities go global by building "specialization-based" R&D laboratories with full global responsibility for a product or technology or process, and "integration-based" R&D laboratories with different units contributing to technology development programs. These integrated R&D laboratories have gotten involved in GPD.

6.4.4 Global R&D Coordination and Communication

1. The role of global R&D units
   Multinational corporations establish R&D facilities in strategic locations around the world as part of the process of achieving the goals set in the corporate

strategy. Depending on the patterns of communication with the parent company, Nobel and Birkenshaw (1998) find that global R&D facilities play one of three roles: local adaptor, international adaptor or international creator.

- Local adaptor, an R&D unit assisting the local manufacturing unit to incorporate and exploit available mainstream technology, with a core role to simplify technology transfer from the parent company to the manufacturing subsidiaries worldwide (Ronstadt 1977).
- International adaptor, with responsibility for developing new and improved products to respond to foreign markets.
- International creator, oriented towards conducting creative research and development as internationally interdependent laboratories rather than improving and adapting existing technologies.

2. The control of global R&D units

MNEs need to determine the degree of control over global R&D units and the ability to influence the decisions and operations of global R&D units. Without sufficient control over foreign operations, MNCs are not able to standardize, coordinate, and integrate global R&D activities, which in turn might result in failure in global competition.

Nobel and Birkenshaw (1998) distinguish three modes of control, depending on the role of global R&D units. Local adaptors mainly adapt and standardize products in global markets, and should be based on formalization. Pugh et al. (1968) explain formalization as a mode of control based on formal rules and routines. International adaptors have a greater strategic importance for MNCs as they develop and introduce new products to the market. The preferred mode of control is centralization in order to retain decision-making with a high degree of control at the headquarters. International creators are linked to each other and exchange much information. Consequentially, the beneficial mode of control is socialization, by developing common expectations and a shared set of values for decision-making.

3. Global R&D units organization

Gassmann and von Zedtwitz (1999) define five types of international R&D organization differing in organizational structure, communication patterns, and coordination mechanisms:

- Ethnocentric centralized R&D, with all R&D activities concentrated in the home country.
- Geocentric centralized R&D, with geocentric external orientation and high sensitivity to local markets.
- Polycentric decentralized R&D, with polycentric orientation in order to respond to customer requests for product adaptation.
- R&D hub model, with tight central control to reduce the risk of suboptimal resource allocation and R&D duplication.
- Integrated R&D network, with central R&D as a competency center among many interdependent R&D units closely interconnected by flexible and diverse coordination mechanisms.

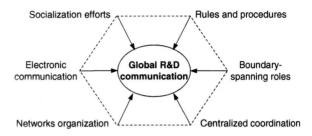

Fig. 6.19 De Meyer global R&D communication approaches

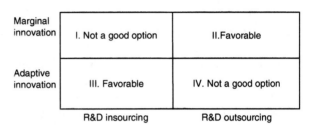

Fig. 6.20 Huang, Chung, and Lin's R&D sourcing strategies

4. The communication approaches of global R&D units

   Communication is critical for effective global R&D since globalization brings geographical and cultural dispersion and increases the difficulty of R&D communication. De Meyer (1991) describes six global R&D communication approaches (see Fig. 6.19). First, firms can use "socialization efforts" including temporary assignments, constant traveling, reinforcing rules, and training programs to stimulate a positive organizational culture and enhance R&D communication. Second, firms implement "rules and procedures" to increase R&D communication. Third, some firms create "boundary-spanning roles" and assign central staff (e.g., called sponsors, liaison, technology coordinators or ambassadors in different firms) to facilitate communication. Many firms use organizational mechanisms, either using "centralized coordination" staff or developing "networks organization". Nowadays, all firms will use electronic communication to improve the efficiency of global R&D communication.

6.4.5   Global R&D Sourcing Strategies

An MNE can use global R&D sourcing strategies to improve operational flexibility, understand local market demand, reduce cost, speed the delivery of new products, and get access to global talent. Global R&D sourcing strategies usually try to achieve two types of product innovation including incremental product innovation to improve the existing product, and radical product innovation to create new products in the industry.

Huang et al. (2009) develop an R&D sourcing strategy matrix (see Fig. 6.20) to help decisions in global R&D sourcing for incremental product innovation including "adaptive innovation" to develop a limited new product incorporating existing technology, and less innovative "marginal innovation" to just improve features and functions of an existing technology.

For marginal innovation, R&D outsourcing is a good option since it has high technological codification and low development cost, and firms face fewer risks in outsourcing existing technologies. For adaptive innovation, R&D insourcing is a good option since it can generate high technological competency and high profits. This model has not answered whether radical product innovation is suitable for outsourcing.

6.4.6 Technology Strategies for Global Sustainable Operations

Technology is an important weapon to help a company link business and society, to achieve sustainable competitive advantage.

- NPD to provide new environmentally friendly products and services
  A firm can use NPD to provide new environmentally friendly products and services. Toyota has launched a hybrid electric vehicle to reduce pollution and oil consumption. In its hybrid models Toyota has developed the "Hybrid Synergy Drive" technology, with one gasoline motor and two small electric motors, to enable the car to use both types of engines.
- NPD to provide new socially responsible products and services
  Technology strategy is also used to provide products and services with social value including healthier food. For example, Dow AgroSciences has developed a line of Omega-9 rich canola and sunflower oils, with zero trans fats and the lowest levels of saturated fats. Since 2005, Omega-9 oils have eliminated nearly a billion pounds of trans fat and 250 million pounds of saturated fat from North American foods.
- Comprehensive R&D programs for sustainable solutions
  This is not only for a specific product but a comprehensive strategy for a range of solutions. For example, GE has invested $10 billion in Ecomagination, the green-focused research and development program to imagine and build innovative solutions to environmental challenges while driving economic growth. The program includes development of compact fluorescent lighting, smart appliances, battery technology, wind turbine manufacturing, a hybrid-powered water heater, and a sustainable aircraft engine.
- Technology education
  In developed countries, there are social problems like shortages of technological workers. Microsoft works together with the American Association of Community Colleges to train IT workers, sends employees to college to help their teaching, and provides financial aid. The shortage of IT workers is a problem not only for Microsoft but also for American society. So by means of the partnership, Microsoft can achieve both economic and social values. Marriott provides training to potential job candidates in the local community to make a social contribution to local communities and reduce its recruitment costs.

- Technology support

  In many cases, sustainable global operations strategy includes training workers and provides them with technologies in developing countries. Nestlé has trained farmers to improve their technologies for milk, coffee and cocoa. Walmart has trained farmers and farm workers in agricultural technological knowledge (e.g., contamination, safety, water treatment, pesticides, postproduction and waste treatment) in Central America, Mexico and China.

Case Example: Microsoft Research Worldwide

Microsoft Research (MSR) was created in 1991 as the research division of the multinational software company Microsoft, and manages at least 13 research laboratories worldwide. In 2011, Microsoft Corporation spent around $9 billion on R&D, representing 13 % of the company's annual revenues.

Each R&D facility has been established in a strategic location. To get access to knowledge and talents, some labs like "Microsoft Research Silicon Valley" and "Advanced Technology Labs Israel" are in world-class innovation centers, and others like "Microsoft Research Cambridge" and "Microsoft Research Station Q" are located on leading university campuses. To get access to mature markets, "Microsoft Research New York City" and "Advanced Technology Labs Europe" (Germany) are located in developed countries. To understand emerging markets and attract talent, "Microsoft Research India" and "Microsoft Research Asia" (Beijing) are in fast-growing countries.

Each of them has specific research fields and hires the specialists, locals or foreigners, in these particular fields. For example, the main research fields of Microsoft Research Asia in Beijing are "advanced user interface, networking and wireless" while Microsoft Research India, based in Bangalore, focuses on "cryptography, security and algorithms". The implementation of such a global strategy is based on powerful communication networks between research facilities.

Microsoft is interacting with all members of the supply chain to ensure the success of its global R&D strategy, and pursue innovation through basic applied research in computer science and software engineering, and it maintains a market-leading position by continuous technological innovation and product development. For example, it provides its vendors with "a range of resources and guidelines for development, training, and testing" (MSR 2011 Annual Report). Microsoft's level of control over MSR is well-balanced in order to help facilitate the development of new products and ideas. The R&D activities of MSR lead to new discoveries and lay the foundation for future technology breakthroughs that define new standards in the industry. The activities of MSR are closely integrated with Microsoft development groups and aim to support the corporate vision of "empowering people through great software anytime and place and on any device".

Microsoft has introduced innovation by collaboration, technology joint venture, and technology acquisition. In addition to Microsoft's product development, MSR vigorously contributes to the global research community.

Researchers at MSR are encouraged to serve as editors of journals, participate in international advisory boards, work in conference program committees and give educational lectures worldwide. MSR collaborates with worldwide researchers and institutions to develop technologies for solving global challenges, and offers research fellowship programs like the "Microsoft Research PhD Fellowship" and "Microsoft Research Faculty Fellowship Program" to enable young researchers to collaborate with colleagues worldwide. Microsoft collaborates with universities, industries and governments to support research in computing sciences, and has built collaborative labs, including at least 13 collaborative Asia-Pacific institutes, three collaborative European institutes, two Latin America institutes, and seven North America institutes. For example, in France, INRIA and Microsoft have built "The Microsoft Research-INRIA Joint Centre". In China, Microsoft and China's Ministry of Education have built the "China Ministry of Education–Microsoft Key Laboratory of Media and Networking Technology" at Tsinghua University. Taking another instance, in 2012 GE and Microsoft have launched a 50-50 joint venture "Caradigm" to enable health systems and professionals to use real-time intelligence for improving healthcare quality and service levels.

(Source: Microsoft Annual Reports 2005–2011).

Case Questions

1. How did Microsoft choose the locations of its global research institutes? What were the benefits of Microsoft's global R&D strategy?
2. Use the open innovation model (see Sect. 6.4.2) to study MSR.
3. Use von Zedtwitz and Grassman's R&D internationalization archetypes (see Sect. 6.4.3) to study MSR.

6.5   Global Operational Risk Management Strategy

6.5.1   Introduction to Global Operational Risks

In global operations, an MNE faces various operational risks including capacity risks, inventory risks, receivables risk, procurement risks, intellectual property risks, forecast risks, and delays risks. Tang and Musa (2011) classify supply chain risks into three flows, and we extend the classification to global operations.

- Material flow risks
  Material flow risks refer to risks in the physical movement between global operational units, including flows of raw materials, components, and finished products. These include risks in raw material purchasing, single and multiple sourcing, production capacity, production processes, outsourcing, and distribution, among others.

- Financial flow risks
  Financial flow risks refer to risks in financial flows between global operational units, including risks in cost changing, price fluctuations, exchange rates, tax, and custom duty.
- Information flow risks
  Information flow risks refer to risks in information flows between global operational units, including risks in demand information accuracy, inventory information accuracy, production capacity information accuracy, information system security, and information sharing.

6.5.2 Basic Operational Strategies to Address Global Risks

Kogut (1985) presents three basic operational strategies including speculative, hedge, and flexible strategies to address risks in the global supply chain. Besides these three strategies, a safety strategy like reserves or redundancy is another operational strategy to address global risks.

- Speculative strategy
  In this strategy, an MNE speculates on a single scenario and overlooks others. For example, when Haier went global, it chose to first build facilities in the US and bet it would win in the US, although Haier knew the potential risks of entering the most competitive market when it was still short of administration skills and market knowledge.
- Hedge strategy
  An MNE can design GOS such that losses in some places can be offset by gains in other places. For example, Huawei simultaneously operates in many locations including Europe, China and the US. Its operations are more profitable in Europe, and can support its growth in the US, where it is developing slowly.
- Flexible strategy
  An MNE can establish flexible GOS to take advantage of different scenarios. With flexible resources, processes, and products, the MNEs can reduce the influence of risks. For example, transshipments between locations can deal with risks of demand fluctuation in some locations. A cross-trained call center can handle risks of service type fluctuation. A centralized warehouse can pool or aggregate demand to deal with demand changes in distributed locations.
- Safety strategy
  An MNE can mitigate operational risks through either a reserves strategy including safety capacity, safety inventory, safety time, or a redundancy strategy including redundant suppliers, redundant distributors, redundant retailers, back-up new products, and redundant processes.

6.5.3 Basic Approaches for Global Operational Risk Management

Tang (1991) summarizes four approaches including supply management, product management, demand management, and information management, to manage

Fig. 6.21 Basic approaches
for global supply chain risk
management

supply chain risks by a coordinated or collaborative mechanism. We extend it to a
global environment and include global finance management (see Fig. 6.21).

* Global supply management
  An MNE can manage global supply chain risks by coordinating or collaborating
  with upstream entities through global network design, supplier selection, supplier order allocation and supply contracts. For example, the MNE can improve
  its network configuration to handle the risks of demand fluctuation as a hedge
  strategy in different locations.
* Global demand management
  An MNE can coordinate or collaborate with upstream entities by global demand
  management like dynamic pricing, shifting demand across time, markets and
  products, which can mitigate risks from changing market and capacity shortages.
  For example, American Airlines uses dynamic pricing to manage customer
  demand and mitigate the risks of over- and under-capacity.
* Global product management
  Product variety design, particularly considering product globalization and localization, can work as a hedge strategy, and postponement and process sequencing
  can work as a flexible strategy to mitigate risks. For example, Dell and Zara use
  postponement to fit to actual local demand and mitigate risks from demand
  forecasting.
* Global information management
  Supply chain visibility, information sharing, and collaborative planning can
  mitigate risks from global information flows. Using VMI, Walmart shares
  information with P&G, reducing demand and inventory risks. With information
  systems, Zara can catch street trends and deliver fashionable products for
  mitigating marketing risks.
* Global finance management
  MNEs use a combination of operational mitigation strategies with financial
  strategies to hedge risks. An MNE can hedge currency risk with forward
  contracts and swaps (a contract between two counterparties to determine the
  exchange of payments for some periods) and hedge demand risks with
  derivatives and options.

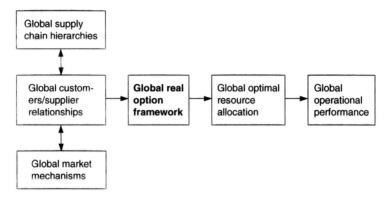

Fig. 6.22 Global supply chain risk management: a real option framework

6.5.4   Kleindorfer's Operational Risk Management Framework

Cohen and Kunreuther (2007) summarize a real option framework for supply chain risk management from Paul Kleindorfer's view of operational risk management, which can be applied in a global environment (see Fig. 6.22). Global supply chain hierarchies, global customer/supplier relationships, and global market mechanisms are the global environment of supply chain risk management. Global supply chain hierarchies include global geography hierarchy, global product hierarchy, and customer hierarchy in the global marketplace. Global customer/supplier relationships determine the incentive/reward structure and contracts, which can be used to mitigate risks. Global market mechanisms like auctions, collaborative forecasting, spot markets, and global sourcing strategies can be used to mitigate supply chain risks.

Then managers input three factors into a two-stage real option framework. In the first stage, the MNE acquires ownership of assets and capabilities based on inputs. In the second stage, when a random contingency outcome is realized, managers deploy and use the acquired assets and capabilities. The outputs will provide global optimal resource allocation, determining operations policy, which leads to operations performance. In this framework, value maximization is achieved by a real option portfolio, which provides hedge and flexibility strategies to mitigate global operational risks.

Case Example: Mattel's Global Risks and Supply Chains

Mattel, the world's largest toy maker in terms of revenue, is an American company founded in 1945. The company has grown fast through its core product, the Barbie doll, and other toys including American Girl dolls, Fisher-Price toys, Hot Wheels and Matchbox toys.

Nowadays, the large retailers in the toy market such as Walmart, Target, and Toys R Us have strong negotiating power. Mattel continually reduces its prices to meet the demand of large retailers. To save costs, Mattel has outsourced its

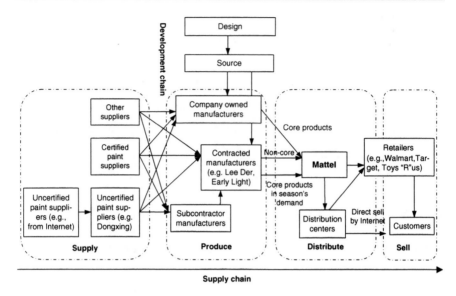

Fig. 6.23 Development and supply chains of Mattel

production to China to reduce production costs and enhance operational flexibility. But this strategic decision brought operational risks to the company and they had to recall a large number of products made in China in 2007. To study its global risks, we present the development and supply chains (see Simchi-Levi et al. 2009, p. 4) of Mattel in Fig. 6.23.

• Risks in development chain

In 2007, Mattel used many small and powerful magnets in toys. These magnets could become dislodged and be swallowed by children, potentially causing serious injury or death. In 2007 Mattel recalled its "Laugh & Learn learning bunny", "Mattel Batman", "Barbie and Tanner play set" for design reasons.

• Risks in supply chain

Mattel produced core products like Barbie in factories it owned and used contracted manufacturers to produce non-core products. In seasons with high demand, Mattel also used contracted manufacturers as additional capacity for some of the core products. Contracted manufacturers may subcontract some produce processes. Contracted manufacturers and subcontractors may purchase from certified suppliers and uncertified suppliers. The complexity of the supply chain increases operational risks.

For example, the paint supplier of a contracted manufacturer Lee Der is Dongxing, which is not on Mattel's list of approved paint suppliers. In 2007, when Dongxing ran out of yellow pigment, it bought from a company providing paint with lead, a neurotoxin that is harmful for children's brain development. Strangely, Dongxing, Lee Der, and Mattel did not test the paint. Finally, Mattel recalled the products and Lee Der's factories were closed. After the recall, the company made a public apology.

- Risk management by Mattel

Recalls are post-risk management. In the aftermath of this recall, Mattel organized inspections in its toy factories in China and decided to suspend or revoke the licenses of many factories based in Guangdong province. In particular, Mattel implemented a three-point check system:

   i. Tested every batch of paint at every vendor and only allowed paint from certificated suppliers to be used.

  ii. Improved safety measures and increased random inspections.

 iii. Tested every production run before shipment.

Case Questions

1. Why did Mattel make the decision to outsource to China? What is the trade-off between in-house production and outsourcing?
2. Which basic operational strategies has Mattel used to address risks? Any suggestions on basic operations strategies (see Sect. 6.5.2)?
3. Is recall a good way to manage risks in global outsourcing? Can Mattel's current risk control approaches handle potential operational risks? Any suggestions on basic approaches to managing the risks of the global development and supply chain in Mattel (see Sect. 6.5.3)?

Case: Tiffany

Tiffany & Co., headquartered in New York City, is a world-leading jewelry corporation engaged in designing, manufacturing and retailing luxury products like jewelry, sterling silver, china, crystal, stationery, fragrances, personal accessories, and leather goods.

1. Product development chain

The company operates in five product categories: "silver and gold jewelry", "engagement jewelry and wedding bands", "statement, fine and solitaire jewelry", "designer jewelry", and others. The "silver and gold jewelry" category primarily consists of non-gemstone, sterling silver or gold jewelry. The "engagement" jewelry is made from platinum. The "statement, fine and solitaire jewelry" category includes jewelry for purposes other than engagement, and contains diamonds, other gemstones or both. The "designer jewelry" category includes only jewelry that bears the name of the company's designers like Elsa Peretti, Paloma Picasso, Frank Gehry and Jean Schlumberger. The other category includes sale of timepieces, sterling silver goods, china, crystal, stationery, fragrances, personal accessories, and leather goods. Product development depends on some celebrated designers and brings operational risks. For example, in 2012 Tiffany and a reputable designer Elsa Peretti could not agree to continue to use her intellectual property rights and designs, accounting for 10 % of net sales.

2. Supply Chain

Tiffany's supply chain strategy is "to increase its control over product supply and achieve improved profit margins through direct diamond sourcing and internal jewelry manufacturing". Tiffany has established strong sourcing and manufacturing capabilities pro-actively over the years. Nearly 60 % of the polished diamonds acquired by Tiffany were produced from rough diamonds sourced directly from the mines. The well-established sourcing network reduces operational risk as Tiffany has better control over the supply chain. Direct sourcing of raw rough diamonds from the mines ensures access to scarce and high-end diamond supplies, and allows better margins as intermediaries are eliminated.

Tiffany procures gems and precious metals from several vendors. The company has established diamond processing operations to purchase, sort, cut and polish rough diamonds at facilities in Belgium, South Africa, Botswana, Namibia, Mauritius and Vietnam, and at joint ventures in South Africa, Botswana and Namibia.

The corporation's in-house manufacturing facilities produce approximately 60 % of its merchandise in New York, Rhode Island, Kentucky and New Jersey, and purchase rose-gold and almost all non-jewelry items from third parties overseas.

3. Demand chain

Tiffany conducts its operations across five geographical segments: Americas, Asia-Pacific, Japan, Europe and others. Tiffany operates 250 stores and boutiques, strategically located based on the demographics of the area, consumer demand distribution, and the proximity of other luxury products. Its stores are located in some of the best "high streets" and luxury malls, and staffed with knowledgeable professionals providing excellent service to customers. Its strong presence in the direct selling channel increases the potential customer base.

Apart from the retail stores, Tiffany's direct marketing consists of Internet and catalogue sales. The company offers a wide range of products through its website tiffany.com, and operates the tiffany.com/business portal to facilitate business-to-business sales. The company is engaged in the distribution of catalogues of selected merchandise to its list of customers and to mailing lists from third parties. Tiffany also engages in business-to-business sales through its business sales executives. Tiffany develops relations with business clients and offers them price allowances for certain purchases. Tiffany's multichannel approach has been extended across geographical markets and caters to the various local preferences of its global customers.

4. Risks

Tiffany is first exposed to market risks from fluctuations in foreign currency exchange rates, since countries outside the US in aggregate represent approximately half its net sales.

Most of the company's jewelry and non-jewelry offering is made up of diamonds, gemstones and precious metals. Changes in the price of diamonds and precious metals or reduced supply availability might adversely affect the company's ability to produce and sell products with the desired profit margins. Acquiring diamonds for the engagement jewelry business has, at times, been difficult because of supply limitations. At such times, Tiffany may not be able to maintain a full selection of diamonds at each location.

The market for counterfeit goods and accessories has been growing, and in turn adversely affecting sales of Tiffany's branded merchandise. In 2009, the Australian Customs and Border Protection Service seized 10,778 counterfeit Tiffany items. Counterfeit crime is difficult to stop especially with the advent of the Internet, where sellers' identities can be concealed. Tiffany has limited power to exercise control over third-party selling sites and this will increase the vulnerability of Tiffany's brand to counterfeit products.

Since 2008, the economic crisis and the credit crunch have had a devastating impact on jewelry retailers. Although Tiffany, a large company with a strong brand, can maintain its market share, its sales are still influenced by the economic slowdown.

(*Source: Tiffany annual reports 2010–2011*)

Case Questions

1. Study Tiffany's global supply chain strategy using the GSCS taxonomy (see Sect. 6.2.1).
2. Study the GPD strategy of Tiffany, and make suggestions for GPD strategy based on the open innovation model (see Sect. 6.4.2).
3. List and categorize the distribution channels of Tiffany.
4. Analyze Tiffany's risks using the Tang and Musa classification (see Sect. 6.5.1), and propose possible basic operational strategies (see Sect. 6.5.2), and basic approaches (see Sect. 6.5.3).

References

Anupindi, R., Chopra, S., Deshmukh, S., Van Mieghem, J. A., & Zemel, E. (2012). *Managing business process flows: Principles of operations management*. Boston: Prentice Hall.

Bartholdi, J. J., & Gue, K. R. (2004). The best shape for a crossdock. *Transportation Science, 38* (2), 235–244.

Bartlett, C. A., & Ghoshal, S. (1986). Tap your subsidiaries for global reach. *Harvard Business Review, 64*(6), 87–94.

Brown, S. L., & Eisenhardt, K. M. (1995). Product development: Past research, present findings, and future directions. *Academy of Management Review, 20*(2), 343–378.

Buegelman, R. A., Maidique, M. A., & Wheelwright, S. C. (1995). *Strategic management of technology and innovation*. Chicago: Irwin.

Cheng, J. L. C., & Bolon, D. S. (1993). The management of multinational R&D: A neglected topic in international business research. *Journal of International Business Studies, 1*, 1–18.

Chesbrough, H. (2003). *Open innovation: The new imperative for creating and profiting from technology*. Boston: Harvard Business School Publishing.

Chesbrough, H. (2006). Open innovation: A new paradigm for understanding industrial innovation. In H. Chesbrough, W. Vanhaverbeke, & J. West (Eds.), *Open innovation: Researching a new paradigm* (pp. 1–14). Oxford: Oxford University Press.

Chiesa, V. (2000). Global R&D project management and organization: A taxonomy. *Journal of Product Innovation Management, 17*, 341–359.

Cohen, M., & Kunreuther, H. (2007). Operations risk management: Overview of Paul Kleindorfer's contributions. *Production and Operations Management, 16*(5), 525–541.

Davenport, T. H., Short, J. F. (1990). The new industrial engineering: Information technology and business process redesign. *Sloan Management Review, 31*(4), 11–27.

De Meyer, A. (1991). Tech talk: How managers are stimulating global R&D communication. *Sloan Management Review, 32*(3), 49–58.

Dunning, J. H. (1995). Re-evaluating multinational enterprises and the globalization of innovatory capacity. *Research Policy, 23*, 67–88.

Ethier, W. J. (1986). The multinational firm. *Quarterly Journal of Economics, 101*(4), 805–834.

Eppinger, S. D., & Chitkara, A. R. (2006). The new practice of global product development. *MIT Sloan Management Review, 47*(4), 22–30.

Fine, C. H., Whitney, D. E. (1996). Is the make-buy decision process a core competency? Working paper. Massachusetts Institute Technology, USA.

Fisher, M. L. (1997). What is the right supply chain for your product? *Harvard Business Review, 75*(2), 105–116.

Forrester, J. W. (1961). *Industrial dynamics*. Cambridge: The MIT Press.

Gassmann, O., & von Zedtwitz, M. (1999). New concepts and trends in international R&D organization. *Research Policy, 28*, 231–250.

Ghoshal, S. (1986). *The innovative multinational: A differentiated network of organizational roles and management processes*. Unpublished doctoral dissertation, Harvard Business School.

Graber, D. R. (1996). How to manage a global product development process. *Industrial Marketing Management, 25*, 483–489.

Guha, S., Kettinger, W. J., & Teng, T. C. (1993). Business process reengineering: Building a comprehensive methodology. *Information Systems Management, 10*(3), 13–22.

Hammer, M. (1990). Reengineering work: Don't automate, obliterate. *Harvard Business Review, 68*(4), 104–112.

Hammer, M., & Champy, J. (1993). *Reengineering the corporation: A manifesto for business revolution*. New York: Harper Business.

Harrison, J. M. (1997). The processing network paradigm in operations management. Working paper, Graduate School of Business, Stanford University.

Hayes, R. H., Pisano, G. P., Upton, D. M., & Wheelwright, S. C. (2004). *Operations, strategy, and technology: Pursuing the competitive edge*. Hoboken: Wiley.

Huang, Y.-A., Chung, H.-J., & Lin, C. (2009). R&D sourcing strategies: Determinants and consequences. *Technovation, 29*, 155–169.

Kleindorfer, P. R., & Van Wassenhove, L. (2004). Risk management in global supply chains. In H. Gatignon & J. Kimberly (Eds.), *The alliance on globalization*. Cambridge: Cambridge University Press. chapter 12.

Kuemmerle, W. (1996). *Home base and foreign direct investment in research and development: An investigation into the international allocation of research activity by multinational enterprises*. Unpublished doctoral thesis, Harvard University.

Kummerle, W. (1997). Building effective R&D capabilities abroad. *Harvard Business Review, 75* (2), 61–70.

Kogut, B. (1985). Designing global strategies: Profiting from operational flexibility. *Sloan Management Review, 27*(1), 27–38.

Lahiri, N. (2010). Geographic distribution of R&D activity: How does it affect innovation quality? *Academy of Management Journal, 53*(5), 1194–1209.

Laseter, T. M. (1998). *Balanced sourcing: Cooperation and competition in supplier relationships*. San Francisco: Jossey-Bass.

Lee, H. L., Padmanabhan, V., & Whang, S. (1997a). Information distortion in a supply chain: The bullwhip effect. *Management Science, 43*, 546–558.

Lee, H. L., Padmanabhan, V., Whang, S. (1997b). The bullwhip effect in supply chains. *Sloan Management Review, 38*(3), 93–102.

Loch, C. (1998). Operations management and reengineering. *European Management Journal, 16* (3), 306–317.

Nobel, R., & Birkenshaw, J. (1998). Innovation in multinational corporations: Control and communication patterns in international R&D operations. *Strategic Management Journal, 19*, 479–496.

Pearce, R. D. (1989). *The internationalization of research and development by multinational enterprises.* New York: St. Martin's Press.

Pearce, R. D. (1991). The globalization of R&D by TNCs. CTC Reporter 31, Spring, pp. 13–16.

Phillips, R. L. (2005). *Pricing and revenue optimization.* California: Stanford University Press.

Porter, M. E. (1985). Technology and competitive advantage, chapter 5. In *Competitive advantage.* New York: Free Press.

Porter, M. E. (1990). *The competitive advantage of nations.* New York: Free Press.

Pugh, D., Hickson, D. J., Hinings, C. R., & Turner, C. (1968). Dimensions of organization structure. *Administrative Science Quarterly, 13*, 67–105.

Ronstadt, R. C. (1977). *Research and development abroad by US multinationals.* New York: Praeger.

Simchi-Levi, D., Kaminsky, P., & Simchi-Levi, E. (2009). *Designing and managing the supply chain: Concepts, strategies, and case studies* (3rd ed.). New York: McGraw Hill.

Subramaniam, M., Rosenthal, S. R., & Hatten, K. J. (1998). Global new product development processes: Preliminary findings and research propositions. *Journal of Management Studies, 35* (6), 773–796.

Talluri, K. T., & van Ryzin, G. J. (2004). *The theory and practice of revenue management.* New York: Springer.

Tang, O., & Musa, S. N. (2011). Identifying risk issues and research advancements in supply chain risk management. *International Journal of Production Economics, 133*, 25–34.

Tang, C. S. (2006). Perspectives in supply chain risk management. *International Journal of Production Economics, 103*, 451–488.

Tushman, M. L., & Anderson, P. (1997). *Managing strategic innovation and change: A collection of readings.* Oxford: Oxford University Press.

Ulrich, K. T., & Eppinger, S. D. (1995). *Product design and development.* New York: McGraw Hill.

Van Mieghem, J. A. (2008). *Operations strategy – principles and practice.* Belmont: Dynamic Ideas.

Vernon, R. (1966). International investment and international trade in the product cycle. *Quarterly Journal of Economics, 81*, 190–207.

Vinod, B. (2005). Alliance revenue management. *Journal of Revenue and Pricing Management, 4*(1), 66–82.

von Zedtwitz, M., & Gassmann, O. (2002). Market versus technology drive in R&D internationalization: Four different patterns of managing research and development. *Research Policy, 31*, 569–588.

Part III

Practice of Global Operations Strategy

Part Objectives

- To study practice of global operations strategy.
- To discuss the global operations strategy across borders, including political separation, cultural separation, physical separation, developmental separation, relational separation.
- To address the global operations strategy across functions, and study integration issues among global operations strategy and marketing, finance, accounting, human resource management, and information management.
- To introduce environmentally friendly global operations strategy, and address environmentally friendly operational practices.
- To analyze sustainable operations, and present global sustainable operational strategies (Fig. III).

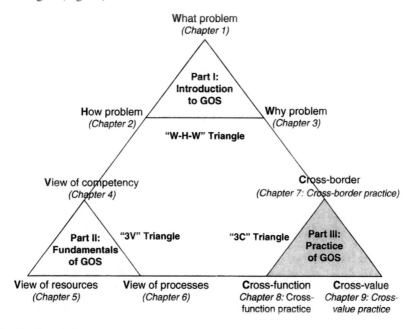

Fig. III The position of Part III in the whole book structure

Cross-Border Global Operational Practice

7

Chapter Objectives

- To address practice across various borders.
- To study the global operations strategy across political separation.
- To discuss types of cultural separation, and study global operations strategy across cultural separation.
- To analyze costs created by physical separation, and study global operations strategy across physical separation.
- To analyze global operations strategy across developmental separation.
- To discuss global operations strategy across relational separation.

7.1 Global Operations Strategy Across Political Separation

7.1.1 Introduction to Political Separation

Different countries have different governments, laws and political environments, which form the external political environment of business activities. When multinational companies do business across multiple political environments and political borders, they may meet political separation.

Political borders separate people, materials, products, financial transactions, and information. Political borders consist not only of visible immigration officers and customs, but also invisible systems to separate political ideas. Political separation imposes restriction on both inward flow and outward flow of financial capitals, by intervention measures such as import restrictions, tax policy, price controls, foreign exchange control, and nationalization policy, which disturb both resource-based and process-based global operations.

Y. Gong, *Global Operations Strategy*, Springer Texts in Business and Economics,
DOI 10.1007/978-3-642-36708-3_7, © Springer-Verlag Berlin Heidelberg 2013

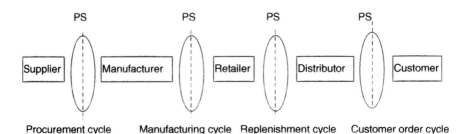

Fig. 7.1 Political separation in global supply chain

Political separation can bring difficulties to multinational corporations. Enterprises engaged in global operations must not only comply with local law system, but must also understand and abide by the foreign legal systems, and relevant international regulations and standards. For example, European states prohibited the sale of lighters without safety protection devices, which restricted the export of low-cost lighters. Taking another instance; in order to handle natural resources shortages and environment pollution, governments strengthen environment protection, with policies and regulations to restrict some business activities. Companies use political strategies to handle political separation in order to ensure competitive advantage, or even just survival.

7.1.2 Political Separation in Global Supply Chain

The processes in a global supply chain can be divided into four process cycles (Chopra and Meindl 2012), at the interface between two successive stages (see Fig. 7.1). Political separation can disturb, influence or even terminate process cycles.

1. Political separation in global procurement cycle.

   Procurement is the most obvious stage influenced by political separation. The procurement of strategic raw materials – defined as those raw materials (e.g., bauxite, chromium, cobalt, copper, iron, lead, manganese, mercury, natural rubber, nickel, phosphate rock, platinum, tin, tungsten, and zinc) essential for the national economy and national defense – has always been associated with politics in human history. For example, in the past 100 years the procurement of oil and gas has been influenced by wars, conflicts, national competition and other political activities. A recent case is rare earth metals, and China now produces over 95 % of the world's rare earth supply, mostly in Inner Mongolia. China has announced regulations on exports, and a crackdown on smuggling. In 2009, China announced plans to reduce its export quota, to conserve scarce resources and protect the environment, which influences the global procurement of rare earth.

Fig. 7.2 Three business responses for handling political separation

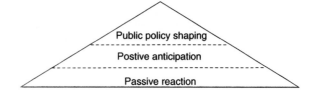

2. Political separation in global manufacturing cycle.

   Political separation seriously influences global manufacturing. The political environment is a factor to drive manufacturing outsourcing. For example, Chinese policies attract outsourcing from Western countries since Chinese chairman, Deng Xiaoping, introduced the "Open Door" policy in 1978. Recently, insourcing, the opposite of outsourcing, has been driven by inner political pressure within Western countries, in the period of economic crisis since 2009. US President Obama has put forward new tax proposals to reward companies that choose to invest in, or bring back jobs to the United States, and to eliminate tax advantages for companies moving jobs overseas. Large manufacturers such as Ford and Caterpillar have announced large investments in US manufacturing facilities. KEEN, a footwear designer, moved its production from China to a location near its corporate headquarters, and, in 2010, opened a large facility to manufacture boots in Portland, Oregon.

3. Political separation in global replenishment cycle.

   Global replenishment is not a cycle influenced frequently by political separation. However, in some special cases, such as weapons, ammunition, nuclear materials, and critical parts of large equipment, political separation will impose an impact on replenishment.

4. Political separation in global customer order cycle.

   In the global customer order cycle consisting of customer arrival, customer order entry, customer order fulfilment, and customer order receipt, political separation mainly influences customer arrival. Different political attitudes will influence customers' judgment on products.

7.1.3   Strategies for Political Separation

There are three general business attitudes to public policy: passive reaction, positive anticipation, and public policy shaping (Weidenbaum 1980). Based on three general responses, we present three general strategies for handling political separation in global operations (see Fig. 7.2).

1. Passive reaction

   With a passive reaction strategy, a firm does not play a role in policy formulation and implementation, and reacts passively to legislation in a foreign country. Before operating in a new country, according to the results of the investigation on political environment, the company may choose to abandon the market because of political separation. Many firms (e.g., Google, Levi's) even quit existing markets for political reasons.

2. Positive anticipation

   With a passive reaction strategy, a firm considers foreign government policy and political separation in global operations strategy, and anticipates adjustments of regulations. Since 2002, Microsoft has attempted to improve its political environment in China, in particular, to improve the environment of intelligence property protection, by maintaining a good relation with Chinese governments: not only the central government, including the National Development and Reform Commission, but also local governments, such as Shenzhen city and Jinan city. With efficient public relation policies, Microsoft enables its largest Chinese government client to purchase legal software successfully, which sets a model for other clients.

3. Public policy shaping

   With a proactive strategy, a firm tries to shape foreign government policies, in order to handle political separation in global operations. Hillman and Hitt (1999) present three proactive strategies:

   - Information strategy. A firm provides information to shape political decision-makers through tactics such as lobbying, publishing research reports, and supplying technical reports.
   - Financial incentive strategy. A firm provides financial incentives to shape or influence political decision-makers through tactics such as contributing to a party, honorariums for speaking and personal services.
   - Constituency-building strategy. A firm provides constituent support to indirectly influence political decision-makers through tactics such as grassroots mobilization of employees, advocacy advertising, and public relations.

Case Example: Microsoft's Political Road in China

Microsoft, an American company, encountered political separation and bumbled for years after entering China in 1992, and its business was a disaster. It figured out that almost none of the basic factors that led to its success in the US made sense in China. After 20 years of learning and trying, today Microsoft has a good political relation with the Chinese government, and maintains a good image with the Chinese people.

- 1992–1998 (CEO Jiabin Du)

In this period, the Chinese Congress did not have mature laws for intelligence property, and the Chinese Government had not taken measures to protect intelligence property. Counterfeit copies could be bought on the street for a few dollars. The Head of Microsoft's Chinese R&D, Ya-Qin Zhang, said: "In China we don't have problems with market share. The issue is how do we translate that into revenue." On July 20, 1998, *Fortune* magazine published an interview with Bill Gates, who said, "people in China are not paying for software, but someday they will. If they want to steal, we want them to steal ours".

- 1998–2002 (CEOs Qunyao Gao, Juliet Wu)

The intellectual property problem became a sensitive political topic between the Chinese and American Governments. Microsoft fought to protect its intellectual property, and sued companies using its software illegally, but lost regularly in court.

The relationship with the Chinese government became worse. In a public government purchase, in 2001, Beijing City Government chose WPS (a product competing with MS Office), and software based on free open-source Linux operating systems, not Microsoft's products. Meanwhile, Chinese security officials and the public showed deep concern that government and military operations depended on Microsoft software made in the US. Its political image was associated with hegemony, monopolization, and arrogance.

To handle the crisis, Microsoft sent 25 of the company's 100 vice-presidents for a week-long "China Immersion Tour". Microsoft hired former Secretary of State Henry Kissinger to advise on political strategy in China. Microsoft tried to convince Chinese leaders that Microsoft wanted to help China develop its own software industry. In 2001, the company commissioned McKinsey: a study recommending the improvement of intellectual property protection.

- 2002–2006 (CEOs Jun Tang, Tim Chen)

Microsoft began talks with Chinese security officials to convince them that Microsoft's software was not a tool of the US Government. In 2003, the company offered China and other countries the right to check the fundamental source code for its Windows operating system, and to substitute certain portions with their own codes. Now, when the Chinese Government organization uses Windows, they can install their own cryptography. With regard to the intellectual property problem, Microsoft openly concedes that tolerating piracy has turned out to be the company's long-term strategy.

In 2006, Microsoft signed a cooperative agreement with a value of RMB 6.2 billion, with the National Development and Reform Commission, to provide human resources, management experience, and technological support. In 2006, Microsoft promised the Chinese Government they would invest USD 3.7 billion. Government relations turned out to be better. When President Hu Jintao visited the Microsoft campus in Redmond, and attended a dinner at Gates' home, Hu told his host: "You are a friend to the Chinese people, and I am a friend of Microsoft. Every morning I go to my office and use your software", When Gates visited China, he met four members of the Politburo on his four-day trip. Very few Fortune 500 companies get the same treatment in China.

With the help of good government relations, the Chinese Government is changing its policies. First, it requires central and local governments to use legal software. Second, the government requires local PC manufacturers to load legal software on their computers. The third mandate requires the gradual legalization of the millions of computers in state-owned enterprises.

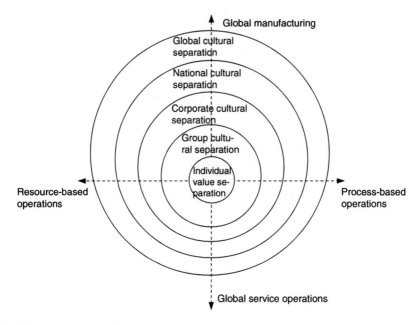

Fig. 7.3 Levels of cultural separation

1. In 1992, what kind of political separation did Microsoft meet in China?
2. To what extent did political separation change the global operations strategy of Microsoft in China?
3. How did Microsoft go beyond the political separation between countries? Which political strategies has Microsoft used to solve the problem of political separation?

7.2   Global Operations Strategy Across Cultural Separation

7.2.1   Introduction to Cultural Separation

Culture is, "the collective programming of the mind which distinguishes the members of one human group from another" (Hofstede 1980, p. 25). As cultures vary, so arises cultural separation, which refers to the phenomenon whereby people with different cultural backgrounds try to retain their original features, instead of being assimilated into other cultures.

In a global environment, both manufacturing and service operations need cross cultural borders at different levels (see Fig. 7.3). So do resource-based and process-based operations. Among these levels, the largest macro-level is global cultural

Table 7.1 National culture separation and their influences on global operations

Dimension	Definition	Global manufacturing	Global service
Individualism versus collectivism	The degree to which people in a country prefer to act as individuals rather than as members of a group	Supply relation, supply contract, manufacturing scale, automation level, production planning	Service concept design, service diversity, service process (standard versus customization) design
Large versus small power distance	The extent to which a society accepts the fact that power in institutions and organizations is distributed unequally	Mass production, facility location, global manufacturing network structure	Service organization structure
Strong versus weak, uncertain avoidance	The extent to which a society feels threatened by uncertain and ambiguous situations	Risk control, quality management, delivery accuracy, Enterprise resource planning	Service demand forecasting, standardization of service process
Masculinity versus femininity	The extent to which the dominant values in society are "masculine"	Manufacturing scale, supplier-retailer relation, automation level	Service concept design

separation, formed by global organizations, global networks, and global institutions across national borders. Then comes national cultural separation since national cultures vary from one to another (Hofstede 1991). Below national level is organizational cultural separation, which is usually shaped by different industries, ownership and value of founders. Organizational culture has four traits: involvement, consistency, adaptability and mission (see e.g., Denison 1990; Fey and Denison 2003). Within an organization, a global operation can meet group cultural separation, such as culture differences of marketing and manufacturing departments. The lowest cultural separation is individual value differences.

7.2.2   Influence of National Cultural Separation

Among these levels, national cultural separation plays an important role in global operations strategy. The values that distinguish countries from each other can be grouped statistically into four clusters (Hofstede 1991), and national cultural separation develops along four underlying value dimensions (Hofstede dimensions): individualism versus collectivism; large versus small power distance; strong versus weak, uncertain avoidance; and masculinity versus femininity (see Table 7.1).

Table 7.1 presents the definition of four cultural separations, and gives examples to show the influence of cultural separation on global manufacturing and global service operations. Firstly, collectivism is characterized by a tight social framework in which people distinguish between in-groups (social groups to which individuals feel they belong as members) and out-groups (social groups for which individuals feel contempt, opposition, or a desire to compete). They expect their in-group to look after them, and in exchange, they feel they owe loyalty to it. With a higher collectivism level, trust and information sharing in the supply chain can be high, while supply relation and supply contract are stable. With a higher individualism level, the operations strategy needs to increase the service diversity and customization of the service process. Secondly, power distance is the extent to which subordinates are not expected to express disagreement with their supervisors, and supervisors are not expected to consult with their subordinates in the decision-making process. With a higher power distance level, the operations strategy may increase the manufacturing scale and use mass production. Thirdly, uncertainty avoidance is the extent to which a society feels threatened by uncertain and ambiguous situations, and tries to avoid these situations by providing greater career stability, establishing more formal rules, not tolerating deviant ideas and behaviors, and believing in absolute truths and the attainment of expertise. With high uncertainty avoidance, a company can enhance risk control, quality management, and improve delivery accuracy. Fourthly, masculinity is the degree to which values, such as assertiveness, performance, success and competition, prevail over values such as quality of life, maintaining warm personal relationships, care for the weak, and solidarity. This dimension influences the manufacturing scale, supplier-retailer relation, automation level, and service concept design.

Besides Hofstede's traditional four dimensions, the fifth dimension is "Long-Term Orientation." Societies with a long-term orientation believe that truth depends very much on situation, context and time, and show an ability to adapt traditions to changed conditions (Hofstede and Bond 1988). The sixth dimension is "Indulgence versus Restraint", referring to the extent to which a society allows the relatively free gratification of basic and natural human drives about enjoying life and having fun.

7.2.3 Strategies for Cultural Separations

We present both strategies to handle static cultural separations, and strategies for dynamic cultural separations and cultural change.

7.2.3.1 Strategic Fit Between Global Operations Strategy and Nation Culture

When formulating and evaluating a global operations strategy, we need to consider its strategy fit to different cultures. Figure 7.4 illustrates an example of the strategy fit between global supply chain and national culture, with increasing collectivism level as we move along the vertical axis, and increasing information sharing as we move along the horizontal axis. In the zone of low efficiency, a global supply chain, with an emphasis on duty and group decision-making, only achieves low trust and information sharing. Its efficiency is low since it can do better in trust and information sharing. In the high cost zone, a global supply chain, with an emphasis on

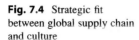
Fig. 7.4 Strategic fit between global supply chain and culture

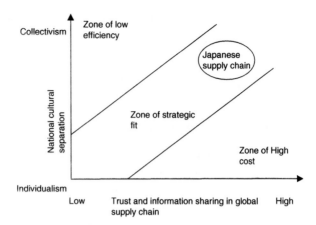

individual achievement, needs high cost to achieve information sharing. To achieve a high level of performance, a global supply chain strategy should move toward the zone of strategic fit. In Japanese society, with a high level of collectivism, companies may share inventory and other business information with partners, to achieve a higher collective performance in global supply chains. Japanese companies may join the *Kyoryoku Kai* (a Japanese term for a supplier association), which is a collection of a company's most important suppliers that work together to develop more efficient production techniques and management methods, through trust building and information sharing.

7.2.3.2 Strategies for Culture Change

If a company cannot achieve the strategy fit between global operations strategy and national culture, it can either change its operations strategy or culture if it decides to enter the market. After considering the trade-off between the cost of cultural change and the benefit of strategic fit, a company can use approaches for cultural change to cross cultural separation. Bate (1994) presents strategies to handle culture changes. Usually, multiple approaches are used in most change processes.

- Progressive. This aggressive approach refers to implementing cultural change rapidly, which is effective in rapid major change, but poor in gaining commitment and ownership of the result.
- Consultative. This approach uses a great deal of communication and involvement, which is effective in gaining commitment, but poor for rapid major change.
- Educative. This approach changes culture by educating and training people, which is poor in people's reaction to rational change.
- Corrosive. This approach "corrodes" people by releasing key messages from the executives at suitable points. The approach is used to manage professionals, who usually resist direct control.

Table 7.2 Comparing two countries according to Hofstede dimensions

	Individualism	Power distance	Uncertainty avoidance	Masculinity
Germany	67	35	65	66
United States	91	40	46	62

Source: http://geert-hofstede.com

Case Example: Culture Separation and DaimlerChrysler

On 7 May 1998, Chrysler announced it would merge with Daimler-Benz, to create the combined entity DaimlerChrysler. The merger turned out to be a failure. Three years after the merger, DaimlerChrysler's market capitalization stood at USD 44 billion, roughly equal to the value of Daimler-Benz before the merger. Chrysler Group's share value had declined by one-third compared to pre-merger values. In 2007, DaimlerChrysler announced the sale of 80.1 % of the Chrysler Group to the American private equity firm Cerberus Capital Management. In 2009, Daimler gave up its 19.9 % remaining stake in Chrysler to Cerberus Capital Management. An important reason for the failure was the cultural separation, which gradually eroded the anticipated synergy.

1. Brand image difference

   Daimler, a representative Germany company and one of the top luxury car makers, dominated the European market. Daimler-Benz, was universally perceived as the fancy special brand, exuding disciplined German engineering with uncompromising quality. Meanwhile, in the mid-1990s, the Chrysler Corporation, founded on June 6, 1925, by Walter Chrysler, was the most profitable automotive producer in the world. Buoyed by record light truck, van, and large sedan sales, its revenues were at an all-time high; Chrysler was acclaimed for producing vehicles that captured the bold and pioneering American spirit.

2. Corporate cultural separation

   Mercedes-Benz valued disciplined German engineering to achieve uncompromising quality competency. Chrysler valued assertiveness and a risk-taking cowboy culture to achieve cost competency. Daimler-Benz encouraged structured decision-making, while Chrysler was characterized by creativity. Chrysler valued efficiency, empowerment, and fairly egalitarian relations among staff, whereas Daimler-Benz seemed to value respect for centralized authority and bureaucratic precision. Germans disliked huge pay disparities, but American executives were highly rewarded.

3. National cultural separation

   Table 7.2 presents German and American national cultural difference according to Hofstede dimensions. Germany is an individualist countries (with a score of 67), but the United States has a highly individualistic culture (with a score of 91). Germany is among the uncertainty avoidant countries (with a score of 65), but American society is described as "uncertainty accepting" (with a score of 46). Consequently, Americans are willing to accept new ideas and innovative products. American employees emphasize freedom, passion, and independence,

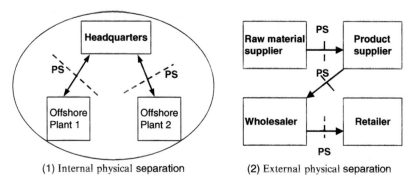

Fig. 7.5 Two types of physical separation

and they perform better in high efficiency. German employees tend to be strictly disciplined, and there are much more regulations to follow.

Case Questions

1. What was the corporate cultural separation between Chrysler and Daimler? What is national cultural separation between American Chrysler and German Daimler?
2. What was the influence of cultural separation on the global operations (e.g., global manufacturing, global R&D) of DaimlerChrysler?
3. What was the role of cultural separation in the failure of the merger? If culture change was an option, what would your approach suggestion be to DaimlerChrysler to avoid the failure?

7.3 Global Operations Strategy Across Physical Separation

7.3.1 Introduction to Physical Separation

Physical barriers separate countries. For instance, China is separated from India by the Himalayas, and from Japan by the East China Sea. This physical separation of geographical distance influences global operations. Generally speaking, although there are exceptions, in international trade, the further apart two countries are, the less they will do business together.

There are two types of physical separation (see Fig. 7.5): (1) Internal physical separation. This happens in global operations between internal units, in different locations, within one company. When a company builds offshore manufacturing facilities in another country, the headquarters and offshore plants will have a physical separation. (2) External physical separation. A global supply chain needs to handle physical separation among business partners in different countries. For a partner in this global supply chain, this physical separation is from the outside.

7.3.2   Influence of Physical Separation on Global Operations

Physical separation leads to four types of trade costs for companies implementing their operation strategies across borders. Transporting goods from one point of the globe to another not only creates transportation costs, but also shipping time costs, communication costs, and transaction costs (see Burns et al. 1985; Hummels 1999).

1. Shipping time

   Globalization has increased the importance of time as the transfer and exchange of goods, labor and knowledge are strategic. Besides, shipping time, resulting from physical separation between trade partners, may imply exchange rate costs. Ocean shipping was the primary mode of large transportation but, nowadays, many others have appeared. Firms pay more to air freight to save time in transit. Shipping containers from European ports to the US. Midwest need two or three weeks, and Far Eastern ports require as long as six weeks, whereas air freight requires only a day or less. For a company which faces a surge in demand, seasonal demand or specific demand (e.g., perishable products), timing becomes a key issue. In a supply chain process, time will regulate the schedule production between actors, and can impact the consumer.

2. Transportation cost

   An empirical fact is that trade is inversely proportionate to distance, but Head (2007) has shown that "a doubling of distance will decrease trade by one half" between two countries. The first cause for this negative distance effect is the transportation cost, and transportation costs are an increasing function of distance. Head (2007, p. 55) presents five reasons to explain the transportations costs: fuel consumption; vehicle building and operating price; infrastructure cost; risk cost; delay compensation for customers.

3. Transaction costs

   Transaction costs are involved in the process of buying or selling between two entities. This process is defined by five steps: searching for a potential partner, engaging in an agreement, negotiating a contract, safeguarding the agreement conditions, and enforcing payment and delivery. This implies that costs could be avoided if the provider and the user are from the same organization. Agreements are more costly to negotiate and enforce when buyers and sellers are from different countries. Networks of trade partners, that are familiar with each other or are not physically separated, have implicit rules (e.g., peer pressure and reputation) to reduce the risks of contract breach. However, physical separation brings greater anonymity between parties, and reduces the trust level, thereby increasing transaction costs.

4. Communication costs

   MNCs have to communicate continuously with their partners, in order to provide enough detailed information, to resolve the potential problems suppliers could encounter. The development of the Internet has definitely modified international business relationships, by improving not only the transmission of texts, but also images and videos all over the world. Communication must be effective between suppliers and consumers, who need to interact in order to design the most needed

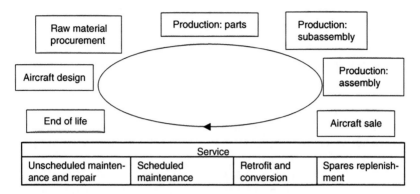

Fig. 7.6 Physical separations in the life cycle of Airbus aircraft

and expected product. Thereby, the quality of telecommunication infrastructures is considered to be a key factor in decisions on investing abroad or not.

Case Example: Physical Separation of Airbus

Airbus, established in 1970, is a leading European aircraft manufacturer. Nowadays, Airbus' product line comprises different families of aircraft ranging from 107 to 525 seats: A320, A330/340, A350, and A380. Operating in the civil aircraft market, in 2010, Airbus had revenues of EURO 29.9 billion.

• Challenges of physical separation

Compared with other industries, physical separation is a larger challenge in the aircraft manufacturing industry. First, it is more difficult to operate global manufacturing and logistics across physical separation, since aircraft parts and end-products are large, irregular and heavy. Second, for an end-product such as the A380, its component parts number millions. This increases the complexity of global manufacturing and logistics across physical separation. Third, this industry widely uses outsourcing, and adopts a huge global manufacturing coordination network, which increases the difficulty for going across external physical separation. Finally, challenges also arise from physical separations in the life cycle of Airbus aircraft (see Fig. 7.6): it is difficult to transport oversize components, parts, spares and aircraft across physical borders at each stage of their lifecycle.

• Internal physical separation

Based in Toulouse, Airbus is a global company which employs 55,000 people in subsidiaries in Europe, the US, China, Japan and the Middle East; with spare parts centers in Hamburg, Frankfurt, Washington, Dubai, Beijing and Singapore; training centers in Toulouse, Miami, Hamburg and Beijing; and more than 150 field service offices around the world.

The company's manufacturing, production and subassembly of parts are distributed across 15 sites in Europe, with jetliner final assembly lines in Toulouse, Hamburg, and Tianjin. This internal industrial system has been expanded to include a regional design office in North America, a joint venture engineering center in Russia, and engineering centers in China and India. Dealing with global logistics is a big challenge for Airbus: they have to transfer the various airframe components mainly to Toulouse for final assembly. Taking the A380, the Airbus flagship, as an example, it is a double-deck, wide-body, two-engine aircraft. The steps to build this aircraft are as follows: operations in Airbus Centers of Excellence (for key production areas: fuselage and cabin; wing and pylon; aft fuselage and empennage; and aerostructures); transport of major aircraft sections; assembly; tests; and, finally delivery to customers.

• External physical separation

Airbus deals with more than 1,500 primary suppliers in 30 countries. The suppliers are organized in three tiers, according to their strategic importance. Airbus Procurement is organized into six commodity departments in charge of purchasing the different categories of goods (aerostructure, materials, equipment & systems, propulsion systems, cabin and general procurement). Airbus created the AIRBUS Supply Platform to communicate and share information with its suppliers. Airbus has worked with local manufacturers to develop some components of the A380, and has an integrated outsourcing approach.

• Global logistics systems across physical separation

Airbus optimizes its global supply chain and logistics by selecting one lead logistics provider, and one lead transport provider. The Airbus strategy selects its lead logistics provider "Kuehne + Nagel" to consolidate all local warehouse facilities into six regional hubs, and to run a pan-European network of logistics hubs, storing aircraft equipment, parts and raw materials to serve Airbus production lines. As the lead transport provider, DHL implements Airbus' transportation system to streamline the flow of materials among Airbus manufacturing plants.

The company develops its own logistics system with a network of transport systems by road, air, river and sea, all over Europe. This involved the construction of a fleet of roll-on/roll-off ships and barges, the construction of port facilities, and the development of new and modified roads to accommodate oversized road convoys. In Saint-Nazaire, a ship trades the fuselage sections from Hamburg for larger, assembled sections, some of which include the nose. The ship unloads in Bordeaux.

Approaches for handling physical separation are featured by oversize cargo transport in aircraft manufacturing. To support its internal supply chain, Airbus developed the Super Transporter Beluga to carry complete aircraft sections from various production sites to the final assembly lines. Beluga has one of the widest fuselage cross-sections of any aircraft, and its main deck's cargo volume is greater than many of the world's leading airlifters. A semi-automated main deck cargo loading system ensures easy and efficient handling of aircraft components. Owing to Beluga's jet speed and efficiency, Airbus can go across physical separation with short transport times, to meet strict production planning.

Table 7.3 Influence of income per capita on global operations (example of benefits)

	Low income per capita	High income per capita
Impact on resources	Cheap labor force, lower capital investment requirement	Qualified labor force, more financial resources available, higher demand
Impact on processes	Low product or service price, closer to potential retailers and customers	Lower risk, speed processes without much corruption, better research and development environment

Case Questions

1. Why are both internal physical separation and external separation significant for Airbus?
2. As a European company, how does Airbus deal with physical separation? Why did Airbus select one lead logistics provider and one lead transport provider, while maintaining its own logistics system?
3. Are the Airbus global logistics systems efficient solutions to the challenges of physical separation?

7.4 Global Operations Strategy Across Developmental Separation

Developmental separation refers to the differences between countries' development, in terms of economic growth (with a national-scope basis) and human development (with an individual-scope basis). Those two types of development are linked closely together, and affect both resources and processes of global operations.

Economic growth is the process by which a nation's wealth increases over time, and is influenced not only by natural, human and capital resources, but also by institutional structure and stability. Human development aims at enlarging people's freedom to do and to be what they value. In practice, human development enables people to lead a long and healthy live, be educated, and have a decent standard of living (see Ranis et al. 2000; Tarun et al. 2005).

The efficient measurement of this relationship is the income per capita index, and the level of income per capita is correlated with consumer price levels, productivity, educational levels, health-care levels, infrastructure, and corruption (see Head 2007). Table 7.3 presents examples of benefits that a low versus high income per capita can provide to operational resources and operational processes. For example, while suppliers receive a competitive advantage by using a cheap labor force in a low income per capita country, a high income per capita country will have a more qualified labor force.

Table 7.4   Gross national income per capita, 2010 (nations relevant to Tata)

Economy	Atlas methodology (US dollars)	Purchasing power parity (international dollars)	Subsidiaries, JVs and associates
Netherlands	49,720 (ranking 15)	42,590 (ranking 23)	Tata Steel Europe
United Kingdom	38,540 (ranking 32)	36,580 (ranking 33)	Jaguar Land Rover
Spain	31,650 (ranking 38)	31,550 (ranking 41)	Tata Hispano Motors Carrocera S. A.
Korea, Rep.	19,890 (ranking 56)	29,010 (ranking 48)	Tata Daewoo Commercial Vehicle Company Ltd
Brazil	9,390 (ranking 82)	10,920 (ranking 96)	Tata Marcopolo Motors Ltd.
Thailand	4,210 (ranking 122)	8,240 (ranking 114)	Tata Motors (Thailand) Limited
India	1,340 (ranking 160)	3,560 (ranking 153)	Headquarters and other subsidiaries

(*Source: World Development Indicators database, World Bank, July 1, 2011*)

Case Example: Tata Across Developmental Separation

Founded in 1868, the Tata Group has expanded from India to more than 80 countries across continents and its companies export products and services to 85 countries. Today's Tata Group comprises over 100 companies in seven business sectors: engineering, materials, services, energy, communications and information technology, consumer products and chemicals, employing over 450,000 people worldwide. The total revenue of Tata companies was USD 100.09 billion in 2010–11, with 58 % of this coming from business outside India. During the process from India to developed countries, Tata has met significant developmental separation (see Table 7.4). We present two Tata companies in this case example.

1. Tata Motors

   Originating in India, Tata Motors might be seen as one of successful car producers in emerging countries. Recognizing the need to integrate its international strategy with its domestic one, the company split its previously independent international business arm into two business units: the Passenger Car Business Unit, and the Commercial Vehicle Business Unit. Tata grew by acquiring foreign brands. Tata entered South Korea by acquiring Deawoo's commercial vehicles division; Spain by controlling Hispano Carrocera; and Brazil by creating a joint venture with Marcopolo.

   In 2008, Tata revealed its true influence by acquiring two well-known British luxury brands, Jaguar and Land Rover (JLR), for USD 2.5 billion from Ford Motor. The acquisition gave Tata Motors access to premium cars, and an opportunity to include two iconic luxury brands in its global image, and to transform Tata Motors from a commercial vehicle and small-car manufacturer to a global player, with marquee brands in its portfolio. Although many critics expressed doubts about Tata's ability across developmental separations, three years after the acquirement JLR profits are up sharply, and it contributes more than 50 % of Tata Motors' profits.

2. Tata Steel

Tata Steel is one of the top ten global steel companies, with an annual crude steel capacity of more than 27 million tons per annum (mtpa), and one of the world's most geographically diversified steel producers, with operations in 20 countries, and a commercial presence in over 50 countries. The challenges of developmental separation come especially from the Tata-Corus acquisition, the largest acquisition by an Indian firm.

Corus, the Anglo-Dutch steelmaker, was formed in 1999 by the merger of British Steel with Hoogovens of the Netherlands. With 47,300 employees working in plants across Britain, the Netherlands, Germany, France, Norway, and Belgium, Corus had the highest cost of production among the world's steelmakers. Tata Steel acquired the Anglo-Dutch steel firm Corus for USD 11.3 billion, in 2007. Tata's acquisition of Corus made it the fifth largest global steel producer. The acquisition gave Tata Steel access to European markets, and to achieving potential synergies in procurement, R&D, manufacturing, logistics, and back office operations.

It is not easy for Tata to integrate Corus. After five years, Tata Steel Europe is still taking restructuring measures, such as restructuring its steel tubes business, cutting jobs, suspending production at a hot strip mill in Wales, stopping work at a blast furnace in England, implementing an efficiency drive plan in the Netherlands, tightening up supply chains by focusing on high-end products in Europe, and looking for new raw material sources.

Among global operation problems, global risk control is critical, since raw material prices have been volatile and buying behavior has been unstable in the global steel industry. To manage global risks, Tata manages fixed costs "by insourcing and outsourcing, by consolidating sites and by optimizing operations at each site" (Koushik Chatterjee, CFO of Tata Steel; see issue 2, Q1 2012, capital insights, *The Financial Times*).

Case Questions

1. What kind of developmental separation did Tata meet in the acquisition of Jaguar and Land Rover? What are the benefits of acquiring Jaguar and Land Rover?
2. What kind of developmental separation did Tata meet in the acquisition of Corus? What are the benefits of acquiring Corus?
3. How did Tata handle developmental separation in its global operations?

7.5   Global Operations Strategy Across Relational Separation

7.5.1   Introduction to Relational Separation

Implementing an operational strategy across borders is affected directly by relational separation. There are two kinds of relational separation: social network, and business network. We care particularly about the case of the business network. Local communities have webs of one-on-one interactions that are social and business networks. We are particularly interested in business networks which comprise relationship between buyers and sellers. In the terminology of network analysis, buyers and sellers are called "nodes". Some nodes are connected to each other by links. There are many types of links. For instance, in a telecommunication network, the links might be fiber optic cable. In a business network, a link usually corresponds to an ongoing history of exchange. Relational separation occurs in business networks when buyers and sellers, residing in one country, are linked mainly to each other, and have few, if any, links with their counterparts in a foreign country. Relational separation may not simply reflect an absence of past interactions. It is likely to also cause a reluctance to engage in future interactions. This is because buyers and sellers that are already connected tend to prefer to continue to trade with each other, and they often shun "outsiders", those with whom they have never interacted before. One of the main activities of business networks is the spread of information. Examples of such "data sharing" include leads (names of peoples who can provide particular items), and blacklists (names of people who are known to be untrustworthy).

7.5.2   Relational Separation and Global Operations

The main influence of relational separation for operations strategy is that some firms tend to operate only in their domestic market, and are reluctant to do international trade. As operations strategy is related to the way the firm adapts its capacity to the needs of the market, we realize that the buyer/seller relationship is a major issue in operational strategy. The supply chain management, which is an important part of operational strategy, is also influenced by this relationship.

We analyze two influences of relational separation. First, the transaction costs are usually higher when business partners want to avoid the risk of not being paid. This happens mainly when business partners do not trust each other, because they do not know each other well. In this situation, to make sure that the transaction will be secure, business partners use financial tools such as letters of credit, which increases the total cost of the transaction. Second, having a strong foreign network is also a way to have access to crucial information about the market. Usually, foreign counterparts know much about the specificity of business in their domestic market. For example, they can give information about the purchasing channel for a particular product because it can vary from one country to another, and then the firm can adapt its operation strategy to this particular demand, in order to be more efficient.

Fig. 7.7 *Guanxi*'s foundation of social philosophy

There are four kinds of outsourcing relationships: The first one is "trust-based partnerships", which may not provide clear incentives to drive improvement, assumes supplier goal congruence, and in which the supplier can capture all value creation. The second one is "balanced sourcing", which drives improvement in both customers and suppliers. The third relationship is "unleveraged purchasing", which typifies the clerical mentality of traditional purchasing, focuses on price rather than total cost, and leaves lots of money on the table. Finally, there is a "Darwinian rivalry" relationship, which requires significant purchasing clout, but does not drive synergetic improvements (see Fig. 6.7).

Case Example: *Guanxi* and Operations in China

"Guanxi" is a Chinese term which literally means "relationships" or "connections" (see Chen et al. 2004). Its background is mainly in Confucianism, a social philosophy to establish harmony through a strong and orderly hierarchy (see Fig. 7.7). The core elements of Confucian social philosophy are "Five Constant Virtues" *(wuchang):* benevolence *(ren);* righteousness *(yi);* manners *(li);* wisdom *(zhi),* and credit *(xin).* Guanxi emphasizes two issues *"Mianzi"* and *"Renqing". Mianzi* (literally, "face") is associated with personal status, and the Chinese enjoy maintaining personal prestige among *guanxi* networks. *Renqing* is a form of social capital that balances interpersonal exchanges of favors with an informal social obligation to others in *guanxi* networks.

In traditional Chinese society, *guanxi* is based on factors that promote shared social experience among individuals, which includes being a close or distant relative, classmate, colleague, teacher/student, having the same birth or ancestral origin, being a former neighbor, or supervisor/subordinate, having the same hobbies, and so on. The Chinese classify *guanxi,* networks roughly into three levels: "family", *"shuren"* standing for familiar people, and *"shengren"* standing for strangers (see Fig. 7.8).

Guanxi is an informal personal relationship rather than a formal official relation. Formal and informal relationships may overlap in an organization, and such overlap often leads to a conflict of interest and causes problems of neutrality and fairness. *Guanxi* is transferable, reciprocal, intangible, and utilitarian (see Park and Luo 2001 and Fig. 7.3). *Guanxi* networks are dynamic not static, since personal status keeps changing. *Guanxi* is an important social resource, which can be used to achieve and maintain sustainable competitive advantage.

Guanxi impacts a resource-based operations strategy. With well-built *guanxi* networks, it is easier to acquire land, as well as financial and human resources.

Fig. 7.8 Social structure of *guanxi*

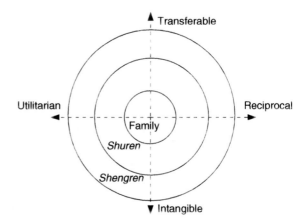

Guanxi networks can provide alternative options for operational decisions, such as facility location selection, logistics development, and supplier selections, and increase operational flexibility.

Guanxi plays an important role in process-based operations strategy in China. It influences four elements of supply chain management in China: global purchasing, outsourcing, supplier development and global risk control (see Lee and Humphreys 2007). In global risk control, purchasing firms build *guanxi* networks with critical suppliers to improve supply trust and communication, and to reduce supply and shortage risks.

Case Questions

1. Why does *guanxi* create relational separation for a Western company which intends to operate in China?
2. How can a Western company crack relational separation through the four principals (transferable, reciprocal, intangible, and utilitarian) of *guanxi*?
3. How is sustainable competitive advantage with *guanxi* networks achieved? How is sustainable competitive advantage maintained by managing *guanxi* dynamics?
4. What are the positive and negative influences of *guanxi* on resource-based operations strategy? What are its influences on process-based operations strategy in China?

Case: Subway Across Borders

Subway, a leading sandwich chain in the world, was founded in 1965, with the first store opened in Connecticut. Subway has more than 38,331 restaurants in 99 countries as of December 2012. The company serves fresh nutritious sandwiches allowing customers to customize their sandwiches by choosing the different types of fillings, bread, and ingredients. There are more than two million sandwich varieties available from its menu choices.

- Cultural separation

Subway had to face cultural problems when the company decided to establish stores in Hindu, Jewish and Muslims countries, with cultural influences and specific religion rules in food and eating habits. To succeed in Israel and the kosher market of the US, Subway decided to become a kosher brand in certain areas. Israel is one of the countries in which Subway decided to adopt the kosher strategy. To run successful restaurants in Israel, Subway decided to customize its products and services according to the needs of the local market.

To become kosher, Subway had to obtain a kosher certificate issued by the Chief Rabbinate and satisfy various conditions. For example, ham and bacon had to be removed from the menu, "cheese" had to be made of soy, and meat and dairy products cannot be mixed in meals. It is usually forbidden to use the same utensils for preparing non-kosher food to make kosher food. To satisfy conditions every store must have two microwaves and ovens to ensure that fish and meat are kept in different areas. A full-time *mashgiach* employed in each store will supervise the *kashrut* status of a kosher store. To please the Jewish community, kosher stores are closed on Saturday and during the Jewish holidays.

Subway also decided to go further and applied for a "glatt kosher" certificate. The difference between "glatt kosher" and kosher is in the way meat is prepared. Kosher meat must come from a kosher animal and be slaughtered in a kosher way. To satisfy the needs of the kosher market, Subway created new sandwiches such as Hot Pastrami, Shawarma sandwich, and Corned Beef. Subway even offered kosher lunch programs to local schools.

- Physical separation

As a global company, Subway needs to go across physical separation. To achieve this goal, Subway built an Internet-based global supply chain to ensure that franchisees worldwide could receive products with the right quality at the right time. All franchisees have to order foods from an approved food distributor for the food quality and cost reduction.

Subway works with local suppliers whose activities are supervised by the Independent Purchasing Cooperative (IPC). IPC is a franchisee-owned and operated purchasing cooperative that negotiates for the lowest prices of goods and services, while maintaining quality and other standards. For example, European Independent Purchasing Company (EIPC) manages the purchasing and supply chain activities for all food, packaging, equipment and services in the UK, Ireland, and other European countries. The IPCs were not only established to ensure quality, but also to coordinate supply chain providers and suppliers. To help franchisees, Subway established regional development offices to help all franchisees with site selection, leasing, design, construction, training, purchasing, internal operations, advertising, and local store marketing.

Although Subway cooperates with the IPCs, it has built many offices to manage these relationships in Europe (franchise offices in Amsterdam, the Netherlands), Asia (franchise offices in Lebanon, Singapore and India), Australia and New Zealand (franchise offices in Australia), and Latin America (franchise support centers in Miami, Florida).

Case Questions

1. Which major problems did Subway face when entering the kosher market? How did Subway cope with cultural separation?
2. Has Subway provided products and services to customers by mass customization? How did it customize its products and services?
3. What strategy did Subway use to deal with the physical separation of restaurants?

References

Bate, P. (1994). *Strategies for cultural change.* Oxford: Butterworth-Heinemann.

Burns, L. D., Hall, R. W., Blumenfeld, D. E., & Daganzo, C. F. (1985). Distribution strategies that minimize transportation and inventory costs. *Operations Research, 33*(3), 469–490.

Chen, C. C., Chen, Y.-R., & Xin, K. (2004). Guanxi practices and trust in management: A procedural justice perspective. *Organization Science, 15*(2), 200–209.

Chopra, S., & Meindl, P. (2012). *Supply chain management: Strategy, planning, and operations.* Upper Saddle River: Prentice Hall.

Denison, D. R. (1990). *Organizational culture and effectiveness.* New York: Wiley.

Fey, C. F., & Denison, D. R. (2003). Organizational culture and effectiveness: Can American theory be applied in Russia? *Organization Science, 14*(6), 686–706.

Head, K. (2007). *Elements of multinational strategy.* Canada: Sauder School of Business, University of British Columbia.

Hillman, A. J., & Hitt, M. A. (1999). Corporate political strategy formulation: A model of approach, participation, and strategy. *Academy of Management Review, 24*(4), 825–842.

Hofstede, G. (1980). *Culture's consequences: International differences in work-related values.* London: Sage.

Hofstede, G. (1991). *Culture and organization: Software of the Mind.* New York: McGraw-Hill.

Hofstede, G., & Bond, M. (1988). *The Confucius connection: From cultural roots to economic growth.* New York: Organizational Dynamics.

Hummels, D. (1999). *Have international transportation costs declined?* University of Chicago, working paper.

Lee, K. C., & Humphreys, P. K. (2007). The role of guanxi in supply management practices. *International Journal of Production Economics, 106*(2), 450–467.

Park, S. H., & Luo, Y. (2001). Guanxi and organizational dynamics: Organizational networking in Chinese firms. *Strategic Management Journal, 22*(5), 455–477.

Ranis, G., Stewart, F., & Ramirez, A. (2000). Economic growth and human development. *World Development, 28*(2), 197–219.

Tarun, K., Palepu, K. G., & Sinha, J. (2005). Strategies that fit emerging markets. *Harvard Business Review, 83*(6), 63–76.

Weidenbaum, M. (1980). Public policy: No longer a spectator sport for business. *Journal of Business Strategy, 3*(4), 46–53.

Cross-Function Global Operational Practice

8

Chapter Objectives

- To study the concept and taxonomy of cross-functional integration, introduce interlinked performance management, present three generations of balanced scorecards, and discuss challenges to cross-functional practice.
- To introduce global marketing strategy and its links to operations, and discuss integration practice across GOS and marketing.
- To introduce global finance strategy and its links to operations, present an integrative framework between finance and GOS, and address cross-functional practice between global operations strategy and finance.
- To introduce global taxation strategy and its links to operations, discuss approaches to integrating GOS and taxation, and present a tax aligned global supply chain framework.
- To introduce global human resources and its links to operations, discuss cross-functional practice between GOS and human resources, and introduce an integrative framework of international HRM.
- To address cross-functional integration problems between global operations strategy and information management, discuss global information management and competitive advantages, and present an integrative framework between information management and GOS.

8.1 Introduction to Cross-Functional Integration

8.1.1 Cross-Functional Integration Mechanisms

Integration means that separate parties work cooperatively to obtain mutually acceptable outcomes (O'Leary-Kelly and Flores 2002). MNEs use two levels of integration to support business processes: intracompany integration, overcoming the boundaries among business functions, and intercompany integration, overcoming individual organizational boundaries (Romano 2003). Cross-functional integration links the processes and activities of each function, such as marketing, finance, human resources, information management and operations (Oliva and Watson 2011), to achieve competencies in a global marketplace.

This section focuses on cross-functional integration, using four mechanisms of cross-functional integration: people-based integration, system-based integration, formalization-based integration and centralization-based integration (Kim et al. 2003).

- People-based integration: This mechanism uses employees to achieve coordination between business functions. It encompasses meetings, teams, training, and the transfer of managers. This mode is more useful when knowledge and information are transmitted face-to-face.
- Information-based integration: This mechanism provides global flow of information through telecommunications systems.
- Formalization-based integration: This mechanism consists of the formalization of cross-functional working protocols and standardization of work procedures, rules, policies and manuals.
- Centralization-based integration: This mechanism centralizes decision-making powers at a high level in MNEs or in global supply chains.

When organizational functions are integrated, functions are interdependent to achieve business objectives. Thompson (1967) presents three classical types of functional interdependency:

- Pooled: The departments work completely separately and each function contributes equally to the whole organization. This creates interdependency because the overall process will fail if one department fails.
- Sequential: Each function is connected in a serial flow with the next function (e.g., an assembly line) and together they support the larger organization.
- Reciprocal: The output of one function is the input for another and vice versa. In this model, departments are in the highest intensity of integration.

8.1.2   Cross-Functional Practice and Performance Management

Previously, executives were mainly concerned with financial measurement, which does not always lead to effective operations. Kaplan and Norton propose four perspectives for performance management. Figure 8.1 presents two methods in multi-dimensional performance management.

The left part of Fig. 8.1 presents a less balanced performance-measurement structure. While executives focus on financial performance measures, such as revenue, profit, and return on investment, since they need to communicate with shareholders, operational managers are concerned about operational measures, such as resource utilization, productivity, product quality, delivery times, and operational flexibility. Managers in the middle level struggle to balance financial and operational requirements. Meanwhile, they need to handle marketing measures, such as customer satisfaction and market share, and growth needs, such as innovation, learning, and researching.

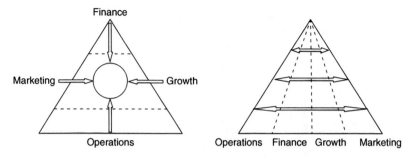

Fig. 8.1 Two multi-dimensional performance management frameworks

However, the structure often leads to functional conflicts and less understanding of the determinants and the results. The right part of Fig. 8.1 presents a balanced and interlinked structure such that managers of all levels can understand relationship among four sets of measures. Figure 8.2 shows an application of such an interlinked structure in the case of the telecommunications company Huawei (see the case in Chap. 2). Through a strategic map (Kaplan and Norton 2004), Fig. 8.2 presents three administration levels: a high level at headquarters, a middle level at its seven regional subsidiaries, and a low level at the basic business units including R&D centers, training centers and service centers. Managers consider four sets of measures, operational, financial, growth, and marketing, and link their measurement to their business strategies.

8.1.3 Strategic Linkage Models and Balanced Scorecard

One of the best methods of linking performance management and strategy is the use of strategic linkage models and balanced scorecards (Kaplan and Norton 1992, 1996a, b). While the application of balanced scorecard is much wider than cross-functional practice, the reputable method provides practical guidelines to cross-functional operations among the finance, operations, marketing, accounting, technology management, information management, and human resources departments. By timeline and evolution, practitioners classify balanced scorecards into first generation (1G), second generation (2G), third generation (3G).

- The first generation of balanced scorecard
  The 1G balanced scorecard is a performance-measurement framework, and translates strategic vision into four notional quadrants reflecting the financial, customer, internal business process, and learning and growth perspectives. To achieve global optimal performance, the balanced scorecard provides a method such that executives can combine financial and non-financial measures, and examine whether they have improved one function at the cost of others (Kaplan and Norton 1992).

  Kaplan and Norton provide five guiding principles. In implementing the balanced scorecard, an organization should translate business strategy into

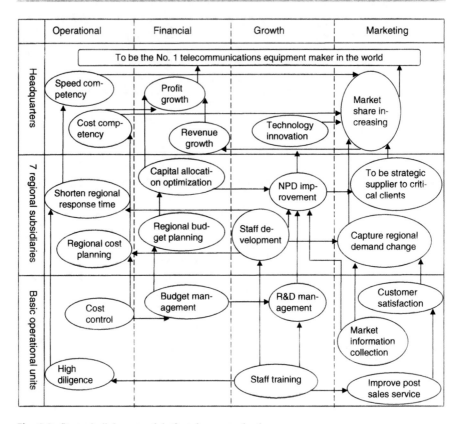

Fig. 8.2 Strategic linkage model of a telecommunications company

operational terms, align the organization to the business strategy, make strategy every employee's job, make strategy a continual process, and mobilize the change through executive leadership.

Since its inception by Kaplan and Norton in 1992, hundreds of organizations have applied the balanced scorecard. Its popularity lies in its flexibility and adaptability. Figure 8.3 shows an application of the 1G balanced scorecard in a leading white goods manufacturer in China. Facing fierce competition in white goods, this company is going global to seek new market opportunities. It first built manufacturing facilities in the US to learn market knowledge and achieve technology leadership to build the brand and become a preferred supplier worldwide.

• The second generation balanced scorecard

By emphasizing the "causality" between measures, introducing the concept of "strategic objectives", and using strategic linkage models, Kaplan and Norton (1996a, b) present the 2G balanced scorecard.

Figure 8.4 shows an example of a 2G balanced scorecard for an airline company in Europe. The primary financial objectives of the airline company

Fig. 8.3   An example of Kaplan and Norton's 1G balanced scorecard for a leading white goods' manufacturer

were to increase revenue and reduce costs. To increase revenue, the airline uses both price-based and capacity-based revenue management. To reduce costs, the airline uses business process reengineering to reduce operational costs, fuel hedging programs to reduce fuel costs, and a negotiation program with the labor union to reduce labor costs.

• The third generation balanced scorecard

A leading management consultancy 2GC and Lawrie and Cobbold (2004) summarize the idea of the 3G balanced scorecard. By introducing the "destination statement" as a reference point for balanced scorecard implementation and simplifying the balanced scorecard with an "outcome" perspective to replace the "financial" and "customer" perspectives and an "activity" perspective to replace the "internal business process" and "learning and growth" perspectives, the 3G balanced scorecard can improve management consensus, research linkages between the strategic activities needed and strategic outcomes desired, and attain better strategic alignment. Figure 8.5 shows a two-perspective strategic linkage model for a smartphone maker, which uses supply chain, risk management, technology innovation, marketing learning, and legal activities to achieve outcomes in customer loyalty, market share, revenue, cost, and profit.

8.1.4   Challenges to Cross-Functional Integration

Although cross-functional integration facilitates the sharing of resources and ideas, the building of mutual understanding and a common vision, and the achievement of

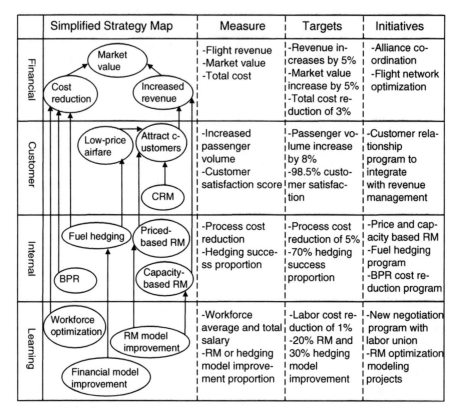

	Simplified Strategy Map	Measure	Targets	Initiatives
Financial	Market value / Cost reduction / Increased revenue	-Flight revenue -Market value -Total cost	-Revenue increases by 5% -Market value increase by 5% -Total cost reduction of 3%	-Alliance coordination -Flight network optimization
Customer	Low-price airfare / Attract customers / CRM	-Increased passenger volume -Customer satisfaction score	-Passenger volume increase by 8% -98.5% customer satisfaction	-Customer relationship program to integrate with revenue management
Internal	Fuel hedging / Priced-based RM / BPR / Capacity-based RM	-Process cost reduction -Hedging success proportion	-Process cost reduction of 5% -70% hedging success proportion	-Price and capacity based RM -Fuel hedging program -BPR cost reduction program
Learning	Workforce optimization / RM model improvement / Financial model improvement	-Workforce average and total salary -RM or hedging model improvement proportion	-Labor cost reduction of 1% -20% RM and 30% hedging model improvement	-New negotiation program with labor union -RM optimization modeling projects

Fig. 8.4 An example of Kaplan and Norton's 2G balanced scorecard for an airline company in Europe

collective goals, it also paves the way to complexity and conflicts in coordinating global decisions.

- Interdependency complexity

  Function interdependency, including pooled, sequential, and reciprocal types, creates unexpected events for other functions, and impacts other functions without direct control and responsibility (Moses and Ahlstrom 2008). Function interdependency increases the complexity of cross-functional practice, and the difficulties in managing communication and the control of its functions.

- Function conflicts

  Functional integration links the processes and activities of each area, such as marketing, finance and operations (Oliva and Watson 2011), which may generate conflicts over different goals and priorities. For example, while the finance department is interested in cost cutting, the operations department considers, not only costs, but also the delivery time and service level. If the corporate strategy has not coordinated all functions, then misaligned functional goals will lead to conflicts.

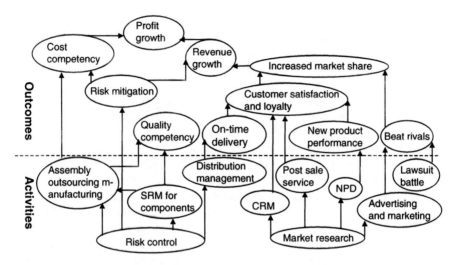

Fig. 8.5 An example of 3G balanced scorecard (Lawrie and Cobbold 2004, Kaplan and Norton 1996a, b) for a smartphone maker

- Operational barriers

  Hutt et al. (1995) identified three cross-functional operational barriers damaging to a strategic change initiative.

  1. Turf barriers. Against loss of status and power, functional units will defend their territory or turf, such as their authority in a function, an important project, the right of access to resources.
  2. Interpretive barriers. Each function has a different interpretation of strategic objectives and functional roles since each has different knowledge, expertise, and functional interests. Cross-functional interpretation is affected by national and corporate cultures when an MNE operates in several countries. The interpretive barriers will reduce the implementation efficiency of cross-functional operations strategy.
  3. Communication barriers. Each functional unit develops shared knowledge, language, and coding to increase internal similarities, but creates cross-functional communication barriers. Cross-functional communication is affected by physical, cultural, and relational separations in a global environment.

Case Example: Philips Electronics and Balanced Scorecard

Philips Electronics, a Dutch multinational electronics company, is a leading electronics company and employs around 122,000 persons across more than 60 countries. To align the company's views at different levels, to train employees from different functional departments to fit to the company's vision, and facilitate continuous learning and improvement, Philips Electronics has implemented balanced scorecards at its quarterly business reviews in global business units.

Philips Electronics' balanced scorecards focus on four perspectives (slightly different from the original BSC) or critical success factors:

- Financial. The company is concerned about value, growth and productivity, using measures of profit growth.
- Customers. The company tries to deliver appropriate value propositions to customers and employees, for customers' delight and employees' satisfaction.
- Processes. The company uses processes as drivers for performance, using indicators of operational excellence.
- Competence. Philips tries to achieve competencies in knowledge, technology, leadership and teamwork, using indicators of organizational development and IT support.

Philips Electronics has implemented the balanced scorecard with four levels including the strategy review card, the operational review card, the business unit card, and the individual employee card. The company uses an information system to link internal systems to the balanced scorecard system such that employees can quickly see the results, and understand how their individual tasks will influence the functional department, and then the whole company.

Case Questions

1. Please draw 1G, 2G, and 3G balanced scorecards (see Figs. 8.3, 8.4, and 8.5) for Philips Electronics.
2. How can Philips Electronics use balanced scorecards to guide cross-functional practice?

8.2   Global Operations Strategy and Marketing

8.2.1   Global Marketing Strategy and Its Links to Operations

Global marketing strategy is a marketing strategy taking advantage of global resources, processes and marketing opportunities to achieve global competitive advantages. The linkage between competitive strategy and global marketing strategies is a precondition to achieve the global business objectives for MNEs. Hill's framework for operations strategy emphasizes the linkage among corporate objectives, marketing strategy, and operations strategy (Hill 2005). Tang (2010) reviews marketing-operations interface models. Although the cooperation between marketing and operational strategies is critical to business success (Berry et al. 1991), MNEs will meet marketing and operations conflicts by the nature of functional separation, incompatible reward systems, and heterogeneous backgrounds of personnel. Three perspectives of global marketing strategy (Lim et al. 2006) fit to different global operations, and each of perspective captures an important aspect of global marketing strategy.

1. Standardization-adaptation

   In this perspective, global marketing strategy is characterized by the degree of standardization. This perspective mainly captures market offering aspect of global marketing strategy (Lim et al. 2006). A standardization marketing strategy applies uniform marketing elements. The associated operation strategy could be uniform across markets. For example, to fit a standardization marketing strategy, an operation strategy will use uniform facility layout and uniform facility location selection criteria. However, to integrate with an adaptation marketing strategy, an operation strategy may select local suppliers and adopt tailored-made facility layout to satisfy local markets.

2. Concentration-dispersion

   Considering geographic distribution, global marketing strategy is featured by the degree of concentration or dispersion. Lim et al. (2006) think this perspective mainly captures structural/organizational aspect of global marketing strategy. The geographic design of global marketing strategy needs synergies with operations strategy. For example, a concentration marketing strategy should optimize the geographic spread of its supply chain to utilize the comparative advantage across locations.

3. Integration-independence

   Regarding independence of subsidiary units, global marketing strategy is featured by the degree of integration or independence. This perspective mainly captures competitive process of global marketing strategy (Lim et al. 2006). The integration design of global marketing strategy needs synergies with operations strategy. For example, an independent subsidiary unit may have more freedom in operations decisions like facility layout and design.

8.2.2   Integration Practice Across GOS and Marketing

8.2.2.1 Integration in Three Phases of Global Marketing Strategy

Douglas and Craig (1989) identify three phases in the evolution of global marketing strategy. Operations strategy should be tailored to these phases in dynamics of international operations (see Fig. 8.6). In the phase of pre-internationalization, the operations mainly focus on domestic market.

In phase one "initial entry", the corporation selects markets to enter. This marketing decision is integrated with location section, an important operational decision. The corporation determines the timing and sequencing of international market entry, relevant to timing decision, another decision in resourced-based operation strategy. The corporation determines operations modes like renting or owning plants, sourcing ways, and supply chain contract structure.

In phase two "local market expansion", the corporation expands within each country or market. The corporation develops new product and service for local customers, organizes product line expansion to achieve economies of scope, and maximizes the profit by optimizing inventory management, facility planning, and distribution management.

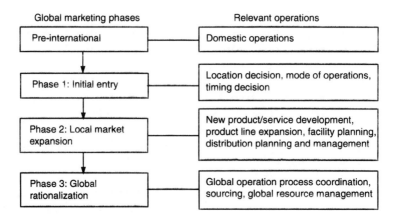

Fig. 8.6 Douglas and Craig (1989) three phases of global marketing strategy

In phase three "global rationalization", the corporation adopts a strategy with global orientation and focuses on global efficiency improvement by coordinated and integrated operations. Instead of considering domestic markets, global operations strategy considers interrelated markets worldwide. In this phase, global operational coordination and integration are critical to rationalize mature operations. For example, optimal global planning and management of facilities, research and development, and production activities can improve global efficiency.

8.2.2.2 Integration Levels of Global Marketing and Operations Strategies

Jüttner et al. (2007) propose the level of marketing and supply chain integration and we extend it to four integration levels of marketing and global operations (see Fig. 8.7).

1. Market losers

   At this integration level, both marketing and operations capacities are not strong. Operations specialists emphasize global operation problems, overlook integration with marketing, and cannot respond to different customer segments. The corporation cannot successfully build competencies to win the marketplace.

2. Operations specialists

   At this integration level, marketing capacities are weak and operations capacities are strong. Although production and service capacities are strong, the corporation is lack of product and service differentiation and cannot capture marketing dynamics on time, leading to ineffective product and service delivery, and suboptimal product development.

3. Marketing specialists

   At this integration level, marketing has strength in a global setting. However, combined with a weak global operation capacity, the corporation may not be able to deliver products and service to satisfy well-developed customer demand at different countries and marketplaces. Both under-delivering and over-delivering will lead to high cost and low customer satisfaction.

Fig. 8.7 Levels of global marketing and operations integration (Jüttner et al. 2007)

4. Marketing winners

At this integration level, both marketing and operation have strength in a global setting. Combined with a strong globally differentiated operation capacity, the corporation is able to deliver products and service to satisfy well-developed customer segments at different countries and marketplaces.

8.2.2.3 Integration Schema

With development of management methods like ERP, JIT, TQM, operation and marketing are integrated with different schemas. For example, ERP systems integrate internal and external management information embracing both operation and marketing to facilitate the flow of information between business functions. JIT integrates operations and marketing by making manufacturing more responsive to the market. Karmarkar (1996) presents three schemas for operations-marketing integration.

1. "Cross-functional" integration

The first schema is called "cross-functional" integration (see Fig. 8.8a). Cross-functional schema integrates elements well developed in marketing and operations departments, and can improve business performance and achieve competencies. For example, cross-functional integration between manufacturing lead time, an operational decision, and customer response time, a marketing decision can enhance time competency. Integration between production quality control, an operational decision, and customer satisfaction, a marketing decision can enhance the competency of quality.

2. "Joint decision-making" integration

The second schema is "joint decision-making" integration (see Fig. 8.8b), characterized by joint decisions between marketing and operation functions. For example, product mix needs joint decision-making considering both marketing demand and production features. Facility location is a typical operational decision problem. Decision makers must consider market demand and revenue management problem in some application settings like supermarket and public storage facility locations.

3. Complete integration

The third schema is complete integration (see Fig. 8.8c), characterized by disappearing of functional distinction between marketing and operation.

Fig. 8.8 Karmarkar (1996) operations-marketing integration schemas (**a**) Integration by cross-functional interactions. (**b**) Integration by joint decision making. (**c**) Complete integration of functions

Karmarkar (1996) thinks service management is one of such cases. For example, the design of service facility for operational efficiency is integrated with the resulting effect on service positioning and customer preferences. Karmarkar (1996) points out coupled supply chain structure cannot easily decomposed into marketing and operations issues.

Case Example: Apple's Operation and Marketing Strategy

Apple, an American multinational corporation that designs and sells consumer electronics, computer software, and personal computers, has 394 retail stores in 14 countries, and an online store as of November 2012. Apple achieves a successful coordination between global operations strategy and marketing.

1. Global marketing strategy
   The core of Apple GMS is "The Apple Marketing Philosophy", written by Mike Markkula (one of the first investors in Apple):
   - *Empathy.* Apple should strive for an "intimate" connection with customers' feelings. "We will truly understand their needs better than any other company", Markkula wrote.
   - *Focus.* Apple should focus efforts on accomplishing main goals, and eliminate all the "unimportant opportunities".
   - *Impute.* Apple should be constantly aware that companies and their products will be judged by the signals they convey. "People DO judge a book by its cover", Markkula wrote.

   The idea of understanding a consumer's needs before they actually need is one of elements in global market strategy of Apple. The idea of empathizing with a consumer before a market is developed is another element. After the financial crisis in 2009, the electronic market experienced a shrink, but Apple was highly ranked in Forbes Global High Performances. Depending on several star products such as iPod, iPhone, and iPad, the sales grow rapidly, and profitability remains high.

   Apple's brand's loyalty is unusually high and Apple has supported the continuing existence of a network of Mac User Groups in the world. Apple Store openings can draw crowds of thousands flying from other countries for the event. The New York city "cube" store had a line of half a mile. John Sculley told The Guardian newspaper in 1997: "People talk about technology, but Apple was a marketing company. It was the marketing company of the decade."

2. Global operations strategy

Apple began improving supply chain management almost immediately upon Steve Jobs's return in 1997. At that time, most computer manufacturers transported products by sea, a cheaper option than air freight. To ensure that the company's new, translucent blue iMacs would be widely available at Christmas the following year, Jobs paid $50 million to buy all the available holiday air freight space. The decision beat rivals like Compaq that later wanted to book air transport. When iPod sales took off in 2001, Apple packed diminutive music players on planes and shipped them directly from Chinese factories to consumers' doors. The decision beat rivals like HP.

Apple exerts influence over nearly the whole supply chain and thereby gets large discounts on production and logistics cost. The operational competency enables Apple to launch massive product with relatively low cost. The former supply chain chief at HP Mike Fawkes says: "Operations expertise is as big an asset for Apple as product innovation or marketing...They have taken operational excellence to a level never seen before."

Apple established many "Apple stores" to increase the customer experience and display products. Businessweek reports another operational advantage in Apple's retail stores. Apple can track demand in the store and by the hour, and adjust production forecasts daily.

(*Source: Satariano and Burrows* 2011, *Apple annual reports 2011*)

Case Questions

1. What are features of operations and marketing strategies in Apple?
2. Have operations and marketing strategies of Apple integrated? If yes, how do they integrate and support each other? If no, how to improve?

8.3   Global Operations Strategy and Finance

8.3.1   A Framework to Integrate Global Operations Strategy and Finance

The development of global cross-functional practice between operations and finance was facilitated by changes in the international trade barriers, the increase of commercial trade and connection among countries, cross-border acquisition and alliances, the advance in telecommunications and information technology, and the rising of new theories such as balanced scorecard and strategic interlinked models to integrate financial and operational measures to achieve strategic objectives.

Operations and global finance strategies depend on each other, but each expects the other to be flexible. For example, while uncertainties lead to tighter global finance control, global operations strategy may need more financial resources to build safety capacity to deal with global operational risks. To handle these challenges, MNEs integrate operations and finance through communication and information sharing, interaction, control, and coordination mechanisms.

Fig. 8.9 A framework to integrate global operations strategy and finance

Figure 8.9 presents a framework to integrate global operations strategy and finance. First, MNEs use finance function to achieve or enhance global operational competencies, in particular, cost, revenue and flexibility competencies. Second, MNEs use cross-functional practice to improve the management of operational resources. Third, MNEs integrate the finance function with global operational processes such as global supply chain, global risk management, global revenue management and global product development. Three parts (operational competency, resource, and processes) are interlinked and all integrated with finance to support each other.

8.3.2 Cross-Functional Practice Between GOS and Finance

8.3.2.1 Finance and Operational Competency
- Finance and cost competency
  By the integration of operations and finance, MNEs can develop strategies to reduce operational costs. For example, airline companies (e.g., Southwest) use jet fuel hedging strategies such as over-the-counter derivatives and futures contracts to reduce fuel costs and risks. Manufacturing MNEs use DPP (direct product profitability) to identify costs attached to a product or an order through the supply chain, to reduce the induced costs by changing the product features and distribution, and to decrease hidden costs and customer's total cost of ownership.

- Finance and flexibility competency
  MNEs can use financial instruments such as various hedging methods and manufacturing facility real asset portfolio optimization to increase operational flexibility. In particular, MNEs can achieve flexibility competency through two real options: the scope option to switch resource allocation for multi-products profit optimization, and the time option (e.g., wait and decision delay, process postponement) to acquire newer valuable information for dynamic profit optimization.
- Finance and revenue competency
  Revenue management companies are using various financial tools such as capacity option (see Hellermann 2006) and price-based financial instruments to achieve revenue competency. Hotel companies use condo hotel finance strategy to improve financial outcomes in rental revenue, appreciation or depreciation, lending and tax deductions. Automotive MNEs have built various finance companies to finance car purchases and improve revenue. Suppliers avoid revenue leaks through electronic abilities to bill the client rapidly after the completion of shipment.
- Finance and other competencies (quality, time, scalability, ubiquity)
  Finance department needs to allocate optimal resource to help MNEs achieve quality or time competency, use scalable and flexible investment to achieve scalability. Ubiquity usually needs a huge number of investments or M&A operations.

8.3.2.2 Finance and Operational Resources

- Global operational resource and real option
  Global operations strategy view capacity as an option of real asset. In particular, MNEs consider option in capacity investment time (e.g., capacity timing decision has an option value of waiting), option in products (e.g., flexible resources have a switching or substitution option for multiple products), and option in location (e.g., global manufacturing network has allocation options to allocate manufacturing to locations), and safety capacity to reduce risks.
- Global capital structure
  Global capital structure decisions are main concern of global finance strategy in MNEs (see Sandberg et al. 1987; Barton and Gordon 1988), using to determine the optimal allocation of debt and capital through capital markets, to issue new capital through the public market, to find new investors for a private firm, and to determine capital expenditures and budget planning. MNEs integrate global capital with global operational configuration to achieve competencies. MNEs utilize offshoring financial centers to evade regulations of investors' origin countries, acquire tax and exchange benefits, particularly at tax havens.
- Global working capital management
  Working capital management is an important method in the short-term operations of the company. MNEs must ensure a strategic cash flow against the required cash outflow to maintain adequate cash flow for meeting short-term operations of the company. Working capital also impacts liquidity, investment

portfolio and the profitability. While too much cash leads to inefficiency, too little cash might be fatal to the organization. Small and medium firms often fail to attract investors by their poor working capital position (Sunday 2011).

- Global strategic facilities planning
  Strategic facilities such as critical manufacturing plants and distribution centers, typically with large physical sizes, huge capital assets, long lifecycle, need irreversible investment and substantial expenditure. Therefore, MNEs must integrate global strategic facilities planning with finance management processes, in particular, capital budgeting process (Steiss 2005), to improve both financial performances such as cost saving and operational performances such as effective facilities.

  To finance strategic facilities, MNEs use various financing options: paying based on current corporate revenue, building reserve funds to accumulate sufficient funds for facility projects in the future, trading stocks or their derivatives to obtain cash, and borrowing from other organizations or investors by bonds. By cross-functional practice between financing and facility planning, MNEs can increase return on investment and use facilities to efficiently deliver products and service.

8.3.2.3 Finance and Operational Processes

- Finance and operational risk management
  MNEs can adopt hedge policies to minimize the exposure to operational and financial risks. The currency exchange rate risk can be hedged by delaying allocation of the capacity to specific markets until both the currency and demand uncertainties are realized or by buying financial option contracts on the currency exchange rate when capacity commitment is made. The use of financial hedges can affect capacity levels by altering global supply chain structural choices, such as the desired location and number of production facilities to be employed to meet global demand (Ding et al. 2007).
- Finance and global supply chain management
  The integration of financial and physical markets is a driving force to global logistics (Kleindorfer and Visvikis 2007). MNEs use derivatives including forwards, options, futures and swaps to help economic agents understand true value of assets, and help MNEs manage risks to undertake large projects. For example, MNEs use exchange based derivatives such as freight future and options, OTC-traded derivatives such as freight forwards, and cleared fright forwards and options to deal with freight rate fluctuation, the largest risk source in shipping.

  The integration of financial and operational contracts can be used to hedge risks in the shipping and global supply chain. For example, shipping companies widely use an OTC freight derivative, EFA (forward freight agreements) contract, between a seller and a buyer to determine freight rates for specific cargo quantities, shipping vessels and trading routes.

- Finance and global revenue management
  Revenue management can influence financial flows and make contributions to corporate finance management. On the other hand, MNEs are using financial instruments to improve global revenue management. Global air cargo companies integrate finance with global revenue management by capacity-option contracts under price and demand uncertainties (Hellermann 2006). Airlines (e.g., Air France, American Airline) and hotels integrate with credit card companies in their frequent-flyer programs, providing customers both operational and financial benefits, to improve global revenue management.
- Finance and global product development
  MNEs use service product development to improve finance service. Merrill Lynch, for example, had developed new service product cash management accounts (CMAs), integrating all of a customer's assets such as checking, savings, and brokerage under one umbrella, to meet customer demand with complying with the complex regulation.

  On the other hand, MNEs use financial instruments or acquire finance resources to improve global product development. At research stage, MNEs consider their current and future investment opportunities, their current and future investment capabilities, and sales potential. At product development stage, MNEs optimize research project portfolio and product development investments across product areas, markets and project types according to product development goals, strategic focus and product priorities. At the stage of product commercialization, MNEs allocate appropriate financial resources and improve operational and contractual arrangements to ensure the performance of the investment products in various market scenarios. In particular, venture capital is an important capital source integrated with global product development for IT and biology industries.

Case Example: Air France-KLM Fuel Hedge Strategy

Jet fuel is the main cost source for global airline companies. Unfortunately, in 2011, the crude oil price was maintained at a high level, as the spot price of Brent averaged $111.26 a barrel, compared with Brent crude which averaged $80 a barrel in 2010. Due to the rise in oil prices, the International Air Transport Association cut its forecast for global airline profits for 2012.

To handle fuel cost fluctuations, the Air France-KLM Group, the largest airline in Europe, had established a well-formulated fuel hedge strategy on commodities including jet fuel, crude oil, gas oil, and diesel. Hedging allows the airline to purchase fuel at prices based on expected fuel needs. The airline does not completely apply a hedging strategy on all fuel, but uses multiple methods to reduce fuel costs. Typically, the airline hedges up to 60 % at a defined time period (e.g., 24 months). Air France-KLM had hedged 53 % of its fuel at an average price of $111 a barrel using the Brent crude price in 2011, 55 % at $112 a barrel from July to September, and 58 % at $111 for the following three months.

Air France-KLM had used options for the right to buy or sell fuel commodities at the strike price within the option period until the options expired, swaps to exchange a floating price for a fixed price over a certain time period with another party, collars to hedge against the risk of losses at the expense of limiting the profit, and futures to help it buy fuel at a fixed price at some future date with exchange trade. Through fuel hedge strategies, Air France-KLM can mitigate the risks of fuel price fluctuation, gain operational time to adapt to market changes, achieve flexibility for cost control, and stabilize cash flow.

Jet fuel hedge strategies are not always successful if inappropriate fuel hedging proportions are chosen or if the wrong forecasting on the oil price trend is made. Air France-KLM and other airlines, such as Emirates, Singapore Airlines and British Airways, had predicted that oil prices would continue to rise when prices were climbing to a record $147 a barrel in July 2008, but spot prices had declined to $40 a few months later. Consequently, Air France-KLM had reported fuel hedging as a primary reason for its heavy losses in 2009. Taking another example, Delta suffered fuel hedging losses of $155 million in the second quarter of 2012 after spot prices were much cheaper than the prices in Delta's futures contracts. Since the oil price fluctuation in 2008, several airlines, such as British Airways, Ryan Air, and Easy Jet, have reduced their fuel hedging programs.

(*Source: Bloomberg, 2011*)

Case Questions

1. How can Air France-KLM use fuel hedge strategies to achieve operational competencies such as cost and flexibility?
2. How can Air France-KLM use fuel hedge strategies to mitigate global operational risks?
3. Why had some airlines (e.g., British Airways) reduced their fuel hedging programs, and regard it as a double-edged sword? How can Air France improve its fuel hedge strategies?

8.4   Global Operations Strategy and Taxation

8.4.1   Global Taxation Strategy and Its Links to Operations

Global taxation strategy deals with taxes levied by different jurisdictions and nations on individuals and enterprises, and consists of decisions in double taxation, thin capitalization, withholding taxes, transfer pricing, migration costs, value-added tax (VAT) and customs duty.

A local operational strategy suffers from disadvantage of not looking into important aspects of global strategy like taxation, global competitiveness and international politics while taking decisions. Increasingly finance departments in global corporations are looking at the link between the tax burden and effective supply chain management to reduce the overall tax expense. Governments are looking to attract corporations to invest by offering various tax incentives. Major consulting firms have initiated ideas such as "tax aligned supply chain" (Deloitte 2004), "tax efficient supply chain management" (KPMG and Ernst &Young).

8.4.2 Approaches to Integrating GOS and Taxation

8.4.2.1 Tax Aligned Global Outsourcing

MNEs are increasingly outsourcing their manufacturing and service to countries with advantages of taxation expenses. In China, a qualified manufacturing FIE (foreign investment enterprise) can enjoy a 5-year tax holiday. MNEs operate in high-tax countries to enjoy interest rate deductions and then shift some of operations and intellectual property to low-tax countries for low royalty payments. This increases their competitiveness in the global markets. A number of destinations like Switzerland, Ireland and Mauritius actively promote them as low tax jurisdiction and encourage companies to shift their facilities there.

8.4.2.2 Transfer Pricing and Global Tax Burden

MNEs use transfer pricing not only to avoid double taxation, but also to increase the profitability of the parent corporation and minimize the MNE's global tax burden. Transfer prices determine tax burden of each subsidiary, and MNEs can use transfer pricing as a strategic weapon for shifting its profits to low-cost jurisdiction. For example, when a home entity sells components to its foreign subsidiary, the transfer price charged is included as its revenue at home. The foreign subsidiary deducts this price as a cost when declaring its profits, making it useful to charge a high transfer price when foreign taxes are high. However, MNEs should calculate and negotiate with both home and host country before making a particular transfer price since penalties for charging an unreasonably high transfer price are heavy.

8.4.2.3 Tax Aligned Foreign Subsidiaries

MNEs build tax aligned global operations strategy by taking advantage of foreign subsidiaries like logistics, R&D, manufacturing, intellectual property holding units.

Tax aligned global operations strategy involves the incorporation of holding or shipping subsidiaries at tax havens. Foreign subsidiaries can also be used to ship the products via a third country to reduce the effective VAT paid in the country of sale. This technique is especially effective when there is a bilateral agreement between the country of sale and the third country being considered (Henkow and Norrman 2011).

Many MNEs generating revenue from intellectual property such as patents, copyrights, and trademarks (the IP Assets) can organize intellectual property holding companies (IPHCs) in a state or in a foreign country with little or no taxes (e.g., Delaware, Nevada, Bahamas, Cayman Islands, Ireland) to reduce federal and state taxes.

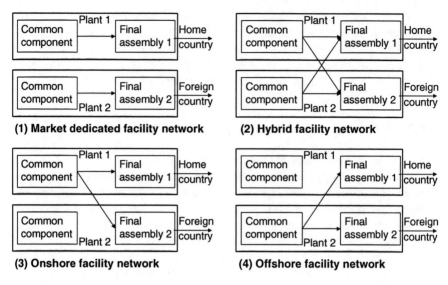

Fig. 8.10 Manufacturing network configurations

MNEs build foreign R&D subsidiaries in countries (e.g., the US, China, Austria) with tax incentive programs. For example, Canada Revenue Agency (CRA) administers "Scientific Research and Experimental Development Tax Incentive Program", a federal tax incentive program giving claimants cash refunds and tax credits for expenditures on eligible R&D, to encourage Canadian businesses to conduct R&D in Canada.

8.4.2.4 Tax Aligned Manufacturing Networks Configuration

Francas et al. (2008) examines several network configurations from Lu and van Mieghem (2009) for a firm that produces products to serve several countries using a common component and regionalized final assembly. MNEs can use tax in choosing an optimal manufacturing network configuration, and build tax aligned global manufacturing networks (see Fig. 8.10).

- The market focused network (Fig. 8.10(1)) would provide higher responsiveness to market and reduce shipping costs. If tariff and custom duty are high, or the penalty of transfer pricing is unacceptable, a company would locate its production plants in the same country to minimize cost.
- The hybrid facility network (Fig. 8.10(2)) is the most flexible and uses Jordan and Graves "chaining" structure. The configuration allows an MNE reaches global optimization to minimize transportation cost, tariff, and custom duty, taking full advantage of low-tax countries and tax incentive policies. Toyota, VW, and GM build both component plants in foreign countries and their home countries.
- Onshore facility network (Fig. 8.10(3)) provides economies of scale and allows risk pooling in component manufacturing. Maintaining component

manufacturing home is help to protect intelligence property. If home country has incentive policy to encourage export, or foreign country has strict customs regulations in importing complete products, MNEs will use onshore facility network. For example, BMW manufactures automobile components at home country and builds assembly plants in Thailand, Malaysia, Russia, Egypt, Indonesia, India, and Brazil, countries with customs regulations in importing complete automobiles.

- Offshore facility network (Fig. 8.10(4)) provides economies of scale and allows risk pooling in component manufacturing, and takes advantage of tax incentive program in foreign countries.

8.4.3 Tax Aligned Global Supply Chain Framework

Supply chain initiatives generally focus on reducing pre-tax costs, and ignore the potential tax savings. Facing a variety of effective tax rates from 5 % to 40 %, MNEs are optimize their supply chains by tax-effective supply chain restructuring process of integrating tax planning into supply chain management. The firms can benefit from tax aligned global supply chain by:

- Restructuring global supply chain with considering tax in location decisions,
- Performing supply chain activities in countries with different tax policies,
- Planning facilities in countries with different tax policies,
- Adopting new supply chain initiatives and a merger or acquisition, and
- Increasing profits by avoiding tax burdens with effective tax planning.

Supply chains can be restructured at the following stages in the value chain, and a number of tax advantages may be obtained.

- Procurement: MNEs cut expenses by integrating tax and sourcing strategies. For example, MNEs centralize procurement as a separate corporate entity in a low-tax country to reduce the total tax and sourcing expenses.
- Manufacturing: MNEs consider tax aligned manufacturing capacity planning to minimize the total tax and manufacturing expenses.
- Distribution: MNEs regularly reconfigure logistics networks by opening and closing facilities, and restructures logistics flows considering the impact of tax on material flow.
- Sales and marketing: MNEs can locate marketing centers in a low-tax region to reduce cost, and integrate sales and tax strategies to realize supply chain efficiencies.

8.4.4 "Double Irish Dutch Sandwich" Structure

Many US companies including Apple and Google are using a "Double Irish Dutch Sandwich" tax structure, building two Irish subsidiaries as the "bread" and a Dutch subsidiary as the "cheese", to reduce their global taxation burden connected with intellectual property and comply with the US tax legislation.

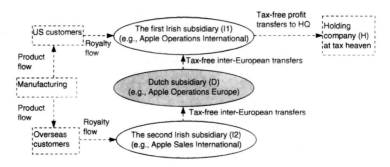

Fig. 8.11 "Double Irish Dutch Sandwich" tax structure

In this structure (see Fig. 8.11), the US parent company transfers its intellectual property to an Irish subsidiary (I1), which is further controlled by a holding company (H) in tax heavens such as Bermuda. Irish subsidiary (I1) sublicenses the intellectual property to a subsidiary (D) in the Netherlands. The Dutch subsidiary (D) sublicenses the intellectual property to a company (I2) tax resident in Ireland, which sublicenses the intellectual property to subsidiary located in jurisdictions outside the US.

For profits from US customers, while the profits would be subject to a federal tax of 35 % in the US, it can be taxed at lower rates if royalties are paid to an Irish subsidiary. The process is:

1. US customers pay royalties to the Irish subsidiary (I1).
2. Irish subsidiary (I1) transfers the profit to its holding company (H) in tax heavens since the profit transfer from a foreign company to its headquarters is tax free in Ireland.
3. In the tax heaven, the company can benefit from zero or low tax rate.

For profits from non-US customers, the company uses "Double Irish Dutch Sandwich" tax structure by taking advantage of taxation rules in Ireland and the Netherlands to reduce the taxation payable on royalties generated from intellectual property. The process is:

1. The companies in non-US jurisdictions pay royalties to the Irish subsidiary (I2) since (I2) has sublicensed the intellectual property to the non-US companies.
2. Irish subsidiary (I2) maintains a margin of these royalties (to be compliant with the minimum required for transfer pricing rules, usually 5–10 %) and transfer the remainder to Dutch subsidiary (D).
3. Dutch subsidiary (D) maintains a small margin of the royalties (to be compliant transfer pricing rules) from (I2) and transfers the remainder to Irish subsidiary (I1).
4. Irish subsidiary (I1) transfers the profit to its holding company (H) in tax heavens.
5. In tax heaven, the company can benefit from zero or low tax rate.

Case Example: Tax Restructuring Strategies of GE

GE is famous for employing one of the largest legal teams in the world, headed by a former treasury chief, to minimize the firm's tax expenditure. In its 2010 annual report, GE reported worldwide profits of $14.2 billion, and claimed that only $5.1 billion were from American operations. The interesting aspect is that GE's tax bill in the US was zero, and it claimed tax benefits of more than $3 billion.

Not only did it lobby the government persistently to alter the tax laws, it also ensured that it could exploit them to the fullest advantage. It started financing the sale of its heavy machinery (e.g., engines, generators) in Ireland instead of in the US. With the profits remaining offshore, GE was not obliged to pay taxes on them, or on the interest generated from them. The savings thus realized by GE are utilized by the firm to offset the tax it does bear on manufacturing operations in the US. While more than 70 % of its revenues and profits were reported in the US in the late 1990s, recently the revenue has been just a shade below 50 % and the profits are a mere 18 % in the US. This has been achieved through tax aligned operations strategies.

Aviation leasing: In 2004, the American Jobs Creation Act prompted GE to shift its aviation leasing division's headquarters to Ireland, where the tax rate is substantially lower than in the US, 12.5 % compared with the 35 % prevalent in its home country. This shift qualifies GE for a tax deferral by reporting income earned on foreign land which, under current law, cannot be taxed in the US.

Health care: In August 2011, the company decided to move the headquarters of the X-Ray division of GE Health Care from Wisconsin, with a high tax rate, to China and, more recently, to invest $2 billion in China. The move would not only help GE invest in China, but also drastically lower its tax bill.

Appliances: GE's appliances groups have considered government tax benefits to invest $432 million in four US centers for appliance product innovation and manufacturing.

Information technology: GE is relocating to a center in Detroit, Michigan, to take advantage of $60 million in incentives over more than 12 years.
(*Source: GE annual report 2009–2011, Gerth and Sloan 2011, Kocieniewski 2011*).

Case Questions

1. How does GE integrate its tax and global operations?
2. What are the benefits of the integration of tax and operations in GE?

8.5   Global Operations Strategy and Human Resource

The globalization of business had made it more important to identify the linkage between human resource management and operations strategy, and to understand how global human resource can facilitate operating globalization and enhance operations effectiveness.

8.5.1 Global Human Resources and Its Links to Operations

MNEs need to employ staff to manage their foreign subsidiaries. There are two kinds of employees at foreign locations.
1. Locals: The employee's nationality is the same as the location of the subsidiary.
2. Expatriates: individuals working outside their home country, including two types:
   • Home country nationals: The employee's nationality is the same as the headquarters country.
   • Third country nationals: The employee's nationality is neither the location of the subsidiary nor the headquarters country.

Heenan and Perlmutter (1979) present a classification system including ethnocentric, polycentric and geocentric approaches in international business. It is widely applied in the international human resource field. For example, Caligiuri and Stroh (1995) apply Heenan and Perlmutter classifications in human resources and demonstrate four international human resource management strategies: ethnocentric, polycentric, geocentric and regiocentric. An MNE can use one of the four approaches, described in Table 8.1, to staff their subsidiaries.

The application contexts of those four approaches are: (1) Ethnocentric practice is mainly used when starting ventures, or finding inadequacy of local labor skills, or needing to maintain close communication with headquarters, or hiring top managers (CEO or CFO) to maintain close control. (2) The context of polycentric practice is the situation where a multinational wants to "act local". (3) Regiocentric approach provides a stepping stone for corporations wishing to move from an ethnocentric or polycentric approach to a geocentric approach. (4) MNEs may use geocentric approach with the desire of an integration of foreign corporations with a worldwide corporate culture, such that the best staff is recruited for positions, regardless of nationalities. Edstrom and Galbraith (1977) find that the geocentric approach "permits the greatest amount of local discretion and greatest amount of decentralization while maintaining overall integration".

8.5.2 Integration Practice Between GOS and Human Resource

8.5.2.1 Integration Objectives

A global human resource strategy should create global competencies to facilitate effective implementation of global operations strategy. Linking with human resource strategy, MNEs can develop competencies, improve business performance and reduce risks in global operations strategy.
1. Building competencies. The integration of operations and human resource strategies can achieve three competencies. The human resource is one of inputs of operations strategy, plays a vital role to develop sustainable competitive advantage, and enables a corporation to supply customers with products and services (Lado and Wilson 1994). With excellent capabilities of the top management team and competent operations managers, a corporation can achieve managerial competencies to accomplish the corporate mission. A competent top

Table 8.1 Comparison of four international staffing approaches

	Description	Positive	Negative
Ethnocentric	Important positions are Parent-Country Nationals, and from headquarters	Good knowledge of corporate issues including goals, values, competitive strategy, culture, products, and procedures	Expatriate executives are expensive. Poor adaptability of expatriates. Lack of opportunity for local managers which lowers their motivation and loyalty
Polycentric	The subsidiaries are managed on a local basis, mainly by local managers, and host country nationals (HCNs)	HCNs are less expensive and their turnover is low. HCNs are more likely to be accepted by people both inside and outside the subsidiaries. Subsidiaries can develop local knowledge	Difficulty of coordinating between subsidiaries and headquarters. While HCN managers have few chances to gain experiences outside their own countries, PCN managers have few chances to gain international experience
Regiocentric	A variation of staffing policy to suit a region, with regional autonomy in decision-making and rare staff transferring between regions	Provide some sensitivity to regional condition, and allow interaction between executives transferred to regional headquarters from subsidiaries	Constrain the corporation from a global view with a regional basis. The career of staff is still limited by regional headquarters
Geocentric or global	The corporation applies the global integrated strategy, and staffs employees on a global basis. The nationality is overlooked in favour of ability	Local autonomy for daily decision-making and regional control over strategic aspects of the subsidiary businesses. Corporations can develop a global executive team. Highly unified corporation culture	Expensive to implement. Reduce independence of subsidiary management

management team and operations managers can develop competencies to manage relationship with external supply chain partners, and enable operations systems to effectively transform inputs into products and services, with relative competitive advantages over other operational systems (Harvey and Richey 2001).

2. Improving performance. Human resource practice including empowerment and staffing can support specific operational practices. For example, De Menezes et al. (2010) use longitudinal data from operations and human resource practices in British manufacturing to show that the integration of human resource and operations practices can improve performance in productivity with lean production. Taking another instance, outsourcing can integrate human resource practices, including accessing local labor with special skills, to improve productivity of supply chain.

3. Reducing risks. In global outsourcing, some human resource issues including job dissatisfaction and turnover may introduce risks to the global supply chain.

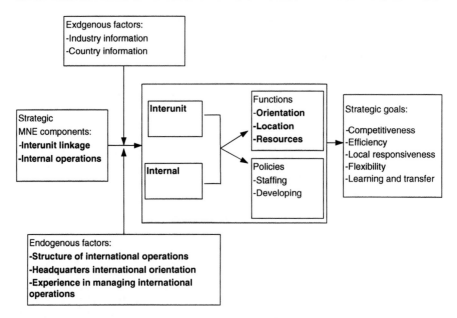

Fig. 8.12 Schuler, Dowling and De Cieri's integrative framework of strategic international human resource management

For example, Jiang et al. (2009) report that high labor turnover rates in China's coastal industrial zones have led to poor quality, low productivity and unfulfilled orders in global supply chains in 2006, and thereby expose the global supply chain to three types of business risks: cost risk, operational risk and reputational risk. The risks can be reduced by performance-based compensation, training and emphasizing commitment towards the organization. Foreign buyers can motivate suppliers to improve labor stability and provide support and guidance.

8.5.2.2 An Integrative Framework

Schuler et al. (1993) propose an integrative framework of strategic international human resource management (see Fig. 8.12), which provides guidance for integration practices of operations and human resource. The framework consists of strategic components including inter-unit linkages and internal operations, endogenous and exogenous factors, functions, policies, and strategic goals including competitiveness, efficiency, local responsiveness, flexibility, learning and knowledge transfer. The elements relevant to operations are highlighted by bold fonts in Fig. 8.12.

In Schuler, Dowling and De Cieri integrative framework, operations play the following vital roles: (1) Interunits linkages among operation units in different regions will influence international human resource management. Differentiation and integration of design, manufacturing, logistics, and distribution units can influence functions, policies and practices of human resources. (2) Internal operations of each operations unit are strategic components of MNEs. Human resource management can facilitate effective internal operations to be responsive in local environment and fit the corporate strategy of MNEs. (3) Some operations are regarded as endogenous factors in the integrative framework of strategic international human resource management. For example, operation elements (including the structure of international operations, MNE's headquarters international orientation, and international operations experiences) will influence international human resource management.

Case Example: P&G Greater China

1. P&G and its corporate strategy
   P&G, American multinational company headquartered in Cincinnati, has more than 127,000 employees in more than 80 countries as of December 2012. The company operates in two distinct markets: (1) Beauty and grooming with trademarks including Gillette, Olay, and Pantene. (2) Household care with trademarks including Pampers, Duracell, Swiffer, Tide, and Downy.

   P&G clearly states its corporate strategy, including basic corporate value, strategic objectives, and competencies. P&G states their expected competencies: consumer understanding, innovation, brand building, go-to-market capabilities, and scale advantage. The following "Purpose Statement" of P&G articulates their strategic objective and corporate philosophy.

   It is the company's goal to offer branded products and services of superior quality and high user value which improve the lives of consumers throughout the world. When we accomplish this, the consumers reward us with very high sales figures and greater profits – which benefit our employees, our shareholders and the communities in which we live and work (P&G).

2. P&G Greater China and its operations
   P&G entered mainland China in 1988 by establishing its first joint venture, P&G Guangzhou Ltd. P&G is the largest consumer products company in China, with annual sales of US$2 billion, with the largest market share position in most categories where it competes. Rejoice, Safeguard, Olay, Pampers, Tide and Gillette are among the largest brands in China's haircare, personal cleansing, skin care, baby care, powder detergent and male grooming categories respectively.

   Company's top scientists and researchers work in hands to innovate and create outstanding products. The company is involved in a highly competitive market. Manufacturing and production, design call for innovation to differentiate P&G products from competitors' products, tackle new segments and be competitive in present segments. HR must provide skilled and competent employees.

   While the company remains committed to "mass prestige", delivering high-quality brands such as Olay, Crest, Tide, and Pampers to the middle and upper classes at a premium price, things are changing and as there are new segments to explore, P&G needs more qualified scientists and researchers to develop low-cost products.

A highly competitive market obliges P&G to be close to customers to understand exactly market needs and meet them efficiently and effectively. It has to work with locals to get an overwhelming understanding of Chinese cultural and business culture.

P&G opened a R&D Lab in Beijing in 1998 as part of a global strategy to adapt products to local conditions and to take advantage of local ideas in improving products around the world. Among the center's staff, roughly 200 scientists is local Chinese and this represents a range of 80–90 % of the total. The center occupies three floors of a building adjacent to Tsinghua University. This center is about the median among P&G's 17 technical centers world-wide, which together employ about 8,500 scientists.

3. Human resource management of P&G Greater China

P&G follows an ethnocentric staffing policy, in which key management positions are filled by parent-country nationals, and global staff with robust links to Cincinnati headquarters. P&G prefers to staff important management positions with US nationals who have been adapted to P&G's corporate culture by years of employment in its US operations. The negative effect of this staffing is obvious. For example, P&G lost $25 million in Japan between 1973 and 1986 when US national managers ran advertisements for its Camay soap in which a Japanese man meeting a Japanese woman for the first time compared her skin to that of a porcelain doll, which advertisement infuriated the Japanese customers.

P&G Greater China uses a workforce consisting of a mix of local and global staff. Acknowledging that specific cultural knowledge is necessary, the company coupled expatriates with host-country employees. Local staff is mostly used in research and innovation. Local staff has a better understanding of Chinese market and can better respond to their needs. P&G's China staff has grown rapidly. More than 97 % of their Chinese workforce is made up by Chinese nationals in 2010. P&G China exports managerial staff to other P&G markets.

It seems that there is an emerging trend calling for more and more local staff in senior positions. In its initial years in China, P&G brought in experienced Americans to manage the country's operations. The company also hired Chinese then but gave them a plan to follow. It trained these locals to think in the American way. As the firm policy is to promote from within the organization, these local staff gained some key positions and became more and more important on strategic decisions. "Build from within" is the overarching human resource management strategy to develop future leaders of the organization in both P&G headquarters and P&G Greater China.

We are totally committed to building and developing our organization from within. We primarily recruit talented people at entry level with the intent of having a long-term productive relationship. Whenever we have vacancies at higher levels, we will fill them with someone from within the Company *(P&G Greater China)*.

The principal hiring tactic at P&G is to assign skilled staff to key managerial positions. Employees' motivation, turnover and competencies development are crucial in business and can lead to unsatisfactory financial performance. Companies with high performance are succeeding in retaining their people, and in getting the returns on their people investments. P&G China has clearly understood the issues surrounding this question and has developed the following tools to anticipate and mitigate the influence of risk related to HRM and GOS:

- Working closely with reputable universities and attract young talents,
- Training sessions for existing employees,
- Overwhelming financial compensation and benefits, and
- Frequent employees' evaluation and promotion.

(*Source: P&G annual report 2011*)

Case Questions

1. Please evaluate the roles of local and expatriate staff in the subsidiary, P&G Greater China.
2. What is the human resources approach (ethnocentric, polycentric, geocentric and regiocentric) of P&G Greater China? Have P&G taken any measures to offset the negative effect of this approach?
3. How does HRM affect operations strategy of P&G Greater China? Particularly, how does "Build from Within" philosophy of human resource strategy integrate with its operations?
4. How does integration of human resource strategy and operations strategy keep alignment with business strategy and corporate strategy of P&G?

8.6   Global Operations Strategy and Information Management

8.6.1   Global Information Management Strategy and Operations

MNEs are increasing using information technology to support their global business strategies (Sia et al. 2010), using IT-based innovation to improve their processes or services and achieve performance excellence, and regarding the information technology as a competitive weapon in corporate strategy (Bakos and Treacy 1986). Global information management strategies consist of acquiring, processing, storing and disseminating information processes across different business units with help of information technology.

As MNEs are challenged by increasing competitive pressures, they are implementing information technological innovations to achieve operational effectiveness, and explore the strategic triangle, the alignment among business strategies, organizational strategies, and information technology strategies (Pearlson and Saunders 2004). Organizations need to be both operationally effective and strategically flexible in continuous innovation to achieve competencies.

8.6.2   Global Information Management and Competitive Advantages

IT can enhance sustainable global competitive advantages in global operation strategy (Palvia 1997). The technological progress in IT has been critical to explain the difference of growth and productivity between the US and Europe (Gust and Marquez 2004). Information management (IM) integrates with global operations strategy and helps MNEs achieve competencies in cost, quality, flexibility, and time.

IM can identify inefficiencies and waste in global operations processes to achieve continuous improvement in the cost performance (Slack et al. 2009). Furthermore, IM models can help MNEs minimize costs in global supply chain. SAP, for example, can provide a solution "Advance Planning and Optimizer" to generate an automatic inventory replenishment plan to reduce supply chain costs.

By bridging the gap between what MNEs can offer and what customers demand, IM can improve product and service quality. For instance, in the healthcare industry, hospitals and clinics use customer relationship management (CRM) systems to get easier access to patients' medical records and histories, and improve the service quality by enhancing bonds between hospitals and patients.

IM can help MNEs achieve flexibility competency to adjust to changes of customer demand in both time and scope (see e.g., Lee et al. 2004). For example, most McDonald's stores have recently installed "the easy order machines" where customers can easily customize their orders using both English and local language menus.

IT can enhance global integration by information control and integration systems, and national responsiveness by managing the interdependencies between the different business units. IT can speed global operations. Walmart, for example, has used information systems to implement cross-docking distribution system, to shorten the total distribution time.

8.6.3   Cross-Functional Practice Between GOS and Information

Information management and GOS can build cross-functional operational mechanisms including global communication, coordination, control, integration and improvement, and apply in fields including global supply chain management, R&D management, revenue management, service management and risk management. Figure 8.13 presents a cross-functional integration framework between GOS and IM.

Fig. 8.13 Cross-functional integration framework between GOS and IM

8.6.3.1 Cross-Functional Operational Mechanisms

- IT-based global communication
  The IT system can facilitate the communication among the different business units to achieve operational competencies. For example, Zara has used information system to collect market information, and enhance communication between sales and design units to speed the process from the design to stores. Walmart has used satellite network to improve the communication of global supply chain.

- IT-based global coordination
  IT can be used to achieve global operational coordination by acquiring instantaneous customer information, improving information sharing between suppliers and retailers, coordinating multiple channels to enable "bricks-and-clicks" mode for maintaining market presence in both Internet and physical stores (e.g., Best Buy), establishing Available to Promise (ATP) to improve response abilities to customer order requests, coordinating pricing and inventory decisions in global supply chains, using collaborative forecasting and advance inventory information to manage global inventory, and collaborating decisions in global operations. For example, Electronic Data Interchange (EDI) can be used to share data between different parts of the supply chain, and information sharing can be used to mitigate bullwhip effect, the distortion of demand information from one end to the other in a supply chain, which can lead to tremendous inefficiencies (Lee et al. 1997).

- IT-based global control
  Intranets and video conferencing can help the top managers better evaluation and control of the global business units. BP and Total, for example, have used CENTUM, an integrated production control system delivered by Yokogawa, to control global production systems.

- IT-based global integration
  Enterprise Resource Planning (ERP) is the most important information system in global integration. A typical ERP (e.g., SAP's R/3) contains and integrates three layers, the "production layer" consisting of manufacturing, the "back-office layer" including human resource and accounting, and "front-office layer" comprising sales and marketing. ERP can achieve three types of integration, "horizontal integration" to integrate ERP with shop floor through manufacturing execution systems (MES), "functional integration" to integrate with R&D, marketing, manufacturing, distribution, sales, human resource and accounting functions, and "external integration" to tie ERP with external systems such as suppliers and customers. In particular, MNEs can use enterprise application integration (EAI) packages to achieve global integration. EAI typically uses XML (extensible markup language) data exchange to achieve three integrations: "application integration" at the data level, "business process integration" to support global business processes, and "business community integration".
- IT-based global improvement
  An MNE can use IT to continuously make innovation and improvement to achieve sustainable competitive advantage since new technology can be duplicated by rivals and global business environment continuously keeps changing. The most common approach is to use IT to implement business process reengineering (BPR), to fundamentally rethink and radically redesign business processes to achieve improvements (see Davenport and Short 1990; Davenport 1993; Hammer 1990).

8.6.3.2 Cross-Functional Application

- Global supply chain management and IM
  MNEs can use IM to improve information sharing and knowledge transfers between suppliers and retailers, reduce the supply chain cost, speed logistics time, and bridge demand and supply in global sourcing, distribution, strategic alliance, SCM coordination and integration. IM makes contribution to "triple A" (agile, aligned and adaptable) supply chains (Lee 2004). For example, global SCM can achieve adaptability by integrating IM with structural shifts, relocating facilities, changing sources of supplies, outsourcing, and flexible product designs.
- Global R&D and IM
  Computer-aided manufacturing (CAM), computer-aided design (CAD), and computer-aided engineering (CAE) digitize R&D activities and facilitate the globalization of R&D. MNEs use R&D information system (RDIS) for collecting, processing, storing and transferring information in R&D, project management information system (PMIS) to manage projects in R&D, new product development information system (NPDIS) to manage NPD activities, and IT-based design platforms (e.g., VW, GM, Toyota) to conduct global production development for global manufacturing.
- Global revenue management and IM
  Global revenue management is a computationally intensive process and information systems infrastructure is a business condition conductive to global revenue

management. For example, hotels, airlines, and rental-car companies use global distribution systems (GDS) to receive bookings. The GDS then communicate with computerized reservation system (CRS) in airlines and property management systems (PMS) in hotels. Retail RM uses retail management system (RMS) to collect information from point of sale (POS) and connect with suppliers' ERP.

- Global service management and IM
  IT can make service innovation including new service development, the innovation of service elements, service organization innovation (e.g., e-bank) and innovation through service. By improving abilities to process information, low cost high bandwidth information logistics, process standardization and higher productivity, IM has shaped information-intensive services like financial service, management consulting, health care and education. Global service management can in turn improve IM. IT service management (ITSM) is implementing IT service to meet business demand with focus on the relationship with customers, not just internal organization.

- Global risk management and IM
  While IT systems create global business opportunities, they may expose MNEs to significant vulnerabilities from "cybersecurity risk", which pushes MNEs to implement information technology risk management (ITRM). On other hand, IT can be used to mitigate global risks with information sharing, demand and supply information acquisition, collaborative forecasting, advance information management, and risk control information systems.

Case Example: Walmart Satellite Communication Network

Walmart, an American retailing corporation with 8,500 stores in 15 countries, employs advanced IT tools and applications in all supply chain functions, starting from demand forecasting, procurement, logistics, distribution and inventory management. The company improves efficiency of the whole supply chain to offer its customers products at the lowest possible prices. From Sam Walton, founder of Walmart, the integration of operations and information seems to be in the DNA of Walmart.

People think we got big by putting big stores in small towns. Really, we got big by replacing inventory with information (Sam Walton).

Walmart introduced the world's largest private integrated satellite communication network in 1987 with 24 million dollar, which made a vast difference from other retailers. This network allows the instantaneous transfer of data between headquarters, distribution centers, suppliers and stores. Satellites allow headquarters to check inventory level, sales at any store, and shelves status. The world's biggest private satellite network gave Walmart a huge informational advantage and the edge to combine size with speed.

The network uses a Ku-band satellite transmission with voice and computer data streaming between headquarters at Bentonville, Arkansas and all other locations. With this system, computer data and voice transmissions can be sent at 56 kilobits per second. Credit card authorizations are faster and more accurate, speeding up checkout services at stores worldwide. The network cuts telephone costs by about 20–30 %, simultaneously offering high speed communications.

Walmart implemented satellite communication systems to create JIT ordering with many of its key suppliers. When the inventory of certain products reaches a reordering point, an automated response is sent out instantaneously via the satellite to the corresponding supplier to organize replenishment. This payment and restocking decreases the inventory cost and streamline supply chain.

The satellite network system allows information to be shared among stores, distribution centers, and suppliers. Walmart satellite network sends point of sale (POS) data directly to vendors. The system consolidated orders for goods, enabling the company to optimize full truckload quantities to reduce logistics cost in its fleet with more than 3,000 trucks and 12,000 trailers.

Walmart was a front-runner to use satellite communication systems to facilitate cross docking. With help of satellite, the requests from stores are converted to orders, which are then forwarded to suppliers who conveyed their willing to supply the products in a specific period. The finished products are directly picked from suppliers, sorted out and directly shipped to the stores. The system reduces handling and storage costs.

Case Questions

1. What are the advantages to own a private satellite communication network? Which competencies can Walmart achieve by satellite communication network? (see Sect. 8.6.2).
2. How can Walmart integrate satellite communication network with global operation strategy? (see Sect. 8.6.3 and Fig. 8.13).

Case: McKinsey & Company

McKinsey & Company, Inc. is a global management consulting firm providing consulting services to its clients in two major areas: industrial practice, such as in the technology, automotive, and healthcare industries, and functional practice, such as in finance, marketing & sales, and strategy. Its clients include corporations, governments, and other organizations, including 100 of the 150 largest companies in the world.

The firm was founded in 1926 by Professor James O. McKinsey. McKinsey provided what was referred to as "management engineering," which largely referred to shop-floor optimization, and other operational issues. The firm continued to grow and develop the fields. In 1959, McKinsey opened its first overseas office, in London. Since then, McKinsey has experienced steady global expansion. Today, there are more than 100 McKinsey offices in more than 50 countries and yearly revenue is estimated, by Forbes, to be $6.6 billion.

McKinsey maintains a decentralized structure, with no global headquarters and without much hierarchy. Instead, the company has a horizontal structure and is divided into 80–100 "performance cells", established on various platforms by industry practice, function practice, and geographic location. Each cell is autonomous and reports only to the managing director. Consultants come together in teams of three to five to complete consulting projects.

- Global operations strategy

Our mission is to help our clients make distinctive, lasting, and substantial improvements in their performance and to build a great firm that attracts, develops, excites, and retains exceptional people (McKinsey).

Rajat Gupta (former managing director of McKinsey) has said that firm's missions and values form a strategy that resides in three critical dimensions: people, knowledge, and connections.

- People: McKinsey aims to recruit the highest caliber staff, and then develop their talents to the highest level.
- Knowledge: As a management consulting firm, McKinsey seeks to be at the forefront of business and economic topics, and up to date with the most cutting edge practices across all industries.
- Connections: McKinsey places high emphasis on the value networks it cultivates among people, whether, clients or employees.

Developing from the interactions among these three dimensions, McKinsey is in a privileged position. It has what could be called "top secret" information on the strategies and practices of some leading organizations, while often advising their competitors. To solve this conflict of interests, McKinsey has developed a strict code of ethics. The firm will not speak at all about the specifics of any companies it advises. Furthermore, consultants are not allowed to advise competing companies in the same industry within two years. Despite this tight code of secrecy, McKinsey can benefit internally from advising competitors. By comparing the information and strategies from different companies competing in the same industry, McKinsey can determine the best practices in that industry.

- Global human resources strategy

With more than 17,000 employees in 2010, McKinsey has developed a special human resources strategy. Traditionally, McKinsey hired professionals with experience. Now McKinsey is recruiting MBA students, particularly from the Ivy League, non-MBA masters and PhD students. Once a new-hire enters McKinsey, either as an analyst or associate, there is little time to relax. The firm maintains an "up or out" policy, under which employees are constantly expected to grow and develop their capabilities. To facilitate this, the firm strives to develop an atmosphere of growth and teamwork. When newly-hired consultants join, they go through a training program to instill in them McKinsey's values and strategy. Throughout their careers, employees have constant access to skill and knowledge development resources. Lower-level consultants are expected to progress to partner level in, at most, nine years after they join the firm. If they stagnate in their roles, they are asked to leave.

Promotion to principal and partner level happens organically within the firm, and newcomers are rarely brought in from outside. The managing director and the chief officers are chosen by the senior partners. The position has a limit of three terms, each lasting 3 years, a policy established in 1994 by Rajat Gupta at the beginning of his tenure as managing director. In general, there is rotation every 3–5 years of the top leadership within McKinsey. Partners retire at 60 and can remain active at the firm under the position of "senior partner emeritus."

Most consultants leave after 2–3 years, and each year approximately 25 % of the company is new. Leaving McKinsey is not the end of the experience, but simply the entrance to McKinsey's huge "alumni network" worldwide. McKinsey recognizes this network as one of its assets, and boasts that among its alumni are more than 200 current CEOs of the world's top companies.

• Global research strategy

Several years ago, when I started as managing director, one of the most important things I emphasized was making sure we were in the forefront of knowledge, in the development of knowledge, and in investments of knowledge (Rajat Gupta).

The McKinsey Knowledge Center is home to the "knowledge network," a set of more than 1,500 consultants who specialize in research. These consultants, known to be the consultants to the consultants, keep the firm stocked with the newest ideas in management research. The firm conducts research through the McKinsey Global Institute, at several locations around the world. At the institute, senior researchers lead teams of consultants who research business and economic topics for a duration of approximately 6–12 months, and then return to consulting.

The McKinsey Quarterly is a business journal featuring articles by McKinsey consultants. The target readerships are McKinsey consultants and other business persons. The journal features articles on topics across McKinsey's industry and functional practice areas.

• Global marketing Strategy

Due to the company's strict code of ethics and confidentiality, the firm is tight-lipped on its consulting methods, even to its clients. This esotericism has led Fortune to call McKinsey, "one of the world's best known, least understood organization." How then does such a well-known, but little understood company market itself? McKinsey claims that it does not use the aggressive strategy of self-promotion, but maintains records of excellence, speaking for itself. McKinsey relies on its deep network of relationships with its clients to bring in repeat business. In the words of a partner at the competing Bain group, "they have these deep relationships with senior management that lead companies to return to McKinsey, unquestioned, time and time again." McKinsey partners are often members of the board of top organizations, along with other executives of their client companies. Naturally, when these companies need consulting, they will visit McKinsey. For those who are not already McKinsey clients, word of mouth and McKinsey's reputation are enough for them to seek the firm's services.

Case Questions

1. In what ways does McKinsey's human resources strategy generate a competitive advantage for the firm?
2. How does the R&D strategy generate a competitive advantage for McKinsey?
3. How are human resources strategy, R&D strategy, and marketing strategy integrated to keep alignment with McKinsey's corporate strategy and business strategy?

References

Bakos, J. Y., & Treacy, M. E. (1986). Information technology and corporate strategy: A research perspective. *MIS Quarterly, 10*(2), 107–119.

Barton, S., & Gordon, P. (1988). Corporate strategy and capital structure. *Strategic Management Journal, 9*(6), 623–632.

Berry, W. L., Klompmaker, J. E., McLaughlin, C. P., & Hill, T. (1991). Linking strategy formulation in marketing and operations: Empirical research. *Journal of Operations Management, 10*(3), 294–302.

Caligiuri, P. M., & Stroh, L. K. (1995). Multinational corporation management strategies and international human resources practices: Bringing IHRM to the bottom line. *International Journal of Human Resource Management, 6*(3), 494–507.

Davenport, T. (1993). *Process innovation: Reengineering work through information technology.* Boston: Harvard Business School Press.

Davenport, T., Short, J. (1990). The new industrial engineering: Information technology and business process redesign. *Sloan Management Review, 31*(4), 11–27.

De Menezes, L. M., Wood, S., & Gelade, G. (2010). The integration of human resource and operation management practices and its link with performance: A longitudinal latent class study. *Journal of Operations Management, 28*(6), 455–471.

Deloitte. (2004). *The tax aligned supply chain.* New York: Deloitte Development LLC.

Ding, Q., Dong, L., & Kouvelis, P. (2007). On the integration of production and financial hedging decisions in global markets. *Operations Research, 55*(3), 470–489.

Douglas, S. P., & Craig, C. S. (1989). Evolution of global marketing strategy: Scale, scope and synergy. *Columbia Journal of World Business, 24*(3), 47–59.

Edstrom, A., & Galbraith, J. (1977). Transfer of managers as a coordination and control strategy in multinational firms. *Administrative Science Quarterly, 22*, 248–263.

Francas, D., Raulwing, M., & Minner, S. (2008). Transfer pricing, taxation and capacity planning in international manufacturing networks. In W. Kersten, T. Blecker, & H. Flamig (Eds.), *Global logistics management* (pp. 3–20). Berlin: Erich Schmidt Verlag.

Gerth, J., Sloan, A. (2011). *Five ways GE plays the tax game.* Pro Publica, 4 April 2011, New York.

Gust, C., & Marquez, J. (2004). International comparisons of productivity growth: The role of information technology and regulatory practices. *Labour Economics, 11*, 33–58.

Hammer, M. (1990). Reengineering work: Don't automate, obliterate. *Harvard Business Review, 68*(4), 104–112.

Harvey, M. G., & Richey, R. G. (2001). Global supply chain management: The selection of globally competent managers. *Journal of International Management, 7*(2), 105–128.

Heenan, D. A., & Perlmutter, H. V. (1979). *Multinational organization development.* Reading: Addison-Wesley.

Hellermann, R. (2006). *Capacity options for revenue management: Theory and applications in the air cargo industry.* Heidelberg: Springer Verlag.

Henkow, O., & Norrman, A. (2011). Tax aligned global supply chains. *International Journal of Physical Distribution and Logistics Management, 41*(9), 878–895.

Hill, T. (2005). *Operational management: Strategic context and managerial analysis.* Palgrave Macmillan, Basingstoke (Hampshire, UK).

Hutt, M. D., Walker, B. A., & Frankwick, G. L. (1995). Hurdle the crossfunctional barriers to strategic change. *Sloan Management Review, 36*(3), 22–30.

Jiang, B., Baker, R. C., & Frazier, G. V. (2009). An analysis of job dissatisfaction and turnover to reduce global supply chain risk: Evidence from China. *Journal of Operations Management, 27*(2), 169–184.

Jüttner, U., Christopher, M., & Baker, S. (2007). Demand chain management-integrating marketing and supply chain management. *Industrial Marketing Management, 36*(3), 377–392.

Kaplan, R. S., & Norton, D. (1992). The balanced scorecard: Measures that drive performance. *Harvard Business Review, 70*(1), 71–79.

Kaplan, R. S., & Norton, D. (1996a). Linking the balanced scorecard to strategy. *California Management Review, 39*(1), 53–79.

Kaplan, R. S., & Norton, D. (1996b). Using the balanced scorecard as a strategic management system. *Harvard Business Review, 74*(1), 75–85.

Kaplan, R. S., & Norton, D. (2004). *Strategy maps: Converting intangible assets into tangible outcomes.* Boston: Harvard Business School Press.

Karmarkar, U. (1996). Integrative research in marketing and operations management. *Journal of Marketing Research, 33*(2), 125–133.

Kim, K., Park, J.-H., & Prescott, J. E. (2003). The global integration of business functions: A study of multinational businesses in integrated global industries. *Journal of International Business Studies, 34*(4), 327–344.

Kleindorfer, P. R., Visvikis, I. (2007). *Integration of financial and physical networks in global logistics.* Risk Management and Decision Processes Center, The Wharton School of the University of Pennsylvania, Philadelphia, USA.

Kocieniewski, D. (2011). *G.E.'s strategies allow it to avoid taxes altogether.* New York Times, 24 March 2011.

Lado, A. A., & Wilson, M. C. (1994). Human resource systems and sustained competitive advantage: A competency-based perspective. *The Academy of Management Review, 19,* 699–727.

Lawrie, G., & Cobbold, I. (2004). Third-generation balanced scorecard: Evolution of an effective strategic control tool. *International Journal of Productivity and Performance Management, 53*(7), 611–623.

Lee, H. L. (2004). The triple-A supply chain. *Harvard Business Review, 82*(10), 102–112.

Lee, H. L., Padmanabhan, V., & Whang, S. (1997). The bullwhip effect in supply chains. *Sloan Management Review, 38*(3), 93–102.

Lee, H. L., Ofek, E., & Cohen, S. (2004). Manufacturer benefits from information integration with retail customers. *Management Science, 50*(4), 431–444.

Lim, L. K. S., Acito, F., & Rusetski, A. (2006). Development of archetypes of international marketing strategy. *Journal of International Business Studies, 37*(4), 499–524.

Lu, L. X., & Van Mieghem, J. (2009). Multimarket facility network design with offshoring applications. *Manufacturing and Service Operations Management, 11*(1), 90–108.

Moses, A., & Ahlstrom, P. (2008). Problems in cross-functional sourcing decision processes. *Journal of Purchasing and Supply Management, 14,* 87–99.

O'Leary-Kelly, S. W., & Flores, B. E. (2002). The integration of manufacturing and marketing/ sales decisions: Impact on organizational performance. *Journal of Operations Management, 20*(3), 221–240.

Oliva, R., & Watson, N. (2011). Cross-functional alignment in supply chain planning: A case study of sales and operations planning. *Journal of Operations Management, 29,* 434–448.

Palvia, P. (1997). Developing a model of the global and strategic impact of information technology. *Information Management, 32,* 229–244.

Pearlson, K., Saunders, C. (2004). *Managing and using information system: A strategic approach* (2nd ed.). Wiley Hoboken, NJ.

Romano, P. (2003). Coordination and integration mechanisms to manage logistics processes across supply networks. *Journal of Purchasing and Supply Management, 9*, 119–134.

Sandberg, C., Lewellen, W., & Stanley, K. (1987). Financial strategy: Planning and managing the corporate leverage position. *Strategic Management Journal, 8*(1), 15–24.

Satariano, A., Burrows, P. (2011). *Apple's supply chain secret? Hoard lasers.* Bloomberg Businessweek, 3 November 2011.

Schuler, R. S., Dowling, P. J., & De Cieri, H. (1993). An integrative framework of strategic international human resource management. *Journal of Management, 19*(2), 419–459.

Sia, S. K., Soh, C., & Weill, P. (2010). Global IT management: Structuring for scale, responsiveness, and innovation. *Communications of the ACM, 53*(3), 59–64.

Slack, N., Chambers, S., & Johnston, R. (2009). *Operations management* (4th ed.). Harlow: Prentice Hall/Financial Times.

Steiss, A. W. (2005). *Strategic facilities planning: Capital budgeting and debt administration.* Oxford: Lexington Books.

Sunday, K. J. (2011). Effective working capital management in small and medium scale enterprises. *International Journal of Business and Management, 6*(9), 271–278.

Tang, C. S. (2010). A review of marketing-operations interface models: From co-existence to coordination and collaboration. *International Journal of Production Economics, 125*(1), 22–40.

Thompson, J. D. (1967). *Organizations in action.* New York: McGraw-Hill.

Cross-Value Global Operational Practice

9

Chapter Objectives

- To introduce triple bottom line (TBL) theory, the basic concept of value integration, and basic practices across values.
- To address environmentally friendly global operational practice, focusing on the link and value integration between economic value and environmental value.
- To address socially responsible global operational practice, focusing on the link and value integration between economic value and social value.
- To analyze sustainable operations and global sustainable operational strategies, considering the link and full integration among economic value, environmental value, and social value.

9.1   Introduction to Practice Across Values

Today's global operational practice is deeply influenced by the TBL theory introduced by Elkington (1994). TBL theory argues that firms should be preparing three bottom lines. The first one is the bottom line of the "profit account", which is the measure of the firm's economic value. The second is the bottom line of a firm's "people account", which is a measure of the social value created by the firm. The third is the bottom line of the firm's "planet account", which is a measure of how environmentally responsible the firm has been. Therefore, TBL consists of three Ps: profit, people, and planet. While there are different definitions on "value", the term "value" used in this chapter is based on TBL theory, and thus refers to economic value, environmental value, and social value.

Y. Gong, *Global Operations Strategy*, Springer Texts in Business and Economics, 283
DOI 10.1007/978-3-642-36708-3_9, © Springer-Verlag Berlin Heidelberg 2013

Fig. 9.1 Global operations strategy across economic, environmental, and social values

What global operations strategy tries to achieve is not only economic value, but also environmental value and social value. Based on TBL theory, it is crucial to formulate and implement a GOS with the consideration of these three values:

- Economic value (profit). Socially and environmentally friendly products are likely to be preferred by consumers. Consequently, socially and environmentally friendly companies may be able to achieve higher profits.
- Environmental value (planet). There is only one planet with finite resources. A number of MNEs are committed to ensuring sustainable resources for the economic value and social value of future generations.
- Social value (people). MNEs need to improve social value by, for example, alleviating poverty and utilizing natural resources in a sustainable manner.

A sustainable GOS considers these three dimensions to achieve a sustainable balance between the people, planet, and profit pillars (see Fig. 9.1).

Sustainable operations management is a developing discipline. The terminologies "environmentally friendly operations", "green operations", "socially responsible operations", and "sustainable operations" are somehow interchanged by different researchers. In this book, we use "environmentally friendly operations" to refer to the value integration between economic value and environmental value, "socially responsible operations" to refer to the value integration between economic value and social value, and "sustainable operations" to refer to full integration among economic value, environmental value, and social value.

We can observe global operations practices across the following four main global operations strategies (see Fig. 9.2):

1. Economy-focused global operations strategy. This global operations strategy focuses on economic value. The firm may or may not consider social and environmental values.
2. Environmentally friendly global operations strategy. This global operations strategy is mainly based on the practice across economic and environmental value.

Emphasizing integration between economic value and environmental value	2. Environmentally friendly GOS	4. Sustainable GOS
Not emphasizing (but may consider)	1. Economy focused GOS	3. Socially responsible GOS
	Not emphasizing (but may consider)	Emphasizing integration between economic value and social value

Fig. 9.2 Four global operations strategies across values

3. Socially responsible global operations strategy. This global operations strategy is based on the practice across economic and environmental value. It is difficult to completely separate this strategy from environmental value since both economic and social values are positively relevant to environmental value. While its focus is the practice across economic value and social one, it does not exclude environmental value.
4. Sustainable global operations strategy. This global operations strategy is based on the practice across the three values. This strategy considers the values of the next generations and time dimensions.

We can hardly claim which one is "best". Global operations strategy selection is a "strategic fit" problem and depends on the social environment, business features, and company characteristics. For the chemical industry, its main concern is environmental pollution. Therefore, such firms typically consider environmental values more than other general social values. The Grameen Bank, which provides financial services to poor people in India, hardly creates environmental pollution as a banking service firm, and so its focus is social value (to help rural areas and poor people).

The 2×2 matrix in Fig. 9.2 is designed for reader convenience. We do not claim that a sustainable GOS is the "most advanced" form of cross-value operations strategy. In terms of implementation motivation, efficiency, and business value creation, a socially responsible strategy such as "Creating Shared Value" (CSV) can be a better integration strategy between economic and social values.

Case Example: Green Logistics in Fujitsu

In April 2006, Fujitsu established a Green Logistics Committee as a company-wide organization to create environmentally friendly logistics that maintains a balance among cost, lead time, and quality throughout the supply chain. To reduce transport-related CO_2 emissions, this strategy focuses on transportation mode shift and intensive vehicle allocation control from parts procurement to product delivery and recovery.

One major part of Fujitsu's green logistics strategy is changing its modes of transportations from airplane and truck to railway and shipping, which emits less CO_2. In the past, Fujitsu and its group companies, retailers, and clients allocated vehicles and transport and delivered parts or goods based on independent local optimization for each company and for each procurement, manufacturing, and sales process. Fujitsu began activities to minimize the number of transport vehicles and reduce CO_2 emissions through global optimization. These activities included:

- Rationalization of distribution centers,
- Standardization of shipping instructions based on fixed rules,
- Revision of operations systems among logistics partners to optimize vehicle allocation, and
- Further reduction of CO_2 emissions through the use of Fujitsu logistics solutions.
  (*Source: Niwa* 2008)

Case Questions

1. What practice is used by Fujitsu to reduce environmental externalities?
2. Can Fujitsu use green logistics to achieve a sustainable balance between economic, environmental, and social values?

9.2   Environmentally Friendly Global Operations

9.2.1 Introduction to Environmentally Friendly Global Operations Strategy

9.2.1.1 Concepts

An environmentally friendly business is one that attempts to minimize its negative effect on the environment during operations, often sustainable with policies for protecting the environment (Bansal and Roth 2000; Buysse and Verbeke 2003). Environmentally friendly operations strategies specify the resources and processes that are not harmful to the environment, with the possibly non-financial benefits.

The incentives for a firm to adopt environmentally friendly strategies can be divided into two categories: internal and external ones. In terms of the former, if properly executed, an environmental strategy can be a way for a firm to obtain competitive advantage. Hart (1997, p. 67–68) argues that savings from excess pollution are the most readily evident savings that a company may reap from adopting environmentally friendly strategies: "Bottom-up pollution-prevention programs have saved companies billions of dollars. However, few executives realize that environmental opportunities might actually become a major source of revenue growth." In terms of the latter, Rosen (2001) identifies three primary sources of external incentives: shifts in international regulation schemes, changes in the market itself, and the worry about the future of humankind.

Environmentally friendly operations strategies have been applied to the manufacturing industry. For example, the chemical industry was regarded as one

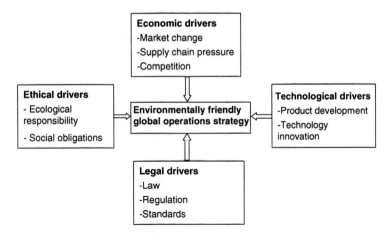

Fig. 9.3 Drivers of environmentally friendly global operations strategies

of the biggest "environmental bullies" in the 1980s, but now they "are among the few large corporations to have engaged the challenge of sustainable development seriously" (Hart 1997, p. 70). However, environmentally friendly strategies have increasingly expanded into services and other sectors, too. For example, Whole Foods Market (WFM) is a US supermarket chain that emphasizes natural and organic products. WFM has promoted sustainable fisheries worldwide and helped preserve fish stocks for future generations. The company has also been helping drive the development of new renewable energy sources for electricity generation. Further, in 2008 it stopped providing plastic bags, which was an effort to follow the "Reduce, Reuse, Recycle" paradigm.

9.2.1.2 Drivers

Companies are driven to implement global environmentally friendly operations by economic, legal, ethical, and technological drivers (see Fig. 9.3).

1. Economic drivers

    Competitiveness pushes companies to adopt an environmentally friendly global operations strategy by engaging in ecologically responsible activities in order to improve long-term profit and by investing in energy and waste management technologies resulting in a higher output-to-input ratio, ecological labeling, and the development of ecological products.

    Companies are convinced that consumer behavior is changing and that future successful products and services will be those that are environmentally friendly. As a consequence, some companies want to be considered as leaders in ecological responsiveness to benefit from sustainable competitive advantage. Firms no longer consider price and quality to be the only parameters for a successful product. They realize customers are pressing for more environmentally friendly products, especially in developed countries. With the motivation of

Table 9.1   European Environmental Law

Categories	Description	Examples
EU constitution and treaties	The legal basis for environmental actions	EU constitution
		Treaty on European Union
Secondary legislation	The most important European environmental regulations to ensure the implementation of the primary legislation	Relevant legislation in air, chemicals, climate change, energy, nature and agriculture, noise, transport, waste, and water
International treaties	The main international treaties relevant to the environment	Agreement for cooperation in dealing with pollution of the North Sea by oil and other harmful substances (Bonn agreement)
		Convention on the protection of the Rhine against chemical pollution (Rhine convention)
National legislation	The main environmental legislation of different countries	Environmental management act (The Netherlands)
		German environmental legislation (Germany)

(*Source: European Environmental Law Network*)

competitiveness, companies are looking for ecological initiatives that will also enhance financial performance.

2. Legal drivers

Environmental law is a set of conventions, statutes, treaties, regulations, and common law to regulate the interaction of humanity and the natural environment (Stewart 1993). Taking European Environmental Law (see Table 9.1) as an example, we explain how it drives global environmentally friendly operations strategy. In the European Union, numerous initiatives have been developed to protect the environment, resulting in a large amount of legislation, policy papers, and judgments by the European Court of Justice and member countries.

Corporations in these markets or those trying to enter these markets have to conform to these laws and regulations or risk losing their licenses or jeopardizing their long-term survival. A well-known case is the European regulations restricting the use of harmful chemicals in the production of textiles and clothing. In 1994, the German government enacted the Second Amendments to the Consumer Protection Act to prohibit the use of azo dyes. The Fifth Amendments to the Act came into force in April 1997. In 1996, the Netherlands also enacted a law prohibiting the use of certain azo dyes. The European ban resulted in hardship to many Chinese textiles, dye, and dyeing enterprises and trading companies. After suffering from losses and high costs, the Chinese textile sector has gradually overcome the difficulties and developed environmentally friendly products.

Driven by laws and regulation, more MNEs are establishing environmental committees or executive environmental positions to oversee environmentally friendly policies, publish social responsibility reports in their annual reports, and develop environmentally friendly products and services.

Another driver is from environmental standards, which are a set of quality conditions for particular environmental requirements. For example, mainly driven by EN13869 (a standard for child security in EU), Chinese manufacturers of lighters have innovated to develop environmentally friendly products.

3. Ethical drivers

Ecological responsibility is a firm's social obligations and values where concerns for social good and ethical aspects are emphasized rather than pragmatism. Companies act out of a sense of obligation, responsibility, or philanthropy rather than out of self-interest.

Some of these initiatives include the launch of a less-profitable green product line (e.g., Renault electrical cars). Other firms prefer donating to environmental interest groups such as the Save Your Logo program, which aims at protecting the species represented in many company logos (e.g., alligators for Lacoste). Further, many companies choose to use recycled paper and recycle office waste. These initiatives improve employee satisfaction and morale. As a result, firms willing to be considered to be ecologically responsible often choose independent and innovative courses of action rather than mimicking other firms whose motive was legitimacy.

4. Technological drivers

Technology innovation makes constant changes and proposes complex initiatives to drive environmentally friendly global operations strategy (Shrivastava 1995). For example, fiber optic technology reduces copper consumption, while concentrated detergent formulas help Procter & Gamble and Unilever reduce the volumes and weights of their products in order to reduce transportation costs and CO_2 emissions.

9.2.1.3 Benefits and Challenges

The benefits of implementing a global environmentally friendly operations strategy are linked to these drivers. Such a strategy can improve sustainable competitive advantage, reduce costs in situations such as green power and reverse logistics, improve public relations in different countries, increase revenue from customers with environmental concerns, build brand image with social responsibility, and improve efficiency in situations such as the paperless office and digital documents.

Although we consider the ecological issue one of today's important priorities, environmentally friendly operations strategies are limited to "risk reduction, reengineering, or cost cutting" (Hart 1997, p. 68) and rarely to strategic levels in many companies. Companies thus face the following structural challenges to the adoption of environmentally friendly operations strategies:

1. Taxes and fines from environmental laws and regulation,
2. Less-productive practices such as environmental auditing and waste treatment,
3. The obsolescence of equipment no longer acceptable in more regulated markets,
4. Banned products in more regulated markets,

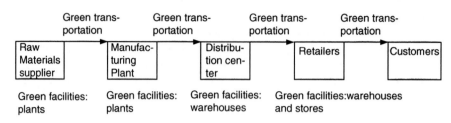

Fig. 9.4 A green logistics flow

5. Supply chain coordination if the supply chain is not wholly committed to the same environmentally friendly objectives,
6. The trade-off between sustainability and profitability, since solutions may be less effective than regular operations and green solutions often involve huge investments with blurry payback horizons,
7. Economic and political lobbying from different levels of commitment in environmental protection on a global scale, and
8. Technological difficulties to create environmentally friendly products and service.

9.2.2   Environmentally Friendly Practice

Of the many global environmentally friendly operations practices, we present several influential green operations.

9.2.2.1 Green Logistics

Green logistics aims to reduce the environmental externalities of logistics operations, such as greenhouse gas emissions, noise, and accidents, and develop a sustainable balance between economic, environmental, and social objectives (see Dekker et al. 2012). It also aims to deploy logistics processes that produce and distribute goods in an environmentally friendly way and optimize resources with a view of reducing waste and conserving resources to achieve sustainable competencies. Green logistics is a management approach by which firms evaluate, manage, and control the environmental impacts of their logistics activities throughout the lifecycles of their products. Lai and Wong (2012) identify the components of green logistics management:

1. Procedure-based practice,
2. Evaluation-based practice,
3. Partner-based practice, and
4. General environmental management practice.

A logistics network consists of nodes and links, and a green logistics network mainly consists of green transportation (links) and green facilities (nodes). From a view of processes, Fig. 9.4 presents a green logistics flow along a supply chain. Every stage of the supply chain can benefit from green logistics, from developing

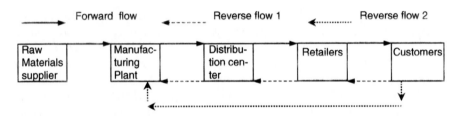

Fig. 9.5 Reverse logistics flows

better methods to extracting raw materials (from the beginning stage) to encouraging customers to reuse materials (at the ending stage).

Green transportation is a viable method of reducing CO_2, NOx, SO_2, and PM (particulate matter or fine dust) emissions as well as energy and wastewater. Green logistics practices include using cleaner fuels, shipping products together rather than in smaller batches, optimizing routing to reduce energy consumption, choosing suitable transportation modes, using alternative vehicles and equipment for manufacturing and shipping, reducing overall packaging, utilizing raw products that are harvested in a sustainable way, and promoting recycling and reuse programs. For example, Cargill uses wind power to propel its kite-powered vessel to reduce greenhouse gas emissions and fuel consumption by as much as 35 % in ideal weather.

Green facilities management includes designing, building, planning, and managing facilities for manufacturing and storage that are environmentally friendly. Green facility practices include the "3Rs":

- Reusing materials handling equipment such as bins, wood pallets, and plastic totes,
- Recycling materials including used packaging and packing material, and
- Reducing energy, water use, and transport.

9.2.2.2 Closed-Loop Supply Chain and Reverse Logistics

Reverse logistics is defined by the Council of Logistics Management as "the process of planning, implementing, and controlling the efficient, cost effective flow of raw materials, in-process inventory, finished goods and related information from the point of consumption to the point of origin for the purpose of recapturing value or proper disposal". Reverse logistics can create competitive advantage for a firm (Jarayanam and Luo 2007) Fig. 9.5 shows two examples of reverse logistics flows. The flows from raw materials to customers are forward flows, while reverse logistics flow 1 is from customers to retailers, distribution centers, and manufacturers and reverse logistics flow 2 is directly from customers to manufacturers.

A closed-loop supply chain usually refers to supply chains comprising return and reverse flows. Moving materials back up a supply chain is not simple and can cause considerable difficulties when the chain is designed largely around moving goods downstream to customers.

Reverse logistics includes activities such as reusing, reconditioning, retransforming, and repackaging components in order to reduce the environmental impact. However, it also covers the aspect of returning goods due to seasonal stock excesses or defects as well as recycling programs for obsolete furniture and dangerous materials.

With the surge in e-commerce, rates of returned goods seem to be higher than in traditional distribution channels. This rising amount of returns can lead to an important loss of environmental and economic value if reverse logistics is not efficiently implemented. The management of returned goods involves the following activities: activities that aim at minimizing or avoiding the source of the returns, activities that control return flow, and activities to allocate and place a return to a destination (relocation market, primary market, outlet, online auctions) before or after the activities of re-processing (remanufacturing, reuse, repair, recycling) or disposal in landfills.

From the access point in the return chain, products can follow seven distinct channels: return to the supplier, reselling in mint condition, selling through a factory or discount store, selling in the secondary market, offering products to charities, remanufacturing or reconditioning, destroying and recycling, and secondary markets.

9.2.2.3 Green Manufacturing

Green manufacturing can be described as a set of activities to reduce harmful waste, reduce emissions, and reduce water and energy consumption during the production process, with an objective of making production sustainable in the long term. There are five main green manufacturing strategies a company can follow (Azzone and Noci 1998):

1. Evangelist strategy. Firms can adopt an evangelist strategy in which green manufacturing is adopted for ethical reasons and their core values.
2. Proactive green strategy. This operations strategy aims to influence the whole value chain.
3. Responsive strategy. This strategy is mostly used by firms that have low bargaining power relative to their suppliers, namely those forced to adopt green manufacturing.
4. Reactive strategy. This aims to react to new customer requirements or new environmental regulations.
5. Unresponsive strategy. Companies adopt a relatively passive attitude to green manufacturing.

Case Example: GoGreen at DHL

DHL is a global logistics and mail group with more than 275,000 employees across 220 countries and revenue of €51 billion in 2010. DHL's services are separated into four divisions: express, mail, supply chain, and global forwarding/freight. Each of these divisions operates on a global scale, with express being the largest in terms of the number of countries and customers served. DHL operates an extensive network of dedicated vehicles, warehouses, offices, and other facilities. DHL's business strategy is to offer an extensive range of high-quality, personalized, customer-focused logistics services on a worldwide scale, without harming the environment, and working towards becoming completely sustainable.

DHL is committed to environmental protection and has taken measures to minimize its impact on nature. As a logistics company, its operations result in a considerable amount of CO_2 emissions, which lead to climate change. DHL has thus set a carbon efficiency target, which is currently to improve CO_2 efficiency in its operations and networks by 30 % compared with 2007.

In 2010, it introduced "GoGreen", an environment protection program that outlines its global environmental policies with the goal of developing sustainable operations. The primary objectives outlined in this program are the following:

- To improve efficiency and minimize environmental impact,
- To increase total transparency of the company's carbon footprint,
- To offer green services to customers,
- To become a global leader in the development of environmental policies and technology, and
- To educate and encourage employees and customers in environmental matters.

To reduce its carbon emissions DHL has optimized its delivery routes and combined multiple transport modes. Its fleet of vehicles are constantly modernized and replaced to improve carbon efficiency, and alternative vehicles using renewable fuels are adopted when possible. From 2008 to 2010, it reduced its air fleet from 227 to 147 aircraft to create a significant CO_2 efficiency. Overall, DHL obtains a third of the energy used to power its various buildings from renewable sources, while in Germany and other EU countries the figure is as high as 85 %. Green technologies such as intelligent energy-efficient lighting are used in its warehouses, offices, and distribution centers to help reduce energy use.

There are other environmental policies for non-carbon related issues. Its "Paper Policy" states that only recycled paper products are used, unless unavailable in local markets, and digital documentation is favored. Its environmental policy prioritizes reuse and recycling over disposal. DHL offers GoGreen options (e.g., carbon-neutral shipping options, green customer reporting, green consultancy) to its customers for many of its services.

Case Questions

1. What is the role of GoGreen in the global operations strategy of DHL?
2. Why has DHL decided to be a leader of green operations strategy among competitors?

Active and internal drivers	Proactive strategy without value integration	Proactive strategy with value integration
Passive and external drivers	Responsive strategy	Infeasible
	Separating economic and social value	Integrating economic and social value

Fig. 9.6 Socially responsible operations

9.3   Socially Responsible Global Operations

9.3.1   Introduction to Socially Responsible Operations

9.3.1.1 Socially Responsible Operations

Socially responsible operations strategy considers both economic value and social value, with an active or passive posture. Socially responsible operations strategy either links economic value and social value or goes further to integrate two values. Such operations concern a broad set of stakeholders instead of just shareholders, and serves stakeholders ranging from consumers to suppliers and from employees to external constituencies.

Socially responsible operations strategy is a developing field consisting of a number of linking and competing theories and methods. Such strategy is a general concept in this book. There are different attitudes to social responsibility (see Fig. 9.6).

(1) Unresponsive strategy. Companies highly focus on economic value and think working towards social value will not help or even harm the development of the corporation.

(2) Responsive strategy. Under social pressure, the company is forced to take some basic measures (e.g., fair trade purchasing) to respond. A company will act as a good citizen, respond to the social concerns of stakeholders, and mitigate the adverse effects of business activities.

(3) Proactive strategy without value integration. The company actively contributes to society. However, social value is separated from economic value.

(4) Proactive strategy with value integration. The company actively identifies the intersection points between the company and society, selects appropriate social issues to address, and creates value for social development. Further, social value is linked or even integrated with economic value. Social value can help the company build competitive advantage.

Among these levels, strategies (2) and (3) are relevant to Corporate Social Responsibility (CSR), while strategy (4) is relevant to CSV.

Table 9.2   An example of a CSR profile along two dimensions

	Share-holders	Employees	Customers	Business partners	Comp-etitors	Gov-ernment	NGO	Local com-munities
Values and governance								
Regulation and controls								
Operations process								
Accountability and disclosure								
Human rights								
Employee rights								
Working conditions								
Business environment								
Social impact of products								
Social impact of investment								
Community development								

Notes: strong interest in black; moderate interest in gray; weak interest in white

9.3.1.2 Corporate Social Responsibility

CSR is a large research field with a number of definitions and views. Of the 250 largest multinational corporations, 64 % published CSR reports in 2005. This book adopts the definition of "The World Business Council for Sustainable Development" in its publication "Making Good Business Sense".

> Corporate Social Responsibility is the continuing commitment by business to behave ethically and contribute to economic development while improving the quality of life of the workforce and their families as well as of the local community and society at large. (Holme and Watts 2000)

Bowen (1953) first presented CSR as a distinct framework for business strategy. From that time, CSR has developed a large set of concerns. Jones (1980) states that CSR should consider a broad set of stakeholders instead of just shareholders. The formulation of a CSR strategy is typically based on these two dimensions: stakeholders and concerns. Table 9.2 shows an example of a CSR profile based on these dimensions.

CSR Stakeholders

A well-devised CSR strategy considers not only the economic value of shareholders, but also the social value of employees, customers, business partners, suppliers, competitors, government organizations, NGOs, pressure groups, and local communities.

The stakeholder list above varies with different companies and stakeholders. For example, some companies may segment customers into classes (e.g., high-end versus low-end, well-educated versus low-educated) with different concerns and interests. Companies may even divide shareholders into groups including company owners, strategic investors, and small shareholders, in order to take account of the different viewpoints on economic and social value.

CSR Concerns

These stakeholders have different concerns. It is critical for CSR strategy to identify the interest levels of different stakeholders on each. Concerns vary with industries, countries, and even companies. Among others, we present the following main concerns:

- Values and governance,
- Regulation and controls,
- Operations process,
- Accountability and disclosure,
- Human rights,
- Employee rights,
- Working conditions,
- Business environment,
- Social impact of products,
- Social impact of investment, and
- Local community development.

9.3.1.3 Creating Shared Value

Going beyond CSR, CSV was first introduced by Porter and Kramer (2006) and further expanded in Porter and Kramer (2011). Many companies including GE, Google, IBM, and Nestlé (see the case later in this chapter) have begun to implement CSR-based strategies.

Porter and Kramer (2011) state that CSR is mainly about responsibility and considers reputation with placing values in doing good. While CSR separates social value from profit maximization and is limited by CSR budget, "shared value" can link social and economic values, enhance competitive advantage, and impose a greater influence without the limitation of a CSR budget. A corporation can create shared value using three methods:

- Reconceiving products and markets.

  This way is relevant to new product development and demand chain management in process-based global operations strategy. Companies can identify new demand and market opportunities from missing and unmet social needs, which were once regarded as constraints of business development, and create value by technology innovation and new product development to meet the demand relevant to social value.

Table 9.3 Differences between CSV and CSR

	CSV	CSR
Theme	About creating value	About responsibility
Objective	Integrated with profit maximization	Separate from profit maximization
Driver	Driven by internal motivations	Driven by external factors
Value	Consider both economic and societal values	Consider reputation with placing values in doing good
Impact	Larger impact	Limited impact by CSR budget
Principle	Expand the overall amount of social and economic values and go beyond trade-off	Trade-off between social and economic values
Scope	Smaller scope of values	Larger scope of values including some not directly linked with economic value

- Redefining productivity in the value chain.
  This way reshapes supply chain management in process-based global operations strategy. Companies can integrate societal progress and productivity in the value chain by reexamining energy use and logistics, improving the utilization of resource use, redesigning procurement process, creating new distribution modes, combining employee productivity improvement with human development, and optimizing business locating activities with considering relevant social value.
- Enabling local cluster development.
  This way influences location strategies in resource-based global operations strategy and supply chain management in process-based global operations strategy. Companies usually operate in local surroundings including supporting companies and infrastructure, which is called a local cluster. To create shared value, companies need to amplify the link between theirs and the economic and social values of their local communities and improve their productivity while developing a local cluster by attracting and developing reliable local suppliers.

Based on Porter and Kramer (2011), Table 9.3 presents the main differences between CSV and CSR in terms of themes, objectives, drivers, values, impacts, and principles. However, CSR proponents argue that the scope of values by CSV is narrower than CSR since not all social values (e.g., human rights and corruption) can be integrated with an economic value and be used to establish firm competitive advantage.

9.3.2 Socially Responsible Operational Practice

Both CSR and CSV are at the level of corporate strategy and work as a guideline to influence operations strategy. In particular, CSV is a solution to manage the link between economic and social value and can influence operations strategy. Table 9.4 presents social responsible practice from three fundamental views: competency, resource, and process.

Table 9.4 Socially responsible practice and global operations strategy

View	Area	Socially responsible practice	Examples
C.	Value-based competencies	Build unique value-based competencies	Crédit Agricole Grameen Bank
		Combine value-based competency and quality competency	WFM, Body Shop
		Combine value-based competency and cost competency	DuPont
R.	Size	Resource allocation between socially responsible projects and normal projects. Size of socially responsible programs	GE
		Size of socially responsible manufacturing capacity	Shougang
	Timing	Time to start socially responsible programs. To be a socially responsible leader or follower	UPS, Nestlé
	Types	Provide a wide variety of socially responsible products and service	Body Shop, WFM
	Location	Build and develop local communities	Walmart, Nestlé
		Select locations in developing countries to help poor people	VisionSpring Grameen Bank
P.	Supply chain	Purchasing (fair trade, direct farm, locally sourcing, educate suppliers, select local suppliers)	Walmart, Nestlé
		Manufacturing (using ergonomics and medicine knowledge to improve working condition)	GE, Johnson and Johnson
		Distribution (to overcome logistical challenges for service supply chain in emerging markets)	Riders for health
		Socially responsible retailing	WFM
	Demand and revenue management	Link customer loyalty program with charities	HHonors
		Shared car ownership program to reduce car numbers	Peugeot
		Combine revenue management with customer relationship management	Harrah's Entertainment
	Technology	R&D to provide new socially responsible products and service	GE Ecomagination
		New product development to provide healthier food	Dow AgroSciences
		Train workers to solve the HR shortage problem in developed countries	Microsoft, Marriott
		Train workers and provide technology to them in developing countries	Nestlé farmers education
	Risks	Control food and customer healthcare risks	Heinz
		Manage children safety	Lighter in EU

9.3.2.1 Competency-Based Socially Responsible Operational Practice

Competency-based operations strategy is influenced by CSV and Porter and Kramer (2006). Although value-based competency is a global issue, it varies by region. There are three types of value-based competencies. The first one is unique value-based competencies, typically achieved through operation model innovation (e.g., VisionSpring's affordable eyeglasses model), product and service innovation (e.g., Toyota's hybrid electric/gasoline vehicle and Crédit Agricole's socially responsible investment solutions), and even social enterprises (e.g., The Grameen Bank and Kiva). The second one combines value-based competency and quality competency (e.g., Carrefour Bio-milk). The third combines value-based competency and cost competency. For example, DuPont simultaneously saves energy use and reduces its costs.

9.3.2.2 Resource-Based Socially Responsible Operational Practice

In resource-based global operations strategy, location strategy and resource type are particularly influenced by social responsibility (for other resource-based socially responsible operational practice, see Table 9.4). Socially responsible operational practice provides a wide variety of socially responsible products and services. For example, The Body Shop provides natural and environmentally minded cosmetics, while WFM sells natural and organic foods throughout North America and the UK.

Many companies select locations in developing countries to help social development (e.g., VisionSpring, Grameen Bank). Sustainable global operations strategy considers building local communities and contributing to local cluster development (e.g., Nestlé).

9.3.2.3 Process-Based Socially Responsible Operational Practice

In process-based global operations strategy, supply chain strategy and technology strategy are particularly influenced by social responsibility (for other process-based socially responsible operational practice, see Table 9.4). Global socially responsible supply chain strategy produces the following practice. First, socially responsible purchasing considers fair trade products (e.g., Nestlé), direct farm sourcing (e.g., Walmart), and local sourcing (e.g., Walmart, Nestlé) to link economic value and social value. Then, socially responsible manufacturing uses ergonomics technology or medicine knowledge to improve working conditions. For example, GE is going to start paying its employees to quit smoking. Third, the distribution system is redesigned to incorporate social responsibility. "Riders for health" is working to make sure health workers in Africa have access to reliable transportation. Retailing incorporates social responsibility into the operations strategy. For example, WFM operates a color-coded sustainability rating program for wild-caught seafood.

Technology strategy is an important weapon to help companies link business and society to provide products and services with a social value. For example, Dow AgroSciences has developed a line of Omega-9 rich canola and sunflower oils, while GE is operating Ecomagination, a comprehensive R&D program for sustainable solutions. In developed countries, Microsoft and Marriott are training job candidates in local communities to solve its worker shortage problem. In developing countries, Nestlé and Walmart are training workers and providing technology to farmers.

Walmart is operating a "global direct farm" program and buying directly from small- and medium-sized farmers, eliminating intermediaries, raising farmer income, and emphasizing sustainability. With no previous access to a large retailer, local farmers did not have the financial resources to pay for logistics (e.g., the containers), marketing information to respond to customers' demands, and agricultural technology necessary to satisfy the requirements of large retailers. To support farmers and their communities, the goals of the program are:

- To sell $1 billion in food sourced from one million small- and medium-sized farmers in emerging markets,
- To train a million farmers and farm workers.
- To increase income by 10–15 % for the small- and medium-sized farmers associated with the program.

Walmart is operating this program in the communities it serves around the world, with considering heterogeneous opportunities, needs, and challenges in each region (see Table 9.5). The program tries to bring benefits to three parties:

- Customers have access to a wider variety of fresh, safe, and locally grown produce.
- Farmers are able to sell more products, earn more income, obtain more training, and obtain information to respond to market needs.
- Walmart is able to reduce shipping costs by sourcing close to its stores and improve produce coverage by bringing locally sourced and fresher produce to its stores.

Case Questions

1. Which economic value has Walmart achieved through the "global direct farm" program? Which social value has Walmart achieved through the "global direct farm" program?
2. How has Walmart integrated economic value and social value through the "global direct farm" program?
3. Is the strategy of Walmart closer to CSV or CSR?
4. How has the "global direct farm" program influenced the global operations strategy of Walmart?

9.4   Sustainable Global Operations

9.4.1   Sustainability: Beyond Greening

Although many companies accept green global operations strategy, they are facing up to challenges beyond environmental pollution: poverty, disease, depleted resources, and migration on a global scale. Nestlé has launched a "fair trade instant

Table 9.5 Walmart "global direct farm" program in different regions

Region	Activities	Results
US	Walmart partnered with Tuskegee University and the USDA, coordinated with a local Walmart distribution center to help local farmers to sell shelled peas in Alabama	In 2011, Walmart sold shelled peas for the first time. Farmers' incomes increased
Central America	The Tierra Fértil program supported the development of 3,774 small- and medium-sized farmers in 2011. Walmart's agronomical engineers advised farmers	This program assisted farmers to respond to market needs
Mexico	As of August 2011, Walmart Mexico had trained 2,447 farmers and farm workers in Best Agricultural Practices	Participants earned certification and acquired knowledge
India	Since 2008, Walmart has helped 3,700 small farmers close the critical gaps in cultivation and postharvest processes	The farmers earned a better price and received expert advice on crop management
Japan	Walmart Japan has directly sourced produce for nearly four decades	Customers benefited from fresher, safer, and lower-priced produce
Brazil	The Producer's Club program, which aims to provide producers access to the retail market, has helped more than 9,000 families in more than 350 cities in 12 Brazilian states	Participating farmers improved their production processes, while gaining access to a new market
Chile	Walmart Chile has collaborated with local government to train small- and medium-sized farmers	By selling directly to Walmart, farmers earned more
China	Piloting farmer training on vegetable production bases in China, including training of women farmers	Farmers acquired vegetable knowledge

(*Source: Walmart International Annual Report 2012, Global Responsibility Report 2012*)

coffee", not for the environment, but for ethical shopping as consumers impose pressure to ensure poor farmers get a better deal. It is committed to providing coffee growers with a fairer price for their products, particularly to help some of the poorest farmers in the world.

Humans must balance simultaneously biological systems, economic systems, and social systems. Companies need to consider not only environmentally friendly strategies (e.g., biological productivity and genetic diversity problems), but also economically friendly strategies (e.g., economic equity and basic needs problems) and socially friendly strategies (e.g., social justice and cultural diversity problems). In 2005, KPMG found that many global Fortune 500 companies had moved from considering simply environmental information to sustainability information including social, environmental, and economic issues (KPMG 2005). Current companies need to go beyond greening, from an "internal, operational focus on greening to a more external, strategic focus on sustainable development" (Hart 1997, p. 71).

Fig. 9.7 Concept of
sustainable development
(Gladwin et al. 1995)

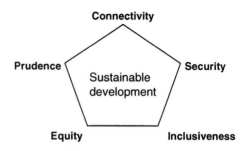

A broad and influential definition of sustainable development is given by the World Commission on Environment and Development (1987): "Development which meets the needs of the present without compromising the ability of future generations to meet their own needs". Further, sustainability is a relationship between faster-changing human economic systems and slower-changing ecological system in which human system can develop without destroying the diversity, complexity and function of ecological system (Costanza et al. 1991). As management scholars, Gladwin et al. (1995, p. 878) define sustainable development as "a process of achieving human development in an inclusive, connected, equitable, prudent and secure manner". This concept includes five components (see Fig. 9.7):

- Connectivity is to link economic, ecological, and social systems.
- Security is to protect from harmful disruption and threats.
- Inclusiveness is to embrace both environmental and human systems and both the present and the future objectives.
- Equity is to guarantee intergenerational, intragenerational, and interspecies fairness.
- Prudence is about demand precaution, safety margin, and preparation actions for uncertainty and unpredictability in ecological and human systems.

9.4.2   Globalization and Sustainable Development

Sustainable development is global. The OECD (2005) reports that CSR initiatives are now an international business trend in both OECD and emerging countries. Likewise, as mentioned earlier, KPMG (2005) finds that more Global Fortune 500 companies are showing concerns about CSR than before.

The globalization of sustainable development is partially from Hart (1997) who identifies three economics on a global scale (see Fig. 9.8). The first type is a market economy, which includes both developed countries and emerging economies. The survival economy in the rural parts of many developing countries is the second, while nature's economy consisting of the natural systems and resources is the third. Unfortunately, these three worlds are not perfectly balanced and they often collide. The collision of the market economy with nature's economy produces pollution, while the collision of the market economy with the survival economy leads to

Fig. 9.8 The globalization background of sustainable development (based on Hart 1997)

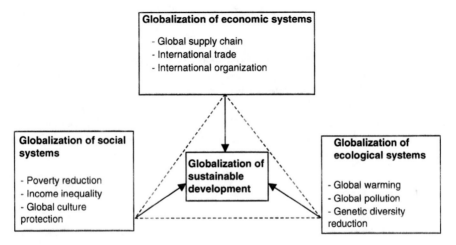

Fig. 9.9 Globalization of sustainable development

poverty. The survival economy may also deplete nature resources. These collisions are important drivers for the globalization of sustainable development.

Globalization influences sustainable development, which tries to balance simultaneously economic, social, and biological systems (see Fig. 9.9). First, global economic growth and economic globalization are globalizing sustainable development. Globalization has brought challenges not only through the creation of trade regimes such as the WTO, but also by business activities such as global supply chain and international trade. For example, Chinese manufacturers of lighters hardly considered environmental problems when they focused on local markets. However, when they exported lighters to European countries, they innovated to produce high-quality lighters to satisfy ISO9994, child-resistant lighters to satisfy EN13869 for children security, and a flameless rechargeable USB lighter to meet environmentally friendly requirements. Second, global social problems such as poverty reduction and increasing income inequality are influencing sustainable strategies. Third, global ecological changes are globalizing sustainable

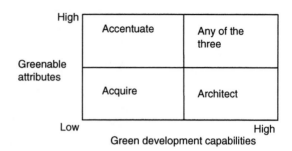

Fig. 9.10 Unruh and Ettenson's strategies for developing sustainable products

development. For example, global warming, the rising average temperature of the Earth's atmosphere and oceans since the late nineteenth century, influences global business activities and imposes pressure on sustainable strategies on a global scale.

9.4.3 Global Sustainable Operational Strategies

1. Unruh and Ettenson's sustainable strategy system
   The main objective of sustainable development is to stabilize or reduce human activity's environmental burden (EB), which is a function of population (P), affluence (A), and technology (T) according to environmentalists Paul Ehrlich and Barry Commoner:

$$EB = P \times A \times T$$

From this formula, it is possible to reduce EB by decreasing P, A, or T. However, since it is infeasible to reduce population and unsuitable to reduce affluence, the feasible method of reducing environmental burden is to improve technology. Sustainable technology management is thus an important part of sustainable operations strategy. Focusing on a product-developing strategy, Unruh and Ettenson (2010) present three strategies (see Fig. 9.10) to develop sustainable products:
   - Accentuate
     This operations strategy aims to highlight and "accentuate" existing or latent green attributes in order to develop sustainable products. This is a simple and direct method that is easy to implement for beginners of sustainable strategy. Dell identifies what it already has in green packaging and makes it greener by switching to compostable bamboo packaging, which is made from mechanically pulped bamboo from a bamboo forest in China, and will compost and biodegrade at a fast rate.
   - Acquire
     This alternative product strategy is to buy a well-built green brand when a company's portfolio does not contain products for accentuation. The number of takeovers of smaller ethical companies by multinational corporations is increasing. While Tom's of Maine was America's top selling "natural"

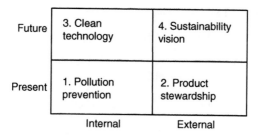

Fig. 9.11 Hart's sustainability portfolio

toothpaste brand against animal testing and with paraben-free products, Colgate Palmolive performed worse in these categories. In 2006, Colgate Palmolive purchased Tom's of Maine to improve its green image. In 2006, L'Oreal acquired The Body Shop, a UK retailer of natural beauty products, which has developed a reputation as "campaigning traders" to campaign vocally against animal testing and other ethical issues.

- Architect

  This is a product strategy for a firm to develop its own green products from scratch for a company with green development capabilities. It may be slower and more costly but it can build competencies over other firms. For example, Toyota has developed a sustainable product (Prius), a full hybrid electric mid-size hatchback among the cleanest vehicles in terms of smog-forming emissions.

2. Hart's sustainable strategy system

   Hart (1997) proposes a theoretical system of sustainable strategies along two dimensions of strategic planning time and organization borders. Stage one is "pollution prevention". The company needs to go beyond pollution control to pollution prevention to reduce or eliminate pollution. The strategy in stage two is "product stewardship", which is based on environment analysis along the entire product lifecycle, including product development, raw materials access and extraction, production and distribution, product use, and disposal. Redesigning products and packaging to satisfy sustainable requests are the results of such an analysis. This ensures that both upstream and downstream value chains follow sustainable practices. Thirdly, in a "clean technology" strategy, companies with a long-run strategic consideration will invest in new technologies for sustainable development.

   Based on these three stages of sustainable strategies, "sustainability version" provides a framework (see Fig. 9.11) to direct practices for achieving sustainable development. Hart's sustainability portfolio is a diagnostic tool to assess sustainable strategy. For example, a sustainable strategy strong in "pollution prevention" in the lower left-hand quadrant but weak in "sustainability version" in the higher right-hand quadrant indicates vulnerability in the future.

Table 9.6   A profile of UPS's sustainability strategy

Areas	Practices (examples)	Results
Economic systems	Transport management solutions by UPS Logistics Technologies. Effective technology utilization for optimizing the amount of miles driven	Saving 1.1 bn miles not driven by customers during 2006–09, leading to 186 m gallons of fuel savings and carbon avoidance
	Healthcare support	Customized logistics infrastructure catering for needs of the healthcare industry
Social systems	Established the UPS foundation for global philanthropy and to cater to needs of society	Total charitable contributions of $97.1 m and over 1.2 m volunteer hours by UPS employees and their families in 2010
	Support organizations for small and diverse businesses	Spending US$826 million with small and diverse and entrepreneurial vendors
Ecological systems	Alternative fuel vehicles (e.g., electric, hybrid electric vehicles.)	28.9 % more fuel-efficient than conventional vehicles
	Airline bio-fuels and noise reduction	Reduce noise emissions by 30 % and fuel consumption by 40–70 gallons per flight
	Carbon neutral shipping (provided its customers with the ability to offset CO_2 emissions)	Providing customers with an opportunity to make their own businesses more environmentally responsible
	Recycling and conservation	Reduce water consumption from 1.54 m^3 in 2007 to 1.19 m^3 per 1,000 packages in 2010

(*Source: UPS sustainability report 2008–2010*)

Case Example: UPS Sustainability Strategy

UPS is a leading company in transportation and logistics, providing package delivery, supply chain, and freight services across more than 220 countries and territories worldwide. The firm recognizes sustainability as an important part of its business strategies. UPS's chairman and CEO D. S. Davis claims: "Our decision-making was led by sustainability principles that have served us well for over a century – a balance of economic prosperity, social responsibility and environmental stewardship."

UPS has been undertaking several sustainability measures focusing on four broad areas – community, marketplace, workplace, and environment. It has made use of technology to optimize the number of miles driven, launched new green products, used alternative fuel delivery vehicles, and leveraged multiple transportation modes to ensure a fuel-efficient delivery network. It undertakes initiatives to conserve resources such as fuel, water, energy, and paper and to reduce the noise and carbon emitted by its airline fleet. Table 9.6 provides practical examples of UPS's sustainability strategy in three main areas: economic systems, social systems, and ecological systems. UPS has won a number of awards for its sustainability measures, scoring on indexes such as the Dow

Table 9.7 Nestlé's CSV framework

Level	Subject	Description
1	Compliance	Commitment to act with honesty, integrity and respect for laws and regulations
2	Environmental sustainability	Use natural resources efficiently, promote the use of sustainably managed renewable resources, and achieve zero waste
3	CSV	Share values for both Nestlé and society, with focuses on nutrition, water and rural development

Jones Sustainability Index for North America and the Carbon Disclosure Leadership Index.

Case Questions

1. Explain five components (see Fig. 9.7) of sustainable development in the sustainability strategy of UPS.
2. Using UPS as an example, explain the globalization of sustainable development (see Fig. 9.9).

Case: Creating Shared Value at Nestlé

1. CSV framework

   The foundation of Nestlé's CSV approach is provided by Porter and Kramer (2006), which state that if firms were to actively examine the links between their activities and the growth and progress of society, they would have considerable potential to contribute to sustainable global growth. Nestlé's CSV framework includes three levels: compliance, environmental sustainability, and CSV (see Table 9.7).

   The first level is compliance, the foundation of how Nestlé does business. Nestlé has a set of global values and principles (e.g., product safety, consumer privacy, responsible infant food). The second level is environmental sustainability referring to the improvement of the environmental impacts of products at all stages of the lifecycle via the use of natural resources efficiently, the promotion of the use of sustainably managed renewable resources, and the reduction of waste. The third one is CSV, focusing on CSV efforts and investments into nutrition, water, and rural development.

2. Value identification and formulation

   A successful sustainable business has to create value not only for its shareholders but also for society. Nestlé identified and formulated shared values for itself and society (see Table 9.8). At all three levels, Nestlé and society can share common values. Taking rural development as an example, Nestlé receives a supply of better quality raw materials at lower procurement costs, while society can benefit from farmers' incomes increasing. These two values link, match, and support each other.

Table 9.8 Value formulation for Nestlé and society

Level	Subject	Representative value for Nestlé	Representative value for society
1	Compliance	Foundation of Nestlé's business	Basic requirement to an MNE
2	Environmental sustainability	Natural resource and cost savings, long-term availability of raw materials and water, profitable growth	Raising environmental standards, waste reduction
3	Nutrition	Deeper understanding of nutrition and health issues, long-term enhanced growth, market share and profitability	Greater access to safe, high-quality, responsibly produced, nutritious food
	Rural development	More secure supply of better quality raw materials, lower procurement costs	Advice and technical assistance for farmers, increased farmer income
	Water	Reduced risks, reduced costs, long-term availability of raw materials and water	Raising water management standards in agriculture, safeguarding farm viability and farmer incomes

Table 9.9 CSV practice and performance

Level	Subject	Representative actions	Representative performance
1	Compliance	Build food traceability system following the "one step up – one step down" principle	Provide consumers with food and beverage products that are both safe and of the highest quality
2	Environmental sustainability	Reducing non-renewable energy consumption, avoiding waste and improving the environmental performance of packaging	Renewable energy consumption is 12 % of total energy consumption
3	Nutrition	Pledge its commitment to the United Nations Every Woman Every Child initiative	Healthy Kids Global Program reaches four million children and is active in more than 50 countries
	Rural development	Increased the scope of the Nestlé Cocoa Plan in Cote d'Ivoire	Rural development programs reached more than 680,000 farmers.
	Water	Implementing good water management practices across complex supply chains	A new SAIN pilot project in India suggests that water use could be reduced by around 30–40 %

(*Source: Nestlé CSV Report 2011*)

3. CSV practice

Based on the CSV framework and values, Nestlé takes relevant actions in compliance, environmental sustainability, and CSV (see Table 9.9). Taking rural development as an example, Nestlé increased the scope of the Nestlé Cocoa Plan in Cote d'Ivoire, while its rural development programs have reached more than 680,000 farmers. This practice creates values for both the firm and society.

Case Questions

1. Why does Nestlé call the program CSV not CSR (hint: Table 9.3)?
2. How does Nestlé integrate the CSV program with its global operations strategy?
3. How is the Nestlé CSV program aligned with its business strategy?

References

Azzone, G., & Noci, G. (1998). Identifying effective PMSs for the deployment of "green" manufacturing strategies. *International Journal of Operations and Production Management, 18*(4), 308–335.

Bansal, P., & Roth, K. (2000). Why companies go green: A model of ecological responsiveness. *The Academy of Management Journal, 43*(4), 717–736.

Bowen, H. R. (1953). *Social responsibilities of the businessman.* New York: Harper & Row.

Buysse, K., & Verbeke, A. (2003). Proactive environmental strategies: A stakeholder management perspective. *Strategic Management Journal, 24*(5), 453–470.

Costanza, R., Daly, H. E., & Bartholomew, J. A. (1991). Goals, agenda, and policy recommendation for ecological economics. In R. Costanza (Ed.), *Ecological economics: The science and management of sustainability* (pp. 1–20). New York: Columbia University Press.

Dekker, R., Bloemhof, J., & Mallidis, I. (2012). Operations research for green logistics – an overview of aspects, issues, contributions and challenges. *European Journal of Operational Research, 219*(3), 671–679.

Elkington, J. (1994). Towards the sustainable corporation: Win-Win-Win business strategies for sustainable development. *California Management Review, 36*(2), 90–100.

Gladwin, T. N., Kennelly, J. J., & Krause, T.-S. (1995). Shifting paradigms for sustainable development: Implications for management theory and research. *Academy of Management Review, 20*(4), 874–907.

Hart, S. L. (1997). Beyond greening: Strategies for a sustainable world. *Harvard Business Review, 75*(1), 66–76.

Holme, L., & Watts, R. (2000). *Corporate social responsibility: Making good business sense.* Conches-Geneva: The World Business Council for Sustainable Development.

Jarayanam, V., & Luo, Y. (2007). Creating competitive advantages through new value creation: A reverse logistics perspective. *Academy of Management Perspectives, 21*(2), 56–73.

Jones, T. M. (1980). Corporate social responsibility revisited, redefined. *California Management Review, 22*(3), 59–67.

KPMG. (2005). *KPMG international survey of corporate responsibility reporting.* Amsterdam: KPMG Global Sustainability Services.

Lai, K.-H., & Wong, C. W. Y. (2012). Green logistics management and performance: Some empirical evidence from Chinese manufacturing exporters. *Omega, 40*(3), 267–282.

Niwa, K. (2008). Fujitsu activities for green logistics. *Fujitsu Scientific and Technical Journal, 45* (1), 28–32.

OECD. (2005). *Corporate responsibility practices of emerging market companies-a fact finding study.* Paris: Organization for Economic Cooperation and Development.

Porter, M. E., & Kramer, M. R. (2006). Strategy & Society: The link between competitive advantage and corporate social responsibility. *Harvard Business Review, 84*(12), 78–92.

Porter, M. E., & Kramer, M. R. (2011). Creating shared value. *Harvard Business Review, 89*(1/2), 62–77.

Rosen, C. M. (2001). Environmental strategy and competitive advantage: An introduction. *California Management Review, 43*(3), 8–15.

Shrivastava, P. (1995). Environmental technologies and competitive advantage. *Strategic Management Journal, 16*(1), 183–200.

Stewart, R. (1993). Environmental regulation and international competitiveness. *Yale Law Journal, 102*, 2039–2106.

Unruh, G., & Ettenson, R. (2010). Growing green: Three smart paths to developing sustainable products. *Harvard Business Review, 88*(6), 94–100.

World Commission on Environment and Development. (1987). *Our common future*. New York: Oxford University Press.

Index

CPSIA information can be obtained at www.ICGtesting.com
Printed in the USA
LVOW10*1836070916

503622LV00015B/150/P

9 783642 367076